THE CHALLENGE OF EFFECTIVE SPEAKING

Fifth Edition

RUDOLPH F. VERDERBER
University of Cincinnati

Wadsworth Publishing Company
Belmont, California
A Division of Wadsworth, Inc.

Senior Editor: Rebecca Hayden
Production Editor: Jeanne Heise
Designer: Adriane Bosworth
Copy Editor: Carol Dondrea
Cover and Illustrations: Dick Cole
Technical Illustrator: Pat Rogondino

Printed in the United States of America
2   3   4   5   6   7   8   9   10—86   85   84   83   82

Library of Congress Cataloging in Publication Data

Verderber, Rudolph F.
   The challenge of effective speaking.

   Bibliography: p.
   Includes index.
   1. Public speaking.   I.   Title.
PN4121.V4   1982   808.5'1   81-10458
ISBN   0-534-01021-0   AACR2

PREFACE

Students and faculty alike have great expectations for the books they use in a course. I'm pleased that through the years both students and faculty have reported that *The Challenge of Effective Speaking* has proved valuable in meeting those expectations. Still, there are always ways of making a book even more valuable to its users. In this fifth edition, I have tried to be responsive to as many suggestions as possible for sharpening, refining, and clarifying ideas. I hope you will be pleased with the result.

In addition to including many new examples and illustrations and to insuring that every key point is as clear as possible, this edition features several important changes. Among the most significant are the following: a new section in Chapter 1 on speaker responsibilities, a differentiation between specific purpose and thesis statement in Chapter 3, an introductory section in Chapter 5 on language, a completely revised section on dealing with fear in Chapter 6, a completely revised discussion of reasoning in Chapter 14, an extended discussion in Chapter 15 of determining how to adapt arguments to audience needs, and an entirely new chapter on speeches for evaluation. Moreover, this edition contains nine new speeches and analyses.

The needs of public speaking students provide the author of a textbook with at least two special challenges: (1) In theory, students must master a great deal of basic information before they give a first speech; yet at the same time, students need to start early giving speeches and present as many as possible during the term. (2) Instructors are likely to want to proceed somewhat differently from what an author might envision, so a book must be flexible. I believe that *The Challenge of Effective Speaking* meets both of these needs.

After the two introductory chapters, you will find a four-chapter unit that presents the fundamental principles of speech making. While this section is long enough to cover the material, it is short enough to be read and assimilated during the first week or two of classes. The remainder of the book is organized to enable the professor to exercise flexibility in assignments. Chapters and units can be presented in any of several orders; some chapters can be used as the bases of speech assignments while others are used for general information. Let us now preview the organization in more detail.

In Part One, Orientation, we lay the foundation for the study of speech principles. In Chapter 1, we examine the importance of public speaking as communication and consider basic speaker responsibilities; in Chapter 2, we focus on listening and on why becoming a good listener is essential to becoming a good speaker. These two chapters can be read as one assignment.

In Part Two, Fundamental Principles, we emphasize the step-by-step procedure used to prepare speech purposes and thesis statements, find material, outline the organization, word the speech, and practice the delivery. The exercises included in this unit will guide you in preparing and delivering a first speech early in the term.

In Part Three, Informative Speaking, we build upon the fundamentals but focus on speeches for information exchange. The unit is constructed to meet any of several approaches. The initial chapter (Chapter 7) focuses on principles of information exchange; the remaining chapters consider the separate skills of using visual aids, explaining processes, defining, describing, and using research material. The material in the unit can be applied in a single informative speech, or in one or more speeches, each concentrating on a specific skill.

In Part Four, Persuasive Speaking, we build upon both fundamental principles and principles of information exchange. The unit focuses on concerns that most relate to persuasion. Again, the unit is constructed so a professor can tailor it to the needs of the student. The initial chapter of the unit (Chapter 13) focuses on principles of persuasion; the remaining chapters consider the separate skills of reasoning with and motivating audiences, and the skill of refutation. The material in the unit can be applied with a single persuasive speech, or with one or more speeches, each concentrating on a specific skill.

In Part Five, Adapting to Other Occasions and Formats, we present material designed for special occasion speech making and for group projects. We also present transcripts of three contemporary speeches to be used for analysis. Use of this unit will, of course, be dictated by both the length of the course and the specific goals.

Although I am responsible for what appears in this book, the content reflects the thoughts of a great number of people. First, I would like to acknowledge the students who contributed speeches and outlines to this edition. In addition, I would like to acknowledge the many instructors who offered insights gained through their use of previous editions, especially Ronald L. Aungst, Manchester College; Thomas L. Bottone, Los Angeles Harbor College; Mary Ann Brohard, Cedarville College; Nelson M. Carpenter, Middle Georgia College; Josh Crane, Texas A&M University; Wedge Crouch, Central Bible College; Michael Dugaw, Lower Columbia College; Jerry Ferguson, South Dakota State University; Norma L. Flores, Southwestern College; Keith H. Griffin, Wingate College; J. C. Hicks, Cameron University; Robert S. Littlefield, North Dakota State University; Patsy Meisel, Mankato State University; Steven Y. Miura, University of Hawaii at Hilo; Charles R. Newman, Parkland College; Charles J. Pecor, Macon Junior College; Bonnie Reule, Missouri Western State College; Mary Anne Rhoades, Catonsville Community College; Mary Jane Richardson, Kirkwood Community College; and Sherwood Snyder III, Chicago State University. My special thanks goes to those who did prerevision or manuscript reviews: Robert H. Coulson, Metropolitan State College; Nicholas M. Cripe, Butler University; Judy Jones, University of Illinois; Gary L. Miller, West Valley College; Janice M. Miller, Washington State University; Henry Tkachuk, Concordia College; Douglas M. Trank, University of Iowa; and Anthony D. Woods, City College of San Francisco. I also would like to thank Rebecca Hayden, Jeanne Heise, and other members of Wadsworth Publishing; and finally my wife Kathie who continues to provide both editing and inspiration.

CONTENTS

LIST OF
SPEECHES

Note: Student speeches, in the first three groups below, are accompanied by outlines prepared by students and commentaries prepared by the author of this book.

PART ONE

ORIENTATION

The material in this section lays the groundwork for your study of public speaking. Chapter 1 considers public speaking as a form of communication; it examines not only the variables to consider and the settings in which communication takes place, but also the responsibilities the public speaker bears. Chapter 2 shows that speaking and listening are part of the same process and that listening improvement is not a separate skill, but should be developed to help you speak more effectively.

Chapter 1 Public Speaking as Communication

On Tuesday, October 27, one week before the national election, Jimmy Carter and Ronald Reagan faced each other in "the Great Debate" of 1980. Just a few days before, the polls had said the election was "too close to call." Although most voters in the United States had made up their minds, a significant number admitted to being either undecided or so unsure of the candidate they had picked that their minds could still be changed. The debate would be a deciding factor in who would be elected. Although guesses vary, perhaps 25 percent of those who voted on November 4 made their decision on the basis of that one debate. Thus, Ronald Reagan's debating was one of the key factors in his landslide victory.

The point is not whether public speaking in general or debate in particular *should* be the deciding factor in such major decisions as who becomes the president of the United States, or who becomes a senator or chairman of the board or a leader of a business, political, or social organization. The point is that public speaking effectiveness *does* affect such decisions. Your effectiveness in public speaking will directly affect many aspects of your life. A successful, responsible, productive citizen must know how to read critically, how to write coherently, and how to speak effectively—which is the subject of this text.

You are now beginning your study of an art form that is nearly as old as humanity. Throughout the centuries famous speakers have changed the history of the world: people like Pericles, Demosthenes, and Cicero in classical times; Patrick Henry, Daniel

Webster, Abraham Lincoln, Susan B. Anthony, and Booker T. Washington during the early years of our nation; and John F. Kennedy, Martin Luther King, Jr., Billy Graham, Betty Friedan, and hundreds of others in our recent history.

Yet, in every period of history some people have tried to diminish the importance of the spoken word. In every age people have heard such statements as "We need less rhetoric and more action," or "That was only empty rhetoric," or "Don't pay any attention to what they say . . . " It's as if what a person says is totally unrelated to what a person really believes or what a person does. More often than not, however, the oral record is a clear statement of both the speaker's philosophy and the speaker's action. Of course, there are and have been deceitful and immoral speakers—just as there are and have been deceitful and immoral doctors, lawyers, scientists, and teachers. But in every art and science we look for and depend upon the best of the group to give us guidance.

Through the study and mastery of public speaking principles, you will not only increase your own effectiveness, but you can also influence the decision making that affects us all. Moreover, you can do it within the moral, ethical framework of our society.

We begin our book by analyzing public speaking as communication, with emphasis on the process, the settings, and the responsibilities.

THE COMMUNICATION PROCESS

When you give a speech, write a letter to your folks, or say to that special man or woman, "I love you," you are communicating. Communication is a process that involves the sharing of meaning. Although it is a dynamic process, for purposes of identifying and explaining the variables involved let us isolate one specific segment. Tom concludes his speech to the student senate by saying, "So, I believe this senate should petition the administration to reinstate a two-day reading period prior to the beginning of final exams." As he concludes the sentence, many of the student senators show their approval of his plan by applauding or by nodding or by saying such things as "right on" or "yes." What took place? The *source* (Tom) presented a *message*, through the *channel* of speech, to a group of *receivers*, who gave Tom a great deal of verbal and nonverbal *feedback*. Let us take a closer look at these variables of source, message, channel, receiver, and feedback, along with one additional variable, noise, and consider how they relate to each other to form a communication transaction.

The Source   The *source* is the sender, the originator of the communication message. The source may be a group of people—a committee, a company, or even a national government. As the author of this book, I am the source of the communication you are reading. In speeches you prepare and deliver, you will be the source.

What the source elects to communicate depends on the field of experience that affects the thoughts and feelings of that source. Thus all of us, I as the author of the book and you in your speeches, are affected by our past and present experiences, moods, feelings, attitudes, beliefs, values, upbringing, sex, occupation, and religion, as well as the aspects of our total environment. You are best able to understand another's perspective by analyzing that person's field of experience. Similarly, how you have lived your life determines what you say and how you say it.

The Message   The public communication process is initiated by the source sending some message. The *message* is the content that the source, the sender, communicates. In this book, my message is how to prepare speeches, particularly informative and persuasive speeches. What you say in your speeches in and out of the classroom will be your message. Messages have at least three components: meaning, symbols expressing the meaning, and a form or organization of those symbols.

Meanings are ideas and feelings. You have *ideas* such as how much to study for your next exam, where to go on vacation, and whether people should be punished for smoking pot. You have feelings such as hunger (for something to eat), anger (with your roommate), and love. The problem is that pure meaning cannot be moved in total from one person's mind to another's. We need some method by which we can bring about the same or analogous meanings in the mind of someone else.

To communicate meaning, you must express the ideas and feelings within you in symbols. *Symbols* are words or actions that stand for or represent meaning. Symbols can be communicated by voice and body. The process of turning ideas and feelings into symbols is called *encoding*. The encoding process is a very complicated one. Because you have been communicating for so long, you probably are not consciously aware of the nature of the encoding process. For instance, when your stomach begins to gnaw at you and you say, "I'm hungry," you are not likely to spend much if any time thinking, "I wonder what symbols I can use to best express what I am feeling." Sometimes we come close to realizing we are encoding when we grope for words, when we have an idea and stutter and stammer to find the word that "is on the tip of our tongue." In encoding, we select verbal symbols—words—to represent our meaning. At the same time, our facial expressions, gestures, tone of voice, and attitudes—all nonverbal cues— accompany our words and affect the meaning of our message.

Messages may be intentional or unintentional. By *intentional,* we mean that the speaker makes a conscious effort to select the symbols used in the communication; the message being sent has a deliberate purpose. By *unintentional,* we mean that the speaker does not consciously select the symbols. Much of the encoding we do is intentional, especially in public speaking, but sometimes the encoding is unintentional, and the meaning that results may surprise, shock, or embarrass us. For instance, you may go to great pains to compliment your audience for its contribution to a charity effort you led. Despite the intended meaning of the words you speak, however, you may notice that members of the audience show signs of being defensive about what you have said. You may have intended to be very gracious with your compliments to the group, but the unintentional nonverbal messages you sent may have given your actual feelings away. For instance, you may have actually been thinking that the group did not do all it could have in helping you. As a result of the negative thought, your voice may have had an "edge" to it that the group perceived as sarcasm. Although unintentional communication can be either verbal or nonverbal, it is more likely to be nonverbal. People do on occasion blurt out something they were not intending to say, but most of us are far better able to control verbal reaction than nonverbal. When unintentional messages compete with intentional ones, receivers are more likely to pay attention to the unintentional because they believe that spontaneous reaction is more likely to be honest. When you deliver speeches, you should make sure that both the verbal and the nonverbal communication convey the same message.

The third component of the message is its *form* or *organization;* this reflects your understanding of the syntax and grammar of the message you wish to send. Again, part of this organization is intentional and part of it is unintentional, influenced by our years of cultural experience as well as by trial and error. Good intentional communication requires message preparation. Although some people look upon message preparation as something that relates only to formal speaking, the process is much the same even when the message is to be sent in conversation on the spur of the moment. For instance, if someone asked you how to get to the post office, your mind would take time to prepare an answer, even though you would be expected to answer nearly instantaneously. In fact, if the route were complicated you might even reply, "Let me think . . . ," to give yourself a few more seconds to prepare your answer. So whether you must speak virtually instantaneously or whether you have considerable time, your mind must still consider idea selection and development, message organization, and the verbal and nonverbal symbols that will convey the message.

At first, putting carefully prepared statements together coherently so they meet all the tests of effective communication will take time and will appear to be quite difficult. Later, as you improve with practice, you will find yourself speaking more effectively, even when message preparation time is nearly instantaneous. Nearly all of Part Two, Fundamental Principles, is devoted to message preparation for any occasion. The remainder of the book deals with the preparation of particular kinds of informative and persuasive messages.

The Channel The *channel* is the *means* by which we convey the symbols. Words are delivered from one person to another by air waves; facial expressions are delivered by light waves. Usually the more channels that can be used to carry a message, the more likely it is that the communication of that message will be successful. Although our everyday interpersonal communication is carried intentionally and unintentionally by any of the sensory channels—a fragrant scent and a firm handshake are both forms of communication—effective public speaking is basically two-channel, that is, carried by sound and sight.

The Receiver The *receiver* is the destination of the message: the listener or reader. Like the source, it may be an individual or a group. You are one of the receivers of the message of this book; in your speeches, the members of the audience will be your receivers. The message is received in the form of symbols that have been carried by sound waves and light waves. The receiver turns these symbols back into meaning. This process of turning symbols back into meaning is called *decoding.* The decoder for most of the communication you receive is your brain.

Just as the source's experience affects the character of the message being sent, so does the receiver's experience affect the way it is received. Thus, the meaning that is stimulated in the receiver may not be the same as that of the source. Much depends upon how the receiver's field of experience affects the decoding process. Like encoding, decoding is a complicated process that is usually accomplished without conscious effort. For instance, when a speaker says, "The water level dropped 2 feet," we have an instant mental picture of the meaning being communicated. We do not consciously think, "Let's see, *water level* means the height of the water, *dropped* means went down, and *2 feet* is a distance of 24 inches—so the water is 24 inches lower than it was." Our mind goes through this process instantaneously. Moreover, we are seldom aware of the potential for misunderstanding within the decoding process. As a receiver, we may not pay too much attention to whether our mental picture of "dropped" is the same as that of the source. Considering the complexity of the encoding-decoding process, however, we are lucky to be able to communicate at all.

But even public communication is not a totally unidirectional event. The process is not completed by a source sending a message by means of one or more channels to a receiver. In public speaking, as in any form of interpersonal communication, messages flow both ways. Thus, the concept of feedback is vital to the understanding of the public communication process.

Feedback   Whether effective communication (the sharing of meaning) really takes place is determined by the verbal and nonverbal *response* of the receiver. This response, called *feedback,* tells the source whether the message was heard, seen, or understood. If feedback indicates that the communication was not received, or was received incorrectly, or was misinterpreted, the source can send the message again, perhaps in a different way.

Different kinds of public communication situations provide for different amounts of feedback. A zero feedback situation exists when it is virtually impossible for the sender to be aware of a receiver's response. Suppose that right now I stated in this book: "Stop what you are doing and draw an equilateral triangle resting on one of its sides." I would have no way of knowing whether you understood what I was talking about, whether you actually drew the triangle, or, if you drew it, whether you drew it correctly. As the source of that message—as well as the other messages in this textbook—I cannot know for sure whether I am really communicating. The lack of direct feedback is a weakness in any form of mass communication. The source has little or no immediate opportunity to test the impact of a message.

Suppose, however, that I am your instructor in a class of fifty students. Now suppose that I asked you to draw an equilateral triangle resting on one of its sides. Even if you said nothing, my presence would enable me to monitor your nonverbal feedback directly. If you drew the triangle, I could see it; if you refused, I would know; in some cases I could see exactly what you were drawing. Now suppose that in this classroom, as I asked you to draw the triangle, you were free to ask me any direct questions and I was free and willing to respond. The free flow of interacting communication that would take place represents the highest level of feedback.

How important is feedback to effective communication? Leavitt and Mueller[1] conducted an experiment similar to the one I just described. They reported that communication improved markedly as the situation moved from zero feedback to complete interaction. In our communication, whether conversation or public speaking, we want to stimulate as much feedback as the situation will allow. In various places in this book we will be concerned with monitoring feedback and responding to it. Although many of your speaking assignments will not allow direct verbal feedback during the regular speaking time, you should learn to take advantage of any nonverbal feedback you get.

An analysis of the communication process is incomplete without consideration of one additional variable—noise.

Noise Our ability to interpret, understand, or respond to symbols is often inhibited by the amount of *noise* accompanying the communication. Noise consists of the external, internal, or semantic interferences that can occur.

---

[1] H. J. Leavitt and Ronald A. H. Mueller, "Some Effects of Feedback on Communication," *Human Relations*, 4 (1951), 403.

External noises are the sights, sounds, and other stimuli that draw people's attention away from the message. For instance, during a lecture in American history, your attention is drawn to the sound of a power lawnmower outside the window. The sound of the lawnmower is external noise. Your attempts to concentrate on the lecture might be fruitless unless the noise is eliminated. External noise does not have to be a sound—a sight can also be distracting. Perhaps during the same lecture an extremely attractive man or woman looks toward you with what you perceive as a particularly engaging look. For the moment at least, your attention is likely to be drawn toward that person.

Internal noises are the thoughts and feelings that find their way into your mind as you are trying to pay attention to someone or something else. Perhaps your economics professor uses an example of food distribution to make a point, and the thought of food causes you to daydream about what you are going to have for lunch. If you tune out the lecture and tune in a daydream, a past conversation, or an irrelevant feeling, you create an internal noise.

The third type of noise, and perhaps the most difficult to cope with, is semantic noise. *Semantic noises* are message symbols that inhibit or prevent shared meaning. Because your perceptions and experiences differ from those of a person speaking to you, you may hold different meanings for even relatively simple words. Suppose a speaker talks of the benefits of democracy in ensuring personal freedom. If the speaker and all the listeners had the same middle-class experiences, then communication would probably take place. However, if listeners had experienced a good deal of social injustice, the concept of "democracy ensuring personal freedom" might well sound like hypocrisy. Communication cannot take place if semantic noise causes the source and the receiver to perceive the symbols of communication differently. The semantic noise factor may be the most important barrier to the communication process. In Chapter 5, on style, we discuss the use of language to convey ideas and feelings clearly, vividly, emphatically, and appropriately.

Model of the Communication Process

Let us look at these six variables in model form. Through a pictorial representation we will be able to see how these variables interrelate. Figure 1-1 illustrates the communication process in terms of a one-to-one relationship, that is, the speaker to one member of an

FIGURE 1-1.   A Model of Communication between Two Individuals

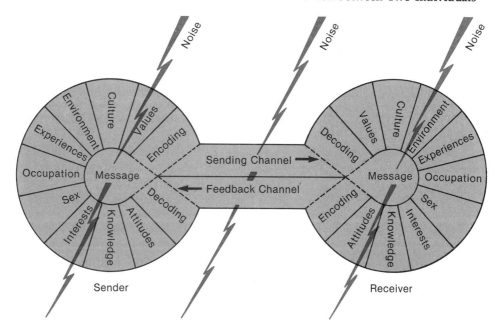

audience. The left-hand circle represents the speaker. In the center of that circle is a message, a thought or feeling that the speaker will send. The nature of that thought or feeling is created, shaped, and affected by the speaker's total field of experience, represented in the outer circle by such specific factors as values, culture, environment, experiences, occupation, sex, interests, knowledge, and attitudes. The bar between the circles represents the channel. The speaker sends the message through the sending channel (upper half of the bar) by words and actions.

The right-hand circle represents the listener. Into the center of that circle comes the message. The received message is turned into meaning for the receiver through the decoding process. This decoding process is affected by the receiver's total field of experience—that is, by the same factors of values, culture, environment, experiences, occupation, sex, interests, knowledge, and attitudes. Upon decoding and interpreting the message, the receiver sends verbal and nonverbal reaction back to the speaker through the receiving or feedback channel (lower half of the bar).

The speaker receives and decodes the feedback in order to interpret the response he or she is getting from the receiver. At the same time this process is taking place, external, internal, and semantic noise may be occurring at various places in the model. These noises may affect the ability of speaker and receiver to share meanings. In a public speaking situation this model is repeated for every person in the audience.

Now let us relate a simple communication act and trace the six variables in operation. As the professor looks at her watch she sees she has only five minutes left. She frowns because she still has one major point to cover, but, aware that time is too short, she says, "That's enough for today." Members of the class gather books, pencils, paper, and coats, and begin filing out.

The professor, the *source,* conveys her *message* in verbal and nonverbal symbols. Her language, "That's enough for today," is the verbal representation of her thoughts; her frown and dejected tone are the nonverbal representation of her frustration at not having more time. In this case, the nonverbal symbols say more than the words about the professor's feelings. Her words and tone of voice are carried by air waves, and her facial expression and bodily action by light waves (the *channel*) to each member of the class. Each member of the class, the *receiver,* records the sound and light waves and then interprets (decodes) the verbal and nonverbal symbols that carried the message. As a result of their interpretation of the message, the class responds, gives *feedback,* by gathering materials and leaving. In this example there were no barriers (*noise*) to the satisfactory completion of the communication.

The variables of source, message, receiver, channel, feedback, and noise are used to analyze the nature of any communication act whether it is accidental or intentional. In discussing these variables we have tried to show how each of them may be considered in the context of effective speaking. We should note that, first, effective speaking is message-oriented; it deals with transmission of information. Second, the meaning of the message is source-selected; a speaker intends to get some point across with his or her communication, and he makes an effort to prepare the message so that it will communicate that point. Third, effective speaking is basically verbal and nonverbal.

COMMUNICATION SETTINGS

Although all communication includes the six variables we have just considered, our communication is not the same under all circumstances. Basically, communication occurs in three overlapping but nonetheless definable settings: personal, small group, and public.

Personal communication is the spontaneous, usually informal communication we engage in with self and others. Intrapersonal communication includes those silent and sometimes verbal conversations we have with ourselves; interpersonal communication is the person-to-person interaction we have with another individual or with a small informal aggregate of people. So, talking to a friend on campus, talking on the phone with a classmate about an upcoming test, discussing a movie with the gang over a beer are all examples of interpersonal communication. Even though the focus of this book is not on personal communication skills, many of the principles we consider may well prove relevant to your personal communication.

Another portion of our communication occurs in group settings. Each of us belongs to many groups: family, social organizations, church organizations, and work committees. The communication in these groups is basically interpersonal; but when several persons combine talents to solve a problem or to make a decision, they form a work group. Because of the importance of the problem-solving group format and because of the public speaking potential of individuals working in these groups, I have devoted one chapter (Chapter 15) to communication in work groups.

The focus of this book, however, is on public speaking. Of all communication settings, public speaking is usually the most difficult for people. Some of the sources of this difficulty are the care required in message preparation, the necessity of facing a large group, and the need to be sensitive to what are often very subtle feedback responses. Public speaking is an art that must be mastered. Why? For one crucial reason—public speaking is a necessary part of modern life, and to succeed you need to equip yourself with these vital skills.

We recognize the importance of the words of our political and religious leaders—but the importance of public speaking is not demonstrated only by a handful of men and women. It is demonstrated daily by people in all walks of life, who use words, for example, to help move information from one person to another, to influence the thinking of others, and to move people to action. Rhetoric, the art of public speaking, is significant for everyone whether (1) through *success,* achieved by speaking effectively, or (2) through *failure,* resulting from either ineffective speaking or, in many instances, refusal to speak at all.

COMMUNICATION
RESPONSIBILITIES

We have stressed the importance of public speaking to us personally and to the society in which we live. Although the First Amendment to the Constitution guarantees freedom of speech, it is interpreted by the courts as carrying certain legal and ethical responsibilities. In 1972, The Speech Communication Association, the national association of teachers of speech communication in America, endorsed the "Credo for Free and Responsible Communication in a Democratic Society." Two paragraphs of that document lay a foundation for an assessment of our communication responsibilities:

> We accept the responsibility of cultivating by precept and example, in our classrooms and in our communities, enlightened uses of communication; of developing in our students a respect for precision and accuracy in communication, and for reasoning based upon evidence and a judicious discrimination among values.

> We encourage our students to accept the role of well-informed and articulate citizens, to defend the communication rights of those with whom they may disagree, and to expose abuses of the communication process.

These two paragraphs provide the overall approach to communication responsibilities; now let us take a look at some specific legal and ethical responsibilities.

Legal Responsibilities

Although there are several legal restrictions to human communication, the following two are especially relevant to the public speaker.

1.   A speaker has the responsibility to refrain from communication that may be defined as a clear and present danger. Behaviors that present *a clear and present danger* are those that incite people to panic, to riot, or to overthrow the government. From the time you began studying civics you learned that a person can't yell "fire" in a public place "just to see what would happen." Such behavior is an example of speech designed to incite panic. You would also be prosecuted for giving a speech that incited a mob of students to riot against the administration or a mob of citizens to riot against the government.

2.   A speaker has the responsibility to refrain from using obscene language. Despite a relaxation of society's attitude toward use of language, a person can still be prosecuted for obscene public

speaking. Since the Supreme Court has defined obscenity as behavior that is outside the boundary of "community standards," what is considered illegal may vary from one place to another.

Ethical Responsibilities   "Ethical issues," according to Richard Johannesen, "center in value judgments concerning degrees of rightness and wrongness, goodness and badness, in human conduct."[2]

While legal responsibilities are codified, what is ethical or not is far more likely to be a personal matter. Still, we expect the society in which we live to hold to certain standards that can be used to help with our personal value judgments. The family, schools, and church all share the responsibility of helping the individual develop ethical standards that can be applied to specific situations. Yet, as we are all aware, ethical judgments are seldom easy. In this initial look at ethical responsibilities for the public speaker we will present two broad guidelines that were reflected in the Speech Communication Association Credo and that are endorsed by most, if not all, communication scholars. Then, in the chapter on principles of persuasion, we will look at several specific behaviors that are considered unethical.

1.   You as a public speaker are responsible for what you say. Your audience has the right to hold you accountable for what you say. If, for instance, you say that Peters (your opponent in a hotly contested political election) received campaign funds from illegal sources, your audience holds you responsible for the truth and accuracy of that statement.

Upholding this ethical responsibility is accomplished in at least two ways. First, you demonstrate accountability by substantiating your statements with solid evidence, not assumption, personal opinion, or hearsay. Before you make any statement about Peters' campaign funds, you are responsible for finding the facts. If you have not found facts to support your claim, it is unethical to present such a claim as if you have the facts.

A second way of demonstrating accountability is by presenting the facts for your audience to examine. You have the right to advocate a position—however unpopular it may be—but the lis-

[2] Richard L. Johannesen, *Ethics in Human Communication,* Columbus, Ohio: Charles E. Merrill, 1975, p. 11.

tener has the right to examine the bases for the conclusions you have drawn. If you state that Peters received funds from illegal sources, you should share the facts that led you to that conclusion with the audience. Although an audience may be willing to trust your judgment on such matters, you owe them, and Peters for that matter, the right to examine the facts for themselves.

2. You as a public speaker have a responsibility to allow the other side to be heard. Freedom of speech applies equally to both sides of an issue or controversy. You do not have the right to suppress the speech of those who hold different views from your own. If you have accused Peters of getting illegal campaign funds, you have the responsibility for allowing Peters to reply to your accusations. Any effort to suppress that right or to deny Peters access to the same audience is unethical.

Everything we say or do in our speeches has a potential effect on the audience to which we speak. If we are assured that we have a solid base for what we say, that we are willing to share the substance upon which our statements are based, and are willing to listen to opposing views, we are reasonably certain that our public speaking will meet the ethical responsibilities we hold.

A better speaker is a better listener.

What kind of listener are you?

Chapter 2 Listening to Speeches

Your goal in this course is to become a better speaker. And, curiously enough, becoming a better speaker is a product of becoming a better listener. Why is that so?

First, being a better listener helps you make the most from the speeches of others. Everyone in class, including your professor, is attempting to model characteristics of effective speaking in classroom speeches and lectures. In contrast to the five to ten speeches you will be giving in this class, you can expect to hear somewhere between one hundred and two hundred speeches—probably more than you will hear during the next several years outside the classroom. Because you will see a much wider selection of methods and techniques in operation than you could hope to try out yourself in your comparatively few classroom speeches, you can use the experience of others to help you. By learning to listen effectively, you can identify both those elements of effectiveness that you want to incorporate in your speaking and those mistakes that you want to avoid.

In addition, through good listening you can help your classmates (as they in turn can help you) by evaluating their effectiveness. Although your instructor will discuss the speeches in terms of his or her standard of speech effectiveness, it will be up to you as part of a sympathetic but critical audience to describe the effect the speech had on you. Effective criticism—honest, accurate appraisal—is invaluable to learning. However, to be able to make more than superficial, obvious comments, you must listen carefully.

As a bonus, your careful listening will enable you to learn about more subjects in this course than in any other course you are taking. Remember, much of what your classmates say will be new information or will give you new insights. You will find that your speech class is truly a liberal arts course, and you will want to make the most of your opportunity to learn. Moreover, you may find the information you take in as a listener today may well be of use to you as a speaker some other time.

WHAT KIND OF LISTENER ARE YOU?

Perhaps you believe you are already a good listener. Unfortunately, most college students are not. Studies indicate that listening proficiency among college students is only about 50 percent—and when a short delay occurs between time of an utterance and testing, average listening efficiency drops to near 25 percent. Ralph Nichols, a leading authority on listening, has conducted numerous studies and has reported the research of others for the last 20 years. All his work points to the same sad figures: 25 to 50 percent efficiency.[1] These percentages are especially important when we realize how much of our daily communication time is spent listening. Paul Rankin's original study, done more than 50 years ago, showed that people spend more time listening than they do in any other form of communication.[2] In a recent study of student communication behavior, Verderber, Elder, and Weiler found that college students spend 8 percent of their time writing, 20 percent reading, 22 percent speaking, and 50 percent of their time listening.[3] What is the difference between hearing and listening? *Hearing* is the ability to record the sound vibrations that are transmitted; *listening* involves making sense of what is heard. Since listening and speaking are by far the most important communication skills, you should try to improve them as much as you try to improve your reading and writing.

---

[1] Ralph Nichols and Leonard A. Stevens, *Are You Listening?* (New York: McGraw-Hill, 1957), pp. 5–6.

[2] Paul Tory Rankin, "The Measurement of the Ability to Understand Spoken Language," doctoral dissertation, University of Michigan, 1926, University Microfilm, 1952, Publ. No. 4352; cited by Nichols and Stevens, *Are You Listening?*, p. 6.

[3] Rudolph Verderber, Ann Elder, and Ernest Weiler, "An Analysis of Student Communication Habits," unpublished study, University of Cincinnati, 1976.

What are the effects of bad listening? Suppose you are listening to a classroom lecture. At least five situations can occur:

1. You can totally miss what your professor is saying. This may occur because you are not paying attention and therefore you do not even hear what was said; or it may occur because you have a physical or psychological problem. If you have a cold, your hearing could be temporarily affected; likewise, if something has happened that affects your behavior deeply, such as something over which you are experiencing a great amount of grief, your emotional state might override your ability to hear.

2. You can take in what is being said (you are hearing the message) but you are unable to ascribe meaning to the message. If your professor attempts to make a point by talking to you in French, for instance, you may hear every word but not have the remotest idea of what is being said. Of course, the speaker need not be talking in a foreign language. If the professor uses English words that you don't know, the result is the same. For instance, if your professor told you that "your implementation is obfuscatory," you may not understand that he's telling you that what you're doing gets in the way.

3. You can take in what is being said (again, you are hearing the message), but you ascribe to it a different meaning than was intended. This means that either you hold different meanings for the words that are used or that you perceive something in the communication process or setting that alters your meanings. For instance, you may elect to stay in a hotel that is "within walking distance" of the convention center. When you get to the hotel you may discover that your understanding of "walking distance" is much different from the hotel's brochure. Or when a person says to you, "Watch what you're doing!" you may perceive some nonverbal element, perhaps a wink, that leads you to take the message differently from the way you normally would.

4. You can listen accurately to the message, but as time goes on, your mind alters the nature of the meaning. For instance, Tom says the report is due by the fifteenth of the month. You listen and understand. But a few days later you may think he said the twenty-fifth rather than the fifteenth.

5. You can listen accurately to the message and then immediately forget it.

In each of the five situations, the speaker has some responsibility for the outcome, but it is unfair to put the entire burden of listening effectiveness on him or her. You as the listener have as much responsibility for effective communication, and in some cases more, as the speaker.

Let us look at the factors that predict which outcome is most likely.

WHAT FACTORS DETERMINE YOUR LISTENING LEVEL?   Your listening is a product of many factors; you have only minimal control over some, but others you can change if you want. Let us consider three factors that are a function of your heredity and environment: hearing acuity, vocabulary, and an "ear for language."

Hearing Acuity   Some people have real hearing problems. Nearly 15 million Americans suffer some hearing impairment.[4] If you are among this number, you may now wear a hearing aid or you may have learned to adapt to the problem. However, if you are not aware of the problem, poor hearing alone may limit your listening effectiveness.

If you suspect you may have a hearing problem, and your school has facilities for testing hearing acuity, have the test done. It is painless and is usually provided at minimal if any cost to the student.

Vocabulary   Listening and vocabulary are definitely related. If you know the meaning of all the words a speaker uses, you are likely to have a better understanding of the material and, as a result, retain more. However, if you do not know the meaning of words used in a lecture or if you are not familiar with the specialized vocabulary of a particular study, you may not understand, and your listening may well be affected. Many "poor students" may have average or better intelligence but be handicapped by a poor vocabulary. If you have a below-average vocabulary, you may have to work that much harder on listening.

When a speaker (your professor, your friend, or a casual ac-

---

[4] Arthur S. Freese, *You and Your Hearing* (New York: Charles Scribner's Sons, 1979), p. 67.

quaintance) uses a word you do not understand in a speech, what do you do? What if that person uses the word in ordinary conversation? Is your behavior the same? People are often reticent to call attention to their lack of understanding of a new word. Why? They do not want to appear foolish—they do not want to "make a spectacle" of themselves. Isn't it equally foolish for them to respond to something they do not understand? This tendency of some people to respond as if they really understand is illustrated by the results of a telephone survey conducted to find out if citizens were continuing efforts to save energy. Most people answered yes to questions about turning out unneeded lights, keeping thermostats set at 68 degrees, and driving at 55 miles per hour; however, a surprising number also said yes to a question about installing a "thermidor" on the family car. Think how foolish these people would feel if they found out they had confirmed that their engines were now equipped with seafood casseroles! You may feel foolish when you need to ask what a word means; however, you are likely to *behave* foolishly if you do not ask.

An Ear for the English Language

If your family is talkative, you will probably have a natural "ear for language," you will have a grasp of good structure, and you will have experience in a variety of kinds and levels of listening. If you have not developed an ear for language at home, then your ear may not be tuned in to the more difficult kinds of listening that you may encounter at school as an adult. Although a student of college age cannot suddenly make up for years of lack of practice with language, you can use your classroom experiences to help you improve, even if your former environment has been a source of your listening problems.

WHAT CAN YOU DO TO IMPROVE?

Assuming that your listening efficiency is about average, what can you do about it? An average listener who is determined can almost double listening efficiency in a few months. In fact, by following a few simple steps, you can improve your listening immediately. A key factor in listening is your own attitude and behavior. Each of the following recommendations can be put into practice *now*.

Get Ready to Listen

The first step to improved listening is to get yourself ready to listen. Good listening takes time, effort, and energy; and, to be frank, many of us are just not willing to work at it. Many Americans consider listening a passive venture; they have fallen into the habit of "watching" television or "listening" to the radio to relax. As a result of years of associating listening with relaxing, many have acquired or developed bad listening habits. The fact is that whereas listening for entertainment may be relaxing, listening for information or listening critically is work. You have to recognize when it is appropriate to "go into high gear" in your listening; and equally important, you have to know what it means to be in high gear!

What characteristics indicate that you are ready to work at listening? An outward sign is whether you look as if you are listening. Poor listeners often slouch in their chairs. Their eyes wander from place to place. They appear to be bored by what is going on. In contrast, good listeners sit upright—sometimes almost on the edge of their chairs. They rivet their eyes on the speaker. These physical signs of attention are indicative of mental alertness.

At first these recommendations may seem shallow or overdrawn, but test these ideas for yourself. When I discuss listening in class, I precede short comprehension tests by saying, "For the next five minutes, I want you to listen as hard as you can. Then I'm going to give a test on what you heard." What happens when the class realizes it has an investment in what will take place? Students straighten up and turn their eyes to the front of the room; extraneous noises—coughing, clearing throats, rustling—drop to near zero.

Getting ready to listen means more than these physical signs show. Getting ready also means concentrating on the subject at hand. At any given moment many stimuli are competing for attention. You must keep your thinking attuned to the subject and not pay attention to those other thoughts, however persistent they may be. For instance, while you are reading these words, a clock may be ticking loudly in the background, a truck may be passing outside your window, or the radiator may be knocking; moreover, a visual impression of a pleasant event that occurred yesterday, or a worry about a paper you have due next week, or a fantasy about a guy or girl in your economics class might all be competing for your attention. Yet *concentration* on your reading may enable you to push all those thoughts out of your mind. These same kinds of intrusions occur while you are trying to listen—and you must work equally hard to concentrate on the speaker's message. Even though you may not be able to listen at peak efficiency for long periods (attention lags of a split second occur whether we want them to or not), you can help keep distracting thoughts from capturing your attention and you can improve your listening—if you maintain a listening posture.

Listen Actively   The second step you can take immediately is to become an active listener. Effective communication involves feedback; the source sends a message and the receiver responds to that message. Research on learning psychology indicates that listeners learn better and faster and make sounder judgments about what they hear when they are mentally and physically active—when the listener is involved. Let us explore the thinking behind such a generalization.

Most of us talk at a rate of 140 to 180 words per minute; we think at a rate between 300 and 600 words per minute. Whether you are listening effectively or not depends a lot on what you are doing during that time difference. Some listeners do nothing; others think about eating, sleeping, a test the next hour, and other things that eventually capture all of their attention. Active listeners use the extra time to weigh and consider what the speaker has said. They may attempt to repeat key ideas, to ask questions related to the topic, or to test the accuracy of the speaker's assertions.

When the speaker says, "The first major election reform bill was passed in England in 1832," active listeners might mentally repeat "reform bill," "England, 1832." When the speaker says, "Napoleon's battle plans were masterpieces of strategy," active listeners might ask themselves, "What were the characteristics of this strategy?" When the speaker says, "An activity that provides exercise for almost every muscle is swimming," active listeners might inwardly question the point, examining the supporting material the speaker offers. Each of these forms of involvement helps the listener master the ideas.

Active listening can also mean taking notes. Whereas poor listeners fidget, doodle, or look about the room, good listeners often make notes on what the speaker is saying. Perhaps they write down words or phrases denoting key ideas; perhaps they write the most important ideas in complete sentences. The physical activity reinforces the mental activity. A speaker might say, "The first artificial orbiting satellite was launched by Russia in 1957"; if a listener jots down, for example, "1st satellite—Russia—1957," the act of writing, coordinated with thinking the country and the year, will provide a better chance for mental recall and the written record itself as later reference.

Keep in mind, however, that notetaking by itself is not a sign of good listening. A person can come out of a history class with pages of notes and have very little idea of what was said during class. Good notetaking *supplements*—but does not replace—good listening.

Withhold Evaluation   A third step to improved listening is to keep an open mind and withhold evaluation of what you hear until your comprehension is complete. This recommendation means you should control both arbitrary judgments about a subject and emotional responses to content. It is a human reaction to listen attentively only to what we like or what we want to hear. Yet, such an attitude is self-limiting and self-defeating. Let us remind ourselves of why we listen in the first place—to learn and to gather data for evaluation. Neither of these goals is possible if we refuse to listen to anything outside our immediate interests. For instance, if a classroom speaker indicates that he or she will talk about the history of unions, you may say you are interested neither in history in general nor in unions in particular. If during the first sentence or two of the speech you find yourself saying, "I don't think I am going to be interested in this topic," you should remind yourself that judgment must follow and not precede the presentation of information. Poor listeners make value judgments about the content after the first few words; good listeners listen objectively.

Even when we are willing to listen to a topic, content elements may so affect us emotionally that we no longer "hear" what the speaker has to say. Ralph Nichols talks about words that "serve as red flags to some listeners." In this category he lists such words as *mother-in-law, pervert, income tax,* and *evolution.*[5] Perhaps these words evoke no emotional response from you, but what if a speaker uses the terms *liberal, racist, abortion, CIA, big business, police officers,* or *gay rights?* Would any of these terms—or the development of them in a speech—turn you off? Often, poor listeners (and occasionally even good listeners) are given an emotional jolt by a speaker invading an area of personal sensitivity. At this point

[5] Ralph G. Nichols, "Do We Know How to Listen? Practical Helps in a Modern Age," *Speech Teacher* 10 (March 1961), 123.

all you can do is be wary. When the speaker trips the switch to your emotional reaction, let a warning light go on before you go off. Instead of quitting or getting ready to fight, work that much harder at being objective. Can you do it? If so, you'll improve your listening.

In trying to change your behavior, you should try not to take on the characteristics of three types of listeners described by Dominick Barbara:[6] first, those who listen with a modest ear—compulsive nodders who shake their heads in agreement when they are not listening at all; second, those who listen with a rebellious ear—chatterboxes who are thinking of their next reply rather than listening to what is taking place; and, third, those who listen with a deaf ear—those who close their ears to unpleasantness.

Since it is easier to pay attention to a speech if it is well presented, the principles in this book are directed to making speeches so clear and interesting that good and poor listeners alike will pay attention. Nevertheless, some of the speeches you hear, in or out of class, will be less than good. In such instances, you will have to work to make the most of the experience. Since attitudes affect our perception of information, the more we allow emotions to intrude into the listening process, the more distorted will be our recollection of what was said.

Listen for Ideas and Meaning

When have we really listened? Some of us mistakenly think we have listened when we can feed back the words or the details that were communicated. Actually, neither of these acts is necessarily characteristic of good listening. Good listeners listen for ideas more than for details. Earlier we suggested notetaking as a means of listening actively. But notetaking does not involve outlining everything a speaker said. Good notetaking refers to getting down key ideas. If you try to master each detail as it comes up, you will be unable to relate detail to principle or for that matter to differentiate the important from the unimportant. Fortunately, listening for ideas is one of the easiest parts of listening to learn. The information we will discuss in Chapter 4, which deals with organizational patterns, will help you separate ideas from details.

Of equal importance is our ability to listen for overall meaning.

---

[6] Dominick A. Barbara, *The Art of Listening* (Springfield, Ill.: Charles C Thomas, 1971).

In Chapter 1, we noted that messages are intentional and unintentional—that it requires a sensitivity to both the verbal and the nonverbal elements of the message to get full meaning from what is said. When a person says, "Isn't this a beautiful day?" when rain pours down, we realize that the meaning being communicated differs from the meaning those words usually carry. In this instance, the vocal tones, body actions, and movements of the speaker (the nonverbal cues) tell us to disregard normal meaning and to recognize the opposite. In addition to contradicting meaning, nonverbal cues may supplement or modify the meaning. When a person says, "I'm really angry," we measure the degree of anger by the nonverbal cues; when a person says, "I'm not sure how much we should give," we measure the extent of assuredness by the nonverbal cues. Since the speaker's real meaning sometimes is communicated unintentionally by nonverbal cues, we must be alert to all aspects of the message.

A good listener, therefore, absorbs all of the speaker's meaning by being sensitive to voice tone, facial expression, and bodily action, as well as to the words themselves. Sincerity, depth of conviction, confidence, true understanding, and many subtle implications may well be revealed, regardless of the words used.

CRITERIA FOR EVALUATION

Let us review the goals of listening to classroom speeches: (1) we can gain information, (2) we can evaluate the speeches, and (3) we can determine the kinds of material that work with audiences and the kinds that don't and should, therefore, be avoided in our own speaking. Improving general listening efficiency will enable you to achieve the first goal. The other two goals require that you have sound criticism standards to apply.

A speech critic evaluates the setting, the audience, the speaker, and the speech. The critic looks at the room itself and other aspects of the setting to determine whether they affect the speaker's chances for success. If a speaker faces several thousand people in a large auditorium but the public address system is bad, the speaker will have little chance for success.

Second, the critic looks at the nature of the audience to determine its affect on speaker effectiveness. The age, sex, occupation, religion, socioeconomic level, attitudes, interests, and knowledge of the audience all affect how that audience will view the speaker's ideas. For instance, an audience of political conservatives is likely to be far more receptive to a speech by William F. Buckley, Jr., than to a speech by Teddy Kennedy.

Third, the critic assesses the speaker. The reputation, appearance, and attitude of the speaker toward the audience will all affect his or her relative success. In the chapter on persuasion we will consider speaker credibility as one of the primary keys to speaker effectiveness. If a speaker is not liked or is not trusted by the audience, this dislike and/or distrust will affect the speaker's prospects for success.

Fourth, the critic analyzes the speech itself. In the final analysis the burden of evaluation will be on the content, organization, and presentation of that speech. With each speech given in class, you should make a complete analysis of content and method.

The following questions are applicable to all kinds of speeches. With each question I have included the page numbers where complete discussion of each question occurs. Your answers will enable you to prepare a complete profile of what you have heard. When you have applied these questions, you will have a sound basis for speech criticism and an awareness of the criteria for effective speaking.

EVALUATION QUESTIONS

•**The Speech Setting:** Was there anything about the room (size, lighting, heating, and the like), distribution of the audience, public address system, or any other aspect of setting that added to or detracted from the speaker's potential success? (See pages 48–51.)

•**The Speech Audience:** Was there anything about the audience size, age, sex, race, religion, socioeconomic level, attitude, interests, or knowledge that added to or detracted from the speaker's potential success? (See pages 45–48.)

•**The Speaker:** Was there anything about the speaker's attitude, dress, demeanor, posture, and the like that added to or detracted from his or her potential success? (See pages 251–255.) (Although this section overlaps somewhat with the section on delivery, these questions are worth considering separately.)

•**The Speech:**

Content:
Was the speaker prepared? (pages 51–61)

Was the specific goal of the speech apparent? (pages 40–45)
Did the speaker have specific facts and opinions to support or to explain his statements? (pages 54–60 and pages 71–74)
Was the support logical? (pages 85–88)
Was the speaker ethical in the handling of the material? (pages 255–257)

Organization:
Did the introduction gain attention, gain good will for the speaker, and lead into the speech? (pages 74–80)
Were the main points clear statements that proved or explained the specific goal of the speech? (pages 64–71)
Did the conclusion tie the speech together? (pages 81–85)

Language:
Were the ideas clear? (pages 95–100)
Were the ideas presented vividly? (pages 100–104)
Were ideas presented emphatically? (pages 104–108)
Was the language appropriate for this audience? (pages 108–116)

Delivery:
Did the speaker sound enthusiastic? (pages 124–125)
Did the speaker look at the audience? (pages 125–126)
Was the delivery spontaneous? (pages 126–127)
Did the speaker show sufficient variety and emphasis of pitch, rate, and volume? (pages 131–132)
Was articulation satisfactory? (pages 132–133)
Did the speaker show sufficient poise and have good posture? (pages 133–134)

Suggested Readings:
Part One

The following works will give you additional information on the two main subjects of this orientation unit: the communication process and listening.

Barbara, Dominick A. *The Art of Listening.* Springfield, Ill.: Charles C Thomas, 1971. This is a relatively short but easy-to-read book.

Barker, Larry L. *Listening Behavior.* Englewood Cliffs, N.J.: Prentice-Hall, 1971. A comprehensive analysis of listening literature.

Barnlund, Dean C., ed. *Interpersonal Communication: Surveys and Studies.* Boston: Houghton Mifflin, 1968. See particularly pages 3 to 29 for a good discussion of communication goals and a worthwhile analysis of the evolution of communication models.

Freese, Arthur S. *You and Your Hearing.* New York: Charles Scribner's Sons, 1979. A short introduction to hearing problems for nonexperts.

Hirsch, Robert O. *Listening: A Way to Process Information Aurally.* Dubuque, Iowa: Gorsuch Scarisbrick, 1979. A 45-page module that considers various aspects of listening. Contains several lists and explanations related to types, barriers, and way to improve.

Johannesen, Richard L. *Ethics in Human Communication.* Columbus, Ohio: Charles E. Merrill, 1975. (Paperback) An excellent analysis of various ethical perspectives. Also includes four case studies.

Kelley, Charles M. "Empathic Listening." In *Concepts in Communication,* edited by Jimmie D. Trent et al. Boston: Allyn & Bacon, 1973. A good, short article that emphasizes becoming more actively involved in the listening process.

Millar, Dan P., and Frank E. Millar. *Messages and Myths.* New York: Alfred Publishing, 1976. Chapters 1 and 3 explore the myths related to the communication process and listening. The entire book provides a unique approach to the study of communication.

31

Mortensen, C. David. *Communication: The Study of Human Interaction.* New York: McGraw-Hill, 1972. See particularly Chapter 2, pages 29 to 64, for a good survey of models, their functions, and their limitations.

Nichols, Ralph G. "Do We Know How to Listen? Practical Helps in a Modern Age." *Speech Teacher* 10 (March 1961), 118–124. Although this article is no longer "modern," it is still well worth the few minutes it takes to read it.

PART TWO

FUNDAMENTAL PRINCIPLES

Although the act of speaking is itself instructive, you should read the basic material that explains and develops four fundamental principles of public speaking before you prepare and present your first major speeches.

Part Two presents material on selecting topics, finding material, organizing material, wording the speech, and delivering the speech. You will find additional material and further development of these fundamentals in later chapters.

Vocation	Interests	Social Problems
Political Sciences	Sports	Urban Renewal
History	Community Relations	Housing
Biography	Family Tree	Civil Rights
	Blacks History	

Frederick Douglass

Henry O. Flipper first black graduate of West Point.

Dr. George Washington Carver

FREE

FREEDOM NOW

WE WILL OVERCOME

Chapter 3 Selecting Topics and Finding Material

PRINCIPLE I:
Effective speaking
begins with
good content.

They say you cannot make a silk purse out of a sow's ear, and indeed, whether it is purses, buildings, or speeches, you can get a lot farther if you have good material to work with. By using a little common sense and by proceeding systematically, you will find that determining what you will say is much easier than you might expect. Let us consider the essentials of good content: selecting your topic, determining your purpose, analyzing your audience and occasion, and finding your material.

I feel a certain frustration in discussing this procedure as four separate steps. This frustration arises from the knowledge that none of the steps can be completed without information gained from completing one of the other steps. For instance, "selecting a topic" may require insights from "finding your material" in order to phrase the topic in a usable form. So, even though I discuss each step separately, please understand that the steps overlap; they are sometimes accomplished in this order, sometimes in another order, and sometimes nearly simultaneously.

SELECTING YOUR TOPIC

For speeches given outside the classroom, this step of selecting your topic may be accomplished for you. A representative of a group who asks you to speak usually indicates what the group wants you to talk about. In the classroom, however, topic selection is usually left to you. For some students, selecting a topic may be the most terrifying part of the preparation period. I have heard many students exclaim, "I know I can give a good speech—if only I could find a topic!"

How can you find a good topic without wasting valuable hours fretting? The answer involves good common sense: Use the same guidelines that determine what you talk about in ordinary conversation. When you are with the gang, do you select topics with conscious effort? I doubt it. You probably just start talking *about topics that concern you.* If you have just seen a good movie or gone to a new restaurant or viewed a particularly good television show, you are likely to talk about the experience. If you are distressed by the performance of a particular sports team or by the city council's position on a public issue or by the lack of progress in development of a national energy policy, you are likely to talk about these topics.

If you talk about what concerns you, you will be in line with most of the important speakers in the country. Just as Leonard Woodcock talks about labor, Gloria Steinem about women, Jesse Jackson about black self-determination, Paul Samuelson about economics, and Billy Graham about God, you as a speaker will do well to talk about subjects that you know something about and that interest you!

Speakers sometimes have trouble in translating their broad subject interests into specific speech topics. If this is your problem, try brainstorming. This is like the old word-association process: think of "snow," and you may also think of "sled," "cold," "shoveling," and "snowman." Likewise, when you suggest a word or idea related to your major areas of interest, you can often put thirty or more other related ideas and concepts down on paper.

To start, take a sheet of paper and divide it into three columns. Label column 1 "Major" or "Vocation"; column 2, "Hobby," "Interest," or "Activity"; and column 3, "Current Events" or "Social Problems." Work on one column at a time. If you begin with column 2, "Hobby," you might write "chess." Then you would jot down everything that comes to mind, such as "master," "Bobby Fischer," "openings," "carving chess men." Work for at least five minutes on a column. Then begin with a second column. Although you may not finish in one sitting, do not begin an evaluation until you have noted at least twenty items in each column.

Suppose that one of your major interests is computers. A ten-minute brainstorming session might yield the following word associations:

history	games	central
hardware	home units	processing unit
software	CRTs	costs
chips	printers	technology
crime	floppy discs	accuracy
application	terminals	time saving
cards	terminology	word processing
language	capabilities	communication
programming		with

After you believe you have exhausted your personal resources, look over your list and check the three or four items that "ring a bell"—that is, that best capture your concerns and interests. Now, the point of this exercise is to enable you to take advantage of a basic psychological principle—it is easier to answer a multiple-choice question than to answer the same question without the choices. Thus, whereas you may be stumped if you saddle yourself with the question "What should I talk about for my speech?" you may find it easy to make a choice from among the twenty or more topics you yourself have listed. For instance, if you are interested in elementary education, you may find it much easier to decide that you like "programmed texts," "reading," or "motivation" from your list than it would be to come up with one of these topics cold.

You may find, however, that the words or phrases you select are still too general to give you direction. If so, start a new list with one of the general topics. For instance, a few additional minutes of brainstorming on "programmed texts" might yield: "writing programs," "principles underlying programs," "use of programmed texts," "effectiveness of programmed learning." From this list you might be inclined to select "principles underlying the construction of programmed texts." If you make a selection of this kind from each of the three columns, you may realize that you have three good topics to choose from for your first speeches.

Exercise 1   *1. Divide a sheet of paper into three columns labeled "Vocation" or "Major," "Hobby" or "Interest" or "Activity," and "Current Events" or "Social Problems." After you identify* *your major ("history"), interests ("computers"), or current events ("space shuttles"), make a list of twenty to forty items in each column.*

2.   Select three items from each list.

3.   If any of these three items seems too broad, continue the brainstorming process until you have limited the topic sufficiently.

4.   In order of preference, indicate the three topics that are most interesting or most important to you.

DETERMINING YOUR SPECIFIC PURPOSE AND WRITING A THESIS STATEMENT

Once you have a topic (whether one that someone suggested for you or one that you selected yourself), continue the speech-building process by deciding what to do with that topic in your speech. This step is called determining your specific purpose and writing a thesis statement. Although completing this process may involve your doing *some* audience analysis and gathering *some* material, let us consider it separately at this point.

A *specific purpose* is a statement that indicates your goal: what you want to do with the speech or what response you want from your audience as a result of the speech. The *thesis statement* (or central idea) refines the specific purpose and is worded to say what the speaker will accomplish in the speech. The purpose can be decided before you go any further in the speech preparation process; final wording of the thesis statement, however, may have to wait until you have gotten most of the information for the speech. The specific purpose, then, is a statement that begins speech preparation; it is the basis for the thesis statement. In the remainder of this section, we assume that you have enough material to write both the purpose sentence and the thesis statement.

I suggest that the specific purpose be stated as an infinitive phrase; the infinitive (for instance, to describe, to explain, or to prove) indicates the intent of the speaker, and the rest of the phrase states the goal. The thesis statement, which refines the statement of purpose, is written as a complete sentence and includes the details of that goal. During brainstorming you identify a subject area and select a topic. Then you determine your specific purpose and write your complete thesis statement. For example, you pick the general subject area of "diamonds" from column 2

("Interest") of your first brainstorming sheet. On a second sheet, you list twenty or more items related to "diamonds," and eventually you select the topic "evaluating diamonds." Using that topic you could determine that your specific purpose (your goal) was "to explain the four major criteria for evaluating a diamond." Then you could write your thesis statement, based on the specific purpose, as follows: "Diamonds are evaluated on the basis of what diamond experts call the four C's: caret (weight), color, clarity, and cutting." Notice the relationship between specific purpose (goal) and thesis statement (refinement of goal).

With any one topic a number of specific purposes are possible; and a specific purpose may be refined by a number of thesis statements. Let us illustrate this relationship among subject area, topic, specific purpose, and thesis statement with two additional examples:

Subject Area: Computers
Topic: Essentials of computer hardware
Specific Purpose: To explain the three essentials of computer hardware.
Thesis statement: The three essentials of computer hardware are the central processing unit, memory, and input/output devices. (This topic is used as the basis for the sample outline at the end of Chapter 4. Turn there and see where the purpose sentence and thesis statements appear on a complete outline.)

Subject Area: Current Events/Issues—Euthanasia
Topic: Legalization of euthanasia
Specific Purpose: To prove that overt euthanasia should be legalized.
Thesis statement: Euthanasia should be legalized because it relieves the pain and suffering of the terminally ill and because it is in keeping with legal precedent.

Since writing a good specific purpose is so important, let us take a step-by-step look at the procedure:

1. Write out several potential wordings of the specific purpose. You probably will not be satisfied with your first idea. In fact, you may find it difficult to arrive at a statement that clearly states your point.

2. Make sure the specific purpose is written as a complete thought. Do not stop with a word, a few words, a vague statement. For instance, suppose you wanted to talk about "capital punishment." You have an idea, but it is just the start of a complete thought. "Methods of capital punishment" indicates the aspect of capital punishment that you want to consider. "Three methods of capital punishment" limits what you will say to a specific number. "To explain three methods of capital punishment practiced in the United States" is a complete, clear statement of specific purpose.

3. Write the specific purpose so that it contains only one idea. "To explain three methods of capital punishment practiced in the United States and to show that all three are inhumane" includes two distinct ideas, either of which can be used—but not both. Make a decision. Do you want to talk about methods? Then the statement "To explain three methods of capital punishment that are practiced in the United States" is the better statement. Do you want to talk about morality? Then the statement "To prove that the methods of capital punishment practiced in the United States are inhumane" is the better statement. Whenever the specific purpose appears in compound or complex form, you are probably trying to give more than one speech. Notice that in the statement "To prove that the methods of capital punishment practiced in the United States are inhumane" you may have to mention the three methods. However, the emphasis or thrust of the speech will be on proving they are inhumane. In contrast, the thrust of "To explain the three methods of capital punishment that are practiced in the United States" will be an explanation of the methods. Whether they are inhumane is not within the scope of *that* speech.

4. Write the specific purpose in declarative form. "Is capital punishment inhumane?" is a good question for discussion, but it is not a good speech specific purpose because it does not show direction. Likewise "Capital punishment—man's inhumanity to man!" may be a clever title, but it too fails as a specific purpose for much the same reason: It does not give clear enough direction. "To prove that capital punishment is inhumane" is a clear declarative form.

5. Precede the statement of thesis with an infinitive or infinitive phrase that shows intent. If you regard your idea as noncontroversial, universally accepted, or an expression of observation, then your intent is basically informative and will be shown with such wordings as "to explain," "to show," "to indicate," "to have the audience understand." However, if your idea is controversial, a statement of belief, or a call to action, then your intent is persuasive and that intent will be shown with such statements as "to convince," "to motivate," "to prove to the audience," "to have the audience act," and so forth.

6.   **Write a thesis statement that refines the specific purpose.** This step may not be completed until the topic is researched. For instance, you may know that you want "to prove that capital punishment should be abolished," but you may not yet have enough material to refine the purpose. After some research you may be able to complete the thesis statement to read, "Capital punishment should be abolished because it does not deter crime, because it is not just, and because it is an inhumane form of punishment."

Most specific purposes can be classified by their general purpose: (1) to entertain, (2) to inform, or (3) to persuade. Because speech is a complex act that may serve many purposes, never hold slavishly to the rigid guidelines these categories might suggest. They are useful only in showing that in any communicative act one overriding purpose is likely to predominate. For instance, Johnny Carson's opening monologue may have some informative elements and may even contain some intended or unintended persuasive message, yet his major goal is to entertain his viewers. Your history professor's discussion of the events leading up to World War I may use elements of entertainment to gain and hold your attention, and the implication of the discussion of those events may have persuasive overtones, yet the professor's primary goal is to explain those events in a way that will enable the class to understand them. Procter & Gamble may seek to amuse you with their commercials, and they may well include some elements of information in their presentation, but there can be no question that their goal is to persuade you to buy their soap.

Because one common way of assigning speeches is by purpose and because methods of development differ according to purpose. The assignments discussed later in this book are made by purpose. Part III deals with informative speeches and Part IV with persuasive speeches.

Why is it so important to have a clearly stated specific purpose early in speech preparation? First, the specific purpose helps you to limit your research. If you know you want "to explain the criteria used to evaluate a diamond," you can limit your reading to criteria for evaluation, and save many hours of preparation time. Second, a good specific purpose will help you organize your ideas. (You will see how this is true in the next chapter.) And, third, the phrasing of a good specific purpose will put your topic in a form that will enable you to apply the necessary tests.

When you believe that your topic is clearly phrased in specific-purpose form, you should test it by asking these five questions:

1.   Am I really interested in the topic? Although you began your selection of the topic on the basis of interest, you should make sure that you have not drifted into an area that no longer reflects that interest.

2.   Does my purpose meet the assignment? Whether the assignment is made by purpose (to inform or to persuade), or by type of speech (expository or descriptive), or by subject (book analysis or current event), your specific purpose should reflect the nature of that assignment.

3.   Can I cover the topic in the time allotted? To explain "three major causes of World War I" can be discussed in five minutes; to present "a history of World War I" cannot. Your time limits for classroom speeches will be relatively short; although you want your topics to have depth, avoid trying to cover too broad an area.

4.   Is this topic one that will provide new information, new insights, or reason for a change of opinion for my audience? Usually, there is no sense taking time to talk about a subject the audience already understands or believes in. To explain "how to hold a tennis racket" would be a waste of time for a group of tennis players; "a comparison of wooden and aluminum rackets by their ability to generate power and spin" would be much better. Likewise, "to persuade you to go to college" would be a waste of time for college students; "to persuade you to take a course in economics" would be much better. When you have decided that your audience already knows much of what you are going to say, or already believes in or is doing what you wish, you should work for a different specific purpose within the same subject area. An audience is making a time investment; it is up to you to make that time worthwhile. Likewise, try to stay away from the superficial, the banal, and the frivolous; "how to tie shoe laces" and "my first day at camp" are just not good topics. If you have worked on your brainstorming lists, superficiality should be no problem.

5. Are my motives for speaking legitimate? Examination of the speech purpose is the starting point for ethical consideration. If you find yourself using the assignment as a platform for airing personal views regardless of audience reaction, you should take time to question your motives. Likewise, if your only purpose is personal gain, you should reexamine your goals.

Exercise 2
1. *For each of the three topics you selected in Exercise 1, phrase one or more specific purposes.*
2. *Evaluate each in terms of the five tests above.*
3. *Write a thesis statement that refines the specific purpose.*

ANALYZING YOUR AUDIENCE AND OCCASION

Since you are planning to give your speech to a specific audience for a specific occasion, you need to analyze the nature of both very carefully. The audience, of course, is the people, individually and collectively, to whom the speech is directed; the occasion is the place, setting, and circumstances under which the speech is given. Although audience and occasion are discussed separately for purposes of analysis, in reality an audience cannot be separated from the place, setting, and circumstances. It is best, therefore, to make a preliminary analysis of each and then put the analyses together to test your conclusions.

Audience

Audience analysis is a method of examining audience knowledge, interests, and attitudes to determine a set of criteria by which you can test the appropriateness of the selected topic and the specific purpose. You use the results of this analysis also to guide your selection of supporting material, organization, language, and delivery. The following three groups of questions provide a working framework for such analysis. As you gain experience, you may modify the phrasing of the questions and add other appropriate questions.

1. What are the nature and extent of my listeners' knowledge of this topic?

Is my listeners' knowledge of the subject area sufficient for them to understand my speech? For some subjects, special knowledge is necessary; for others, a certain level of information may be necessary (an explanation of calculus, for example, requires that the audience understand certain mathematical information).

Will developmental material provide new information to most of my listeners? A speech that provides neither new information nor new insights needs to be reconsidered.

What kinds of development and language will meet their level of knowledge most suitably? Each audience is receptive to material that fits best into its members' general frame of reference.

2. What are the nature and extent of my listeners' interest in this topic?

Do my listeners already have an immediate interest? If not, can I relate my topic to their interest? Only rarely does a topic create an automatic interest; some topics require a special creative approach to make them interesting.

What kinds of material are most likely to arouse or maintain their interest? Each audience responds differently to ways of stimulating interest.

3. What are the nature and the intensity of my listeners' attitude toward this topic?

Will my listeners be sympathetic? apathetic? or hostile? Knowing or at least attempting to determine audience disposition beforehand will probably help you determine procedure.

Can I expect them to have any preconceived biases that will affect their listening, understanding, or emotional reactions?

If they are sympathetic, how can I present my material so that it will take advantage of their favorable attitude?

If they are hostile, how can I present my material in a way that will at least not increase their hostility?

If you could give your audience a comprehensive exam and an aptitude test, and then take an opinion poll, you could answer these questions with no difficulty. Since such methods are impractical, you have to approach the problem more indirectly. You must gather as much data about the audience as you possibly can, and then use the data to make judgments about knowledge, interests, and attitudes.

Data about your listeners are gathered in a variety of ways. If you know them, if you have spoken to them before, you can gather data by direct observation and experience. Any group you know well such as your family or the group you live with, your political group, your service organization, or your speech class can be analyzed in this way.

If you are not familiar with the group, you can ask the chairperson or group contact to provide you with information. If you cannot learn anything about the audience beforehand, you can make qualified guesses based on such things as the kind of group most likely to attend a speech on this topic, the location of the meeting place, and the sponsor of the speech.

Before you speak you usually have a chance to observe the audience, and often you have an opportunity to talk with a few of the members. For instance, if you are scheduled to speak after a dinner, you can observe the physical characteristics of your audience directly; your informal conversation with those around you will often reveal information that substantiates and supplements your observations.

What clues are you looking for in audience analysis? Judgments (guesses) about audience knowledge, interests, and attitudes can be made by gathering the following data:

•**Age:**   What is the average age? What is the age range?

•**Sex:**   Is the audience all or predominantly male? female? Or are the sexes in the group reasonably evenly balanced?

•**Occupation:**   Is everyone in the same occupation, such as nurses? bankers? drill press operators? Is everyone in a related occupation such as professional people? educators? skilled laborers?

•**Income:**   Is average income high? low? average? Is range of income narrow? large?

•**Race, Religion, Nationality:**   Is the audience primarily of one race, religion, or nationality? Or is it mixed?

•**Geographic Uniqueness:**   Are all the people from one state? city? region?

•**Group Affiliation:**   Is the audience composed of members of one group such as a fraternity or sorority, professional organization, political group?

Remember, your goal is to determine how the members of the audience are alike and how they differ. The more similar or homogeneous the members of the group, the easier it is to learn about knowledge, interests, and attitudes. Suppose, for instance, that you are scheduled to talk to a group of fifth graders about the role of computers in business and industry. The members of the class have many things in common: (1) They are roughly the same age, (2) they go to the same school and have had similar educational experiences, (3) they live in the same city or the same part of a city or the same geographic area. Their total knowledge will be far more limited than that of an adult audience—especially their knowledge of the use of computers in general; their interests will be similar since they are all about the same age; their attitude about computers is likely to be open, and they are likely to be quite inquisitive. In your speech, then, if you talk about uses of computers in an educational setting and about computers in relation to toys, games, and other objects within their realm of experience, you will be adapting your speech directly to them.

Yet, even when members of the audience are dissimilar or heterogeneous, you can uncover similarities that will provide a base for adaptation. Suppose the speech on computers is to be given to a local adult community organization. If that is the only information you have available, you could still make some good guesses about similarities: (1) Because the organization is an adult organization, you can assume that the audience will be mostly adult—most will be married and many will have homes and families; (2) because the organization is a local community organization, they have a geographic bond. Since they are adults, some knowledge about computers in general can be assumed; their interest will relate in part to home, family, and neighborhood; their experience with computers will be varied—some may regard computer technology as a path to Big Brother, the all-pervasive presence in George Orwell's novel *1984*. In your speech, then, if you allude to the influence of computers; talk about effects of computer technology in home, neighborhood, and community; and state ideas that will show benefits and drawbacks, you will be adapting to that audience.

Occasion   You can determine the nature of the occasion and the effect it will have on both speech preparation and presentation by considering the following three questions: When will the speech be given? Where will the speech be given? What facilities are necessary to give the speech? Let us consider each.

1. When will the speech be given? The general question of *when* covers several other questions: whether the speech is part of some commemorative occasion, what time of day it occurs, and where on the program it occurs.

Some speeches arise from a special occasion. The Fourth of July, the anniversary of the founding of an organization, and Martin Luther King's birthday are all special commemorative occasions. If your speech is given in honor of any of those occasions, the occasion itself will control the nature and direction of the speech. If the speech falls on some special occasion by coincidence, you may want to allude to the occasion in the speech.

The time of day the speech is given is likely to be equally important. Different times of day present different problems. For instance, speaking to an audience just before a meal presents a different problem from speaking to a similar audience after they have just eaten. The before a meal audience is likely to be anxious, short of patience, and hungry; the after a meal audience is likely to be lethargic, mellow, and at times on the verge of sleep.

At what point your speech occurs on the program is also important. If you are the featured speaker, the sole reason for the audience to be gathered, you have an obvious advantage. You are the focal point of audience attention. Your class is a good place to practice speaking at different positions in a program. For each round of classroom speeches there will be three to seven other speakers. Your place on the schedule may well affect how your speech is received. I have been in meetings where four speakers were each supposed to have 15 minutes to speak, and I have seen the frustration of the last speaker, whose time has been reduced to 5 minutes because the meeting got started late or one or more speakers went overtime—in this case speaking order certainly affected the speech. You must be aware of when you are scheduled to speak and you must be ready to adjust your speech to meet the circumstances.

In your classroom speech you will be guaranteed enough speaking time, but going first or last will still make a difference. For instance, if you go first, you may have to be prepared to meet the distraction of a few class members strolling in late; if you speak last, you must counter the tendency of the audience to be a bit weary from listening to several speeches in a row. If you anticipate the nature of the problems you may encounter, you will be in a much better position to deal with them effectively.

2.   Where will the speech be given? The room in which you are scheduled to speak will have a great bearing on your presentation. Consider your own speech classroom for a minute. If you are fortunate, the room is large enough to seat the class comfortably, with no student more than eight to ten rows away. But classrooms obviously vary in size. Perhaps the room is square, with a nicely constructed speaker's stand at the front. But perhaps it isn't. One day all the chairs may be in neat rows, the floors swept and polished; another day, the room might look like a tornado hit. In some rooms your voice will carry to all corners at a conversational volume; in others, you must nearly shout to be heard. Every aspect of the room can affect your speech.

I have focused on the classroom because that is where you will be giving your speeches this term. But you should study every place in which you are scheduled to speak before you make final speech plans. If possible, visit the place and see it for yourself. If you cannot see it for yourself, ask about such things as size, shape, number of seats, light, heat, and so forth.

Find out where you will be speaking from. Ideally, you will be speaking from behind a speaker's stand or lectern. Most places have such a formalized setting. But you can never assume that this will be the case. Let's reconsider the classroom setting. One day the room may contain a table on which a portable speaker's stand rests; the next day both the stand and the table may be missing. (How many times have I scurried from room to room trying to retrieve the speaker's stand!) You should be prepared to speak from a stand or from behind a table, and you should know what you will do if neither is available.

3.   What facilities are necessary to give the speech? For many speeches you will have no special needs. But for some you may want a microphone, a chalkboard, an overhead projector, or slide projector and screen. If the person who has contacted you to speak has any control over the setting, make sure you explain what you need. But always have alternative plans in case what you asked for does not arrive.

Exercise 3   1.   *Analyze your public speaking class based on demographic information. Draw conclusions about that audience based on answers to the questions posed on pages 45–46.*

2.   Analyze the occasion. Draw conclusions about the effect occasion will have on your speech; base your conclusion on the three questions discussed on pages 49–50. What will you most have to take into account in order to be prepared to adapt to that occasion?

FINDING YOUR MATERIAL: WHERE TO LOOK

What you say about the topic you have selected is going to determine much of your effectiveness as a speaker. Knowing where to look for material is a starting point for finding the best possible information on your topic. Most speakers find that the best way to look for material is to start from within their own experiences and work outward to other sources. Let us explore what you can expect to find from exploring your own knowledge, and from observation, interviewing, and reading.

Your Own Knowledge

What do you know? At times you may have questioned the extent and the accuracy of your knowledge; yet, when you test yourself, you discover that you really know quite a lot, especially about your major interests. For instance, athletes have special knowledge about their sports, coin collectors about coins, detective-fiction buffs about mystery novels, do-it-yourself advocates about house and garden, musicians about music and instruments, farmers about animals or crops and equipment, and camp counselors about camping. As a result of such special knowledge, you should be your first, if not your best, source of information for the topics you have selected. After all, firsthand knowledge of a subject enables a speaker to develop unique, imaginative, original speeches. Regardless of what topic you have selected, take the time to analyze and record your knowledge before you go to any other source.

The first speech assignment in this textbook (see pages 139–140) will be based almost entirely on your own personal knowledge and experience. You may find that your own knowledge is the basis for most of the information you present in your first two or three classroom speeches.

Of course, you must not accept every item you know or remember without testing its accuracy. Our minds play tricks on us, and you may find that some "fact" you are sure of is not really a fact at all. Nevertheless, you should not be discouraged from using your previous knowledge. Verifying a fact is far easier than discovering material in the first place.

Observation   Take advantage of one of your best resources, your power of observation. Many people are poor observers because they just do not apply their critical powers. Why are police officers better observers than most eyewitness reporters? Because they have been trained to use their powers.

You, too, can be a better observer if you try. Get in the habit of seeing and not just looking. Pay attention to everything about you. The development of nearly any topic you select can profit from the use of materials gained by observation. Are you planning to give a speech on how newspapers are printed? Before you finish your preparation, go down to your local newspaper printing plant and take a tour. The material drawn from your observation will provide excellent additions to your speech. Are you planning to evaluate the role of the city council in governing the city? Attend a couple of council meetings. Do you want to talk about the urban renewal of your downtown area? Go downtown and look around. Remember, through observation, you can add a personal dimension to your speech that will make it more imaginative and probably more interesting.

Interviewing   The time it takes to set up and conduct an interview usually multiplies itself in speaker benefits. Through the interview you get the ideas and feelings of a person involved firsthand. Although some public officials appear to be too busy to take time to talk with a student, you will be surprised to find that most people in public positions are approachable. The reason? Publicizing what they do and how they do it is an important part of their public relations. Moreover, many officials have a vested interest in keeping their constituents informed. Are you concerned with the way a recent Supreme Court ruling will affect police work in your community? Make an appointment with a local judge, the chief of police, or a precinct captain to get varying views on the subject. Are you interested in more information on some aspect of your college? Make an appointment with the head of a division, the chairperson of a department, or even a dean, the provost, or the president. Make sure, however, that you are trying to see the person who is in the best position to answer your question. The old adage "When you want to know something, go to the top" has its limitations. A better approach is "Discover who has the information you need, and go see that person."

When you interview someone it is important that you have a

good idea of the questions you wish to ask. People are far more likely to grant interviews when you tell them that you have three or four specific questions you would like them to answer. Moreover, the interviewee is likely to be impressed by your careful preparation, and might be more open with you than you would expect. We discuss the interview as a means of getting material for informative speeches in detail in Chapter 12.

A variation of the interview is the survey. When you have a topic for which you need individual comments, you can conduct a poll of students, dorm residents, commuters, or any segment of the group whose views you want. Again, if you prepare a few well-worded questions, you are more likely to get answers. You may be surprised at how often the answers to your questions are worth quoting in your speech. Of course, you will want to make sure that you have polled a large enough group and that you have sampled different segments of the larger group before you attempt to draw any significant conclusions from your poll.

Reading Material For many of your speeches, most of your material will probably come from what you read. My experience indicates that the most effective speakers are also effective researchers. Whether your library is large or small, well equipped or poorly equipped, its contents are of little value to you unless you know how to find what you need. Later, on pages 211–212, we discuss library research in considerable detail. For now, you should have a good working knowledge of the card catalog and *Readers' Guide to Periodical Literature*.

The card catalog indexes all your library's holdings by author, title, and subject. Your principal use of the card catalog will be to locate the best available books on your topic. In all probability your library will have at least one or two books on almost any subject you choose to consider.

Readers' Guide to Periodical Literature is a yearly index of articles in some 125 popular American journals. Articles indexed by topic come from such diverse magazines as the *Atlantic, Ebony, Business Week, New Yorker, Newsweek, Reader's Digest, Vital Speeches,* and *Yale Review. Readers' Guide* is by far the most valuable source for topics of current interest. You can probably find listings for at least a couple up to a hundred or more articles in just one or two of the most recent volumes.

Until you become adept at research, you will find that the

reference librarian is a good person to know. Do not hesitate to ask library staff for help; helping library patrons is a major professional responsibility and, with very few exceptions, librarians are delighted to help. They should be every bit as much a part of your educational experience as your professors and textbooks.

Exercise 4   *For one of the three specific purposes you wrote for Exercise 2, list three sources that would provide information (don't forget personal knowledge and/or observation).*

FINDING YOUR MATERIAL: WHAT TO LOOK FOR   The whole point of reviewing your own knowledge about a subject, and of observing, interviewing, surveying, and reading is to discover material that you might use in your speech to explain and support the points you make. Some of the material you find may be used as is. For instance, an example of how a cut in budget affects your school's academic program printed in the school paper can be reported in the form you found it. Some other material you find will be used to create a different form of material. For instance, the height of a building that you find in an almanac may be used to create a comparison in your speech on "The Changing Face of the City." In this section we focus on material that you can find and use as is; later in Chapter 12, Expository Speeches, we discuss the creation of different forms of development or support using the same basic factual material. Most of the material you are looking for is factual information, which takes a variety of forms.

Eventually you will subject the information you collect to at least two tests: (1) how well it supports, amplifies, or proves the points you wish to make; and (2) how interesting the material will appear to your audience. As you survey sources of material, you should look for examples and illustrations, anecdotes and narratives, statistics, quotable explanations and opinions, comparisons, definitions, descriptions, and visual aids.

Examples and Illustrations   As you speak, your audience is going to be looking for examples. Good examples are indispensable to your ability to explain or prove a point. An *example* is a single instance supporting or developing a generalization; an *illustration* is a more detailed example. Consider the following statements: As accurate as they are, computers have made some colossal errors; The University of Oklahoma has produced many of the NFL's best running backs; New cars in the late 1980s are going to have standard features that few if any cars offer now as options. In every case you are likely to say "Give me an example."

The examples you find will be of three kinds: *real* examples, which give actual specifics; *fictitious* examples, which allude to instances that are or have been made up to explain the point; and *hypothetical* examples, which suggest what would happen in certain circumstances. For instance:

•**Real:** Automobile companies are making major efforts to increase gasoline mileage in even the largest models. "Full-sized cars" are as much as 3 feet shorter than 1977 models; weight has been reduced by as much as 1,000 pounds or more; engine horsepower has been lowered considerably.

•**Fictitious:** Just because a person is slow does not mean that he is or should be considered a loser. Remember the story of the tortoise and the hare: the tortoise, who was much slower, still won the race.

•**Hypothetical:** Dogs do very poorly on simple tests of intelligence. If a 10-foot section of fence were put between a dog and a bone, he would try to paw through the fence rather than go the 5 feet or so it would take to get around the fence.

In the following passage, notice how the speaker uses examples to support his point about the importance of family education:

I have received from my first family—things of value. Things you couldn't obtain anywhere for all the gold in Zurich. Just take education: I learned to do all the basic things from my family before I ever went to school. And I learned to learn, as all children do, years before I was packed off to kindergarten—well fed, clothed, scrubbed clean and socialized.

The real tough teaching jobs were left up to my Mom and Pop: things like tying my shoes; not playing with fire; learning my way to the potty; picking up my own toys and socks; not hitting my brother or sister; standing up to the bully down the block; learning when to be quiet around my father while he worked. In short, I learned to be a worker, a citizen, a neighbor, a friend, a father, a husband and—I hope—a civilized human being—all under the tutelage of this marvelous university called the family—and all before I set foot in a school.[1]

---

[1] Mario M. Cuomo, "The Family," *Vital Speeches*, February 15, 1980, p. 268.

Because examples are such excellent aids to clarity and vividness, you should keep a constant lookout for them and use them frequently.

Anecdotes and Narratives

Anecdotes are brief, often amusing stories; *narratives* are accounts, tales, or lengthier stories. Each of these does about the same thing—relates material in story form. Because interest is so important to any kind of communication, and because our attention is always focused by a story, anecdotes and narratives are worth looking for, and/or creating. For a 2-minute speech, you have little time to tell a detailed story, so one or two anecdotes or a very short narrative would be preferable. In longer speeches, however, including at least one longer anecdote or narrative will pay dividends in audience attention. Remember the last time one of your professors said, "That reminds me of a story"? Probably more people listened to the story than to any other part of the lecture.

In his speech about the importance of supervision, Joseph Toot was making the point that good supervision is a lost art. To lay the groundwork for his point, he related the following story:

> I can perhaps best approach the theme of my remarks this evening by recalling to you the story of the construction foreman who was very big, very husky, and *very* tough. He invariably ruled his crew with an iron hand and enjoyed a fearsome reputation. One day, he lined up his new crew and announced to them—as was his custom—"The first thing I want you to know is that I can lick any man in my crew." At this point stepped forward one young fellow, obviously even bigger, huskier, and tougher than the foreman, who said in a quiet but self-assured voice, *"You can't lick me."* The foreman sized him up carefully, nodded his head in agreement, and replied, "You're right . . . you're *fired*."[2]

But neither the anecdote nor the narrative need be humorous to be effective. In a speech entitled "The Soviet Threat," the speaker was trying to make the point that the people of Russia are aware of the nature of their suppression and are willing to communicate their feelings to tourists. Near the beginning of his speech he narrated several experiences that illustrate the point. The

---

[2] Joseph F. Toot, Jr., "The Lost and Crucial Art," *Vital Speeches,* February 1, 1980, pp. 236–237.

final one in the series uses description, dialogue, and climax, which are a part of the narrative form:

> One late afternoon after returning to Moscow from Novosibirsk, I was walking through Red Square on my way to Hotel Rossia when a man walked beside me and said, "Aren't you one of the Americans who visited Moscow University recently?"
>
> I said "Yes, I was there."
>
> He said, "When you get home will you tell your friends that we are not free to study, free to travel, free to read foreign journals, free to go from county to county, or place to place as you are." With this abrupt message, he disappeared in the crowd.[3]

Statistics   Statistics are numerical facts. Statements such as "seven out of every ten voted in the last election" or "the cost of living rose three-tenths of one percent" enable you to pack a great deal of information into a small package. When statistics are well used, they can be most impressive; when they are poorly used, they may be boring and, in some instances, downright deceiving.

Your first and most important concern should be the accuracy of the statistics you find. Taking statistics from only the most reliable sources and double-checking any startling statistics with another source will help you avoid a great deal of difficulty. In addition, record only the most recent statistics. Times change; what was true five or even two years ago may be significantly different today. For instance, in 1981 only 15 out of 435 members of Congress were women. If you wanted to make a point about the number of women in Congress today, you would want the most recent figures.

If you are satisfied that you have found recent, reputable statistics, you will also want to be careful with how you use them. Statistics are most meaningful when they are used for comparative purposes. To say that industry offered the nation's supermarkets about 5,200 products this year does not mean much unless we know how many products are already on the shelves.

In comparisons, we should make sure that we do not present a misleading picture. For instance, if we say that during the past six months Company A doubled its sales while its nearest competitor, Company B, improved by only 40 percent, the implication would

---

[3] John D. Garwood, "The Soviet Threat," *Vital Speeches,* May 15, 1980, p. 459.

be misleading if we did not indicate the size of the base; Company B could have more sales, even though its improvement was only 40 percent.

Although statistics may be an excellent way of supporting material, be careful of overusing them. A few well-used statistics are far better than a barrage of numbers. When you believe you must use many statistics, you may find that putting them on a visual aid, perhaps in the form of a chart, will help your audience understand them more readily. The following passage from a speech about chemical waste is an excellent example of how statistics can be made meaningful by use of comparison.

A generation ago we measured the presence of chemicals in terms of parts per million. If the concentration was less than one part per million, it was considered to be of no consequence—in effect, zero or non-existent.

Today we commonly measure the presence of chemicals in terms of parts per billion and, in the case of some chemicals, in terms of parts per trillion.

For those of you who have trouble imagining those proportions, let me give you two simple analogies.

One part per billion is the equivalent of one drop—one drop!—of vermouth in two 36,000 gallon tank cars of gin—and that would be a very dry martini even by San Francisco standards!

One part per trillion is the equivalent of one drop in two thousand tank cars.[4]

Quotable Explanations and Opinions

Whether you find that a writer's *explanation* or *opinion* is valuable either because of what the writer said or the way the writer said it, you may record the material precisely as stated. If you use the material in the speech, you should remember to give credit to your source. Use of any quotation or close paraphrasing that is not documented is plagiarism, an unethical procedure that violates scholarly practice. Many of our most notable quotations are remembered because they have literary merit. Winston Churchill's "I have nothing to offer but blood, toil, tears, and sweat," included in his first speech as prime minister in 1940, and John F. Kennedy's "Ask not what your country can do for you—ask what you can do for your country," from his 1961 inaugural address, are examples

---

[4] Donald L. Baeder, "Chemical Wastes," *Vital Speeches,* June 1, 1980, p. 497.

from speeches that are worth remembering and repeating. At other times, you will find that the clear, concise manner in which ideas were stated is worth repeating, even if the words themselves have no literary merit.

In the following passage, notice how the speaker helps add force to his point with the use of a short quotation.

> I believe we have one critical task: *to go public*. We must take our message directly into American homes . . . to the people . . . to the ultimate deciders of our society's fate. We need nothing less than a major and sustained effort in the marketplace of ideas. As Judge Learned Hand noted, "Words are not only the keys to persuasion but the triggers of action."[5]

In your speeches you have an opportunity and a right to use the words of others, as long as you keep quotations to a minimum in both number and length, and as long as you give credit where it is due.

Comparisons   One way to discuss a new idea in terms that can be understood is to compare the new idea with a familiar concept. *Comparison* involves showing the similarities between two entities. Although you will be drawing your own comparisons in later stages of speech preparation, you should still keep your eye open for comparisons in your research.

Comparisons may be figurative or literal. A *figurative* comparison expresses one thing in terms normally denoting another. We may speak of a person who is "slow as a turtle," meaning that he or she moves extremely slowly in comparison to other persons. A *literal* comparison is an actual comparison. We may describe a ball as being about the same size as a tennis ball. In this instance, we mean that both balls are about 2½ inches in diameter.

Occasionally a comparison is cast as a *contrast*, which focuses on differences rather than on similarities. "Unlike last year, when we did mostly period drama, this year we are producing mostly comedies and musicals," is a contrast. As you do your research, try to find comparisons that will help you express your ideas more meaningfully and more interestingly.

---

[5] Willard C. Butcher, "Going Public for the Private Enterprise System," *Vital Speeches*, February 15, 1980, p. 266.

Definitions   A *definition* is a statement of what a thing is. Our entire language is built on the assumption that we, as a culture, share common meanings of words. Of course, most of us can define only a fraction of the words in the English language. For instance, a standard collegiate dictionary may have more than 100,000 entries, whereas first-year college students may have vocabularies ranging from 10,000 to 30,000 words. Since many of the words we want to use may not be totally understood by our audience, we need to offer definitions when they are appropriate. Remember, though, that the nature of the definition will determine whether the audience really understands. The types of definitions, their uses and functions, are discussed in detail in Chapter 11.

Descriptions   *Description* is the act of picturing verbally or giving an account in words. We think of description in relation to concrete, specific materials. Thus, we try to describe a room, a city, a park, a dog, or any other object, place, person, or thing with the goal of enabling the audience to hold a mental picture that corresponds to the actual thing. The elements of description are discussed in Chapter 10.

Visual Aids   The *visual aid* is a form of speech development that allows the audience to see as well as hear about the material. A speaker will rarely try to explain complicated material without the use of visual aids, such as charts, drawings, or models. In information exchange, visual aids are especially important in showing how things work, are made, are done, or are used. Some common visual aids and their use are considered in Chapter 8.

FINDING YOUR MATERIAL: HOW TO RECORD   In your research (including observation, interviewing, and knowledge, as well as printed sources), you may find a variety of examples, illustrations, quotations, statistics, and comparisons that you want to consider for your speech. How should you record these materials so they will be of greatest value? You will be able to use only a fraction of the material you find. Moreover, you can never be sure of the order in which you will use the materials in the speech. Therefore, you need a method of recording that will allow you to use or select the better materials and to order these materials to meet your needs.

　　The *notecard method* is probably the best. As you find materials, record each item separately on 3-by-5-inch or 4-by-6-inch cards. Although it may seem easier to record materials from one source on a single sheet of paper or on a large card, sorting and arranging material is much easier when each item is recorded on a separate card. In addition to recording each item separately, you should indicate the name of the source, the name of the author if one is given, and the page number from which it was taken. You will not necessarily need this material, but should you decide to quote directly or to reexamine a point, you will know where it came from. Figure 3-1 illustrates a useful notecard form.

How many sources should you use? As a rule, you should never use fewer than three sources. One-source speeches often lead to plagiarism; furthermore, a one-source or two-source speech just does not give you sufficient breadth of material. The process of selection, putting material together, adding, cutting, and revising will enable you to develop an original approach to your topic.

How you go about organizing, developing, and adapting material to your audience will be considered in the next two chapters.

Exercise 5   *For one of the specific purposes you plan to use for a speech this term, gather examples of each kind of developmental material discussed: example, illustration, comparison, statistics, and quotation. Make sure that you draw your material from at least three and preferably from four or more sources.*

FIGURE 3-1.   Example of a Notecard Recording Information

```
Topic: Costs for auto owners

"A 1981 midsized car that is driven 15,000
miles a year for four years costs 28 cents for
every mile it travels.  That represents an 11
percent increase just since last June (1980)."

"A typical front-wheeled-drive compact car
turns out to be almost as expensive--25.1 cents
per mile."

"Autos: Guzzling More Dollars," U.S. News and
World Report, March 23, 1981, p. 74.
```

The eternal search for missing parts... One years wait for one headlamp.

Bruised and battered and bandaged and forever greasy hands

"All it takes to restore the Classic automobile"

The patience of family and friends.

THE UNITED STATES OF AME

ONE DOLLAR

lots of this

Chapter 4 Organizing Speech Materials

PRINCIPLE II:
Effective speaking
involves organizing
material so that it
develops and heightens
the speech's specific
purpose.

Now that you have a clear, well-worded specific purpose and a clear, well-worded thesis statement, and have gathered the material to explain, develop, or support both of them, you are ready to give form to the speech. A speech can be organized in many different ways. You want to find or create the way that makes the most sense and will best achieve your goal.

As a starting point in your speech organization, you will need to begin outlining the material. A speech outline is a short, complete-sentence representation of the speech that is used to test the logic, organization, development, and overall strength of the structure before the wording is prepared or the delivery is practiced. In this chapter, we discuss the development of each part of the outline: the body, the introduction, and the conclusion. We conclude the chapter by examining a complete outline and discussing the tests you should make before going on to wording the speech.

PREPARING THE BODY OF THE SPEECH

Many students assume that, since the introduction is the first part of the speech to be heard by the audience, they should begin outlining with the introduction. If you think about it, however, you will realize that it is very hard to work on an introduction until you know the nature of the content you will be introducing. Most speakers find they work most efficiently if they complete the body of the speech first. Organizing the body of the speech involves selecting and stating main points, determining the best order, and

63

then selecting and developing the material that explains or supports the main points.

Selecting and Stating Main Points   *Main points* anchor the structure of your speech. In terms of what you hope the audience will remember, they are next in importance to the goal of the speech; therefore, they should be carefully selected and phrased. If your specific purpose is well written, the main-point ideas will already be stated or suggested. As a result, selecting the main points should be easy. For instance, what would be the main points for a speech developing the specific purpose, "To explain the four most important considerations for choosing a location for roses" and the thesis statement, "Roses should be planted in an area that receives morning sun, that is close to a supply of water, that contains well-drained soil, and that is away from trees and shrubs"? The answer seems obvious. Written in outline form, the main points would be:

I. Roses should be planted in an area that receives four to six hours of morning sun.
II. Roses should be planted close to a supply of water.
III. Roses should be planted in an area with good, well-drained soil.
IV. Roses should be planted in an area away from other trees and shrubs.

The key to determining your main points is the clarity of the specific purpose and thesis statement. A shortcut in writing the specific purpose is likely to lead to poorly conceived and poorly stated main points. For instance, what would be the main points of a speech based on the specific purpose, "To talk about airplanes"? Since the phrase "about airplanes" gives no clue to the intended line of development, a thesis statement would be very difficult to write and the main points could not be determined.

Once you have selected the main points, you need to state them in complete sentences that are specific, vivid, and parallel in structure. *Specific* means describing the main points exactly— telling exactly what you mean—*vivid* means stating the main points in a way that will arouse interest, and *parallel* means stating them with the same structural pattern, perhaps using the same introductory words. Since you want the audience to remember the main points as stated, you want to phrase them with care. To illustrate careful phrasing that meets the three tests cited, let us examine three contrasting ways of saying the same main points:

Specific Purpose: To explain the insights our clothes give us into our society.

Thesis Statement: Our clothing gives us insight into the casual approach, youthful look, similarity in men's and women's roles, and lack of visual distinction between rich and poor in our society.

	Set 1		*Set 2*		*Set 3*
I.	Casual	I.	They are casual.	I.	Our clothes indicate our casual look.
II.	Youthful	II.	They are youthful.	II.	Our clothes indicate our emphasis on youthfulness.
III.	Similarities	III.	There is a similarity between men's and women's.	III.	Our clothes indicate the similarity in men's and women's roles.
IV.	Little distinction	IV.	There is little distinction between rich and poor.	IV.	Our clothes indicate the lack of visual distinction between the rich and poor.

The labels in the first column indicate the subject areas only. Although the words *casual, youthful, similarities,* and *little distinction* relate to the purpose and indicate the subject areas of the thesis statement, the nature of the relationship is unknown. In the second set, the complete-sentence main points are more meaningful than the labels. Nevertheless, the use of *they* and *there* along with the verb *to be* makes the statements vague, indirect, and generally unclear. The speaker might get the point across, but any effectiveness would be a result of speech development rather than a result of the clear statement of main points. The third set is considerably better. The main points include each of the classifications; moreover, they explain the relationships of the categories to the purpose sentence, and they are specific, vivid, and written with parallel construction. If the audience remembers only the main points of set 3, they will still know exactly what our clothes tell us about our society.

As you begin to phrase prospective main points, you may find your list growing to five, seven, or even ten points that seem to be main ideas. If you will remember that every main point must be developed in some detail and that your goal is to help the audience retain the subject matter of each main point, you will see the impracticality of more than two to five main points. More than five is usually a sign that your thesis statement needs to be limited or that similar ideas need to be grouped under a single heading.

Determining Best Order   You will find that the main points are more easily understood and remembered if they follow some identifiable order. For most speeches that you will give in class and out, you will find that the four basic speech patterns of time order, space order, topic order, and problem-solution order will meet your organizational needs for informative or persuasive speeches quite well. On pages 257–263, we will consider variations of these basic orders.

TIME ORDER   Time order is a kind of organization in which each of the main points follows a chronological sequence; it is used mostly in informative speeches, and is especially relevant to narrative speeches. Time order tells the audience that there is a particular importance to the sequence as well as to the content of those main points. This kind of order often evolves when you are explaining how to do something, how to make something, how something works, or how something happened. For each of the following examples notice how the order is as important to the fulfillment of the purpose as the substance of the points.

Specific Purpose: To explain the four simple steps involved in antiquing a table.

Thesis Statement: Antiquing a table can be accomplished by following the four steps of cleaning the table, painting on the base coat, applying the antique finish, and shellacking.

I. Clean the table thoroughly.
II. Paint the base coat right over the old surface.

III. Apply the antique finish with a stiff brush, sponge, or piece of textured material.

IV. Apply two coats of shellac to harden the finish.

Specific Purpose: To explain the path followed by the Roman citizen as he progressed upward in government office.

Thesis Statement: As he progressed upward in government office, the Roman citizen followed the path of gaining military experience, serving as quaester, serving as aedile, serving as praetor, and finally obtaining a consulship.

I. Before he was eligible for office, a young Roman needed ten years' military experience.

II. At age twenty-eight, he was eligible for the office of quaester.

III. The office of aedile, next in line, could be skipped.

IV. After serving as aedile, or quaester if he skipped aedile, a Roman could become a praetor.

V. Finally, at age forty-two, the Roman could obtain a consulship.

SPACE ORDER   Space order is a kind of organization in which each of the main points indicates a spatial relationship. Space order is likely to be used in descriptive informative speeches. If a speaker's intent is to explain a scene, place, object, or person in terms of its parts, a space order will allow him to put emphasis on the description, function, or arrangement of those parts. Because we remember best when we see a logical order of items, the speaker should proceed from top to bottom, left to right, inside to outside, or any constant direction that will enable the audience to follow visually. For each of the following examples, notice how the order proceeds spatially.

Specific Purpose: To describe the Cape Hatteras Lighthouse.

Thesis Statement: The Cape Hatteras Lighthouse has two parts: a body and a top.

I. The body of the Lighthouse is 192 feet tall.

II. The top of the Lighthouse is 15 feet tall.

Specific Purpose: To describe the three layers that comprise the earth's atmosphere.

Thesis Statement: The earth's atmosphere comprises the troposphere, the stratosphere, and the ionosphere.

I. The troposphere is the inner layer of the atmosphere.

II. The stratosphere is the middle layer of the atmosphere.

III. The ionosphere is the succession of layers that constitute the outer regions of the atmosphere.

TOPIC ORDER   Topic order is a kind of organization in which each of the main points arbitrarily develops a part of the purpose. Although the points may go from general to specific, least important to most important, or may follow some other logical order, the order is still at the discretion of the speaker and is not a necessary part of the topic. With this kind of order, the content of the topics and not their relationship to each other is of paramount importance. You will find that topic orders are appropriate for organizing either informative or persuasive speeches. Although the relationship of the wording of the topics to the thesis statement is arbitrary, the following four examples illustrate some of the major possibilities.

In many informative speeches, the main points are written to spell out the topics that are stated in the thesis statement. This first example illustrates the identification of topics.

Specific Purpose: To explain major roles of the presidency.

Thesis Statement: The president is chief of foreign relations, commander-in-chief of armed forces, head of his party, and head of the executive branch.

I. The President is the chief of foreign relations.

II. The President is commander-in-chief of the armed forces.

III. The President is the head of his party.

IV. The President is the head of the executive branch.

This second example illustrates writing main points as definitions of the topics stated in the thesis statement.

Specific Purpose: To indicate three elements of extrasensory perception.

Thesis Statement: Telepathy, clairvoyance, and precognition are three elements of extrasensory perception.

   I. Telepathy refers to the communication of an idea from one person to another without benefit of the normal senses.

  II. Clairvoyance refers to seeing events and objects that take place elsewhere.

 III. Precognition refers to the ability to know what is going to happen before it happens.

This third example illustrates writing each topic stated in the thesis statement as a cause.

Specific Purpose: To explain the major causes of juvenile crime.

Thesis Statement: The major causes of juvenile crime are poverty, lack of discipline, and broken homes.

   I. One major cause is poverty.

  II. A second major cause is lack of discipline.

 III. A third major cause is broken homes.

This fourth example illustrates writing each topic stated in the thesis statement as a reason. Although a statement-of-reasons order may be appropriate for an informative speech, it is more likely to be the organization for a persuasive speech.

Specific Purpose: To convince the audience that nuclear power should be used to generate electricity.

Thesis Statement: Nuclear power should be used because it is efficient, cheap, clean, and safe.

   I. Nuclear power is more efficient.

  II. Nuclear power is cheaper in the long run.

 III. Nuclear power is cleaner.

 IV. Nuclear power is safe.

PROBLEM-SOLUTION ORDER   Problem-solution order is a kind of organization in which the main points are written to show (1) that there is a problem that requires a change in attitude or behavior (or both), (2) that the solution you are presenting will solve the problem, and (3) that the solution you are presenting is the best way to solve that problem. Since the problem-solution organization is used when you are attempting to prove to the audience that a new or different procedure is needed to remedy some major problem, the organization is most appropriate for a persuasive speech.

Specific Purpose: To convince the audience that a minimum annual cash income should be guaranteed to families with an income below $7,500.

Thesis Statement: A minimum annual cash income should be guaranteed to families with an income below $7,500 because nearly 20 percent of the people in the United States live on incomes below this level, because such a guaranteed income would eliminate poverty, and because such an income is better than welfare.

I. Nearly 20 percent of the people in the United States are living on incomes below the poverty level of $7,500.

II. A guaranteed cash income would eliminate the problem of poverty for these people.

III. A guaranteed cash income is a much better solution than the present welfare system.

Let us summarize the guidelines for stating main points:

1.   State each main point as a complete sentence.

2.   State each main point in a way that develops the key words in the thesis statement. If the thesis statement speaks of "several insights" then each main point should be an insight; if the thesis statement speaks of the "steps" involved, then each main point should be a step.

3.   State each main point as specifically and as concisely as possible. For example, "The clothes in our society indicate the emphasis most of us are likely to place on trying to look as youthful as we

can" is less specific and less concise than "Our clothes indicate our emphasis on youthfulness."

4.   State main points in parallel language wherever possible. If the first main point begins with the words "Our clothes indicate . . . ," then each of the other main points should begin "Our clothes indicate. . . ."

5.   Limit the number of main points to a maximum of five.

6.   Organize the main points so they follow a time order, a space order, a topic order, or a problem-solution order.

Selecting and Outlining Developmental Materials

Taken collectively, your main points outline the structure of your speech. Whether your audience understands, believes, or appreciates what you have to say usually depends, however, on how you develop those main points. In Chapter 3 you learned that examples, illustrations, statistics, comparisons, and quotations were the materials to look for; now you must select the most relevant of those materials and decide how you will use them to develop each main point.

First, write down each main point and under it state the information that you believe develops that main point. For example, for the first main point of the speech on diamonds:

> I. Carat is the weight of a diamond.
> Recently standardized.
> Used to be weighed against the seed of the cabob.
> Now the weight is a standard 200 milligrams.
> Weight is also shown in points.
> How much a diamond costs depends upon how big.
> But the price doesn't go up in even increments—it multiplies.
> So, whereas a ½-carat diamond is $600, a 1-carat diamond is $3,000.
> The reason involves the amount of rock that has to be mined.

Once you have put down the items of information that make the point, you work to subordinate material so that the relationships between and among ideas are shown. You accomplish this organization by using a consistent set of symbols and by indenting some ideas more than others. For instance, organization of the statements developing the main point might evolve into the following outline form:

I. Carat is the weight of the diamond.
   A. Diamond weight has only recently been standardized.
      1. Originally, merchants measured weight of diamonds against the seed of the cabob.
      2. Now the carat has been standardized as 200 milligrams.
   B. As diamond weights increase, the costs multiply.
      1. A ½-carat stone will cost about $600.
      2. A 1-carat stone will cost about $3,000.

For each of the subpoints you would have various examples, illustrations, anecdotes, and other material to use in the speech itself. You put down enough material on paper so you can test both the quality and the quantity of your material.

What rules should you use to guide your writing of the development of the speech? The following five rules will help you test your thinking and produce a better speech. In my years of working with beginning speakers, I have found ample proof of the generalization that there is a direct relationship between outlining and quality of speech content.

1.   Use a standard set of symbols. Main points are usually indicated by Roman numerals, major subdivisions by capital letters, minor subheadings by Arabic numerals, and further subdivisions by small letters. Although greater breakdown can be shown, an outline is rarely subdivided further. Thus an outline for a speech with two main points might look like this:

I. _____
   A. _____
      1. _____
      2. _____
   B. _____
II. _____
   A. _____
   B. _____
      1. _____
         a. _____
         b. _____
      2. _____

2.   Use complete sentences for major subdivisions as well as for main points. We have already discussed the importance of stating main points as complete sentences. The same reasoning holds for at least the A, B, C, subdivisions. Further development can be shown with phrases, but the more you can stick with the complete-sentence rule, the more sure you will be of the logic of the material. Furthermore, unless you write key ideas out in full, you will have difficulty accomplishing the next two rules.

3.   Each main point and major subdivision should contain a single idea. By following this rule, you can assure yourself that development is relevant to the point. Let us examine a correct and an incorrect example of this rule:

Incorrect	*Correct*
A. Diamond weight was only recently established and diamond cost varies.	A. Diamond weight was only recently established.
	B. Diamond costs vary with size.

Development of the incorrect example will lead to confusion, for the development cannot relate to both the ideas at once. If your outline follows the correct procedure, you will be able to line up your supporting material with confidence that the audience will see and understand the relationships.

4.   Minor points should relate to or directly support major points. This principle is called *subordination*. Consider the following example:

I. Proper equipment is necessary for successful play.
   A. Good shoes are needed for maneuverability.
   B. A good racquet helps you develop maximum power.
   C. A lively ball provides sufficient bounce.
   D. And a good attitude doesn't hurt.

Notice that the main point deals with equipment. A, B, and C (shoes, racquet, and ball) relate to the main point; D (attitude) is not equipment and should appear somewhere else, if at all.

5.   The total number of words in the outline of the body should equal about one-third of the total number anticipated in the speech. An outline is a skeleton, a representation of a speech—not a manuscript with letters and numbers. One way of testing the length of an outline is by computing the total number of words that you could speak during the time limit, and then limiting your outline to one-third of that total. Since approximate figures are all that are needed, you can assume that your speaking rate is about average—160 words per minute. Thus, for a two- to three-minute speech, which will include roughly 320 to 480 words, the outline should be limited to 110 to 160 words. The outline for an eight- to ten-minute speech, which will contain roughly 1,200 to 1,500 words, should be limited to 400 to 500 words.

PREPARING THE INTRODUCTION

At this stage of preparation, the substance of the speech, the body, is ready for practice. Now you must concern yourself with the strategy of getting your listeners ready for what you have to say. What you say before you get to the body may well determine whether they will really listen to you. Although your audience is captive (few of them will get up and leave), having an audience present physically does not mean having an active, alert, listening audience. It is the introduction that brings the audience to this state.

Any introduction has at least three potential purposes: (1) to get initial attention, (2) to create a bond of goodwill between speaker and audience, and (3) to lead into the content of the speech. These three things are not necessarily synonymous. A speaker may get attention by pounding on the stand, by shouting "Listen!" or by telling a joke. The question is whether any of these approaches will prepare the audience for the body of the speech. If the attention does not relate to the speech topic, it is usually short-lived.

Let us look at each of the three potential purposes in detail.

Getting Attention

The members of the audience would not be present if they were not expecting a speech, but this presence does not ensure their attention. The sound of your voice may be enough to jolt them alert, especially if they already have a great deal of respect for you or have great interest in what you are about to say. However, many audiences are like the one you will face in class: a group of people who, though they won't throw tomatoes, have little motivation for giving undivided attention. They hope they will like your speech, but if they do not, they can think their private thoughts.

So, your first goal is to determine what you can do to win your listeners' undivided attention.

Creating a Bond of Goodwill

Your listeners may be totally familiar with you and what you stand for. Even before you begin, they may be thinking about your last speech and looking forward to hearing you again. On the other hand, they may not know you at all. Or they may know you but view you as a potential threat—as someone who may tell them things they do not want to hear, who may make them feel uncomfortable, or who may make them do some work. If they are going to invest time in your words, they have to be assured that you are OK. So, your second goal is to determine what you can do or say that will make the audience feel good about listening to you. Especially in an opening for a persuasive speech this goal is paramount, although for information exchange the goodwill of the audience is less crucial and often no effort is made to establish it.

Leading into the Speech

You have to focus the audience's attention on the goal of the speech. In an informative speech you need to tell your listeners what you are going to be talking about in a way that will sustain their attention. In a persuasive speech, whether or not you tell them what you are planning to do depends on audience attitudes, the nature of the proposition, and other factors. Whereas an audience will appreciate a statement such as "Now let's look at the five steps in creating this gourmet's delight," it may not appreciate a statement like "Now I'm going to give you material that will persuade you to vote for Jones." If you intend to persuade, you may want to move from attention and goodwill right to the heart of the speech. You need to determine how you can focus attention on the content without alienating audience attitudes about you and the topic.

For informative speeches—and most other speeches as well—lead into the body of the speech by stating your thesis statement as a forecast of what you plan to do in the speech. In the model outline on pages 85–88, the thesis statement is the last point in the speech introduction. If there is some strategic reason for *not* stating the thesis statement at that point, then write it at that point anyway, but put parentheses around it—this means that your speech has a thesis statement, but that you are withholding statement of it for some reason.

**Suggested
Introductions**

A survey of suggested introductions would produce as many as twenty different ways of beginning a speech, most of them directed at getting attention. The following are some representative approaches that will work for short and long speeches; but keep in mind that how you begin depends largely on your imagination. The only way to be sure that you have come across a winner of a speech introduction is to try out three to five different ones and pick the one that seems best.

How long should the introduction be? Introductions may range from a sentence or two to nearly half the speech. How long should yours be? Long enough to put the audience in a frame of mind to hear you out. Let us look at some examples.

STARTLING STATEMENT   Especially in a short speech—the kind you will be giving in your first few assignments—you must obtain your listeners' attention and focus on the topic quickly. One excellent way to do this is to make a startling statement that will penetrate various competing thoughts and get directly to the listeners' minds. The following openings illustrate the attention-getting effect:

> Without casting aspersions on the chef, let me tell you that the luncheon you just finished contained hundreds, perhaps thousands, of potentially toxic substances. In spite of that—God willing—we'll all be around this evening to enjoy another nourishing meal. I think you'll agree that the negligible risk of eating our lunch was well worth the benefits derived. Risks and benefits are the major element of a broader theme I'd like to discuss today. . . .[1]

> History reveals the startling fact that twenty-two civilizations have risen and declined or disappeared during the life of man upon this earth. Nothing that I learned in college or since has intrigued me more.[2]

QUESTION   The direct question is another way to get the audience thinking about ideas you want it to think about. Like a startling statement, this opening is also adaptable to a short speech. The question has to have enough importance to be meaningful to the

---

[1] John W. Hanley, "Has Emotion Tipped the Scales on Consumer Safety?" *Vital Speeches,* November 15, 1977, p. 92.

[2] Howard E. Kershner, "Why Civilizations Rise and Fall," *Vital Speeches,* January 15, 1974, p. 216.

audience. Notice how a student began her speech on counterfeiting with a series of short questions:

> What would you do with this ten-dollar bill if I gave it to you? Take your friend to a movie? Buy some new clothes? Treat yourself to a few beers and a pizza? Well, if you did any of those things, you could get in big trouble—this bill is counterfeit!

QUOTATION   In your research you may well have discovered several quotable statements that are appropriate to your speech. If a particular quotation is especially vivid or thought provoking, you may decide to open your speech with it. A quotation is best suited to a speech introduction when it is short, concise, and attention getting. The speaker then usually works from the quotation itself to the subject of the speech.

Notice how the following three quotations lead directly into a speech on politics and politicians:

> A few decades back it was considered a great joke when the humorist Artemas Ward declared: "I am not a politician, and my other habits are good." Boise Penrose, the editor of *Collier's* magazine claimed that, "Public office is the last refuge of the scoundrel."
>
> Even as learned an observer as Walter Lippmann said politicians are ". . . insecure and intimidated men who advance politically only as they placate, appraise, bribe, seduce, bamboozle, and otherwise manage to manipulate the views and opinions of the people who elect them."
>
> Recent events make these jokes especially amusing. They are more timely than ever. They are equally erroneous.
>
> Obviously, I am here to talk about politics and politicians.[3]

ANECDOTE, NARRATIVE, ILLUSTRATION   Nearly everyone enjoys a good story. However, anecdotes, narratives, and illustrations can be the best or the worst ways of beginning a speech, depending on how they relate to the topic. Some speakers who are so taken with the notion that a story is worth telling may begin with one whether it relates to the topic or not, with the result that the audience enjoys the story and ignores the speech. Since most good stories take time to tell, they are usually more appropriate for speeches of eight to ten minutes or longer.

---

[3] James M. Thomas, "Politics and Politicians," *Vital Speeches,* September 15, 1974, p. 731.

The following illustrates the use of a story to begin a speech on the importance of sense of direction in private enterprise.

A story is told of a knight who returned to his castle at twilight. He was a mess. His armor was dented, his helmet askew, his face was bloody, his horse was limping, the rider was listing to one side in the saddle. The Lord of the castle saw him coming and went out to meet him, asking, "What hath befallen you, Sir Knight?" Straightening himself up as best he could, he replied, "Oh, Sire, I have been laboring in your service, robbing and raping and pillaging your enemies to the west." "You've been WHAT?" cried the startled nobleman, "but I haven't any enemies to the west!" "Oh!" said the knight. And then, after a pause, "Well, I think you do now."

There is a moral to this story. Enthusiasm is not enough. You have to have a sense of direction. Private enterprise, like the bedraggled knight, is not at its best these days. This morning I want to pose to you the possibility that the troubles which beset the business community may arise because it does not have a very clear idea of who its opponents are and as a result, is focussing much of its defensive energies upon the wrong targets. The sense of direction is amiss.[4]

PERSONAL REFERENCE Since the audience is the object of all communication, a direct reference to the audience or occasion may help achieve your goals. Actually, any good opening has an element of audience adaptation to it. The personal reference is directed solely to that end. Although we have learned to suspect insincere use of this method by individuals who are only after our votes, proper use of personal reference is particularly effective.

The following is a good example of the personal reference opening; it was used in a speech to the Toledo Rotary Club on the subject of problems in the legal system.

Good afternoon, and thank you for the generous introduction. It is an honor to be here and to have the privilege of addressing not only the distinguished group of Rotary members, but also the judges present today in honor of the celebration of Law Day.

I have never had any active association with Rotary, but my respect for it stems from my association with one of your former members here, the late Judge Frank L. Kloeb. Judge Kloeb was an exemplary person—as an individual, as a judge and I'm sure as a Rotarian. He influenced me greatly when I was an assistant United States attorney

---

[4] John Howard, "Curing the Unrecognized Malady Which Afflicts Private Enterprise," *Vital Speeches,* May 15, 1980, p. 450.

here starting in 1959. I remember many conferences in his chambers when my eye would wander to the little blue stand with the Rotarian Four-Way Test on it. Particularly the test "Is It Fair to All Concerned?" comes back to me even now, and is very pertinent to the thoughts I wish to express today about the current problems I believe to exist in the operation of our legal system.[5]

SUSPENSE   An extremely effective way of gaining attention is through suspense. If you can start your speech in a way that gets the listeners to ask, "What is this leading up to?" you may well get them hooked for the entire speech. The suspense opening is especially valuable when the topic is one that the audience might not ordinarily be willing to listen to if started in a less dramatic way.

Consider the attention-getting value of the following:

It cost the United States $20 billion in *one* year. It has caused the loss of more jobs than a recession. It caused the death of more than 35,000 Americans. No, I'm not talking about a war; but it is a problem just as deadly. The problem is alcoholism.

COMPLIMENT   It feels good to be complimented. We like to believe we are important. Although politicians often overdo the compliment, it is still a powerful opening when it is well used. Consider the following opening on the free economic system:

Thank you, Ladies and Gentlemen. I am honored to be a member of this panel of distinguished speakers—and to be speaking to such a fine group of concerned Americans.

Your membership in the United States Industrial Council, and your presence at today's National Issues Seminar, affirm your belief in the central role played by millions of individual businesses in creating jobs, wealth and managerial skills for a world that desperately needs all three.

Despite, or perhaps because of, our visible successes, the free economic system we support has been under sustained attack for some time now.[6]

How do you know whether the introduction you have worked up meets the goals for your speech? You cannot tell unless you

---

[5] Carl F. Larue, "Modern Dreams and Demands," *Vital Speeches,* July 15, 1980, p. 591.

[6] Rafael D. Pagan, Jr., "A System That Works," *Vital Speeches,* July 15, 1980, p. 594.

have something to compare it with. I suggest that you work on three or four introductions, then pick the one you like best.

Consider the following introductions for a speech on computers.

> In 1946 it took an entire room filled with vacuum tubes to power the ENIAC computer. Today the capacity of that entire room filled with vacuum tubes can be duplicated in one single chip—a technological advancement that has revolutionized the computer industry and made it possible for each of us to have a home computer system for surprisingly little money. Today I'd like to talk with you about the essentials of a computer hardware system that you would need for a home system.

> Last Christmas the hottest selling item was the electronic game; this Christmas the computer game was the big seller. It's very likely that by next Christmas or shortly thereafter the hottest Christmas item will be the complete home computer. Sound farfetched? It's not—we're in the midst of a technological revolution that will soon bring the computer to every household in the land. Today I'd like to talk with you about the potential of the home computer for the American family. I'd like to focus on the three essentials of a hardware system.

> Walk through any work area of a modern bank, department store, or business office and you'll overhear such words as *CRT, mainframe, floppy discs, chip*—all of these are the words of computer language. Today computers may still be outside the realm of your everyday world—but tomorrow every family in America will have one in the home. The language frighten you? It need not. Today I'd like to explain to you the three essentials of any computer hardware system.

Which introduction do you prefer?

Although each type of introduction has been discussed individually, the various types may be used either alone or in combination, depending on the time you have available and the interest of your audience. The introduction is not going to make your speech an instant success, but an effective introduction will get an audience to look at you and listen to you. That is about as much as you have a right to ask of an audience during the first minute of your speech.

Exercise 6   *For any topic that you might use during this term, prepare three separate introductions that would be appropriate for your classroom audience. Which is the best one? Why?*

PREPARING THE CONCLUSION

Shakespeare said, "All's well that ends well," and nothing could be truer of a good speech. As you complete the body of your speech you are suddenly seized with the notion that you have got only one last chance to hit home with your point. Although a poor speech certainly is not going to be saved by a good conclusion, a good speech can be lost for lack of a good conclusion, and any speech can be enhanced by the presence of an outstanding conclusion. Unfortunately, all too many speakers, knowing that they have only this one last chance, ramble on incessantly as they try to find those words that will save the day. However, like a good introduction, a good conclusion is not a matter of accident; it is a carefully planned occurrence.

What is a conclusion supposed to do and how can you do it? A conclusion has two major goals: (1) wrapping the speech up in a way that reminds the audience of what you have said and (2) hitting home in such a way that the audience will remember your words or consider your appeal. Here are kinds of conclusions that will work for both short and long speeches.

The Summary

By far the easiest way to end a speech is to summarize the main points. Thus, the shortest appropriate ending for a speech on the causes of juvenile delinquency would be, "In conclusion, the three major causes of juvenile delinquency are poverty, broken homes, and lack of discipline." The virtue of such an ending is that it restates the main points—the ideas that are the three main ideas of the speech. Although such a conclusion is appropriate, easy, and generally satisfactory, it is not very stimulating. A better one would lead up to the summary more interestingly. Notice how the following conclusion improves the overall effect:

> Each of us is concerned with the problem of juvenile delinquency; likewise, each of us realizes that no real dent can be made in the problem until and unless we know the causes. I hope that as a result of what I've said you have a better understanding of the three major causes of juvenile delinquency: poverty, broken homes, and lack of discipline.

Because the conclusion may be so important to heightening the emotional impact of the speech even when you are using a summary, you may want to supplement it in some way so that your message is impressed upon the audience. Speakers have found numerous ways to supplement and occasionally supplant the summary. Let us look at a few.

Illustration or Personal Experience   Since the goal of the conclusion, at least in part, is to leave your subject on a high point, the illustration or personal experience is often an excellent way to end. In his speech, "Profitable Banking in the 1980s," Edward Crutchfield ends his speech with a personal experience that puts his message in perspective.

> The importance of the data processor should be obvious. But many banks need to get him out from behind the disc packs and the line printers and into the mainstream of banking. At First Union, the head of data processing reports directly to the CEO and he is on a level equivalent to the head of our corporate and consumer banking groups.
>
> I see the 80s as an era of shake-out and consolidation for the banking industry. The strong will get stronger and the weak will merge or fade away. During the 1980s, I believe we will see the evolution of very large regional banks. They will be capable of tackling the most awesome of non-bank competitors.
>
> Before we go about our planning to be one of these large banking institutions, let me leave you with a hard lesson learned many years ago.
>
> I played a little football once for Davidson—a small men's college about 20 miles north of Charlotte. One particularly memorable game for me was one in which I was blindsided on an off-tackle trap. Even though that was 17 years ago, I can still recall the sound of crackling bones ringing in my ears. Well, 17 years and 3 operations later my back is fine. But, I learned something important about competition that day. Don't always assume that your competition is straight in front of you. It's easy enough to be blindsided by a competitor who comes at you from a very different direction.[7]

Humor   Whether in the beginning, the middle, or the end of a speech, humor is always effective if it is appropriate to the material. By and large, a humorous conclusion will leave you in good standing with your audience—and perhaps because they feel good about you, they may well adopt your message.

The following conclusion of a speech about economics is an excellent illustration:

> You have been patient to listen to my economics lecture tonight . . . I know how dismal this science can be. There was a joke going around Moscow last year. It seems that in the big May Day parade, the final

---

[7] Edward E. Crutchfield, Jr. "Profitable Banking in the 1980s," *Vital Speeches*, June 15, 1980, p. 537.

vehicle, following all of those rockets and tanks, was a truck carrying three solemn-looking, middle-aged men. Chairman Brezhnev turned to one of his aides and asked what in the world those men were in the parade for.

"Those men are *economists,* Comrade," the aide replied. "Their destructive capability is enormous!"

Amen to that, and thank you for letting me get some of that destructive capability out of my system.[8]

The Appeal

The appeal is a frequently used conclusion for a persuasive speech. You are telling your listeners that now that they have heard all the arguments, you will describe the behavior you would like them to follow.

Notice how this speaker blends a short quotation with a direct appeal for internationalism:

It's a tall order. But after two decades dominated by welfare state economics and hang-the-expense environmental clean-up, we are obliged now to shift our national priorities and concentrate our major resources on a major drive to restore the economic and technological leadership that provides the material basis for our standard of living and our programs of social welfare. This same program of economic restoration is also essential to support a modernization of our national defense system and make us competitive again in world markets.

Recalling Ben Franklin's admonition, "You may talk too much on the best of subjects," I'll conclude these remarks by saying that the strength of the free world requires strong U.S. leadership.

Our economy, like Gulliver in Jonathan Swift's masterpiece, is a giant potential source of strength when freed to serve the nation. But thousands of Lilliputian disincentives and regulations—no one perhaps in itself disabling—are weakening the ability of the business community to serve.

Let's untie Gulliver. The world community will be better served by a United States that has domestic and international vitality than by a weakened giant.[9]

The Challenge

Like the appeal, the challenge calls for an audience to try something new. However, rather than touching an emotional chord, the challenge takes the "I dare you" approach.

---

[8] Ruth A. Bryant, "Inflation: The Seven Percent Solution," *Vital Speeches,* June 15, 1980, p. 522.

[9] Reginald H. Jones, "The Export Imperative," *Vital Speeches,* November 1, 1980, p. 36.

In this speech, Richard Daschbach challenges his audience to tap the reserve within us. Notice how he uses a quotation to lead into the final portion of his challenge conclusion:

> As U.S. citizens, you must demand excellence in the performance of your government and your nation, and you must actively contribute to that objective.
>
> D'Israeli once said, "It is a wretched taste to be gratified with mediocrity when the excellent lies before us." The record of U.S. shipping, U.S. trade, and the U.S. economy is currently not excellent. But the excellence we have demonstrated in the past not only lies before us, it lies *within* us. We must work together to tap that reserve of excellence within us to restore America to its full potential.[10]

Emotional Appeal   Of all the conclusions possible, none is more impressive than one that truly affects the emotions of the audience.

The ending to General Douglas MacArthur's famed address to Congress in 1951 is a classic in the use of emotional impact.

> I am closing my fifty-two years of military service. When I joined the Army even before the turn of the century, it was the fulfillment of all my boyish hopes and dreams. The world has turned over many times since I took the oath on the plain at West Point, and the hopes and dreams have long since vanished. But I still remember the refrain of one of the most popular barrack ballads of that day, which proclaimed most proudly that—
>
> "Old soldiers never die; they just fade away."
>
> And like the old soldier of that ballad, I now close my military career and just fade away—an old soldier who tried to do his duty as God gave him to see that duty.
>
> Good-bye.[11]

As with introductions, it is difficult to tell whether a conclusion you have worked up is effective unless you have something to compare it with. I suggest that you work on several conclusions for any speech you are called upon to prepare, then choose the one that seems best to you.

Consider the following possible conclusions for the speech about computers.

---

[10] Richard J. Daschbach, "U.S. Shipping's Critical Choice for the 1980s," *Vital Speeches,* October 15, 1980, p. 32.

[11] Douglas MacArthur, "Address to Congress," in William Linsley, *Speech Criticism: Methods and Materials* (Dubuque, Iowa: Wm. C. Brown, 1968), p. 344.

So, the three basics of a computer hardware system are the central processing unit, memory, and input/output devices.

So, if you decide to explore the world of the home computer you can now talk intelligently about the three basics of the hardware system: the central processing unit, memory, and input/output devices.

I think that you can see that by having the basic knowledge of the central processing unit, memory, and input/output devices, you can talk intelligently about the essentials of the home computer system.

So before you get too involved in the home computer mania of the 80s, you'll want to make sure that you understand the central processing unit, memory, and input/output devices.

Which of the conclusions would you select?

Exercise 7   *For the same topic used in Exercise 6, prepare a short summary conclusion. Is there any way you can supplement the summary to give the conclusion greater impact?*

THE COMPLETE OUTLINE   Now that we have considered the various parts of an outline, let us put them all together for a final look. The following outline illustrates the principles in practice. In the analysis of the outline, I have tried to summarize and emphasize the various rules we have considered separately.

Does a speaker really need to write out an outline? Most of us do. Of course, there are some speakers who do not prepare outlines, who have, through trial and error, learned alternate means of planning speeches and of testing their structure that work for them. Some accomplish the entire process in their head and never put a word on paper—but they are few indeed. As a beginner, you can save yourself a lot of trouble if you learn to outline ideas as suggested. Then you will know that your speech has a solid, logical structure and that it really fulfills the intended purpose.

Analysis

Writing the specific purpose at the top of the page before the outline of the speech reminds

Outline: For a Speech (4–6 minutes)

Specific Purpose: To explain that a computer system may be reduced to three essentials.

the speaker of the goal. The speaker should refer to the specific purpose to test whether everything in the outline is relevant. The substance of the specific purpose will probably appear as part of the speech introduction.

The word *Introduction* sets this section apart as a separate unit. The content of the introduction (1) is devoted to getting attention, (2) may be used to gain goodwill, and (3) leads into the content of the speech.

The thesis statement refines the specific purpose; in this case the refinement is the clear statement of the three essentials that will be discussed in the speech.
The thesis statement appears as the last section of the speech introduction. In an informative speech, the thesis statement is likely to be presented as written; in a persuasive speech presentation of the thesis statement may be withheld if there is some strategic reason for so doing—if so, it should be written in parenthesis.
The introduction may be modified considerably before the speaker is ready to give the speech.

The word *Body* sets this section apart as a separate unit.
Main point I reflects a topical relationship of main ideas. It is stated as a complete, substantive sentence.
The main point could be developed in many ways. These two subdivisions, shown by consistent symbols (A and B)

Introduction

I. Main frame, floppy discs, CRT—these are computer terms—the language of tomorrow.

II. For many of us the idea of the computer is still a total mystery.

Thesis Statement: The three essential elements of a computer are a central processing unit, memory, and input/output devices.

Body

I. The first element of a computer is the central processing unit.
  A. The CPU, as it is called, is the "brain" of the computer.
  B. The CPU is composed of two interlinking functions.
    1. The first does the directing.
      (a) It reads instructions.
      (b) It tells the computer what to do.

indicating the equal weight of the points, consider the label and the functions.

Main point II continues the topical relationship. The sentence is a complete, substantive statement paralleling the wording of main point I. Furthermore, notice that each of the main points considers one major idea. The degree of subordination is at the discretion of the speaker. After the first two stages of subordination, words and phrases may be used in place of complete sentences in further subdivisions.

2. The second performs the operations.
    (a) It does the arithmetic.
    (b) It does the logical operations in decision making.

II. The second is the main memory unit.
    A. The main memory is the storage component.
        1. This is where instructions are stored when they are not being used.
        2. This is where information is housed while the computer is working on it.
    B. It is sometimes called the "core" memory.
        1. Each core is magnetized.
        2. Each core has its own "address."
        3. By stacking cores together, memory can be increased.
    C. The two units together, the CPU and memory, are called the "main frame."
    D. All circuits can be combined in a single chip the size of a fingernail.
        1. Chips are used as CPUs and memory in microcomputers.
        2. One chip contains all the circuits that used to take up a whole room.
    E. Information can also be stored on auxiliary memory units.
        1. Floppy discs and drums are two of the most common.
        2. Each has a RAM—random access memory.

Main point III continues the topical relationship, is parallel to the other two in phrasing, and is a complete, substantive sentence.
Throughout the outline, notice that each statement is an explanation, definition, or development of the statement to which it is subordinate.

III. Computer inputs and outputs take many forms.
    A. Computer inputs have three common sources.
        1. Input can be made through punchcards.
        2. Input can be made through paper tape.
        3. Input can be made through scanners.
    B. Computer outputs have two common sources.
        1. Output can be made through high-speed printers.
        2. Output can be made through plotters for maps and graphs.
    C. Input and output can be combined in a terminal.
        1. The CRT is the most common.
        2. A phone hookup is a second.

Conclusion

The word *Conclusion* sets this apart as a separate unit.

I. The computer necessities are the central processing unit, memory, and input/output devices.

The content of the conclusion is a form of summary tying the key ideas together. Although there are many types of conclusions, a summary is always acceptable for an informative speech.
In any speech where research was done, a bibliography of sources should be included.

II. So the next time people speak of home computers and computer hardware, you'll know what they're talking about.

Bibliography

"Computers." *Encyclopedia Americana.* 1977 ed.

O'Brien, Linda. *Computers.* New York: Franklin Watts, 1978.

Osborne, Adam. *An Introduction to Microcomputers.* 2d ed. Berkeley, Calif.: Osborne & Associates, 1979.

Exercise 8   *Complete an outline for your first speech assignment. Test the outline to make sure that it conforms to the assignment.*

From the time you were three to five years old you had learned enough vocabulary to communicate most of your basic ideas.

Chapter 5 Speech Wording

At this stage of speech preparation, you have an outline that indicates the structure of your speech. Now you are ready to begin thinking about presenting that speech. Your emphasis switches from what you plan to say to how you plan to say it. The next two chapters deal with the question of how you get from the outline stage of preparation to being ready to give the speech.

If you were preparing a paper, a newspaper article, or a magazine story, you would write out drafts of the work, criticize what you had written, and rewrite until you were satisfied. "Writing out" a speech in a similar way may help you. However, good writing and good speaking are not necessarily the same; good speech is not measured by the eye, but by the ear. Instead of thinking of "writing out" a speech, think of "speaking it out"— think of building upon your own conversational style. The tape recorder rather than the typewriter is the instrument you should use to record what you say. If you do not own a tape recorder and cannot borrow one, get friends or relatives to listen to various wordings and to share their reactions with you. Or, if you are self-conscious about practicing in front of an audience of friends or relatives, train your ear to really listen to what you say while you are practicing. You do this by sampling various phrasings of ideas over several practice periods; your mind retains wordings that seem especially effective and seeks to modify awkward, hesitant, or otherwise ineffective expressions of ideas. Unless a speech is to be delivered from a manuscript, the wording never really becomes final until it is actually presented to the audience.

Written and oral language are not totally different, but if you compare tapes of what people say orally with sections of books and magazines, you are likely to find that oral language has more personal pronouns, more contractions, shorter sentences on average, more simple sentences, greater use of one- and two-syllable words, and many more common or familiar words.

Despite these quantitative differences, however, both oral and written styles are tested by the same criteria: clarity, vividness, emphasis, and appropriateness. Before we examine these criteria and show how you may meet them in your speeches, let us take a brief look at some aspects of language that provide a basis of understanding for anyone who hopes to use language well in either speech or writing.

LANGUAGE

Because of the way that words and meaning are related, a skilled communicator must be careful when making assumptions about either word selection or word understanding. Although such expressions as "picking exactly the right word" leave the impression that a master of language need only learn enough words, the role of language in communication is far more complicated. You can get a proper perspective on language if you are consciously aware of how words get their meaning and of what complicates the use of words in speech or writing.

Words and Meaning

You are likely to have a better appreciation for meaning if you understand that whatever meaning we assign a word is arbitrary, conventional, and learned.

When we say that meaning is *arbitrary*, we mean that it is a matter of choice. Whether the word is *chair, sister,* or *predilectory* we know that someone at some time had to use those letters (sounds) in that order for the first time. So someone chose to try a certain word to convey some meaning. What happened then?

Before a word begins to carry any standard meaning, its use must become *conventional*. That is, the arbitrary choice must become the choice of a large number of people. At some point in history it may have been a single person's idea to call a female sibling a sister. But the use of *sister* as a symbol with a specific meaning wasn't possible until others started using that word when they wanted to express the idea of female sibling. Every day some person may use certain new sound patterns for the first time to stand for something, but the word does not become part of the language until other people have used the word often enough to make it conventional.

Finally, meaning is *learned.* Because of the arbitrary, conventional nature of words, each new generation must learn the language anew. Children's brains enable them to think, and their vocal mechanism allows them to form any number of sounds. But determining which sounds go together to form which words is a skill that must be taught from generation to generation.

By the time you were three to five years old, you had learned enough vocabulary to communicate almost all of your basic ideas and feelings, and had mastered enough grammar to be understood. Since then, you have enlarged your vocabulary and sharpened your understanding of grammar.

Because meanings are learned, they are subject to the limitations of the learning process. That is, people do not all learn exactly the same meanings for words, and they do not learn exactly the same words. You must never assume, therefore, that another person will know what you are talking about just because that person uses words that you have learned. And of course, as your understanding of the language affects your ability to listen, so it affects your ability to communicate with others, either by writing or by speech.

Complications in Using Words

Until we develop some form of telepathy (and I doubt any of us are going to see that day), we must share our ideas and feelings indirectly through a system of symbols, that is, through words. This symbol system is often an imperfect means of sharing. If you are going to be effective as a communicator, you must be able to distinguish, for example, between denotative and the connotative meanings of words; and you must be able to apply your understanding to your speaking.

DENOTATION *Denotation* means the direct, explicit meaning or reference of a word; denotation is the meaning given in a dictionary. Knowing dictionary definitions is useful in communication, but even with a firm grasp of word denotations, you can still encounter problems. Let us examine a few.

A great many words carry multiple meanings. If we looked up the 500 most commonly used American words in any dictionary, we would be likely to find more than 14,000 definitions. Some of these definitions would be similar, but some would vary greatly. Take the word *low,* for instance. *Webster's New World Dictionary* offers twenty-six meanings for *low.* Number 1 is "of little height or elevation"; number 8 is "near the equator"; and number 16 is "mean; despicable; contemptible."[1] No matter how we look at these three definitions we have to admit that they are quite different.

As words get more difficult, we begin to find fewer and fewer definitions. Thus, it is usually with our most common words that we get into the most trouble. These common words have so many different meanings that unless we examine the context carefully, we may get (or give) the wrong idea. However, if we use a more precise word, some in our audience may not be familiar with it.

A second problem is that meanings of words change with time. According to W. Nelson Francis, in the 700 years *nice* has been in the English language, it "has been used at one time or another to mean the following: Foolish, wanton, strange, lazy, coy, modest, fastidious, refined, precise, subtle, slender, critical, attentive, minutely, accurate, dainty, appetizing, agreeable."[2]

If we think about it, we all know some words that have changed their meaning over a relatively short period of time. The word *gay* is one example. Although *gay* meaning joyous is still heard, it is becoming obsolete. If you describe another person as "gay," and you mean happy or joyous, you will probably be misunderstood; others will think you mean "homosexual."

A third problem is the influence of context. The position of a word in a sentence and its relationship to the words around it may change the denotation. When a young girl says, "Dad, you owe me a dime," the meaning is somewhat different from when she says, "Dad, I need a dime for the machine." In the first case, any combination of coins adding to ten cents will probably be acceptable; in the second case she is looking specifically for that small coin that we call a "dime."

Examples of the influence of context abound. Think of the difference between "George plays a really mean drum" and "The way George talked to Sally was downright mean."

---

[1] *Webster's New World Dictionary,* 2d college ed. (Cleveland, Ohio: William Collins & World, 1978), p. 839.

[2] W. Nelson Francis, *The English Language* (New York: W. W. Norton, 1965), p. 122.

CONNOTATION Whereas denotation refers to the most basic, explicit definition of a word, *connotation* refers to the feelings that a particular word arouses.

If a person has had any experience with the referent of a word that is spoken (especially a specific, concrete word for which there is a clearly defined referent), the person is likely to have some feelings about that word. Take the word *home*. If *home* to you is a place filled with fun, love, understanding, warmth, and good feelings, it means something far different to you than it would if *home* were a place filled with fighting, bickering, punishment, confinement, and harsh rules.

Any word has potential feelings and values attached to it for the person using the word. As a speaker, then, you must take into account both the standard denotative meaning and the potential connotative meaning of the word to the specific person or persons with whom you are communicating. If in a speech Carol says, "Americans have very special feelings about dogs," Carol must understand that her sentence denotes a domesticated mammal, a denotation that her audience is likely to share. But if she is planning to communicate ideas of warmth and happiness with her sentence she may not succeed since members of her audience may not share this meaning—this connotation—of *dogs*.

If you understand how your audience may feel about the words you use, you can better understand and communicate with its members. A congressional representative who is going to use words like *busing, schools,* and *taxes* in a speech to her constituency must consider the connotations these words are likely to have for her audience. Then she must make a special effort to use the words in a way that will increase the likelihood of her audience getting the same meaning she was intending.

Now that we have looked at language in general, let us discuss the four criteria that we apply to the use of words in speeches: clarity, vividness, emphasis, and appropriateness. Our goal is not to establish an absolute or arbitrary standard for each (this word or sentence is clear; this word or sentence is not); rather, we will give guidelines you can apply to help make your wording *clearer, more vivid, more emphatic,* and *more appropriate.*

CLARITY Clear speaking is free from ambiguity and confusion. Suppose you tried to explain a distressing incident by saying, "Some nut almost got me a while ago." The receiver could not tell what had almost happened to you—the message would not be clear. Suppose instead you said, "An older man in a banged-up yellow Datsun crashed the light at Calhoun and Clifton and almost hit me as I was crossing the street." Phrased this way, the wording eliminates ambiguity and confusion. The listener has a fairly detailed mental picture of what happened—the message is clearer.

Clarity is achieved by precise, specific, uncluttered phrasing. Let us consider each of these characteristics separately.

Precision   Speaking precisely requires that you select the word that best represents the idea. Since meaning is affected by various aspects of denotation and connotation, you can never be completely sure that your use of a word will create a meaning in the minds of your audience that is exactly the meaning you intended. But the less precise your wording, the greater the potential for confusion. For example, if you said, "Tom often sprinted for the bus each morning," you could not be completely sure that everyone had a mental image of Tom running as fast as possible for the bus. But if that was indeed the idea you were trying to get across, you would have much less chance of conveying that meaning if you said, "Tom often ambled toward the bus each morning." In fact, failure to communicate would almost be guaranteed, for *amble* means to "move at a slow, easy pace"; and few if any members of an audience would picture running as fast as possible if you said "amble"!

The problem of precision is multiplied by the shades of meaning that many words carry. Take the simple verb *said*. Notice the changes in meaning when a person uses such other words as *stated, averred, growled, indicated, intoned, suggested, pleaded, shouted, purred, answered,* or *asked.* Successful communication requires an understanding of words—not only what they mean in general but also how they relate to each other.

When the elder William Pitt, regarded by some as one of England's greatest speakers, was a teenager he gained an understanding and an appreciation of the language by reading Bailey's dictionary, a famous work of the day, *twice.* Even today, dictionary reading is still a good way to sharpen your understanding of words. An interesting method of practice is to play "synonyms." Think of a word, then list as many words as you can that mean about the same thing. When you have completed your list, refer to a book of synonyms, like *Roget's Thesaurus,* to see which words you have omitted; then try to determine the shades of difference among the words. Refer to a dictionary for help—it is useful to look up words even when you are sure you know their meaning. You may be surprised to find how many times the subtle meaning of a familiar word escapes you. The goal of this exercise is not to get you to select the rarest word to project an idea—the goal is to encourage you to select the word that *best* represents the idea you wish to communicate.

Specificity and Concreteness

Specificity and concreteness go hand in hand in sharpening meaning by reducing choice on the part of the listener. In ordinary conversation, under the pressure of having to talk with little or no previous planning, we tend to use general and abstract words, words that allow the listener the choice of many possible images rather than a single intended image. The more the receiver is called upon to provide his own image, the more likely it is that the meaning he or she sees will be different from the meaning the speaker intended.

Compare the following sentences:

- He brought several *things* with him.
- He brought *four bags of potato chips, a pound of ham, and a case of beer* with him.

- Listen, she lives in a *really big house.*
- Listen, she lives in a *fourteen-room Tudor mansion.*

- What I like about the lot is that it has *trees* to work with.
- What I like about the lot is that it has *two large maples and several smaller evergreens* to work with.

- She drives a real honey of *a car.*
- She drives a *'76 silver Corvette* that's a real honey.

- You have to say this for Morgan—he's *fair.*
- You have to say this for Morgan, he uses *the same standards for all students.*

- I just don't like people who *aren't honest* in class.
- I just don't like people who *cheat on tests* in class.

What are the differences? In the first sentence of each example the italicized words and phrases are vague. Vague language is marked by words that are general rather than specific and abstract rather than concrete. *Things, trees,* and *car* are general—they communicate no definite visual image; *Four bags of potato chips, two large maples,* and *'76 silver Corvette* are specific—they limit what you can picture. *Fair* and *aren't honest* are abstract—they cover a variety of possible behaviors; *the same standards for all students* and *cheat on tests* are concrete—they reduce choice to a single specific behavior.

You can test your ability to speak precisely and specifically by recording portions of your practice. As you listen to the playback, write down words you believe are imprecise and general or abstract. Then try to think of words that would create a clearer mental picture. If your speech is not clear, probably your thinking is not very clear. For practice, look around the room you are in and label various objects about you. Perhaps you see an object you identify as a "lamp"; instead of saying "lamp," however, try to create a clearer word picture of the object. Perhaps you are looking at a yellow, metal floor lamp. Or how about the bookcase you see—is it a four-shelf, wooden bookcase? Or the book on your desk—is it your chemistry book? The more success you have in practice sessions in thinking clearly and using precise, specific language to communicate a thought, the more success you will have in your speeches.

Lack of Clutter

One of the greatest enemies of clarity in speech is verbal clutter. This clutter includes such vocal interferences as "uh," "um," "well uh," "OK," and "you know." Not only do such filler expressions clutter speech and crowd out meaning, they are also likely to drive your listeners to distraction. Although we may tolerate such irritating expressions in ordinary conversation, we are less likely to accept them from public speakers. This kind of clutter is particularly noticeable in the early stages of speech practice when a person is unsure of what to say. Clutter is also noticeable when a person is extremely nervous or under a great deal of tension. Regardless of the cause, however, if you find that you overuse such clutter, work to eliminate as much of it as possible. I recommend that you try these suggestions:

1.   Become aware of usage. A major problem in overcoming clutter is that people are usually not aware of their use of vocal interferences. For instance, you may believe that you never use them, when in fact they may be a major part of your sending style. There are two easy ways to become aware. One way is to tape-record yourself talking for several minutes, then listen to the recording. Turn the recorder on and talk about the game you saw yesterday, the course you plan to take next term, or anything else that comes to mind. When you play it back, you can notice your usages. A second way is a little more traumatic, but may bring even quicker results. Instruct a close friend to raise his or her hand every time you say "uh," "you know," or any other filler sound. Seeing a reaction like that will help you train your ear to listen for verbal clutter. Once you can hear what you are doing, you can plan a program of improvement.

2. Schedule regular practices. If you can speak for long periods of time in practice without vocal clutter, you will do better in conversation and in public speaking. Set up practice periods two or three times a week. Start out by trying to talk for fifteen seconds without a vocal interference. Continue to increase the time until you can talk for two minutes or more without an interference. In these practices, meaning may suffer. You may spend a disproportionate amount of time and energy avoiding clutter. However, you should soon realize success. As you find you can do pretty well, try to create in your practice sessions situations that tend to cause vocal interferences. For instance, if you are likely to lapse into vocal interferences when you are under pressure, try to mentally recreate a situation where you were required to speak under pressure. Likewise, if interferences occur when you are speaking to people in authority, create a practice situation where you are speaking to your parents, a group of college professors, and so forth.

3. Monitor your regular conversations, but do not worry a great deal about any lapses. You may be making real headway when in the heat of a conversation you recognize lapses. However, do not make a conscious effort to reduce clutter in these situations. Improvement in conversation should come naturally enough as a result of improvement in practice sessions. Just as an athlete works on skills in practice but concentrates on the game in competition, so you should work in practice to reduce clutter, but concentrate on communicating meaning in conversation and public speaking.

Ridding yourself of these habits is hard work. You must train your ear to catch your own usages. However, the work is worth it.

Conversation and speaking in public would be a lot more pleasant if everyone would work to reduce clutter by just 50 percent.

In the following example, note how John Cunningham, author and historian, uses accurate word selection and specific, concrete language to sharpen the clarity of his point that the good old days were not really so good:

> I could take you through a full century, chick by chick, onion by onion, Irish potato by Irish potato. I could read some poetry from William Cullen Bryant and a stanza or two from Longfellow to prove in lyrics that for farmers those long-ago times were the good old days.
>
> I will spare you that, for in truth those were NOT the good old days, regardless of poetry and Currier and Ives Lithographs. Those were days of backbreaking toil, or horrible farm failures brought on by unknown natural killers of plants and animals. Those were days when farmers stayed down on the farm chiefly because they were born down on the farm and knew no way out. It was much easier for William Cullen Bryant to catch the charm of farming on a weekend visit down from Boston than it was for the farmer's wife who toiled in the farm house 365 days a year. And Currier and Ives never seemed to be around when disease felled a half-dozen cattle.[3]

VIVIDNESS

Clear language helps the audience see the meaning; vivid language paints meaning in living color. *Vividness* means full of life, vigorous, bright, and intense; it means producing strong impressions or distinct mental images. If your language is vivid, your audience will picture your meanings in striking detail. Consider the following two sentences:

> No one [salesperson] ever left the hotel to look for business.
>
> Nobody, but nobody, ever left the palace, crossed the moat at Fifth Avenue, and went looking for business.[4]

The first sentence is clear; the second is vivid. Vividness gives language staying power—it makes it memorable. How many lines can you remember from the many presidential speeches you have probably heard during the past four years? Any? However, there is

---

[3] John Cunningham, "How Are You Going to Keep Them Down on the Farm?" *Vital Speeches,* March 15, 1971, p. 346.

[4] James Lavenson, "Think Strawberries," *Vital Speeches,* March 15, 1974, p. 347.

a good chance that you have heard and remember the following lines:

> Speak softly, but carry a big stick.
>
> The only thing we have to fear is fear itself.
>
> The buck stops here.
>
> Ask not what your country can do for you—ask what you can do for your country.

Each of these statements—by Theodore Roosevelt, Franklin Roosevelt, Harry Truman, and John Kennedy—is memorable; each is a vivid statement of the idea it represents. Of course, every sentence in a speech is not going to be remembered for all time, but there is no reason why some of the statements you make cannot be truly vivid.

Vivid speech begins with vivid thought. You must have a striking mental picture before you can communicate one to your audience. If you cannot feel the bite of the wind and the sting of the nearly freezing rain; if you cannot hear the thick, juicy T-bone steaks sizzling on the grill; if you cannot feel that empty yet exhilarating feeling as the jet climbs from takeoff—you will not be able to describe these sensations vividly. The more imaginatively you can think about your ideas, the more vividly you will be able to state them.

Aside from thinking imaginatively and describing detail, what specific means can you use in your efforts to achieve vividness? My recommendation is to use one or more figures of speech. Some thirty "figures" of speech are used in modern writing and speaking. I want to discuss briefly just seven that I believe you are already familiar with and that you can use relatively easily. The first three are comparative, the next two involve sound patterns, and the final two are based on contradiction.

Comparative Figures Remember that by definition *vividness* means producing a strong or clear impression on the senses or producing a distinct mental image. These ends can be achieved through comparisons with pictures your audience can already identify.

An extremely easy comparison to create is the simile. A *simile* is a direct comparison of dissimilar things. Similes usually contain the words *like* or *as*. Many of the clichés we use are similes. We may say, "He runs like a turtle" or "She's slow as molasses" to make a point about lack of speed; we say "He swims like a rock" or "She's built like a pencil" to dramatize a negative description. The problem with clichés is that their overuse has destroyed the vividness they once possessed. Similes are vivid when the base for the direct comparison is imaginative or different. Examine the nature of the simile Robert Schertz used in his speech about trucking: "They also seem to regard trucks as monstrous boxcars that can eat highways for breakfast."[5] This simile provides a sharp image with a humorous touch.

Another common comparative form is metaphor. Metaphors are much like similes. Instead of a direct comparison using *like* or *as*, however, *metaphors* build a direct identification. Metaphors are such a common part of our language that we seldom think of them as special. For years the Pittsburgh Steeler line was known as the "Steel Curtain"; cars are referred to as "lemons"; a woman may be "kittenish"; a man may be a "bull in a china shop"; a team's infield may be a "sieve."

Since metaphors are vivid, you should consider ways of using them in your speeches. As with the simile, avoid the trite or hackneyed. The following are three short metaphors that contemporary speakers used to help create vivid impressions in their speeches:

> Speaking out, ladies and gentlemen, is part of the rent we must pay for our room on earth.[6]
>
> As a result, this essential million-person industry finds itself enmeshed in a web of myths, misrepresentations, distortions and outright fabrications.[7]
>
> The current law, which was intended to reform, hit the wrong target and began to kill off the parties.[8]

This final one is a personal favorite:

> I can attest to the fact that this fair city must surely be the one place on earth where sound travels faster than light. Here is a circus of curved

---

[5] Robert H. Schertz, "Deregulation: After the Airlines, Is Trucking Next?" *Vital Speeches*, November 1, 1977, p. 40.

[6] John W. Hanley, "Has Emotion Tipped the Scales on Consumer Safety?" *Vital Speeches*, November 15, 1977, p. 95.

[7] James N. Sites, "Chemophobia, Politics and Distorted Images," *Vital Speeches*, December 15, 1980, p. 151.

[8] Lee Sherman Dreyfus, "People or Money . . . Which Will Rule the State?" *Vital Speeches*, April 1, 1980, p. 364.

mirrors and distorted images of lights and shadows, of leaks and red herrings—where it daily becomes more difficult to separate fact from fiction.[9]

Although the figurative similes and metaphors will work well for you, don't forget the *simple comparison*. When well constructed, it is every bit as powerful for building vividness. You will seldom find a passage more vivid than the following comparison:

> And while technology has gone through the roof, its costs have gone through the basement. If the automobile industry had done what the information industry has done in the last 30 years, a Rolls Royce would cost no more than $2.50 and get two million miles per gallon![10]

Vividness Through Sound Patterns

Vividness can also be built with sounds. Parallelism creates vividness through word sound patterns, alliteration through specific sound repetition. *Parallelism* is a balance in structure of words, phrases, and sentences. The following statement develops parallelism through repetition of introductory words: "Today is the day we must think; today is the day we must weigh and consider; but perhaps most important, today is the day we must act!" Contrast this with the following statement, which achieves parallelism through balance in structure: "Bill will get accepted to graduate school. Sally will get her job with the ad agency. Paul will get his commission. What will you get?"

With a little thought you can build parallelism into your speeches very easily. As with most of the devices we are considering, however, your use must be judicious. Overuse of any of these will become tiring.

Alliteration is repetition of sounds in words or in stressed syllables within words. "Her audience represented a chorus of culinary klutzes" shows alliteration through the repetition of the /k/ sound at the start of three key words. Such phrases as "forget your furry friends," "guard the grandeur," "sing a song of sadness," and "hit the heights" are all alliterative. Even more than any of the other devices we have considered, alliteration must be used sparingly if it is to have a positive effect.

---

9 Sites, "Chemophobia," p. 154.
10 Robert G. Scanlon, "The Year 2000," *Vital Speeches,* September 15, 1980, p. 728.

Contradictions   The final two devices we will consider—irony and paradox—depend on apparent contradiction for their effect.

Irony is especially effective for building vividness. Irony implies a state of affairs that is opposite to expectation or a difference between what is stated and what is meant. Speaking of a math teacher who is audited by the IRS for errors in computation suggests irony—the situation is the opposite of one you would generally expect. Saying "Here comes the club scholar" to a person who is having difficulties with grades is sarcasm; as a difference between what is stated and what is meant, *sarcasm* is a form of irony.

Similar to irony is *paradox*—an apparent contradiction. Notice how Stephanie Bennet builds a paradox in her speech about women:

> If she displays typically feminine behaviors, she is rejected as incompetent; if she does not display typically feminine behaviors, she is rejected as inappropriate.[11]

There is, of course, irony in both clauses—the result, however, is paradox.

In this section we have considered only a few of the many devices you can use to achieve vividness.

EMPHASIS   A third criterion for evaluating language is emphasis. In a 500-word speech, all 500 words are not of equal importance. You neither expect nor necessarily want an audience to retain the memory of every word you utter. Thus, throughout your speech preparation you must be concerned with ways of emphasizing those words and ideas that are more important than others and should therefore be remembered. Emphasis may be made through organization by idea subordination, through delivery by voice and bodily action, and through language itself. Consider three elements of language that will enable you to make ideas stand out: proportion, transition, and repetition.

Proportion   One way of emphasizing points is through proportion, the amount of time spent on each of the ideas in the speech. The psychological importance of proportion can be illustrated by a hypothetical ex-

---

[11] Stephanie M. Bennet, "The Re-entry Woman," *Vital Speeches*, June 1, 1980, p. 497.

ample. Let us assume for a moment that proportion can be considered independently. If in a ten-minute speech on the causes of juvenile delinquency, the three main points (poverty, broken homes, and permissiveness) are discussed for about three minutes each, the audience might perceive the ideas as having equal weight. If, however, the speaker spends five minutes on poverty and only two minutes on each of the other two causes, the audience will perceive poverty, the five-minute point, as the most important one in the speech. Now, if poverty is indeed the most important cause, proportion will emphasize the point; if, however, broken homes are really a more important cause of juvenile delinquency, audience perception will differ from speaker intent.

You will probably find that your ideas have the greatest effect if proportion is correlated with position. Thus, in a ten-minute speech, if you put the most important point first, you should spend four or five minutes on it. If you put the second most important point last, spend three or four minutes on it. The rest of the time should be divided among the points you put in the middle. Since audiences are likely to remember best those points that were discussed in greater detail, the artful speaker takes care that the most important points receive the greatest amount of discussion.

Proportion is brought about by amplification. If a point is important but is not properly developed, you should add a few examples or illustrations to build its strength. Remember, do not add words for the sake of words. If a point really is important, you should have valuable information to include. If you find that you have to invent "padding," you might want to reevaluate the importance of that particular point.

Transition A second kind of emphasis is the carefully phrased transition. Transitions are the words, phrases, and sentences that show idea relationships. Transitions summarize, clarify, forecast, and in almost every case emphasize. Of the three methods of emphasis discussed here, phrasing good transitions is perhaps the most effective, yet the least used. We will look at two important types of transitions.

INTERNAL TRANSITION Internal transitions grow from the relationships among the ideas themselves. Our flexible language provides us with numerous words that show relationships. Although the following list is not complete, it indicates many of the common transition words and phrases that are appropriate for speech.[12]

Transitions	*Uses*
also and likewise again in addition moreover	You will use these words to add material.
therefore and so so finally all in all on the whole in short	You will use these expressions to add up consequences, to summarize, or to show results.
but however yet on the other hand still although while no doubt	You will use these expressions to indicate changes in direction, concessions, or a return to a previous position.
because for	You will use these words to indicate reasons for a statement.
then since as	You will use these words to show causal or time relationships.
in other words in fact for example that is to say more specifically	You will use these expressions to explain, exemplify, or limit.

---

[12] After Sheridan Baker, *The Complete Stylist* (New York: Thomas Y. Crowell, 1966), pp. 73–74.

Because these particular words and phrases give the oral clues needed to perceive idea relationships, you should accustom yourself to their use.

EXTERNAL TRANSITION   External transitions call special attention to words and ideas. Since internal transitions can be missed if the audience is not paying close attention, you can use direct statements, both for the sake of variety and for additional emphasis, to call attention to shifts in meaning, degree of emphasis, and movement from one idea to another. These statements tell the audience exactly how it should respond.

First, external transitions tell the audience where you are in a speech. As listeners, we range from very good to very bad. As a speaker, you do not want to take a chance that we have missed something just because we are not very good listeners. As listeners, we always want to know the relationship between the idea presently being expressed and the rest of the speech. Thus, an effective speaker spends at least a part of his or her time acting like a tour guide, showing us exactly where we are in the progress of the speech. Speakers make use of the following kinds of statements:

> This speech will have three major headings.
>
> Now that we see what the ingredients are, let's move on to the second step, stripping the surface.
>
> We'll start by showing the nature of the problem, then we'll consider some of the suggested solutions.

Second, external transitions tell the audience the importance of the particular point that is being made. As the speaker, you know which ideas are most important, most difficult to understand, most significant. If you level with the audience and state such opinions, it will know how it is supposed to be reacting to those points. Thus, speakers should make use of the following kinds of statements:

> Now I come to the most important idea in the speech.
>
> If you haven't remembered anything so far, make sure you remember this.
>
> Pay particular attention to this idea.
>
> Are you sure you have this point? It is the most important one.
>
> But maybe I should say this again, because it is so significant.

These examples are only a few of the possible expressions that leave the flow of ideas and interject subjective keys, clues, and directions to stimulate audience memory or understanding. Although these are not very subtle, experimental studies have indicated that they are effective in helping emphasize points.[13]

Repetition
: The third and perhaps most common means of emphasis is repetition. Repetition may be an exact duplication of idea or it may be a restatement. If you want the audience to remember the exact words, you should use repetition. If you want the audience to remember the idea, restatement is probably preferable. For instance, the explanation "Even a three hundred hitter only gets three hits in every ten times at bat—that means for every three hits he gets, he is put out seven times" reiterates the idea and not the words.

APPROPRIATENESS

The final way of achieving instant intelligibility is through appropriateness. Appropriateness involves using language that adapts to the needs, interests, knowledge, and attitudes of the audience without offending or angering its members, or in some way turning them off. Appropriate language helps cement the bond of trust between the speaker and the audience. Let us see how you can learn to adapt your language to your audience and how you can avoid usage that will alienate audiences.

Adapt Your Language to Your Audience

You have worked hard to prepare a good outline, so you should feel comfortable with the quality of the material you are planning to present. Now you face the challenge of adapting what you have found to your audience. What is audience adaptation? It is the means by which you get the members of the audience to feel that the speech relates directly to them. The process begins when you examine the materials you are planning to use to develop the points in your speech, and it continues with efforts to phrase those materials so the audience will perceive them as related to its experience.

---

[13] Ronald Stingley, "An Experimental Study of Transition as a Means of Emphasis in Organized Speeches," unpublished masters thesis, University of Cincinnati, Cincinnati, Ohio, 1968, p. 36.

The following three suggestions are guidelines by which you can evaluate the audience adaptability of your developmental material:

1. If you have a choice between two kinds of material, use audience adaptation as the major criterion for making the selection. If two examples are equally informative and one of them relates more directly to the audience, choose it.

2. If you have a variety of developmental material that supports your point, but none of it relates to your audience, create an adaptation. Remember, you can invent comparisons, hypothetical examples, and narratives.

3. If most of your developmental material is composed of statistics, detailed explanations, or elaborate quotations, make a special effort to find additional material that has built-in audience appeal. Illustrations, anecdotes, narratives, comparisons, and contrasts are more interesting. Their novelty alone will often gain audience attention.

Let us see how these three suggestions can be applied to a typical problem of idea development. Suppose you were working on the main point "Japan is a small, densely populated nation." This sentence calls for you to show Japan's area and population. Using material from the 1981 *World Almanac,* you could say:

> Japan is a small, densely populated nation. Her 116 million people are crowded into a land area of 143,000 square miles. The density of her population is 800 persons per square mile.

The essential statistics about population and area have been given. Although the statistics are accurate and the unit is clear, the development is neither as interesting nor as meaningful as it could be. Now compare the following development, which incorporates the suggestions listed above:

> Japan is a small, densely populated nation. Her population is 116 million—only about half that of the United States. Yet the Japanese are crowded into a land area of only 143,000 square miles—roughly the same size as the single state of California. Just think of the implications of having one-half of the population of the United States living in California, where 22 million now live. Moreover, Japan packs 800 persons into every square mile of land, whereas in the United States we average about 58 persons per square mile. Japan, then, is about thirteen times as crowded as the United States.

This second development was built upon an invented comparison of the unknown, Japan, with the familiar, the United States and California. Even though most Americans do not have the total land area of the United States (let alone California) on the tip of their tongue, they know that the United States covers a great deal of territory and they have a mental picture of the size of California compared to the rest of the nation. It is through such detailed comparisons that the audience is able to visualize just how small and crowded Japan is.

Now let us examine several specific language devices that will increase the degree of adaptation. Although no device will give the impression of adaptation if you do not have a sincere interest in your audience, the following four will help you phrase your audience concern more directly.

Use Personal Pronouns

Personal pronouns by themselves are a form of direct audience adaptation. Saying "you," "us," "we," "our," whenever possible will give the audience a verbal clue to your interest in it. Too often, speakers ignore this simplest of devices by stating ideas impersonally. Suppose you wanted the audience to consider buying a house. You could say, "When an individual eventually gets enough money for a down payment on a house, he needs to ask himself some very serious questions." Notice the psychological difference if you were to phrase the same idea this way: "When you eventually get enough money for a down payment on a house, you need to ask yourself some very serious questions." In one sentence you would be able to show *three* times that you are thinking about your audience. Although this may seem a very small matter, it may make the difference between audience attention and audience indifference. You will notice that the four speeches in Chapter 19 illustrate this form of adaptation.

Use Audience Questions

One of the secrets of audience adaptation is inducing audience involvement. Public speaking is not direct conversation; your audience is not going to respond vocally to each of your ideas. How, then, can you create the impression of direct conversation? How can you generate some sense of personal involvement? One way is by asking audience questions.

In her classroom speech explaining people's reasons for wearing clothing, a woman said: "There are certain decisions you must make and there are factors affecting these decisions. One reason we wear clothing is to protect our body from any visible harm." Although she included personal pronouns, she might have augmented the directness of the statement and improved the adaptation by saying:

> There are certain decisions you must make and there are factors affecting these decisions. Why do we wear clothes at all? What is a motivation for anyone to wear clothes? One reason we wear clothing is to protect our body from any visible harm.

Audience questions generate audience participation, and, of course, once an audience is participating, the content will be even more meaningful to it. Because direct audience questions seeking verbal audience responses may disrupt your flow of thought (and sometimes yield unexpected answers), the rhetorical question, a question seeking a mental rather than a vocal response, is usually safer. Rhetorical questions encourage the same degree of involvement and they are easier to handle. Moreover, questions are appropriate at any place in the speech where special emphasis is needed.

Notice how this woman speaker uses audience questions to get her largely male audience thinking with her:

> You may even know the anguish—the very real, the very understandable anguish—that men are now suffering as they take up The Problem of Women in Business Today, or, as someone suggested for these remarks, Business and the New Woman.
>
> What's wrong? Why this real pain? Why this soul-searching? Why all this brow-beating and brain-wrinkling?[14]

Despite their value, one caution about the use of questions is in order: Unless the speaker is really interested in asking a question, his delivery will sound artificial. Get used to asking questions naturally and sincerely.

Allude to Common Experience
Alluding to common experience also brings about audience involvement. Earlier we were talking about giving a speech to a group of fifth graders. If you can remember how you felt when *you* were in fifth grade, your job of adapting to the audience will be

---

[14] Jean Way Schoonover, "Why Corporate America Fears Women," *Vital Speeches,* April 15, 1974, p. 415.

much easier because you can refer to common experiences. You can often adapt directly by relating an anecdote, narrative, or illustration that shows an experience both you and the audience have in common. For instance, if you are expressing the idea that a store in a shopping center often does not have a person's size or color, you might say:

> I'm sure we've all had the experience of going to a shopping center for some item that we had particularly in mind only to find when we got there that either the store didn't have the color we wanted or they didn't have our size.

You want the audience to identify with the common experience. Identification stimulates thought. If an audience is thinking with you, it will be listening to you. The following example shows how this method can be built into the speech unobtrusively and effectively. The speaker, a business person, is talking to other business people, so he can discuss the problem as common to speaker and audience:

> The deterioration of costly service is partly our fault, Gentlemen. We experience the consumer's service problems every day. As businessmen, we know that the same kind of treatment is being given to our customers. Still, we don't do much about it. We tolerate the terrible, when it comes to service.[15]

Build Hypothetical Situations   Since audience involvement is so important to audience attention, you can often stimulate involvement by placing the audience in a hypothetical situation. The hypothetical situation can incorporate the entire framework for the speech, or it can be used to reinforce a single item of information. Suppose you wanted to show the audience how it could turn a cast-off table or chair into a fine piece of refinished furniture. You could start the speech by placing the audience in the following hypothetical situation:

> Many times we relegate our cast-off end tables, a desk, a record cabinet to the land of the lost—the storage room of our basement. We know the piece of furniture is worth saving—but we don't know why. That cast-off is probably a lot heavier and a lot more solid than most furniture being made today. So, what are we going to do with it?

---

[15] Edward Reavey, Jr., "The Critical Consumer Need," *Vital Speeches,* October 15, 1971, pp. 25–26.

> Why not refinish it? Let's assume for this evening that you have just such a piece of furniture in your basement. Let's take it out of that storage room and go to work on it. Where do we start? Well, first of all, we have to gather the right material to do the job.

Whether members of the audience actually have such pieces of furniture is somewhat irrelevant. Because of the hypothetical situation, they can involve themselves in the procedure.

The hypothetical situation can also be used to illustrate a single part of the speech. In your speech on the same topic, refinishing furniture, you might explain the final step, putting on the varnish, by saying:

> The final step in the process is to varnish the piece of furniture. Now, varnishing appears to be a very simple task—and it is if you do it the right way. Let's assume that you've got a good-quality 2-inch brush in your hand, with a good quality of transparent varnish open and ready to go. Now, how are you going to apply that varnish? Many of you may be used to the paintbrush method, you know, back and forth until the piece is covered. But in varnishing, this may well lead to a very poor finish. Instead, start about 4 inches from the edge with the grain, and move your brush to the edge. Now, don't go back the other way. Pick the brush up and make another stroke adjacent to the first—always keep the stroke in the same direction. After you've covered the width go back another 4 inches (now 8 inches from the edge). Move the brush in one direction and continue right over the part you did first. If you will continue doing it in this way you will leave no brush marks in your work and you will have a smooth, even finish.

Whether you used a visual aid or not to illustrate the procedure, the hypothetical example would involve each member of the audience in the actual varnishing. The hypothetical situation is just another way of inducing audience involvement.

Avoid Inappropriate Language

Appropriate language has the positive value of cementing the bond of trust between the speaker and the audience. During the last two decades or so of experimentation with the principles of speaking, we have learned a great deal about what makes people behave as they do. And we have found that at the base of effective communication is speaker personality. If members of an audience like you as a speaker, they often believe you. Through appropriate language you can create this situation. The more hostile the audience is likely to be to us or to our ideas, the more care we need to take to use language that will be accepted by that audience. Under strain we can and often do lose our temper. When we lose our temper, we often say things we do not really mean or we express our feelings in language that is unlikely to be accepted by strangers. If we do that, we may lose all we have gained.

Almost everyone at one time or another in childhood replied to a particularly scathing remark, "Sticks and stones may break my bones, but words will never hurt me." I think this little rhyme is so popular among children because they know it is a lie, but they do not know how else to react. Whether we are willing to admit it or not, words do hurt—sometimes permanently. Think of the great personal damage done to individual persons throughout our history as a result of being called "hillbilly," "nigger," "wop," "yid." Think of the fights started by one person calling another's mother, sister, or a girlfriend a "whore." Of course, we all know that it is not the words alone that are so powerful; it is the context of the words, the situation, the feelings about the participants, the time, the place, or the tone of voice. You may recall circumstances in which a friend called you a name or used a four-letter word to describe you and you did not even flinch; you may also recall other circumstances in which someone else called you something far less offensive and you became enraged.

As a result, we must always be aware that our language may have accidental repercussions. When the sender does not understand the frame of reference of the audience, he or she may send messages in language that distorts the intended communication. It does not take a whole speech to ruin a speaker's effect—a single inappropriate sentence may be enough to wreak havoc with the total message. For instance, the speaker who says, "And we all know the problem originates downtown," may be referring to the city government. However, if the audience is composed of people who see downtown not as the seat of government but as the residential area of an ethnic or a social group, the sentence takes on an entirely different meaning. Being specific can help you avoid problems of appropriateness; recognizing that some words communicate far more than their dictionary meanings will help even more.

In addition to accidental repercussions of our language, we should caution against using words for their shock value. The entire fabric of protest rhetoric is imbued with shock language; yet shock language often backfires on the user. The goal of arousing anger and hostility toward an issue often results in anger and hostility toward the speaker.

Avoiding inappropriate language requires a sensitivity to the feelings of an audience. Some of the mistakes we make are a result of the inadvertent use of expressions that are perceived as sexist to women and racist to minorities. There is usually no intent to offend. In fact, the speaker may be totally unaware of offensiveness; yet the audience may take legitimate offense nonetheless.

Sexist or racist language is any language that is perceived as negative and that occurs solely because of differences in sex, race, or national origin. Since women and minorities have traditionally been the object of such language, they are likely to be the most sensitive to its use.

The following are a few of the kinds of usage problems that arise with such language.

1. Using words that have built-in sexism; police*man,* post*man,* chair*man.* Much more acceptable are such labels as police officer, mail carrier, and chairperson.

2. Modifying generic labels with sexual or racial words: *Black* or *female* modifying such words as *doctor, professor,* and *athlete*— words that have, in the past, been associated with male and/or white occupations. For example, saying "Carson is a good female professor" instead of just "good professor"; saying "Roberts is a highly respected Black surgeon" instead of just "surgeon"; "Connors is quite a female athlete" instead of just "athlete." In each case, the modification takes away from the value of the praise. Thus "Carson is a good female professor" means "Carson is good for a woman, although compared to men she's nothing special."

3. Using male pronouns when no sexual reference is intended. Consider the following sentence: "A doctor is a revered member of a community; he is respected; he is deferred to; and he stands as a role model." Grammatically, the sentence is correct, but women often find such usage offensive. Better would be: "Doctors are revered members of their community: they are respected; they are deferred to; and they stand as role models." The change may seem small, but it may be the difference between persuading an audience or failing.

4. Using common stereotypic expressions: "Morgan acts like an old lady" and "That was really white of you, Smith" will both be perceived as offensive.

Very few people escape all sexist and racist language. By monitoring your usage, however, you can guard against frustrating all communication by assuming that others will react to your language the same way you do and you can guard against saying or doing things that offend others and that perpetuate outdated sex roles and race stereotypes.

Gesture and body movement.

Eye Contact

Spontaneity

Enthusiasum!

Chapter 6 Practicing the Delivery

PRINCIPLE IV:
Effective speaking
requires good delivery.

When Demosthenes, the famous Athenian orator, was asked, "What is the single most important element of speaking?" he answered, "Delivery." Even now in the 1980s we are inclined to hear and perhaps to say, "It's not what you say, but how you say it that counts."

Why do people place such emphasis on the importance of delivery? Primarily because delivery is the source of our contact with the speaker's mind. Delivery is what we see and what we hear. Think of delivery as a window: When it is cracked, clouded over, or dirty, it obscures the most beautiful of scenes; when it is clean, it allows us to appreciate the scene more fully. Although delivery cannot improve the ideas of a speech, it can provide a physical medium through which ideas are perceived.

If delivery is monotonous, harsh to the ear, or in any way unpleasant, content will lose effectiveness. If, on the other hand, the delivery of the speech is vibrant, inspiring to listen to, or generally pleasant, the speaker will gain maximum value from the words and ideas.

In Chapter 5 we focused on wording; in this chapter we focus on the elements of speech delivery that can be improved or perfected with practice. Then we consider how we can go about practicing both the wording and the delivery of the speech itself. But first let us look at an issue that is fundamental to our ability to improve speech delivery.

DEALING WITH
FEAR

Most people love to talk, but even the most talkative person is likely to become a bundle of nerves at the thought of "having to give a speech." This fear of speaking in public seems to be universal. In a survey conducted by R. H. Bruskin Associates, respondents were asked to indicate what they fear most. Only 32 percent reported a fear of heights, only 22 percent reported a fear of financial problems, only 18 percent reported a fear of either sickness or death, but a whopping 40.6 percent reported a fear of speaking in public—a percentage that was higher than for any other item tested!

Not only is fear of speaking common, it is a very normal reaction. People naturally become nervous under pressure. First, of course, the realization that we are standing in front of a group whose eyes are all focused on us heightens our natural tendency to be self-conscious. Couple this tendency to be self-conscious with the knowledge that what we say will be analyzed and evaluated and you can see that we're bound to be anxious. Even speakers with professional experience find themselves more nervous in class when they can see the professor and students taking notes and preparing to evaluate.

Not only are nearly all of us nervous, we nearly all experience the same effects. Before the speech we are likely to experience an inability to eat or sleep; at the time of the speech we are likely to experience trembling, perspiring, shortness of breath, and increased heartbeat; and if we allow ourselves to concentrate on our nervousness, during the speech we may experience excessive self-doubt, loss of contact with the audience, a jumping back and forth from point to point, and occasional lapses of memory.

Although we all experience nervousness, it need not result in speech problems. In fact, most people can and do control their fears. It is important to note that our goal is "controlling fear" and not "getting rid of it." Let's start by looking at four factors that you have working in your favor.

1. You are in good company. Not only do 40 percent of the population regard public speaking as the thing they fear most, but many experienced speakers confess to nervousness when they speak. I can hear you now: "Don't give me that line—you can't tell me that [and you fill in the blank with some person you know] is nervous when he [or she] speaks in public!" You doubt me? Ask the person. He or she will tell you. Even famous speakers like

Abraham Lincoln and Franklin D. Roosevelt were nervous before speaking. The difference in nervousness among people is a matter of degree—good speakers learn to channel their nervousness. The following statement may surprise you: I would be disappointed if you were not nervous. Why? Because you must be a little nervous to do your best. Of course I do not mean that you should be blind with fear, but a bit of nervousness gets the adrenalin flowing—and that brings you to speaking readiness.

2.   Despite nervousness, you can make it through a speech. Very few persons are so bothered that they are literally unable to function. You may not enjoy the experience—but you can do it.

3.   Your listeners aren't nearly as likely to recognize your fear as you might think. Inexperienced speakers find their fear increases because they perceive their audiences as recognizing their nervousness. This recognition makes the speaker more self-conscious, more nervous. The fact is that people, even speech instructors, will greatly underrate the amount of stage fright they believe a person has.[1] Once you realize that your audience doesn't really recognize the fear that you as the speaker believe is so noticeable, you'll no longer experience the acceleration of nervousness.

4.   But perhaps the factor you have going for you the most is that the more experience you get in speaking, the more able you become to cope with nervousness. As you gain experience, you learn to think about the audience and the message and not about yourself. Moreover, you come to realize that audiences are more often than not very supportive. You will come to find that having a group of people listening to *you alone* is a very satisfying experience.

Now that we have looked at four factors that operate almost automatically to help you cope with fear, let's consider some of the specific behaviors that you can put into operation before and during the speech itself.

The very best behavior for controlling nervousness is to pick a topic you know something about and that you are interested in. Public speakers cannot allow themselves to be content with a topic

---

[1] Theodore Clevenger, Jr., "A Synthesis of Experimental Research in Stage Fright," *Quarterly Journal of Speech*, 45 (April 1959), 136.

they don't care about. An unsatisfactory topic lays the groundwork for a psychological mindset that almost guarantees nervousness at the time of the speech. By the same token, having a topic that you know about and are truly interested in lays the groundwork for a satisfying speech experience. In Chapter 3 we placed a great deal of emphasis on how to ensure that you had the best topic possible. Heed that advice and you will be well on the way to reducing nervousness.

Then, give yourself enough time to prepare fully. If you back yourself into a corner where you must find material, organize it, write an outline, and practice the speech all in an hour or two you will almost guarantee failure and destroy your confidence. On the other hand, if you will do a little work each day for a week before the assignment you will experience considerably less pressure and you will feel an increase in confidence.

Giving yourself enough time to prepare fully includes sufficient time for practice. Later in this chapter we will go through the steps of effective speech practice. Follow them closely. Your goal is to build habits that will take over and control your behavior during the speech itself. If our national love affair with big-time athletics has taught us anything, it is that careful preparation enables an athlete (or a speaker) to meet and overcome adversity. Among relatively equal opponents, the team that wins is the team that is mentally and physically prepared for the contest. When an athlete says, "I'm going into this competition as well prepared as I can possibly be," he or she is more likely to do well. In this regard, speech making is no different from athletics. If you assure yourself that you have carefully prepared and practiced your speech, you will do the kind of job that will make you proud.

During this preparation period you can also be "psyching yourself up" for the speech. If you have a good topic and if you are well prepared your audience is going to profit from listening to you. That's right—even though this is only a class and not a professional speaking experience—the audience is going to be glad they have heard you. Now before you say "Come on, who are you trying to kid!" think of speeches you have heard. When someone had really good ideas weren't you impressed? Of course you were. The fact is that some of the speeches you hear in class are going to be some of the best and most valuable speeches you are ever going to hear. Students learn to put time and effort into their speeches and many of them turn out to be quite good. If you work at it, your class is going to look forward to listening to you.

In addition to what you can do before the speech the some behaviors that you can put into operation at the time speech to reduce fear. Research indicates that it is during the period right before you walk up to give your speech and the time when you have your initial contact with the audience that your fear is most likely to be at its greatest.[2]

To make the most of these research findings, you must know yourself. Are you better off "getting it over with"? That is, being the first person to speak that day? If so, you can usually volunteer to go first. But regardless of when you speak, there is at least one additional thing you can do to help yourself: Don't spend your time thinking about yourself or your speech. At the moment the class begins, you have done all you can to be prepared. This is the time to get your mind on something else. Try to listen to each of the speeches that comes before you. Get involved with what each speaker is saying. Then when your turn comes, you will not be overly "worked up."

As you walk to the speaker's stand, remind yourself that you have good ideas, that you are well prepared, and that your audience is going to want to hear what you have to say. So, even if you make mistakes, the audience will profit from your speech.

When you reach the stand, pause a few seconds before you start. Take a deep breath; this may help get your breathing in order. Try to get movement into your speech during the first few sentences. Sometimes a few gestures or a step one way or another is enough to help break some of the tension.

Remember that the college classroom may be the best place for developing speaker confidence. The bibliography at the end of this part includes sources that you may wish to consult for more details about reducing stage fright.

WHAT TO PRACTICE: STANDARDS OF DELIVERY

Delivery is the use of voice and body to help convey the message of the speech. Although the best delivery will not save a poorly prepared speech, particularly poor delivery may harm your speech so that even exceptional content and organization are negated. Speech delivery may be the deciding factor in the audience's estimation of your effectiveness.

---

[2] Larry W. Carlile, Ralph R. Behnke, and James T. Kitchens, "A Psychological Pattern of Anxiety in Public Speaking," *Communication Quarterly*, 25 (Fall 1977), 45.

As you begin speech practice, what qualities and characteristics should you be seeking? You are trying to develop a conversational quality that is characterized by *enthusiasm, eye contact,* and *spontaneity;* and you are trying to maximize effectiveness through *voice, articulation,* and *bodily action.* Let us examine these six topics.

Enthusiasm A review of speech research leads to one inescapable conclusion: By far the single most important element of effective speaking is speaker enthusiasm. A speaker who looks and sounds enthusiastic will be listened to and that speaker's ideas will be remembered.

Think of the speakers who have impressed you most. Probably every speaker on your list presented his or her ideas enthusiastically. The source of enthusiasm is a real, sincere *desire to communicate.* When you listen to Billy Graham and Barbara Jordan, you know they feel strongly about what they are saying. Speakers like Graham and Jordan today and Henry Clay, Susan B. Anthony, William Jennings Bryan, Franklin D. Roosevelt, and Martin Luther King, Jr., in the past all have had an enthusiasm that grew from their deep and overpowering desire to communicate. They have wanted to speak, and their enthusiasm *showed* it!

Enthusiasm cannot be faked. If you really want to communicate, if you really care about the topic, your voice will have an enthusiastic quality—and your audience will listen.

Of course the amount of enthusiasm you can project "naturally" is a matter of individual difference. If you are an outgoing person who displays feelings openly, you may find it easy to project your enthusiasm in a speech. If you are rather reserved, your audience may not be able to pick up the more subtle signs of your enthusiasm as readily. The reserved person who seldom displays feelings openly must do more in the speech than "what comes naturally." If you are more reserved, you must work to intensify your feelings about what you are doing so that the emotions can be communicated. Developing this intensity will require an extra effort on your part, but it can be done. How? Make sure your topic excites you. You cannot afford to select a topic about which you are lukewarm at best. The outgoing person might be able to show enthusiasm about an uninspiring topic—the reserved person cannot. To be perceived as enthusiastic, you must be truly excited. You must get involved with the material. Try to develop vivid mental pictures of what you are trying to say. Mental activity will lead to physical manifestation. Finally, you need to remind yourself constantly that your speech will truly benefit the audience. If you can convince yourself that your audience really ought to listen, you can bring up the level of perceived enthusiasm.

Eye Contact Although perception of speech communication seems to be primarily auditory, we concentrate better on the message when a visual bond is established between speaker and audience. In fact, in face-to-face communication we expect speakers to look at us while they are talking. If the speakers do not look at us, we lose our need to look at them, and, thus, our desire to pay attention to them. The result is a break in the communication bond and a proportional loss of attention. As a speaker, then, you maintain a certain amount of control over your listeners' attention simply by looking at them.

Not only does good eye contact help attention, it also increases audience confidence in the speaker. What do you think of individuals who do *not* look you in the eye when they speak with you? Your attitude toward them is probably negative. On the other hand, when speakers *do* look you in the eye, you are probably more willing to trust them. Eye contact is not material evidence of a speaker's sincerity, but it is regarded as psychological evidence.

As you gain skill in speaking you will become aware of the most beneficial aspect of good eye contact—that is, your ability to study audience reaction to what you are saying. Communication is two-way. You are speaking with an audience, and it, in turn, is responding to what you are saying. In daily conversation, response is verbal; in public speaking, response is shown by various cues. An audience of people who are virtually on the edges of their seats with their eyes on you is paying attention. An audience of people who are yawning, looking out the window, and slouching is not paying attention. You can determine what adjustments, additions, changes, and deletions you need to make in your plans by being aware of audience reaction. As you gain greater skill, you will be able to make more and better use of the information learned through eye contact.

How do you maintain audience eye contact? It is, of course, physically impossible to look at your whole audience at once. What you can do is talk to individuals and small groups in all parts of the audience throughout your speech. Do not spend all of your time looking front and center. The people at the ends of aisles and those in the back of the room are every bit as important as those right in front of you.

Spontaneity   The third characteristic fundamental to effective speech delivery is spontaneity—the impression that the idea is being formed at the time it is spoken. At some time, you may have had to memorize some bit of prose or poetry. Remember when you were working on the assignment, you were not nearly so concerned with the meaning of the words as you were with the process of memorizing the flow of words. If you or other classmates had to recite, you will remember that the class was seldom inspired by the presentations. Why? Since the words sounded memorized, any semblance of meaning was lost. What was missing was spontaneity, the particular characteristic of voice that makes an idea sound new, fresh, and vital, even if you have practiced saying it for days. Although good actors can make lines they have spoken literally thousands of times sound original, most of us do not have the ability or the know-how. Have you ever wondered why a public official often sounds so much better in off-the-cuff interviews than when reading a speech? Once the word is memorized or written down, it is no longer spontaneous communication, and the speaker is then required to become somewhat of an actor to make the idea sound spontaneous.

How can you make a planned speech seem spontaneous? The answer lies in how you use characteristics of your own conversational method. Since there is a tremendous difference between knowing ideas and memorizing them, you need to have a mastery of content, not words. If I asked you to tell me how to get downtown, you would be able to tell me spontaneously because you have made the trip so many times that the knowledge is literally a part of you. If I asked you to tell me about the tennis game you just finished, you could do it spontaneously because key parts of the game would be vivid in your memory. If, however, I asked you to tell me a little about the material you studied for a history class, your ability to do so spontaneously would depend on the quality of the effort you had made to master the material. If you had weighed and considered the material, for example, if you had tried to understand the concepts rather than just memorize the details, you would have enough understanding to discuss the content spontaneously. Spontaneous presentation of prepared materials requires experience with the facts, vivid images of the facts, and true understanding of the facts.

Students often say they speak better on the spur of the moment than they do when they try to give a prepared speech. What they mean, of course, is that given a topic about which they had experiences, vivid images, and understanding, they can communicate reasonably well on the spur of the moment. Since you have the opportunity to weigh and consider your subject matter, there is no reason why you should not be equally spontaneous with a prepared speech. Spontaneity is considered further when we examine speech practice later in this chapter.

These three concepts—enthusiasm, eye contact, and spontaneity—when taken together, give a speaker what has come to be called a conversational quality. Speech making and conversation are not the same. However, by using the best characteristics of conversation in the formal speech situation, the speaker gives listeners the feeling that he or she is conversing with them. These three characteristics of conversational quality provide the foundation for good delivery. Now let us look at the mechanics of delivery: voice, articulation, and bodily action.

Voice Just as our words communicate, so does the sound of our voice. The meanings expressed by the way we sound (called *paralanguage*) may tell our audience what we intended and may contribute to the meanings of our words. However, *how* we sound may interfere with stimulating meaning and may at times even contradict our words.

Our voice has all the capabilities of a musical instrument. How we use it makes the difference between success or failure. To begin our discussion, let us take a brief look at the speech process.

Speech is a product of breathing, phonation, resonation, and articulation. During inhalation, air is taken in through the mouth or nose, down through the pharynx (throat), larynx, trachea, bronchial tubes, and into the lungs (Figures 6-1 and 6-2). We get the power for speech from exhaling the air we breathed. As air is forced from the lungs back up through the trachea and larynx by controlled relaxation of the diaphragm and contraction of abdominal and chest muscles, the vocal folds that help protect the opening into the trachea are brought closely enough together to vibrate the air as it passes through them. This vibration is called *phonation*, the production of sound. The weak sound that is emitted (like the

FIGURE 6-1.   **Section of the head area, showing the relationship of the nose, mouth, pharynx (throat), and larynx**

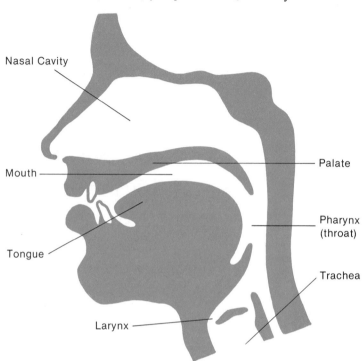

Nasal Cavity

Mouth

Tongue

Palate

Pharynx (throat)

Trachea

Larynx

sound made by vibrating string) travels through the pharynx, mouth, and in some cases the nasal cavity. Each of these three cavities helps to resonate the sound. This resonated sound is then shaped by the articulators (tongue, lips, palate, and so forth) to form the separate sounds of our language system. These individual sounds are then put together into words, or distinguishable oral symbols. We call the sound that we produce *voice*.[3] Now let us examine the major characteristics of voice pitch, volume, rate, and

---

[3] If you are interested in a more detailed analysis of the anatomy and physiology of the process, ask your instructor to recommend one of the many excellent voice and articulation books on the market. Two such books are Hilda Fisher, *Improving Voice and Articulation*, 3d ed. (Boston: Houghton Mifflin, 1981), and Virgil A. Anderson, *Training the Speaking Voice*, 3d ed. (New York: Oxford University Press, 1977).

FIGURE 6-2.   **Section of the breathing apparatus, showing a lung, bronchial tubes, and trachea that lead to the cartilage area housing the larynx**

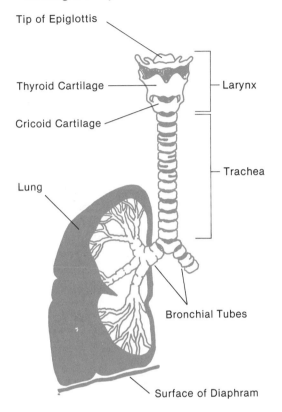

Tip of Epiglottis

Thyroid Cartilage — — Larynx

Cricoid Cartilage

— Trachea

Lung

— Bronchial Tubes

— Surface of Diaphram

quality that work together to give us the variety, expressiveness, and precision in meaning that assist communication.

PITCH *Pitch* refers to the highness or lowness of the voice. As mentioned, voice is produced in the larynx by vibration of the vocal folds. In order to feel this vibration, put your hand on your throat at the top of the Adam's apple and say "ah." Just as the change in pitch of a violin string is brought about by making it tighter or looser, so the pitch of your voice is changed by the tightening and loosening of the vocal folds. Although you have no conscious control over the muscles that change the tension in the vocal folds, you can feel the change of position of the entire larynx by placing your hand on the Adam's apple again and saying "ah," first at a very high pitch and then at a low pitch. The pitch that one uses most frequently is called the "key" of the voice. Fortunately, most people talk in a pitch that is about right for them. Occasionally a person talks in a pitch that seems abnormally high or low. If you have questions about your pitch, ask your professor. If you are one of the very few persons with a pitch problem, your instructor will refer you to a speech therapist for corrective work. Since for most of us our normal pitch is satisfactory, the question is whether we are making the best use of the pitch range we have at our disposal.

VOLUME *Volume* is the loudness of the tone we make. When we exhale normally, the diaphragm relaxes, and air is expelled through the trachea. When we wish to speak, we need to supplement the force of the expelled air on the vibrating vocal folds by contracting our abdominal muscles. This greater force behind the air we expel increases the volume of our tone. To feel how these muscles work, place your hands on your sides with your fingers extended over the stomach. Say "ah" in a normal voice. Now say "ah" louder. Now say "ah" as loud as you can. If you are making proper use of your muscles, you should have felt the stomach contraction increase as you increased volume. If you felt little or no muscle contraction, you are probably trying to gain volume from the upper chest and neck; this results in your voice sounding tired and strident, and lacking sufficient volume to fill a large room. Under ideal circumstances, you should be able to increase volume without raising pitch. Each of us, regardless of size, is capable of a great deal of vocal volume. The problem is that most of us do not use our potential. If you have trouble getting sufficient volume, work on exerting greater pressure from the abdominal area.

RATE *Rate* is the speed at which we talk. As mentioned earlier, a normal rate is somewhere between 140 and 180 words per minute. Rate, like pitch, is an individual matter. There is no one rate that is best for everyone. Since some people talk more rapidly and some more slowly than others, the test is whether an audience can understand what a speaker is saying.

If your instructor believes you talk too rapidly or too slowly, he or she will tell you; and before improvement in normal conversation is possible, you must adjust your ear to a more appropriate rate. The most effective method is to read passages aloud, timing yourself to determine the exact number of words per minute you speak. Then you must make a conscious effort to decrease or increase the number of words per minute accordingly. At first, a different speech rate will sound strange to your own ear. But if you practice daily, within a few weeks you should be able to hear an improvement and you should be able to accustom your ear to the change.

QUALITY   *Quality* is the tone, timbre, or sound of your voice. Voices are characterized as clear, nasal, breathy, harsh, hoarse, strident, and so on. If your voice has too great a degree of some undesirable quality, consult your professor. Although you can make some improvement on your own, improvement requires a great deal of work and a rather extensive knowledge of vocal anatomy and physiology. Severe problems of quality should be referred to a speech therapist.

VOCAL VARIETY AND EXPRESSIVENESS   In determining effectiveness of delivery, these qualities are not nearly so important individually as they are in combination. It is through the variety of pitch, volume, rate, and occasionally quality that you are able to give the most precise meaning to your words. An expressive voice is not flawed by the two most common faults of speech melody: monotone and constant pattern.

A *monotonous voice* is one in which the pitch, volume, and rate remain constant, with no word, idea, or sentence differing from any other. Although very few people speak in a true monotone, many limit themselves severely by using only two or three tones and relatively unchanging volume and rate. The effect of an actual or near monotone is that the audience is lulled to sleep. Without vocal clues to help them assess the comparative value of words, members of an audience will usually lose interest. To illustrate what proper vocal emphasis can do for meaning, say the sentence, "I want to buy ice cream," in such a way that the pitch, rate, and volume are held constant. Such a delivery requires the listener to decide what the sentence means. Now say "buy" in a higher pitch, louder, and perhaps more slowly than the other words in the sentence. Through this vocal stress alone, you are communicating the idea that you want to *buy* ice cream rather than make it or procure it in some other way. With this sentence, meaning can be changed significantly by changing only the vocal emphasis of "I," "want," "buy," or "ice cream." During an actual speech, you should give such vocal clues in almost every sentence, to ensure audience interest and understanding.

The other prevalent fault detracting from expressiveness is the *constant vocal pattern,* in which vocal variation is the same for every sentence regardless of meaning. The resulting vocal pattern is nearly as monotonous as a true monotone. For instance, a person may end every sentence with an upward pitch or may go up in the middle and down at the end of every phrase. Vocal variety is of little value unless it is appropriate to the intended meaning. The best cure for a constant pattern is to correlate changes in voice with meaning. If you suffer from a relatively severe case of monotone or constant pattern, you should set up a work program that you can pursue every day. One method you can use is to read short passages aloud to a friend. Ask your friend to tell you which words were higher in pitch, or louder, or faster. When you find that you can read or speak in such a way that your friend will recognize which words you were trying to emphasize, you will be showing improvement in using vocal variety to clarify meaning.

Articulation   Characteristics of voice are most noticeable on the vowel sounds. Whether or not our words are understandable depends on how we form our consonant sounds. This process is called *articulation,* the shaping of speech sounds into recognizable oral symbols that go together to make up a word. Articulation is often confused with *pronunciation,* the form and accent of various syllables of a word. Thus, in the word *statistics,* articulation refers to the shaping of the ten sounds (*s, t, a, t, i, s, t, i, k, s*); pronunciation refers to the grouping and accenting of the sounds (*sta- tis'-tiks*). If you are unsure of pronunciation, look it up in a dictionary. Constant mis-pronunciation labels a person as ignorant or careless or both.

Although true articulatory problems (distortion, omission, substitution, or addition of sounds) need to be corrected by a speech therapist, the kinds of articulatory problems exhibited by most students can be improved individually during a single term. The two most common faults among college students are slurring sounds (running sounds and words together) and leaving off word endings. "Wutcha doin' " for "What are you doing" illustrates both of these errors. If you have a mild case of "sluritis," caused by not taking the time to form sounds clearly, you can make considerable headway by taking ten to fifteen minutes a day to read passages aloud, trying to overaccentuate each of the sounds. Some teachers advocate "chewing" your words, that is, making sure that you move your lips, jaw, and tongue very carefully for each sound you make. As with most other problems of delivery, you must work conscientiously every day for weeks or months to bring about significant improvement.

Bodily Action   Bodily action serves many key functions in our communication. It stands for words—a nod means "yes," arms extended palms down means "safe," thumbs down means disapproval. It supplements meaning—"The house is over there" (pointing), "It's about so big" (using hands to show the size), "You really make me mad" (stamping the foot). It shows our feelings—wide-open eyes for surprise, a scowl for anger, palms pressed against temples to express a mistake. In normal conversation, bodily action often *defines* the meaning of ideas, and the same is true in public speaking. Consider the principal variables of bodily action, namely, facial expression, gesture, and movement.

FACIAL EXPRESSION   The eyes and mouth communicate far more than some people realize. You need only recall the icy stare, the warm smile, or the hostile scowl that you received from someone to understand the statement that the eyes (and mouth as well) are the mirror of the mind. Facial expression should be appropriate to what we are saying. We are impressed by neither deadpan expressions nor perpetual grins or scowls; we are impressed by honest and sincere expressions that reflect the thought and feeling being communicated. Think actively about what you are saying, and your face will probably respond accordingly.

GESTURE   By gesture we mean the movement of hands, arms, and fingers. Gestures are usually descriptive or emphatic. When the speaker says "about this high" or "nearly this round," we expect to see a gesture accompany the verbal description. Likewise, when the speaker says "We want you" or "Now is the time to act," we look for a pointing finger, pounding fist, or some other gesture that reinforces the point. If you gesture in conversation, you will usually gesture in speech. If you do not gesture in conversation, it is probably best not to force yourself to gesture in a speech. I suggest that you try to leave your hands free at all times to help you "do what comes naturally." If you clasp them behind you, grip the sides of the speaker's stand, or put your hands into your pockets, you will not be able to gesture even if you want to. If you wonder what to do with your hands at the start of the speech so they do not seem conspicuous, you may either rest them on the speaker's stand partially clenched or hold them relaxed at your sides, or perhaps with one arm slightly bent at the elbow. Once you begin the speech, forget about your hands—they will be free for appropriate gestures. If, however, you discover that you have folded your arms in front of you or clasped them behind you, put them back in one of the two original positions. After you have spoken a few times, your professor will suggest whether you need to be more responsive or somewhat restrained with your hands and arms.

MOVEMENT Some speakers stand perfectly still throughout an entire speech. Others are constantly on the move. In general, it is probably better to remain in one place unless you have some reason for moving. However, a little movement adds action to the speech, so it may help you maintain attention. Ideally, movement should help focus on transition, emphasize an idea, or call attention to a particular aspect of the speech. Avoid such unmotivated movement as bobbing and weaving, shifting from foot to foot, or pacing from one side of the room to the other. At the beginning of your speech, stand up straight and on both feet. If during the course of the speech you find yourself in some peculiar posture, return to the upright position standing on both feet.

With all kinds of bodily action, be careful to avoid those little mannerisms that often are so distracting to the audience, like taking off or putting on glasses, smacking the tongue, licking the lips, or scratching the nose, hand, or arm. As a general rule, anything that calls attention to itself is bad, and anything that helps reinforce the idea is good.

A PROGRAM OF SPEECH PRACTICE The first thing we need to consider in terms of speech practice is the mode of delivery we will be using. Speeches may be delivered impromptu, by manuscript, by memorization, or extemporaneously.

Impromptu speaking is done on the spur of the moment, without previous specific preparation. Although nearly all of our conversation is impromptu, most people prefer to prepare their thoughts well ahead of the time they face an audience. Regardless of how good you are at daily communication, you would be foolhardy to leave your preparation and analysis for formal speeches to chance. Audiences expect to hear a speech that was well thought out beforehand.

A common and often misused mode is the *manuscript* speech. Because the speech is written out in full (and then read aloud), the wording can be planned very carefully. Although presidents and other heads of state have good reason to resort to the manuscript (even the slightest mistake in sentence construction could cause national upheaval), most speakers have little need to prepare a manuscript. Often their only excuse is the false sense of security that the written speech provides. As you can attest from your listening experience, however, few manuscript speeches are very interesting. Because manuscript speeches are not likely to be very spontaneous, very stimulating, or very interesting and because of the natural tendency to write a speech devoid of audience adaptation, you should usually avoid manuscript speaking, except as a special assignment. Since learning to use a manuscript can be important, we will talk about using manuscripts properly in Chapter 18, on speeches for special occasions.

A *memorized* speech is merely a manuscript committed to memory. In addition to the opportunity to polish the wording, memorization allows the speaker to look at the audience while speaking. Unfortunately for beginning speakers, memorization has the same disadvantages as the manuscript. Few individuals are able to memorize so well that their speech sounds spontaneous. Since a speech that sounds memorized affects an audience adversely, you should also avoid memorization for your first speech assignment.

The ideal mode is one that has the spontaneity of impromptu, yet allows for careful preparation and practice. The *extemporaneous* speech (the goal of most professional speakers) is prepared and practiced, but the exact wording is determined at the time of utterance. Most of the material in this text relates most directly to the extemporaneous method. Now let us consider how a speech can be carefully prepared without being memorized.

So far, we have discussed the standards of delivery, or what you should practice. Now we can apply the theory showing *when* and *how* you should practice your delivery. Novice speakers often believe that preparation is complete once the outline has been finished. Nothing could be further from the truth. If you are scheduled to speak at 9:00 A.M. Monday and you have not finished the outline for the speech until 8:45 A.M. Monday, the speech is not likely to be nearly as good as it could have been had you allowed yourself sufficient practice time. Try to complete your outline a day in advance for a two- to five-minute speech and two or even three days in advance for longer speeches. The only way to test the speech itself is to make proper use of the practice period. Practice gives you a chance to revise, evaluate, mull over, and consider all aspects of the speech.

Like any other part of speech preparation, speech practice must be undertaken systematically. In order to make the practice period as similar to the speech situation as possible, you should stand up and practice aloud. The specific procedure may be outlined as follows:

1. Read through your outline once or twice before you begin.
2. Put the outline out of sight.
3. Look at your watch to see what time you begin.
4. Begin the speech. Keep going until you have finished the ideas. If you forget something, don't worry about it—complete what you can.
5. Note the time you finish.
6. Look at your outline again.

Now begin your analysis. Did you leave out any key ideas? Did you talk too long on any one point and not long enough on another? Did you really clarify each of your points? Did you try to adapt to your anticipated audience? Unless you are prepared to criticize yourself carefully, your practice will be of little value. As soon as you have finished analyzing your first attempt, go through the six steps again. After you have completed two sessions of practice and criticism, put the speech away for a while. Although you may need to practice three, four, or even ten times, there is no value in going through all the sessions consecutively. You may well find that a practice session right before you go to bed will be extremely beneficial. While you are sleeping, your subconscious will continue to work on the speech. As a result, you will often note a tremendous improvement at the first practice the next day.

Should you use notes in practice or during the speech itself? The answer depends on what you mean by notes and on how you plan to use them. My advice is to avoid using notes at all for the first short speech assignments. Then, when assignments get longer, you will be more likely to use notes properly and not as a crutch. Of course, there is no harm in experimenting with notes to see what effect they have on your delivery.

Appropriate notes are composed of key words or phrases that will help trigger your memory. Notes will be most useful to you when they consist of the fewest words possible written in lettering large enough to be seen instantly at a distance. Many speakers condense their written preparatory outline into a brief word or phrase outline (see Figure 6-3).

For a speech in the five- to ten-minute category, a single

FIGURE 6-3.   Typical Set of Notes Made from Preparatory Outline on Pages 85–88

```
Essentials of Computers

   Central Processing Unit
      Brain
      Functions
         Instructions
         Operations

   Memory
      Storage
      Core
      Mainframe
      Chip
      Auxiliary units

   Input/Output
      Input sources
      Output sources
      Combination
```

3-by-5-inch notecard should be enough. When your speech contains a particularly good quotation or a complicated set of statistics, you may want to write them out in detail on separate 3-by-5 cards.

During practice sessions you should use notes the way you plan to use them in the speech. Either set them on the speaker's stand or hold them in one hand and refer to them only when you have to. Speakers often find that the act of making a notecard is so effective in helping cement ideas in the mind that during practice or during the speech itself they do not need to use the notes at all.

How many times should you practice? This depends on many things, including your experience, familiarity with the subject, and the length of the speech. What you do not want to do is to practice the speech the same way each time until you have it memorized. An effective speaker needs to learn the difference between learning a speech and memorizing it. One has to do with understanding ideas; the other has to do with learning a series of words.

When people memorize, they repeat the speech until they have mastered the wording. Since emphasis is then on word order, any mistake requires backtracking or some other means of getting back to the proper word order. Unfortunately, this kind of practice does not make for mastery of content, it does not give additional insight into the topic, and it does not allow for audience adaptation at the time of presentation. Another way that speakers memorize is to say the speech once extemporaneously and then repeat the same wording over and over again. The result is about the same in both instances.

When people stress the learning of ideas, instead of words, they practice their speech differently each time. Using principles of proper speech practice, the wording of the point concerning the capacity of a computer chip might evolve as follows:

First Practice: The circuits of a computer can be combined in a single chip the size of a fingernail. In the first computers this capacity took a whole room full of machinery.

Second Practice: Miniaturization is the key to computer development. The workings of a computer that used to fill a whole room can now be combined into a single chip the size of a fingernail.

Third Practice: Today we take the miniaturization of computer circuitry for granted. But just imagine: The workings of a computer used to fill an entire room—now the circuits necessary to run a computer can be combined into a single chip. How large? The size of your fingernail!

Notice that in all three versions the same facts were included—they were the facts included in the outline. These are the facts that you will attempt to include in every one of your practices. You should find that each practice gets a bit better—it begins to sound more and more like a speech. For most speakers, at least three complete oral rehearsals are necessary. As you continue to practice, at some time you will reach that point of diminishing returns where additional practices do not help and may actually hurt. You have to learn how many times you must practice to cement the key ideas in your mind and to get that oral, conversational, spontaneous quality that is so important to good speaking without getting stale or beginning to memorize.

Exercise 9   *Make a diary of the practice program for your first formal speech. How many times did you practice? At what point did you feel you had a mastery of substance? How long was each of your practice periods?*

Assignment   *A first speech assignment is likely to achieve one of two purposes: (1) to diagnose the speaker's strengths and weaknesses; this would be a speech of any type that illustrates the speaker's understanding of the principles discussed thus far or (2) to emphasize the speaker's delivery and a few basic speech principles; this would be a speech that is relatively easy to prepare. The following two assignments meet these two goals.*

1.   Diagnostic Speech
Prepare a two- to five-minute speech. The speech may be of any type. An outline is required. Criteria for evaluation will include essentials related to all four aspects of the speech: (1) Content—whether the topic was well selected, whether the specific purpose was clear, and whether good material was used to develop or to prove the points; (2) Organization—whether the speech had a good opening, clearly stated main points, and a good conclusion; (3) Wording—whether the language was clear, vivid, emphatic, and appropriate; and (4) Delivery—whether voice and body

were used to show enthusiasm, whether speaker looked at the audience, showed spontaneity, and achieved vocal variety and emphasis. The point of this diagnostic critique will be to show you where your major strengths and weaknesses seem to be as evidenced by this first speech.

2.   Alternative: Narrative Speech

Prepare a two- to five-minute narrative speech. Review your experiences and select one that you think your audience will enjoy hearing about. In short, this narrative is to be a personal experience speech. Criteria for grading will include how well you are able to hold audience attention, clarity and vividness of the experience, and delivery. Although all three criteria will be considered, major emphasis will be on speech delivery. Let us review some elements of narration.

A narrative *is a story, a tale, or an account—it is a telling of events. A narrative can be long or short. The more details are included, the longer a narrative will be. Usually a narrative has a point to it, a climax that the details build up to. A joke has a punch line; a fable has a moral; a narrative has an ending that makes the story interesting. Most narratives follow a time-order organization. Some follow a topic order with time-order subpoints. Remember, a narrative is primarily to build interest—its goal is audience interest. A narrative can present information; it can have a persuasive message, but most of all, it should be of interest.*

The following speech is a good example of a narrative form that has some informative impact; most of all, however, it is interesting.

Since this outline is for the first speech given, notice the way it is written. Test each part against the recommendations for outlining on pages 72–74. Also note that this outline contains 267 words, a good length for a four- or five-minute speech. Although the outline and the speech are good illustrations for either assignment, they are especially appropriate for the narrative speech assignment.

Outline: First Speech

Specific Purpose: To share with you the experience of the high dive.

Introduction

  I. This summer I had a rather extraordinary job.

 II. I would like to share with you the experience of the high dive.

Thesis Statement: Completion of the high dive involves readying the apparatus, preparing, taking the long climb to the top, making the dive itself, and finishing with the critical reentry.

Body

  I. The high-dive apparatus is composed of a set of interlocking ladders.
    A. They are fastened to the ground by guy wires.
    B. The platform is approximately 1 foot square.

 II. The high dive takes a great deal of preparation.
    A. It took me about a month to perfect my dive.
    B. I executed it first at lower heights and then moved up.

III. The climb up the ladder is one of the more difficult parts.
    A. While climbing you are aware of the danger involved.
    B. During the climb I usually questioned why I was doing it.
    C. Try never to rush, because it is so easy to slip.
    D. Upon reaching the top you will be confronted with mixed feelings.
      1. On one hand is the feeling of power.
      2. On the other hand is the feeling of fear.

 IV. The dive itself produces one of the most exhilarating feelings you will ever experience.
    A. As you prepare to leave the platform, you will find it hard to swallow and your heart will beat wildly.
    B. As you leave, nothing exists but you and the water.
    C. Hitting the water rushes you immediately back to reality.

  V. The entry into the water is a most critical part of the dive.
    A. The diver must stretch and lock out every muscle.
    B. Locking-out and stretching helps you pierce the water.
    C. I hated the entry because it concluded my journey and because the water always felt too hard.

Conclusion

  I. Completion of the dive left me with a tremendous feeling of accomplishment.

 II. I don't recommend this dive to everyone.

Read the sample speech through aloud in its entirety.[4] After you have judged its quality, read the speech again, noting the criticism included in the other column.

Analysis

This is a particularly good opening. It uses a question to get initial attention, identifies with audience interest, and reveals the novel topic in a vivid way. From these first words, the speaker was guaranteed a listening audience.

His first point gives an overall picture of the apparatus. He tries to describe both the physical and the psychological setting.

The second point explains the dive and the diver's preparation for it.

Throughout the development the speaker reminds us of the potential danger. This adds to the excitement of the speech.

His next three points (climb, dive, and entry) are all developed in second person. He says "Come with me" and he then leads us through the dive. In these three points audience involvement is at its peak. We get a vicarious thrill as we listen. This is the narrative portion of the speech.

Speech: The High Dive

How many of you would like to work at an amusement park? Think of it—free rides and a summer of fun and excitement. Maybe you'd like to try out for the job I had last summer. But you'd better hold on for a few minutes before you volunteer—you see, my job was daredevil high diver. From 100 feet in the air I dove into a tank of water only 14 feet deep. I'd like to share with you the experience of the high dive.

The high-dive apparatus consists of a set of interlocking ladders that are fastened down by guy wires to the ground. The perch or platform that the diver stands on to execute his dive is approximately 1 foot square. So, when I stood atop the 100-foot span, all I had was a small foot rest, a little ladder to hang on to, and a lot of air.

I can honestly say that the high dive is not an easy task, but with good coaching and complete concentration an experienced diver can learn to execute the dive without fear. It took me approximately one month to learn my dive. I perfected a double somersault with a half twist, from the lower heights. I then worked my way up the ladder about 6 to 10 feet at a time—always aware that I had to adjust to the increase in height each time, because one slight miscalculation and it would have been all over.

Come with me as we go through the dive step by step. The 100-foot climb up the ladder is one of the more difficult parts of the act. While climbing the ladder, you're conscious of the danger. I was constantly asking myself just what I was doing here. You should, of course, never rush up the ladder, because one slip and you would fall helplessly to the ground below. Upon reaching the top of the long span, you're confronted with mixed feelings of power, looking out onto the audience of people watching every move you make—and the feelings of fear, wondering if you're going to survive this dive.

---

[4] Speech given in Fundamentals of Speech class, University of Cincinnati. Printed by permission of Tim McLaughlin.

In this fourth point, the dive, the speaker helps us feel the exhilaration.

As a result of his method, we actually feel the *smack* of the water.

This fifth point is well introduced. The development would be even better had the speaker defined "locking-out" better. We get the idea, but he does not help us to be sure of our understanding.

The conclusion is satisfactory. Although the speaker does not summarize his points, his caution, "I don't recommend this line of work" reminds us of the danger and I believe brings back the picture of the 100-foot descent. The topic is excellent—it is attention-getting and has great potential for informative and interesting development. In addition, the speech lives up to audience expectation. The speaker has good material and good organization—his wording is excellent. The speech is vivid and well adapted to the audience. I believe this is an excellent model for a first speech round.

The dive itself is one of the most exhilarating experiences you will ever feel. As you make the decision to leave the platform, you'll find your heart beating wildly, and find it very hard to swallow; but when you have actually left the platform, all your problems will seem to disappear behind you. The world just seems to stop for a few seconds and nothing exists but you and the water below—and then, *smack,*—hitting into the water you are instantly rushed back to reality.

The entry into the water is the last and perhaps most critical part of the dive. To enter properly, the diver must stretch and lock out every muscle in his body to prepare for impact of the water. By locking-out and stretching, you are able to pierce the water and prevent injury. I always hated the entry, because it concluded the tremendous journey I just experienced and also because, uh, I never really hit the water too smoothly—I never completely locked out.

The successful conclusion of a high dive left me with a tremendous feeling of accomplishment. I knew that I had not only entertained my audience, but I had also conquered the 100-foot tower for another day. I don't recommend this line of work for everyone; I believe that an equal feeling of exhilaration and excitement can be achieved in other areas. But I do believe my experience this summer was extraordinary, and also one I'll never forget.

Suggested Readings: Part Two

The following books are recommended as additional reading for the fundamentals unit:

Adler, Ronald B. *Confidence in Communication.* New York: Holt, Rinehart and Winston, 1977. Although the focus of the book is on assertiveness training, Chapter 5, "Managing Communication Anxiety" presents a method for relaxation and desensitization that you may find useful for reducing tension.

Anderson, Virgil A. *Training the Speaking Voice,* 3d ed. New York: Oxford University Press, 1977. Although there are many good books on voice and articulation, this has proved to be one of the best.

Blankenship, Jane. *A Sense of Style.* Belmont, Calif.: Dickenson, 1968. Ms. Blankenship packs a great deal of valuable information about style into a short paperback volume.

Brownstein, Samuel C., and Mitchel Weiner. *Basic Word List.* Woodbury, N.Y.: Barron's Educational Series, 1977 (paperback). An excellent vocabulary building book.

Clevenger, Theodore Jr. "A Synthesis of Experimental Research in Stage Fright," *Quarterly Journal of Speech* 45 (April 1959), 134–145. This article draws some 11 conclusions about stage fright that are still consistent with recent data.

Eastman, Richard M. *Style.* New York: Oxford University Press, 1970. This paperback book is a little longer than the Blankenship work, but is also a little more comprehensive.

Gibson, James. *Speech Organization: A Programmed Approach.* San Francisco: Rinehart Press, 1971. The programmed approach enables you to check your understanding of organization systematically.

Knapp, Mark L. *Essentials of Nonverbal Communication.* New York: Holt, Rinehart and Winston, 1980 (paperback). Excellent analysis and summary of research studies.

McCroskey, James C. "Oral Communication Apprehension: A Summary of Recent Theory and Research," *Human Communication Research* 4 (1977), 78. A companion article to the Clevenger article cited above.

Mehrabian, Albert. *Silent Messages.* 2d ed. Belmont, Calif.: Wadsworth, 1981. A short, highly readable book focusing on the role of nonverbal communication in social interaction.

Newman, Edwin. *Strictly Speaking: Will America Be the Death of English?* New York: Warner Books, 1975 (paperback). A highly readable and popular look at contemporary problems of English usage. A best seller.

PART THREE

INFORMATIVE SPEAKING

A great amount of your speaking will involve information exchange. The material in this unit builds on and amplifies the fundamentals presented in the first four chapters. The focus, however, is on mastering the skills that are necessary for clear, understandable informative speaking. After presenting several principles of information exchange, the unit considers use of visual aids, process explanation, description, definition, and use of source material.

I feel that
we should all
take a long
hard look at
the inefficiencies
within our
Social Security
system.

Chapter 7 Principles of Informative Speaking

In order to make any decision, we must have information. In spite of our advanced technology for information retrieval and dissemination, we still send and receive an amazing amount of the information we want or need through the spoken word. Yet, as much as we talk, most of us are not nearly as good at information exchange as we could be. Although speech purposes overlap, studying informative speaking as a separate purpose gives us an opportunity to focus on creating understanding. Whether your intention is to explain how a zipper is made, describe your new library, discuss Thor Heyerdahl's findings on the Ra expeditions, or explain how scientists are working to predict earthquakes, your ultimate purpose is to create understanding. Chapters 8 through 12 consider different forms in which information can be presented. Here we examine some general principles of information exchange that will be useful to your development of *any* informative speech.

GOALS OF INFORMATION EXCHANGE

During this course you will probably be asked to give one or more informative speeches. On the surface, your goal appears to be simple enough: present information. But to what end? Of what value is the oral presentation of information? As a speech purpose, giving information is best justified by the fact that it facilitates the learning process. Although educational psychology questions whether you can "teach" another person anything, you can help another person in his or her learning of that material. How?

1. **By opening the person to the information—helping him or her to become receptive:** As students we are quick to make value judgments about information that is being presented, and, thus, about whether or not we will listen to it. Therefore, helping a person become receptive to information is vital to the learning process.

2. **By helping the person to understand the material:** Think of the thousands of times you have seen people nod that they understand what is being said and then, through actions, demonstrate that they really do not understand. You can help a person relate information to his or her own experiences and you can help a person's ability to apply that information.

3. **By devising means of helping a person retain the material he or she has received:** The minute we take in information we begin losing some of it. Within a relatively short time we may lose anywhere from one-third to all of that information. You can help a person develop means to retain more over a longer period of time.

An informative speech can focus on any or all of the purposes of developing reception, understanding, and retention.

MEANS OF FACILITATING LEARNING Now let us consider in some detail several basic principles that lead to the reception, understanding, and retention of information.

1. **Information is more likely to get audience attention when it is perceived to be relevant to audience experience.** Rather than acting like a sponge and absorbing every bit of information that comes our way, most of us act more like a filter—we retain only that information we perceive as relevant.

The ultimate in relevance is information perceived as vital, that is, information that is truly a matter of life and death. Just as police cadets are likely to pay attention when the subject is what to do when attacked, so members of your audience will pay attention when they think what you have to tell them is critical to them. Although very little of what you tell an audience will literally help them stay alive, you can focus on points that will improve the quality of life. Students pay attention when the professor is telling them what is going to be on the midterm; men and women pay attention when someone talks about what can be done to ensure the fidelity of their boy friend, girl friend, or spouse; college seniors applying for graduate school pay attention to suggestions for increasing scores on graduate entrance exams.

If your speech material can promise vital information you can and should take advantage of it. But even when what you have to say seems remote from audience experience, you can usually build relevance into it if you think creatively and take the time to work at it. A speech on Japan can focus on the importance of Japanese manufacturing to our economy; a speech on the Egyptian pyramids can be related to our interest in building techniques. There is literally no subject for which some audience relevance cannot be shown. It is up to you to find the relevance and make a point of it in the speech.

A good way of achieving relevance is to consider information as an answer to stated or implied questions that grow from perceived audience needs. Consider your need to know as related to today's weather. If you are planning to stay in your room all day to study, you probably have little need to know about outside temperatures and weather conditions; if, however, you are planning to go to a football game or a picnic, or take a hike, weather information will meet a felt need, and you will seek out and listen closely to weather forecasts. What do the people you are planning to talk to need to know? How does your information meet their needs?

2.   Information is more likely to get audience attention when it is perceived as new. When people think they know something already, they are less likely to pay attention. It is up to you as speaker not only to find information that will be new to your audience but also to concentrate on the newness.

Even when you are talking about a topic that most of the people in your audience are familiar with, you can uncover new angles, new applications, new perspectives on the material. Listen to commercials for such products as cellophane wrap, kitchen towels, and cheese. Nearly every commercial points to a new and different use for the various products. When it comes to speech material, the tests of newness are whether the information adds to audience knowledge or gives new insights to information members of the audience already possess.

New information is received even more readily when it is novel. *Novelty* is newness with a twist, something that commands our involuntary attention. Novelty begins with the topic itself. In the speech about the summer job of the high diver, which you read at the end of Part Two, the audience listened because it found the topic truly novel. But if the topic itself is not novel, the next best thing is to take a novel approach to the material by focusing on the features that make the information unusual. A Rolls Royce grill makes a standard Volkswagen novel; solar energy heating makes a three-bedroom ranch-style house novel. Novelty is often the product of the creative mind. We consider creativity in speech making in greater detail in Chapter 12, which is on expository speaking.

3. Information is more readily received when it is startling. When something startles you, you are taken aback or given an emotional jolt. If your professor wears a new sports coat, it may get your attention; if your professor comes to class wearing a toga, a bear skin, or a loin cloth, it would be startling. Whereas novelty implies a long-lasting impression (a speech on the high dive is novel from beginning to end), what is startling has only momentary impact. As a result, the best use of the startling is as an attention getter—either to get attention initially or to rekindle attention at flagging moments.

The startling is often accomplished through action. Blowing up a balloon and letting it sail around the room to illustrate propulsion is startling. Taking off one's outer clothes in class to reveal a gym suit underneath would be startling. Sometimes, however, what you do may be so startling that the audience never recovers. So be careful. Although startling actions may get momentary attention, they can disrupt a speech if they are too overpowering.

Similar to the startling action is a really good anecdote, illustration, example, or particularly provocative statement. For instance, consider this part of a speech to high school graduates:

> Our Bibles tell us that we are allotted three score and ten years on earth. Seventy years, more or less. Barring pestilence and wars, natural disasters and automobile accidents, today's average American can anticipate that life expectancy. So you members of the class of 1974 must realize that you have already consumed about one-quarter of your allotted years.
>
> Feeling old already?[1]

---

[1] Theodore Sendak, "Anchors and Rudders," *Vital Speeches,* August 1, 1974, p. 635.

4. Information is more readily received and retained when it is presented humorously. You do not have to be riotously funny or sprinkle your speech with jokes—in fact, both are likely to be more detrimental to your information than useful. To be most effective, humor should be related to the topic. If you discover an amusing way of developing some point in your speech, your audience will listen. For instance, here is how one speaker heightened audience interest in his speech on hotel management:

> Frankly, I think the hotel business has been one of the most backward in the world. There's been very little change in the attitude of room clerks in the 2,000 years since Joseph arrived in Bethlehem and was told they'd lost his reservation.[2]

If trying to be funny makes you feel self-conscious, then do not force humor into your speech. However, if you think humor is one of your strengths, then make the most of it.

5. Information is more likely to be understood and retained if it is associated. When you walk into a room full of people, you seek out the familiar faces. Likewise, when you are confronted with information that you do not readily understand, you ear listens for certain familiar notes that will put the new information into perspective. A speaker can take advantage of this tendency on the part of the audience by associating new, difficult information with the familiar.

Association is defined as the tendency of a sensation, perception, or thought to recall others previously coexisting in the consciousness with it or with states similar to it. Thus, when one word, idea, or event reminds you of another, you are associating. A speaker can associate through vivid comparisons and contrasts. For instance, if you are trying to show your audience how a television picture tube works, you can build an association between the unknown of the television tube and audience knowledge. The metaphor "a television picture tube is a gun shooting beams of light" is an excellent association between the known and the unknown. The image of a gun shooting is a familiar one. A gun shooting beams of light is easy to visualize. If you make the association striking enough, every time your audience thinks of a televi-

---

[2] James Lavenson, "Think Strawberries," *Vital Speeches*, March 15, 1974, p. 346.

sion picture tube, they will associate it with guns shooting beams of light. If you can establish one or more associations during your speech, you are helping to ensure audience retention of key ideas.

6. Information is more likely to be understood and retained when it is related visually. You are more likely to make your point if you can show it as well as talk about it. Visual aids are effective in simplifying and emphasizing information as well as in holding interest. Their impact is a result of the fact that they appeal to two senses at the same time: hearing—we listen to the explanation—and sight—we see the substance of the explanation. This double sensory impact helps cement the ideas in our mind. Since visual aids are so important in information exchange, the entire next chapter, Chapter 8, is devoted to their use in speeches.

7. Information is more likely to be remembered when it is repeated. The potential of repetition is unquestioned by those who study the memory process. For instance, when you meet someone for the first time, you will be more likely to remember the person's name if you repeat it a few times immediately after being introduced; when you are trying to learn a new definition, a formula for a compound, or a few lines of poetry, you will master them only after you have repeated them often enough to remember. We all know that some of the most effective, as well as the most irritating, television commercials are based on the simple device of repetition. As a student of public address, you should learn when and how to take advantage of this potent device. Unfortunately, for beginning speakers the words that are most often repeated are of the nature of "uh," "well," "now," and "you know." The artful speaker determines the two, three, four, or five most important words, ideas, or concepts in the speech, and thinks of ways of repeating them for emphasis.

Putting repetition into speeches is perhaps one of the easiest things you can do. If you want the audience to remember exactly what you have said, then you can repeat it once or twice: "The number is 572638, that's 5,7,2,6,3,8"; or, "A ring-shaped coral island almost or completely surrounding a lagoon is called an atoll—the word is *atoll*."

There may be times in a speech when you want the audience to remember an idea but not necessarily the specific language you use. Under these circumstances you will probably restate the idea rather than repeat it. Whereas repetition is the exact use of the same words, *restatement* is saying the idea again but in different words. For instance, "The population is 975,439—that's roughly one million people"; or "The test will be composed of about four essay questions—all the questions on the test, about four, will be essay."

8. Information is more likely to be understood and retained when it is well organized. A clear, well-developed outline is the starting point of good speech organization. In addition to your speech having a clear organization on paper, an audience must be consciously aware of the *presence* of that good organization. The old journalistic advice, "Tell them what you're going to tell them, tell them, and tell them what you've told them," recognizes the importance of emphasizing organization. The speaker who states, "In my speech I will cover three goals, the first is . . . the second is . . . and the third is . . ." will often have more success getting an audience to remember than one who does not. Likewise, such reminder statements as "Now we come to the second key point" or "Here's where we move from the third stage of development and go to the fourth" have proven effective in directing audience thinking. When listeners perceive the clarity of idea development, they are likely to remember the material.

Now that we have examined principles of informative speaking, we can begin to put what we have learned into practice. In Chapters 8–12 we pursue skills relating to using visual aids, explaining processes, describing, defining, and using resource material.

Assignment   *Prepare a four- to six-minute informative speech. An outline is required. Criteria for evaluation will include means of ensuring reception and retention of information. The following questions can be used as a basis for evaluation of your speech:*

Did you develop the relevance of the information?

Did you present information in a novel, startling, or humorous fashion?

Did you use visual aids, association and/or repetition to emphasize the information?

Did you help the audience follow your organization?

Outline

Specific Purpose: To explain four major classifications of nursery rhymes.

Introduction

I. "Hey diddle diddle, the cat and the fiddle, the cow jumped over the moon. The little dog laughed to see such sport, and the dish ran away with the spoon."

II. Did you know that there are four major classifications of nursery rhymes?

Thesis Statement: The four classifications of nursery rhymes are ditties, teaching aids, historically based, and modern use.

Body

I. Ditties are nursery rhymes with a prophetic purpose.
   A. A fortune-telling rhyme is told while counting the white spots on the fingernails.
   B. Just as in *Poor Richard's Almanack,* by Benjamin Franklin, Mother Goose had her merry wise sayings.
   C. Traditionally, a rhyme on the topic of love fidelity is said while plucking the petals of a daisy.

II. Some nursery rhymes were used as teaching aids.
   A. "Hickory Dickory Dock" is an example of onomatopoeia, which is an attempt to capture in words a specific sound.
   B. Song rhymes helped the children with their coordination.
      1. Historical background.
      2. Children's usage.
   C. Numbers in nursery rhymes obviously retain the traces of the stages by which prehistoric people first learned to count.

III. Many nursery rhymes have historical significance.
   A. Religious problems entered into the nursery rhymes with "Jack Sprat."
   B. In England it is believed that some of these country rhymes may be relics of formulas used by the Druids in choosing a human sacrifice for their pagan gods.
   C. Cannibalism is quite prevalent in nursery rhymes.

IV. A modern classification of the nursery rhyme is the parody.

A. The famous prayer "Now I lay me down . . ." was first published in 1737, but has now been parodied.

B. A joke has been created out of "Mary and Her Lamb."

Conclusion

I. Every song, ballad, hymn, carol, tale, singing game, dance tune, or dramatic dialogue that comes from an unwritten, unpublished word-of-mouth source contributes to the future culture of our nation.

II. Remember that with your next cute saying, teaching aid in the form of a rhyme, reference to our history, or modern use of nursery rhymes, you may become the next Mother Goose.

Bibliography

Baring-Gould, William S., and Cecil Baring-Gould. *The Annotated Mother Goose.* New York: Clarkson A. Potter, 1962.

Bett, Henry. *Nursery Rhymes and Tales—Their Origins and History.* New York: Henry Holt, 1924.

Ker, John Bellenden. *An Essay on the Archaeology of Popular Phrases and Nursery Rhymes.* London: Longman, Rees, Orme, Brown, Green, 1837.

Mother Goose. *Mother Goose and the Nursery Rhymes.* London: Frederick Warne, 1895.

Read the speech at least once aloud.[3] *Examine it to see how the speaker made information relevant; whether she presented information in a novel, startling, or humorous way; whether she used association or repetition for emphasis; and how she helped the audience follow the information. After you have studied the speech, read the analysis in the other column.*

Analysis

The speaker uses a common rhyme to capture our attention. From the beginning the novelty of the topic and the development get and hold our

Speech: Classifications of Nursery Rhymes

"Hey diddle diddle, the cat and the fiddle, the cow jumped over the moon, the little dog laughed to see such sport and the dish ran away with the spoon." You recognize this as a nursery rhyme, and perhaps you always considered these nursery rhymes

---

[3] Speech given in Fundamentals of Speech class, University of Cincinnati. Printed by permission of Susan Woistmann.

attention. Notice the clever wording "There's more to nursery rhymes than meets the ear."

To increase our understanding, information should be presented clearly. Throughout the speech, the speaker leads us through the organization. She begins the body of the speech by identifying the first classification. The next sentence gives us the three subdivisions of the major classification. The commendable part of this and all sections of the speech is the use of specific examples to illustrate the various types and subtypes. As far as real information is concerned, this main point does not go much beyond labeling and classifying our own knowledge. The last part is of some interest in that it shows the evolution of wording.

Again the main point is clearly stated. She begins this section with an interesting look at a common rhyme. Once more, there is an excellent use of specifics to illustrate the point she is making. Although speech language should be informal, it should not be imprecise. Notice that the antecedent for "he" in "he's trying to show the ticking" is unclear. You should be careful to avoid these common grammatical errors. This section of the speech illustrates how information can sometimes be communicated in such an interesting way that we are not even aware that we have learned anything.

as types of nonsense poetry with little if any meaning. As we look at the four classifications of nursery rhymes, I think that you'll see as I did that there's more to nursery rhymes than meets the ear.

One of the major classifications of nursery rhymes is ditties. Ditties are fortune-tellings, little wise sayings, or little poems on love fidelity, and they are the most popular form of nursery rhyme. There are various ways of telling your fortune through ditties. One is saying, "A gift, a ghost, a friend, a foe; letter to come and a journey to go." And while you say this little ditty, this fortune-telling, you count the little white spots on your fingernails. Or you can say, "Rich man, poor man, beggarman, thief, doctor, lawyer, merchant, chief," and count your buttons. Whichever button you end on is the type of guy you are going to marry. Another kind of ditty is the wise saying. Just as in *Poor Richard's Almanack* by Benjamin Franklin, Mother Goose had her own little sayings. She said, "A pullet in the pen is worth a hundred in the fen," which today we say as "A bird in the hand is worth two in the bush." Love fidelity, the third kind of ditty, can be proven while plucking the petals off a daisy. "Love her, hate her, this year, next year, sometime, never." But today's usage has brought it up to "Love me, love me not, love me, love me not."

Another classification of nursery rhymes is those used as teaching aids, such as the saying "Hickory dickory dock." This is the use of onomatopoeia, which is trying to develop a sound from the use of words. In this case, he's trying to show the ticking of a clock. "London Bridge," although it has some historical background, is used for teaching children coordination, such as running around the circle raising their hands up and jumping back down. Similarly, in the ancient times, man made up rhymes in order to make things easier for him to remember, such as in the saying, "one, two, buckle my shoe; three, four, close the door." And as time went on, he eventually found out that he could use the fingers and toes to count. This is where "This little piggy went to market and this little piggy stayed home" originated.

Again the speaker moves smoothly into the statement of the main point. As far as the quality of information is concerned, this is probably the best section of the speech. Notice that she continues to use her examples and illustrations very well.

Of all the single examples in the speech, this is probably the best.

Once more we are aware of the statement of a main point. The speaker returns to classifying and labeling information that as an audience we have in our possession.

From the foregoing criticism it can be seen that the speech is a very clear, extremely interesting informative speech. Two possibilities for strengthening the speech are worth considering. Since the third main point is so informative, it might have been better for the speaker to limit the entire

Also, did you know that nursery rhymes have historical background? The third classification of nursery rhymes are those of historical significance. In the Middle Ages, which is when most nursery rhymes were formed, the saying, "Jack Sprat could eat no fat, his wife could eat no lean; and so betwixt the two of them, they licked the platter clean," refers to the Catholic Church and the government of the old Roman Empire. This is when the Catholic Church was blessing tithes, and wiping the country clean. The government came in and collected the taxes; and between the two of them, the country had no wealth and no money. The Druids, in their relics of old formulas for selecting human sacrifices, used the "eeny meeny, miny, moe." And cannibalism is quite prevalent in almost all the nursery rhymes. Such as in "Jack and the Beanstalk," the big giant eater, and "Fee, Fi, Foe, Fum, I smell the blood of an Englishman. Be he alive or be he dead, I'm going to use him to make my bread." This also came up again in Shakespeare with *King Lear* and *Midsummer Night's Dream.* "Little Jack Horner" is about a man named Jack Horner, who was steward of the abbot of Glastonberry. And in 1542, he was sent by this abbot to King Henry VIII of England with a pie. And in this pie were documents which were the documents of the ownership of land around the Abbey of Glastonberry, in Somersetshire. And on his way to the king, he stuck in his thumb and pulled out a document to the ownership of Meld, which he kept to himself. And until this day, over in Somersetshire, the Manor of Meld belongs to the Horner family.

The fourth classification of the nursery rhyme is the modern use, parodies and jokes, such as in "Mary had a little lamb, its fleece was white as snow." Today the kids go around saying, "Mary had a little lamb and was the doctor ever surprised." Or else they tend to make parodies of these nursery rhymes. Such as the famous little prayer, "Now I lay me down to sleep. I pray the Lord my soul to keep. If I should die before I wake, I pray the Lord my soul to take." It was first published in 1737, so you can see the age of this prayer. But, nowadays, the children say in joke, "Now I lay me down to sleep with a bag of peanuts at my feet. If I should die before I wake, you'll know I died of a stomach ache."

speech to this particular subject. She could have mentioned the other three classifications in the introduction, then told us why she would focus on historical significance. The advantage of such a revision would, of course, be that the information level of the speech would have been better. Secondly, since the bibliography accompanying the outline shows the amount of research, she should have taken better advantage of the research by including some of the scholarly methodology involved. She could have told us where the scholars uncovered their information. She could have told us which aspects of the analysis were fact and which were theory.

This conclusion ties the speech together pretty well. The wording of the summary gives the conclusion a necessary lift. The speech is light but still informative. Most importantly, information is presented in a novel way. Through the excellent examples, the speaker gets and holds attention throughout the speech. This is a good example of an informative speech.

So every song, ballad, hymn, carol, tale, dance rhythm, or any cute little saying that you might come up with may contribute to the future culture of our nation. So remember, the next time you start spouting wise sayings, using rhymes as a teaching aid, referring to our history, or when you start making jokes of the traditional nursery rhymes, who knows, you might be the next Mother Goose.

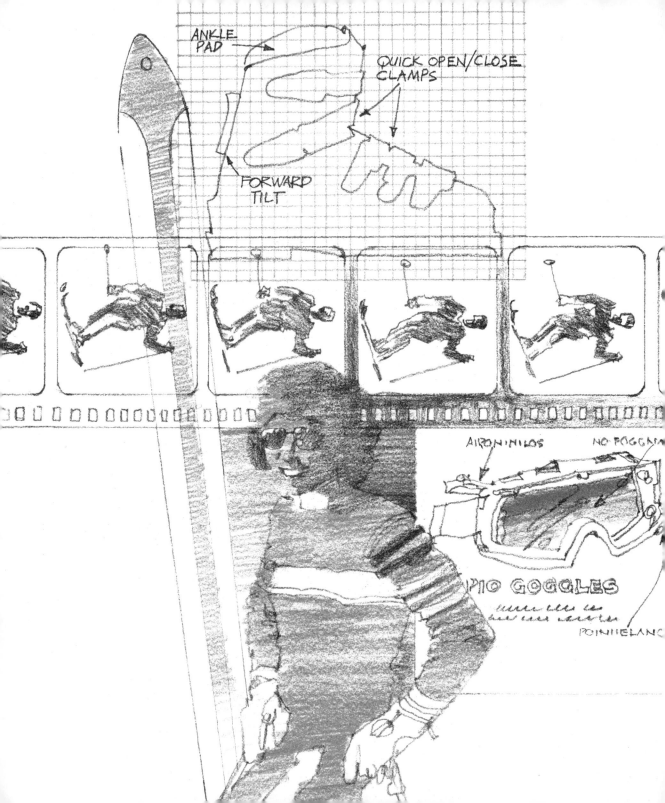

Chapter 8 Using Visual Aids

The visual aid is a unique form of speech development, for it gives the speech a new dimension. Speech, being primarily verbal, appeals to the ear; visual aids appeal to the eye. With the use of visual aids, the ideas of the speech gain a double sensory impact. Whether a picture is worth a thousand words or not, research has shown that people learn considerably more via the eye than via the ear.[1]

Although visual aids may be used in any kind of speech, they are more likely to be used in informative speeches—especially in the process or demonstration speech. Because of the nearly inseparable link between visual aids and demonstration, the discussion of explaining processes follows in Chapter 9, and these two chapters together may be considered as a single unit.

Now let us consider the various kinds of visual aids and how they can be used effectively.

KINDS OF VISUAL AIDS

By definition, anything that is used to appeal to the visual sense of the audience is a visual aid. Going from the simple to the complex, the most common types are the speaker; objects; models; chalkboard; pictures, drawings, and sketches; charts; and films, slides, and projections.

---

[1] See *Speech Monographs* 20 (November 1953), 7.

The Speaker   Sometimes the best visual aid is the speaker. Through the use of gesture, movement, and attire, the speaker can supplement the words. For instance, descriptive gestures can show the size of a racquetball, the height of a volleyball net, and the shape of a lake. Posture and movement can show the correct stance for skiing, a butterfly swimming stroke, and methods of artificial respiration. Attire can illustrate the native dress of a foreign country; the proper outfit for a mountain climber, a spelunker, or a scuba diver; and the uniform of a fire fighter, a nurse, or a soldier.

Objects   Objects are usually excellent visual aids since they eliminate most of the possible distortions of size, shape, and color. If you talk about a vase, a basketball, a braided rug, or an épée, the object itself is most suitable for display. Unfortunately, most objects are too small to be seen or too large to be carried to class, or to be maneuvered or shown. As a result, even though the actual object might be the best visual aid, its use may be impracticable.

Models   A model is a representation used to show the construction of an object or to serve as a copy. When the object itself is too large to bring to class, a model is usually a worthwhile substitute. If you are to talk about a turbine engine, a racing car, the Great Pyramid, or a dam, a model might well be the best visual aid. Especially if you are able to obtain or construct a working model, the speech usually benefits from its use. Your most important test is whether the model is large enough to be seen by the entire audience. Some model cars, for instance, may be only 3 or 4 inches long—too small to be used for a speech; on the other hand, a model car made to the scale of 1 inch to 1 foot (perhaps 12 or 18 inches long) would be large enough. Although models distort size, their shape, color, and maneuverability make them excellent visual aids.

Chalkboard   Because every classroom has a chalkboard, our first reaction is to make use of it in our speeches. As a means of visually portraying simple information, the chalkboard is unbeatable. Unfortunately, the chalkboard is easy to misuse and to overuse. The principal misuse students and teachers make of it is to write a volume of material while they are talking. More often than not what we write while we talk is either illegible or at least partly obscured by our body while we are writing. Furthermore, the tendency is to spend too much time talking to the board instead of to the audience.

The chalkboard is overused because it is so readily available. Most people use it in an impromptu fashion, whereas good visual aids require considerable planning to achieve their greatest value. By and large, anything that can be done with a chalkboard can be done better with a prepared chart, which can be introduced when needed.

If you believe you must use the chalkboard, think about putting the material on the board before you begin, or use the board for only a few seconds at a time. If you plan to draw your visual aid on the board before you begin, get to class a little early so that you can complete your drawing before the period. It is not fair to your classmates to use several minutes of class time completing your visual aid. Moreover, it is usually a good idea to cover what you have done in some way. If you do plan to draw or to write while you are talking, practice doing that as carefully as you practice the rest of the speech. If you are right-handed, stand to the right of what you are drawing. Try to face at least part of the audience while you work. Although it seems awkward at first, your effort will allow your audience to see what you are doing while you are doing it.

Pictures, Drawings, and Sketches

Pictures, drawings, and sketches probably make up most of all visual aids used in speeches in or out of the classroom. Because they may be obtained or made much more easily and inexpensively than models, their use is undoubtedly justified. Obviously, any picture, drawing, or sketch gives up some aspect of realism in size, shape, color, or detail. Nevertheless, the opportunities for emphasis of key features usually outweigh any disadvantages.

Pictures are readily obtainable from a variety of sources. When you select a picture, make sure that it is not so detailed that the central features you wish to emphasize are obscured. Colored pictures are usually better than black and white. Above all, however, the picture must be large enough to be seen. The all-too-common disclaimer, "I know you can't see this picture, but . . ." is of little help to the audience.

Many times you will have to draw your own visual aid. Don't feel that you are at any disadvantage because you "can't draw." If you can use a compass, a straightedge, and a measure, you can draw or sketch well enough for speech purposes. If you are making the point that a water skier must hold his or her arms straight, back

FIGURE 8-1

straight, and knees bent slightly, a stick figure (see Figure 8-1) will illustrate the point every bit as well as an elaborate, lifelike drawing. In fact, elaborate, detailed drawings are not worth the time and effort and may actually obscure the point you wish to make. Although actual representation is not a major problem, size, color, and neatness often are. For some reason, people tend to make drawings and lettering far too small to be seen. Before you complete your visual aid, move as far away from it as the farthest student in class. If you can read the lettering and see the details, it is large enough; if not, you should begin again. Color selection may also cause some problem. Black or red on white are always good contrasts. Chartreuse on pink and other such combinations just cannot be seen very well.

A chart is another graphic representation of material that enables a speaker to compress a great deal of material and show it in a usable, easily interpreted form. A frequently used type is the word chart. For the speech on computers, the speaker might make a word chart, for example, printing the items shown in Figure 8-2. To make the chart more eye-catching, the speaker may have a picture or a sketch to portray each word visually.

The chart is also used to show organization, chains of command, or the steps of a process. The chart in Figure 8-3 illustrates the organization of a student union board. Charts of this kind lend themselves well to what is called a strip-tease method of showing. The speaker prints the words on a large piece of cardboard, covers

FIGURE 8-2

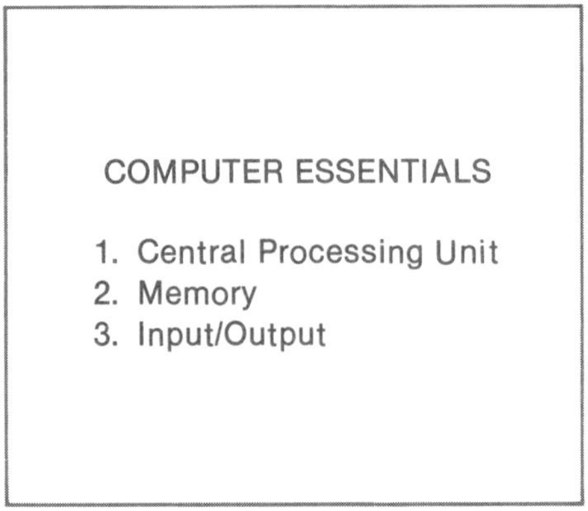

COMPUTER ESSENTIALS

1. Central Processing Unit
2. Memory
3. Input/Output

FIGURE 8-3

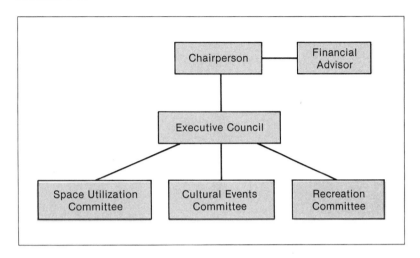

each word or phrase with pieces of cardboard or paper mounted with small pieces of cellophane tape, then removes the cover to expose that portion of the chart as he or she comes to each point.

Maps are valuable in indicating key elements of a territory. For instance, through various maps you have the opportunity to focus on physical details such as mountains, rivers, and valleys; or on the location of cities, states, nations, parks, and monuments; or on automobile, train, boat, and airplane routes. A professionally prepared map may have artistic advantages, but a map you make yourself can be drawn to include only the details you wish to show. Whether you use a professionally prepared map or your own drawing, the features you wish to point out should be easy to see. The weather map in Figure 8-4 is a good example of a map that focuses on selected detail.

If your speech contains figures, you may want to find or draw some kind of graph. The three most common types are the line graph, the bar graph, and the pie graph. If you were giving a speech on the population of the United States, you could use the *line graph* in Figure 8-5 to show population increase, in millions, from 1790 to 1970. If you were giving a speech on gold, you could use the *bar graph* in Figure 8-6 to show comparative holdings of the International Monetary Fund (IMF) and of world governments in gold (1980). In any speech where you want to show distribution

FIGURE 8-4

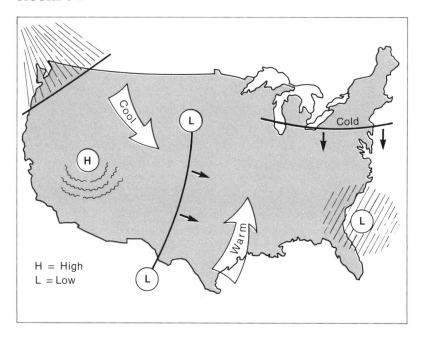

of percentages of a whole, such as total federal budget in 1975, a *pie graph* like the one in Figure 8-7 could be used.

To get the most out of your charts, however, you should be prepared to make extensive interpretations. Since charts do not speak for themselves, you should know how to read, test, and interpret them before you use them in speeches. The obvious tests of size and color are the same as for drawings.

Films, Slides, and Projections   I include discussion of films, slides, and projections with mixed emotions. On the one hand, their use may be a requirement for professional speakers in education, business, and industry. On the other hand, their use creates obstacles that may be nearly insurmountable for the beginner. The scheduling of projectors, the need for darkened classrooms, and the tendency for these visual aids to dominate the speaker all combine to outweigh possible advantages of their use. Beginning speakers find it difficult enough to control the speaking situation without having to cope with the problems that films, slides, and projections involve.

FIGURE 8-5.   Population 1790–1970

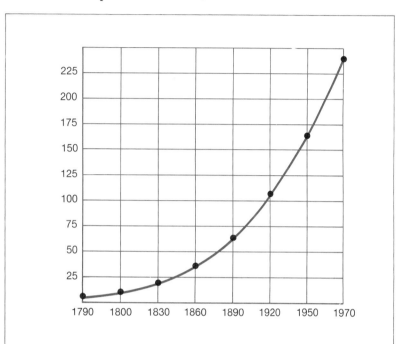

Because they may be so important to professional speakers and because they can make a classroom speech more exciting, however, we need to consider three types of mechanical aids: slides, opaque projections, and overhead projections. *Slides* are mounted transparencies that can be projected individually. In a speech, you might use a few slides; you would use them much the same way you do pictures. For instance, for a speech on scenic attractions in London, a speaker might have one or more slides on the Tower of London, the British Museum, Buckingham Palace, and the Houses of Parliament. He or she could show the slides and talk about each of them as long as necessary. Opaque and overhead projections can be used in a similar way. An *opaque projector* is a machine that enables you to project right from a book, a newspaper, or a typed page. It is especially useful for materials that would be too small to show otherwise. An *overhead projector* is a machine that requires special transparencies. The advantage of an overhead is that the room need not be darkened and you can write, trace, or draw on

FIGURE 8-6.   Comparative Holdings of Gold by the IMF and by World Governments That Are IMF Members (in millions of fine troy ounces)

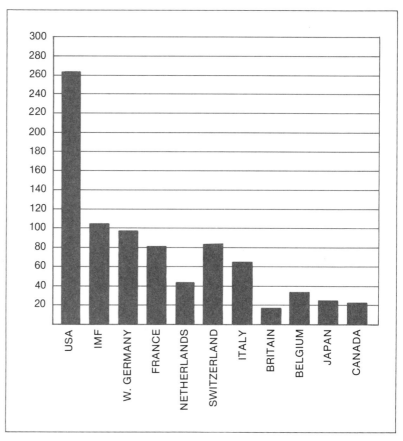

the transparency while you are talking. Overheads are especially useful for showing how formulas work, for illustrating various computations, or for analyzing outlines, prose, or poetry. Many of the kinds of things teachers use a chalkboard for can be done better with an overhead projector.

With each type of projection, you need to practice using the visual aid as often as you practice the speech itself. Notice that it takes longer to prepare mechanically projected visual aids than charts or sketches. It is often to your advantage to use a partner to

FIGURE 8-7.   Gas and Electric Expenditures

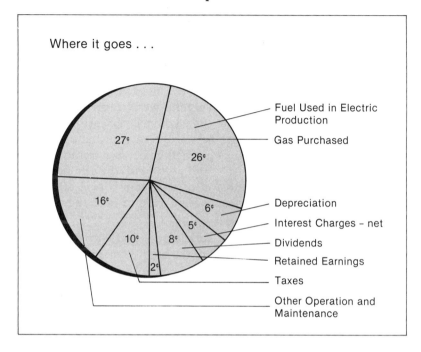

run the machinery from the back of the room while you give your speech from a position next to the projection.

USING VISUAL AIDS

Since visual aids are very powerful types of speech amplification, you should take care to use them to your advantage. The following are some guidelines that will help you get the most out of your visual aids:

1.   Show visual aids only when you are talking about them. It takes a very strong-willed person to avoid looking at a visual aid while it is being shown. And while people are looking at a visual aid, they will find it difficult to pay attention to the speaker's words if the words are not related to that visual aid. So, when you show a visual aid, talk about it; when you have finished talking about it, put it out of sight.

2. **Conversely, you should talk about the visual aid while you are showing it.** Although a picture may be worth a thousand words, it still needs to be explained. You should tell your audience what to look for; you should explain the various parts; and you should interpret figures, symbols, and percentages.

3. **Show visual aids so that everyone in the audience can see them.** If you hold the visual aid, hold it away from your body and let everyone see it. Even when the visual aid is large enough, you may find yourself obscuring someone's view inadvertently if you are not careful in your handling of it. If you place your visual aid on the chalkboard or mount it on some other device, stand to one side and point with the arm nearest the visual aid. If it is necessary to roll or fold your visual aid, you will probably need to bring transparent tape to hold the aid firmly against the chalkboard so that it does not roll or wrinkle.

4. **Talk to your audience and not to your visual aid.** Even though most of the members of the audience will be looking at your visual aid while you are speaking, you should maintain eye contact with them. The eye contact will improve your delivery, and you will be able to see how your audience is reacting to your visual material.

5. **Don't overdo the use of visual aids; you can reach a point of diminishing returns with them.** If one is good, two may be better; if two are good, three may be better. Somewhere along the line, however, there is a point at which one more visual aid is too many. Visual aids are a form of emphasis; but when everything is emphasized, nothing receives emphasis. If there are many places in your speech where visual aids would be appropriate, decide at which points the visual aids would be most valuable. Remember, a visual aid is not a substitute for good speech making.

6. **Think of all the possible hazards before you decide to pass objects around the class.** Since we are used to professors passing out materials, we sometimes become insensitive to the great hazards of such a practice. Audiences cannot resist looking at, reading, handling, and thinking about something they hold in their hands; and while they are so occupied, they are not listening to the speaker. More often than not, when you pass out materials you lose control of your audience, thus lessening your chances of achieving your purpose. Even when only two or three objects are passed around, the result may be disastrous. Most members of the class become absorbed in looking at the objects, looking for the

objects, wondering why people are taking so long, and fearing that perhaps they will be forgotten. Anytime you pass something around, you are taking a gamble—a gamble that is usually not worth the risk.

Assignment   *Prepare a three- to six-minute informative speech in which visual aids are the major kind of speech development. Criteria for evaluation will include selection and use of visual aids. For an example of a speech using visual aids, refer to the sample speech on explaining a process on pages 180–185 of the following chapter.*

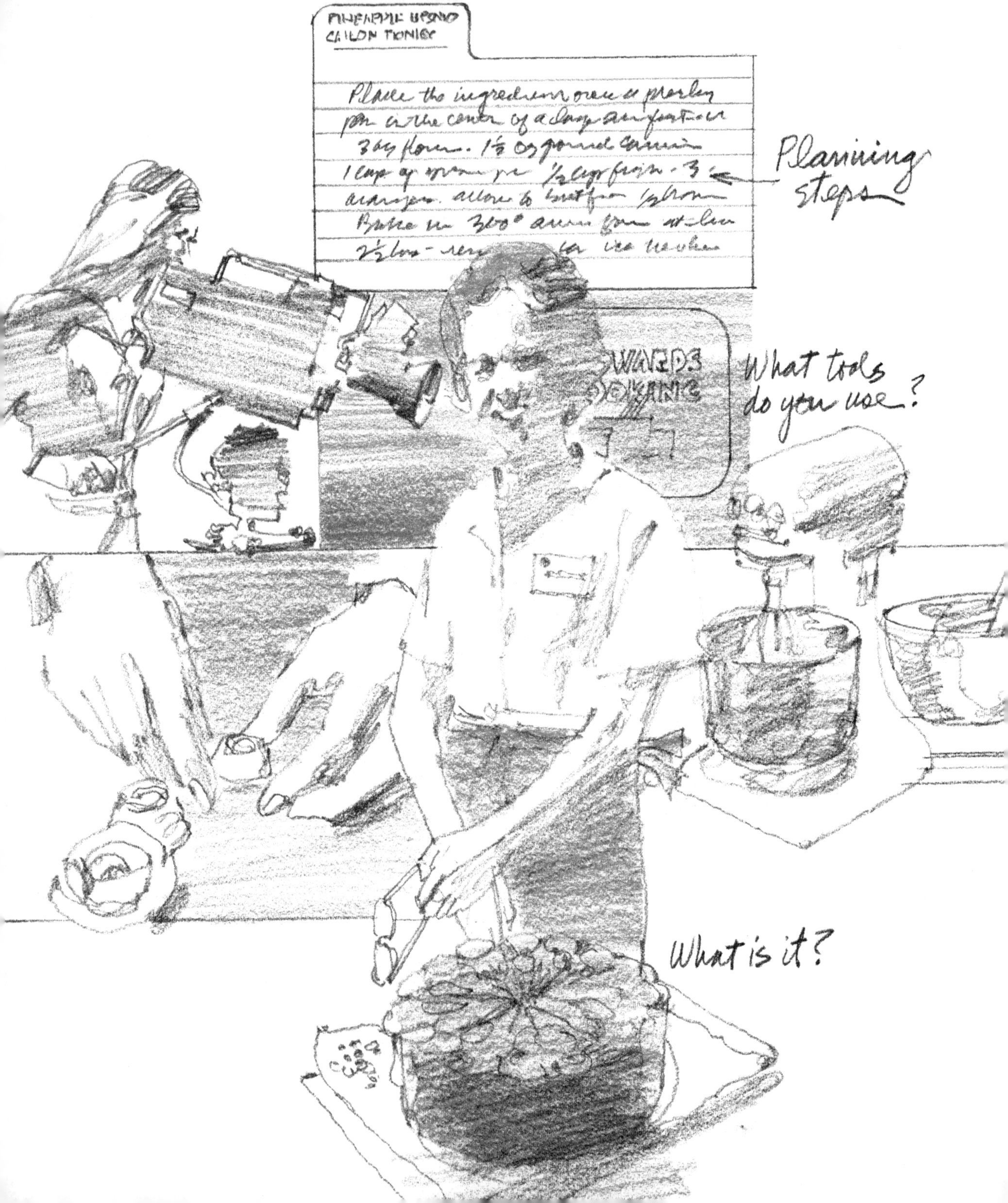
Planning steps
What tools do you use?
What is it?

Chapter 9 Explaining Processes

Much of our daily information exchange involves explaining processes: telling how to do something, how to make something, or how something works. We give instructions to our partner on how to get more power on a forehand table-tennis shot; we share ideas with our neighbor on how to make gourmet meals with ground meat; and we talk with an employee of the water works on how the new water-purification system works.

Your explanation of a process is a success when an audience understands the process well enough to apply it. The more complicated the process, the more care you need to take with your explanation. Although an explanation of a process is often considered one of the easiest types of informative speeches to give—it deals with specific, concrete procedures—you still need to consider the essentials carefully.

In this chapter we consider the four major issues of topic selection, speaker knowledge and experience, organization of steps, and visualization.

TOPIC SELECTION Chances are that the brainstorming lists you developed earlier contain several ideas that relate to processes. Because topics of this kind are so abundant, you may be tempted to make your selection too hastily. For instance, "how to bowl" may sound like a good topic for a bowler. When we apply the tests outlined in Chapter 3, however, we see that the topic fails on at least two counts. First, because nearly all college students have bowled and because many bowl frequently, a topic this general is unlikely to provide much new information for most of the class. Second, the topic is so broad that you are unlikely to be able to get into the topic in much depth within the time limits. If bowling is your hobby, your brainstorming sheet should contain such ideas as "spare bowling," "scoring," "automatic pin setters," "selecting a grip," "altering the amount of curve," and "getting more pin action," any of which would be better than "how to bowl." For explaining a process, a principle for topic selection should be to reject such broad-based topics as "how to bake cookies," "how clocks work," and "how to play tennis," in favor of more informative and more specific topics such as "judging baked goods," "how a cuckoo clock works," or "developing power in your tennis strokes."

The following are some topics that can be used for process speeches:

How to Do It	*How to Make It*	*How It Works*
Racing start	Soufflé	Football zone defense
Racquetball kill shot	Fishing flies	Helicopter
Hanging wall board	Paper figures	Television picture tube
Macramé	Bird feeders	Automatic teller
Mulching roses	Wood carvings	Video disc
Grading meat	Home swimming pool	Xerox

SPEAKER KNOWLEDGE AND EXPERIENCE

Good, clear explanation requires knowledge and experience of the process. Have you ever used a recipe? A recipe is an example of the clear explanation of a process. If you can read a recipe, you can make the dish. Right?—Wrong. As many of us have discovered, in the hands of a novice the best recipe in the world for beef stroganoff may lead to disaster. Why? Because cooking requires both knowledge and experience. Just because Julia Child can turn a recipe into a gourmet's delight does not mean we can. However, after watching Julia Child explain how to make a dish, we can often come up with something that tastes quite good. A recipe includes ingredients, quantities needed, and a way to proceed. The success of the dish depends on the execution of that recipe. Only our knowledge and experience tells us whether two eggs are better than one, whether an additional few minutes in letting dough rise is beneficial or disastrous, or whether the product will taste even better if one of the suggested ingredients is omitted or substituted. If you are experienced, you will have tried the many variations. During the speech, you can speak from that experience; and you will be able to guide your listeners by explaining whether alternate procedures will work equally well or whether such procedures might be ill suited for this recipe.

In addition to giving necessary know-how to otherwise barren instructions, knowledge and experience build speaker credibility. In explaining a process, you are projecting yourself as an authority on that particular subject. How well an audience listens will depend on your credibility as an authority. We listen to Julia Child tell us how to make chicken cacciatore, Steve Carlton tell us how to pitch a curve, and Neil Armstrong tell us how a moon rover works. And your audience will listen to you if you make them confident of your knowledge and experience of the process you are explaining.

ORGANIZATION OF STEPS

All but the simplest processes require many steps in the explanation. In Chapter 4, in our discussion of outlining, we talked about limiting main points to no more than five, yet your process may have nine, eleven, or even fifteen steps. Of course, you cannot leave any of them out. One of your problems will be to group the steps into units that can be comprehended and recalled. A principle of learning states that it is easier to remember and comprehend information that is presented in units than that which is presented as a series of independent items. Although you should not sacrifice accuracy for listening ease, you should employ this principle whenever possible. The following example of a very simple process illustrates this principle:

A	*B*
1. Gather the materials.	1. Plan the job.
2. Draw a pattern.	A. Gather materials.
3. Trace the pattern on the wood.	B. Draw a pattern.
	C. Trace the pattern on wood.
4. Cut out the pattern so that the tracing line can still be seen.	2. Cut out the pattern.
	A. Saw so the tracing line can be seen.

5. File to the pattern line.

6. Sandpaper edge and surfaces.

7. Paint the object.

8. Sand lightly.

9. Apply a second coat of paint.

10. Varnish.

B. File to the pattern line.

C. Sandpaper edge and surface.

3. Finish the object.

A. Paint.

B. Sand lightly.

C. Apply a second coat of paint.

D. Varnish.

Although both sets of directions are essentially the same, the inclusion of the arbitrary headings in B enables us to visualize the process as having three steps instead of ten. As a result, most people would tend to remember the second set of directions more easily than the first. Most processes provide an opportunity for such an arbitrary grouping. The "plan–do–finish" organization is a common type of grouping for explaining how to make something. A little thought on the best way of grouping similar steps will pay dividends in audience understanding and recall.

The example also illustrates the major kind of organization for most process speeches. Both sets of directions represent a *time-order* organization: Each point is a step in the process that must be accomplished before the next step can be taken. Because a process does require a step-by-step procedure, time order is the preferable organization form. Occasionally, however, you will find your material falling into a *topic order*. In such cases, the subdivisions of each topic will usually be discussed in a time order. For instance, you might want to show that there are three ways of making spares in bowling. Your main points would be the three ways: spot bowling, line bowling, and sight bowling; then each of the methods would be explained in terms of the steps involved.

VISUALIZATION

Although you can enable your audience to visualize a process through vivid word pictures—in fact, in your impromptu explanations in ordinary conversation, it is the only way you can proceed—when you have time to prepare, you will probably want to make full use of visual aids (see Chapter 8 where we discussed types and uses).

When the task is relatively simple, you may want to complete an actual demonstration. If so, you will want to practice the demonstration many times until you can do it smoothly and easily. Remember that, under the pressure of speaking before an audience, even an apparently easy task can become quite difficult. Since demonstrations often take longer than planned and since motor control will be a little more difficult in front of an audience than at home (did you ever try to thread a needle with twenty-five people watching you?), you may want to select an alternate method even though the process could be demonstrated within the time limit.

One alternative is the modified demonstration. Suppose you had worked for a florist and you were impressed by how floral displays were made. Making a special floral display would be an excellent topic for this speech. The following example illustrates how one speaker accomplished her goal with a modified demonstration. For her speech on flower arranging, she brought several bags containing all the necessary materials. Since her second step was to prepare the basic triangle to begin her floral arrangement, she took the necessary ingredients from one bag and began to put the parts together in their proper relationship. Rather than trying to get everything together perfectly in the few seconds she had available, she drew from a second bag a partly completed arrangement that illustrated the triangle. Her third point was to show how additional flowers and greenery could be added to bring about various effects. Again, she began to add flowers to give us the idea of how a florist proceeds, and then she drew from a third bag a completed arrangement illustrating one of the possible effects that could be made. Even though she did not complete either of the steps for us, we saw how a florist handles materials. In effect, the speaker's use of visual aids was every bit as professional as the floral arrangement she showed us.

Technically, this was not a demonstration, for she did not go through all the steps in their entirety. Since discretion is the better part of valor, however, it is probably better with any complex subject to have some of the steps completed beforehand.

ADDITIONAL CONSIDERATIONS Your speech will be even better if you keep the following pointers in mind as your prepare.

1. Consider your materials. The effectiveness of your explanation may depend on the nature and the number of materials, parts, equipment, or ingredients you select to show. In your consideration, separate the essentials from the accessories. A bowler needs a ball, bowling shoes, and access to an alley. Wrist bands, thumb straps, finger grip, and fancy shirts are all accessories that may not be worth mentioning. For some speeches, you will want to bring all the materials for display; for other speeches, a list of materials may suffice.

2.   **Speak slowly and repeat key ideas often.** In most speeches the audience need retain only the ideas behind the words. When you explain a process, it is important for an audience to retain considerably more detail. Do not rush. Especially during the visualization steps, you want the audience to have a chance to formulate and retain mental pictures. Give sufficient time for your words and your visual aids to sink in. It is a good idea to repeat key ideas to make sure the audience has command of the material.

3.   **Work for audience participation.** We learn by doing. If you can simulate the process so that others can go through the steps with you, it will help reinforce the ideas. If the process is a simple one, you may want to give materials to the audience to work with. For instance, in a speech on origami—Japanese paper folding—you may want to give members of your audience paper so they can go through a simple process with you. You can explain the principles; then you can pass out paper and have the audience participate in making a figure; finally, you can tell how these principles are used in more elaborate projects. Actual participation will increase interest and ensure recall.

Assignment   *Prepare a three- to six-minute speech in which you show how something is made, how something is done, or how something works. An outline is required. Criteria for evaluation will include quality of topic, listeners' belief in your knowledge and experience with the topic, your ability to group steps, and the visualization of the process.*

Outline: Speech Using Visual Aids (3–6 minutes)

Specific Purpose: To explain the three steps involved in executing a successful grab start.

Introduction

   I. One distinction that I can draw between competitive swimming and recreational swimming is that competitive swimming involves three specialized techniques that recreational swimming does not: the grab start, racing stroke, and racing turn.

  II. Since competitive swimming goes on in a racing setting, where time is the most crucial element, I'm going to limit myself to the beginning—the grab start.

 III. I want to discuss with you the three steps of the grab start that are used in getting the swimmer into the water in an expedient, rapid way.

Thesis Statement: A grab start is executed by mastering the three steps of assuming a "get-ready" position, coordinating the body to provide thrust, and entering the water at the proper angle.

Body

   I. In the first step, a swimmer assumes a "get-ready" position.
     A. The swimmer places his arms on the racing block, grabbing the block with his hands.
     B. His arms are placed between his legs, and the legs must be spread a little wider than the spread of the shoulders.
     C. The swimmer's arms must be bent slightly.
     D. His toes must grab the edge of the block.

  II. In the second step, the swimmer coordinates his body in a way that provides thrust of entry.
     A. The swimmer must pull down hard with his arms to pull himself even more forward than he was in the "get-ready" position.
     B. Then he projects his arms out and almost simultaneously uses his legs to supplement the thrust provided by the arms.

 III. In the final step, the swimmer enters the pool at a slight angle, but almost parallel with the surface.
     A. This allows the swimmer to surface rapidly.
     B. He can commence his stroke more quickly.

Conclusion

I. The grab start is a specialized technique.

II. The three steps involved in the execution of a grab start are: assume a "get-ready" position, provide the necessary thrust, and enter the water at a slight angle.

Study this speech in terms of informative value of topic, apparent knowledge and experience of the speaker, clarity of the steps, and visualization of the process.[1] Read the speech through at least once aloud. After you have read and analyzed the speech, turn to the detailed analysis in the other column.

Analysis

This opening paragraph serves several purposes. First, it establishes the speaker's authority to talk on this topic—we learn that he has done competitive swimming. Second, it gives us the three major contrasts. And, third, it focuses on the subject of this speech, the grab start. Had he not mentioned the other two, we might wonder whether this is the only difference. The introduction's only weakness lies in the very beginning. The speech would profit from a question or startling statement to secure attention to the opening.

Speech: The Racing Start

Before I became a member of a competitive swim team, I never realized the difference between competitive swimming and recreational swimming.

Now, I can draw one clear distinction between the two: Competitive swimming involves three very specialized techniques that recreational swimming does not. These are the techniques of the swimmer's grab start, the swimmer's stroke, and the swimmer's racing turn. Today, I am going to deal with one of these techniques, the swimmer's grab start.

Since there are three major contrasts, and since we will agree that the speaker can talk only about one in the time limit, we are likely to ask, "Why the grab start?" By talking about

Before I do, I think it is important to note the purpose of this technique. Competitive swimming goes on in a racing setting— the most crucial element of this setting is time. Everything the swimmer does is directed toward the goal of maintaining maximum expediency. Therefore, the purpose of the grab start is to

---

[1] Delivered in Speech class, University of Cincinnati. Printed by permission of Craig Newburger.

the importance of speed, the speaker shows us that the grab start is the first step and any second saved here will be important to a race of any length. Still, I would like him to have pointed out that the grab start would be especially important in shorter races.

The speaker states the first step of the process clearly.
Notice that the speaker clearly describes each of the aspects of the position. The steps of this position are clearly stated, and easily followed. The stick-figure visual aids help make the points simply and clearly, yet require little artistic ability.

permit the swimmer to enter the water in a way that is most expedient, most rapid. The grab start involves the following steps:

First, the swimmer assumes a "get-ready" position atop a racing platform. The racing platform [visual aid] is simply an object that provides additional elevation between the swimmer's body and the water. In assuming the "get-ready" position, the swimmer first places his arms on the racing block, grabbing the block with his hands. His arms are placed, or positioned, between his legs [visual aid]. The legs must be spread a little wider apart than the spread of the shoulders, and, thirdly, the swimmer's arms must be bent slightly. Finally, the swimmer's toes must grab the edge of the block. All of these things must be coordinated with precision to allow the swimmer to complete the next step with expediency and efficiency.

In this section the speaker does a little "uh-uhing." Although vocalized pauses should be avoided, a few will creep into almost anyone's speech, and

The next step is called, uh, providing thrust. Thrust is exactly what the word says; the swimmer in this step uses his body in such a way and coordinates himself in such a way that he may provide himself with enough thrust to enter the water effectively. In this step, the swimmer, after hearing the bang of the starter's

probably will not even be noticed by the listener.
Again, the main point is clearly stated. Each of the aspects of "providing thrust" is clearly stated and shown.

signal, uh, must pull down hard—very hard with his arms to pull himself even more forward than he was in the get-ready position [visual aid]. Secondly, he projects his arms out as we see here, and shortly after, almost but not quite simultaneously, he uses his legs to supplement the thrust provided by the arms. He does this by springing his legs forward [at this point the speaker leaps forward] to provide the final push that will allow him to enter the water properly.

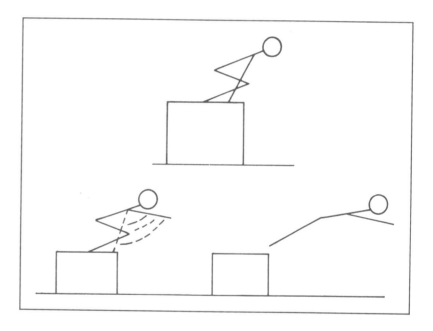

This is a good, clear transition from the second to the third and final main point of the speech. And again the step is clearly stated.
I like the way the speaker emphasizes "slight angle." Apparently entering at too much of an angle is one of the major problems in learning the grab start. By contrasting slight angle with the improper angle, the speaker is able to make his point especially clear.

This brings us now to the third and final step in the grab start, which is entering the water at a slight angle. It is important once the swimmer has departed from the racing platform to maintain his body posture at an angle whereby he can enter the water at a slight angle [visual aid]. Now, it is important for me here to emphasize the words *slight angle*. By entering the water at a slight angle, the swimmer can surface rapidly and commence his stroke—whereas the swimmer who enters the water at more than a slight angle, as we see here [visual aid], runs the risk of having to expend, as our swimmer is doing here, more time, precious time, and additional energy in reaching the surface to a point where he can commence his stroke.

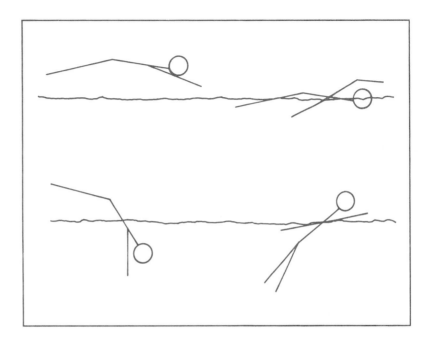

To finish his speech, the speaker uses a simple but effective summary of the main points. In his summary, he make a minor but common mistake. He begins to enumerate the steps, drops the enumeration with the second point, and picks it up again with the third. If you wish to enumerate, and it will help achieve clarity, carry the enumeration through.
By and large, this is a clearly explained, easily visualized process.

Therefore, I think that we can all see that the grab start is a very specialized technique that involves the following steps [repeats all visual aids]: first, the swimmer assumes the "get-ready" position; then he provides the necessary thrust for which his body needs to, uh, dive into the water—enter the water properly; and, third, the swimmer must enter the water at a slight angle.

Painting the "Word Picture".

"The windmills of Holland spider-y giants reaching for the sky, their slow turning arms akimbo"

Poor Don Quixote saw them as monsters and mounted an ill-fated attack much to the consternation of his man Sancho.

The artist Rembrandt found their forms irresistable and often included them in his landscapes.

Chapter 10 Descriptive Speeches

"What does it look like?" "How do the parts fit together?" Questions like these are answered by our describing what we see. At least some of the informative communicating we do every day is descriptive. But like any of the skills of information exchange, description must be carefully worded to be effective.

A descriptive speech assignment provides an excellent opportunity for mastering this important language skill. Since the goal of description is to give an accurate, vivid, informative picture, we first look at the essentials of description. Then we consider the preparation of the descriptive speech, including topic selection, organization, and language suggestions.

ESSENTIALS OF DESCRIPTION
A speech is descriptive when it provides word pictures for the audience. How do you describe accurately and vividly? Effective description requires at least two skills: (1) observing and (2) communicating the observation. I cannot overemphasize the point that descriptive speaking requires alert observation. Since effective description reflects firsthand observation, you must first know what to look for. You must be conscious of size, shape, weight, color, composition, age and condition, and the relationships among various parts; then you must create ways of reporting the essentials—ways that will be accurate and vivid.

Size
How large is the object? Size is described subjectively by "large" and "small" and objectively by dimensions. But neither descrip-

tion nor dimension is likely to be meaningful unless it is compared. For instance, neither "The book is a large one," nor "The book is 9 inches by 6 inches," itself creates an image. However, "The book, 9 by 6 and 3 inches thick, is the same length and width as your textbook, but more than twice as thick" is descriptive.

Shape   What is its spatial form? Shape is described in terms of common geometric forms. "Round," "triangular," "oblong," "spherical," "conical," "cylindrical," and "rectangular" are all descriptive. A complex object is best described as a series of simple shapes. Since most objects do not conform to perfect shapes, you can usually get by with approximations and with comparisons to familiar objects. "The lake is round," "The lot is pie-shaped," and "The car looks like a rectangular box" all give reasonably accurate impressions. Shape is further clarified by such adjectives as "jagged," "smooth," and "indented."

Weight   How heavy is it? Weight is described subjectively as "heavy" or "light" and objectively by pounds and ounces. As with size, descriptions of weight are clarified by comparisons. Thus, "The suitcase weighed about 70 pounds; that's about twice the weight of a normally packed suitcase" is descriptive.

Color   What color is it? Color, an obvious necessity of description, is difficult to describe accurately. Although most people can visualize black and white, the primary colors (red, yellow, and blue), and their complements (green, purple, and orange), very few objects are these colors. Perhaps the best way to describe a color is to couple it with a common referent. For instance, "lime green," "lemon yellow," "brick red," "green as a grape," "banana yellow," or "blue as the sky" give rather accurate approximations. Just be careful with how far you carry the comparisons. Paint companies, fabric dealers, and cosmetics manufacturers stretch our imagination to the breaking point at times with such labels as "blimey blue" or "giddy green."

Composition   What is it made of? The composition of an object helps us visualize it. A ball of aluminum does not look the same as a ball of yarn. A pile of rocks gives a different impression than does a pile of straw. A brick building looks different from a steel, wood, or glass building. Sometimes you refer to what the object *seems* like rather than what it is. An object can appear metallic even if it is not made of metal. Spun glass can have a woolly texture. Nylon can be soft and smooth as in stockings or hard and sharp as in toothbrush bristles.

Age and Condition   How old is it? What condition is it in? Whether an object is new or old can make a difference in its appearance. Since age by itself may not be descriptive, an object is often discussed in terms of condition. Condition is difficult to describe objectively, but it can be very important to an accurate description. The value of coins, for instance, varies tremendously depending on whether they are uncirculated or their condition is good or only fair. A 1917 Lincoln penny in fair condition may be worth two cents, whereas an uncirculated 1960 penny may be worth ten cents. Books become ragged and tattered, buildings become run down and dilapidated, land is subject to erosion. Age and condition together often prove valuable in developing informative descriptions.

Relationship Among Parts   How does it all fit together? If the object you want to describe is complex, its parts must be fitted into their proper relationship before a mental picture emerges. Remember the story of the blind men who described an elephant in terms of what each felt? The one who felt the trunk said the elephant was like a snake; the one who felt a leg said the elephant was like a tree; and the one who felt the body said the elephant was like a wall. Not only must we visualize size, shape, weight, color, composition, age, and condition, but we must also understand how the parts fit together.

Since the ultimate test of description is that it enables the audience to visualize, the speaker probably should include too much detail rather than not enough. Moreover, if some particular aspect is discussed in two or three different ways, everyone might get the mental image, whereas a single description might make the image vivid to only a few. Begin your practice sessions with more material than you could possibly get into the time limits for your speech. As you gain a mastery of the material in practice, you can begin to delete until you get the speech down to a workable length. Keep in mind, however, that with the descriptive speech perhaps more than with any other you will have to resist the desire to memorize.

PREPARING
DESCRIPTIVE
SPEECHES

Although preparing a descriptive speech follows the same steps of speech preparation as any other speech, there are some especially important aspects to it; we focus on those in this section.

Topic Selection

Since the goal of the descriptive speech is to give an accurate, vivid, informative description of something specific and concrete, the topic should be an object, a structure, a place, an animal, or a person. Animals and people may seem like obvious subjects, but the tendency to describe them in terms of subjective reaction rather than objective analysis makes them less suitable topics for informative description. I would also caution against selecting the first thing that comes to mind: your pencil sharpener on the wall, the statue on the shelf, or your favorite chair. Even though the goal is description, you should select your topic by using the methods and applying the tests outlined in Chapter 3. If you discover that your original lists do not include any subjects that would be appropriate for description, continue the brainstorming process until you have several possibilities. For instance, if your hobby is camping, you might list "turtleback campers," "camp site," "kerosene lantern," "tent trailers," "tents," "sleeping bags," and other topics associated with camping. If your major is medieval history, you might list "moats," "castles," "jousting spear," "coat of mail," or "crossbows."

In evaluating your topic selection, remember that it must meet the principal test of informative speeches—it must have the potential for new information. Description itself is, and must be, subordinate to informative intent. You want to describe what the object, place, or building looks like, but your intent must be informative rather than poetic. You want to create an accurate, vivid, verbal picture of what you are describing.

Examples of topics that are appropriate for a descriptive speech are as follows:

Structures	*Natural*	*Objects*
Cape Hatteras Lighthouse	The Grand Tetons	Corkscrew
Washington Monument	Natural Bridge	Rattan chair
Golden Gate Bridge	Grand Canyon	Racing ice skate
Super dome	Cave formation	Fisherman's seine

Organization   Since at least one of the goals of a descriptive speech is to give the audience a visual image of your subject, arrangement of main points by *space order* often proves the most workable. A description of a jet-powered racing car might go from back to front, front to back, outside to inside, or inside to outside. A description of a painting might go from foreground to background, background to foreground, left to right, or top to bottom.

Although space-order organization should be used most often, when you are describing a class of objects you might use a *topic order* with a space order of subdivisions. For instance, in a description of your campus, you might want to speak on the topics of buildings, the walk system, and the wooded park areas. Or, in a description of Yellowstone Park, you might talk about Old Faithful geyser and the Fountain Paint Pot as the two main topics. You would then develop each of these main topics with a space-order arrangement of subordinate detail.

A significant benefit of a space-order organization is that your decision about placement of main points is simplified. Once you determine that you will go from left to right, top to bottom, or inside to outside, every key feature that the eye encounters will become either a main point or an important subdivision of a main point.

Language   Although a descriptive speech has several goals, its major benefit is as a language exercise. With this assignment you can concentrate on *clarity, vividness, emphasis,* and *appropriateness,* fundamental qualities of style that we discussed in Chapter 5. You want to make your description so vivid that the audience will be able to visualize your subject accurately. The descriptive speech then is an excellent opportunity for you to use comparative language, including simile and metaphor.

As you consider the wording of your speech, remember the function of description. You want your speech to be informative, not poetic. Be on the lookout for florid description, emotive words, and excessive adjectives and adverbs. A descriptive speech should not sound like a page from a literary magazine. By keeping an emphasis on the informative nature of the topic and not the beauty, by keeping an emphasis on the functional nature of the language and not the poetic, you should be able to make your speech clear, vivid, emphatic, and appropriate without being affected or artificial.

Developing Description   Now let us see how description can be developed. As you work with your speech you will revise language from general to specific. How may this be done? Consider the following sentence:

> Tom was a writer; at all times several pencils were on his desk.

The sentence labels Tom as a writer and it begins to describe some of the tools of his work. Now let's revise the sentence to make it more descriptive:

> Tom was a writer; at all times at least five pencils adorned his desk.

"Five" is more specific than "several" and "adorned" carries a more descriptive picture than "on." Let us look at two further revisions that contrast potential descriptions:

> Tom was a writer; at all times at least five finely sharpened pencils lined the side of the desk, side by side in perfect order from longest to shortest.
> Tom was a writer; five stubby pencils, all badly in need of sharpening and all well chewed were scattered about his desk.

These examples just begin to show the different pictures that can be created depending on how you use the detail you have observed.

Earlier you were cautioned about not memorizing a speech. Since you can describe any part of your speech in unlimited ways, keep the essentials in mind during each practice, and try to use slightly different wordings each time to express your descriptions. By adapting to your audience and by having a true spontaneity, you will be able to avoid memorization.

Assignment   *Prepare a two- to four-minute speech describing an object, a building, or a place. An outline is required. Criteria for evaluation include clarity, vividness, emphasis, and appropriateness of the description.*

Outline: Descriptive Speech

Specific Purpose: To describe the exterior of the Cape Hatteras Lighthouse.

Introduction
  I. How many of you have been to America's tallest lighthouse?
 II. I recently visited the Cape Hatteras Lighthouse, the tallest in the United States.

Thesis Statement: The Cape Hatteras Lighthouse, located along the Outer Banks of North Carolina, has a 193-foot body and a 15-foot top that I will describe.

Body
  I. The lighthouse is located along the Outer Banks of North Carolina.
     A. It stands on the beach.
     B. It stands in stark contrast to its surroundings.
 II. The major portion of the lighthouse consists of its body.
     A. It is 193 feet tall.
        1. This would be the same as twenty stories.
        2. The interior has approximately 400 steps.
     B. The body is shaped like a cylinder, with the base wider in diameter than the top.
     C. The walls are made of brick.
     D. Black and white stripes spiral the sides of the body.
     E. There are three windows on both the north and south sides.
     F. It was built in 1870.
III. The top of the lighthouse sits on a fenced platform in which the actual light is enclosed.
     A. The height from the top of the body to the tip of the lighthouse is 15 feet.
     B. The platform's base is shaped like a half cone, with the base of the cone fitting on top of the main portion.
     C. The platform and the tip of the lighthouse are made of black steel.
     D. The section containing the light is made of clear glass.

Conclusion
  I. Although the Cape Hatteras Lighthouse is only 208 feet tall, it really looks taller against the background.
 II. America's tallest lighthouse is a major scenic attraction of Cape Hatteras.

As you read this speech analyze the descriptions of size, shape, weight, color, composition, age, condition, and relationship among parts.[1] Which descriptions are clear? Which are vivid? Which need more or better development? After you have read the speech at least once aloud, read the analysis in the other column.

Analysis

The speaker begins by trying to develop common ground with the audience. The question is used to heighten audience attention.

This sentence locates the lighthouse.

In this section the speaker does a good job of giving meaning to "200 feet."

In this context, "somewhat cylindrical" is descriptive.

The specific dimensions add to the overall picture.

Mention of the age of the lighthouse gives a little more feel for the condition.

The 10-foot-wide stripes "spiral their way up the entire body" is quite descriptive.

Use of geometric form helps sharpen the description.

Speech: The Cape Hatteras Lighthouse

I'm sure that some of you may have been atop the tallest building in this city or that country. But have any of you been up the tallest lighthouse? I've had a chance to visit the Cape Hatteras Lighthouse, the tallest lighthouse in America, and tonight I'd like to describe it to you.

The lighthouse is located along the outer banks of North Carolina. It stands on the beach in stark contrast to its surroundings. The lighthouse stands over 200 feet tall. Now, many of you may not think 200 feet is very much, but it is for a lighthouse, especially when it doesn't contain an elevator, and you try to climb the 400 steps that comprise the twenty flights of stairs. When you stop to think of it, that's the equivalent of a 20-story building!

Now 193 feet of this structure is the body. The body is a somewhat cylindrical figure with the base wider than the top; the base is about 50 feet wide and the top is about 15 feet wide. The outside walls are made of brick, which seems to last pretty well since the lighthouse was built in 1870 right after the Civil War, some 110 years ago. Still this is relatively young for a lighthouse; most famous lighthouses date from the sixteenth or seventeenth centuries. The body of the lighthouse is painted black and white stripes all the way up; the stripes are about 10 feet wide, and they spiral their way up the entire body.

On top of this main structure is a 24-foot-wide steel platform which contains the glass structure that has the light inside it. This platform has a half cone shape body with the bottom of the cone fitting exactly on the top of the base of the main structure. Inside

---

[1] Delivered in Speech class, University of Cincinnati. Printed by permission of Karen Zimmer.

a fenced area is the solid glass paned structure that contains the light. On top of the glass structure is a tip with a pointed roof that's like an upside-down cone. Now the tip of this roof and the steel platform are all black. And the glass is clear so the light can be seen from all directions.

I particularly like the phrasing "an upside-down cone."

Although the Cape Hatteras Lighthouse is only 208 feet tall, it really looks taller against the background. The black and white stripes make it stand out against the blue background of the ocean and sky whether it's day or night. America's tallest lighthouse is a major scenic attraction of Cape Hatteras.

The conclusion emphasizes the overall picture. Although the speech is not especially creative, it does present a clear, descriptive picture. I believe an audience can "see" the lighthouse as the speaker finishes.

jay'walk' (jā'wôk'), v. ...
dangered by the traffic —
Colloq.
jazz (jăz), n. — [Creole jazz to speed up;]
of Am. Negro, and prob. African, origin]
can music, characterized by melodiou
dance rhythms, and varied orchestral col
c A quality suggestive of ja... usic, es
pertaining to, or characte... jazz
Into, or infuse wi... jazz
jeal'ous (jĕl'ŭs) ... zeal
VL. zelosus ... 2. a
erant of riva... on... b
terest and ...
fears

"If you have
to ask what
jazz is,
you'll never
know"
Louis Armstrong

Chapter 11 Speeches of Definition

The 1980 election was described by the media as a move toward more conservative political views—a move away from the liberal politics of the 1960s and 1970s. What do "conservative" and "liberal" mean—explain them. Like so many words we use every day, clear, sharp, and accurate definitions of words like *conservative* and *liberal* are difficult to come up with on the spur of the moment. As a result of our problems with vocabulary, our attempts at communicating with others often fail. Sometimes we do not know the meaning of a word and sometimes we accept one meaning when the communicator intended another. Since we cannot solve problems, or learn, or even think without meaningful definitions, the ability to define clearly and vividly is essential for the effective communicator. From the time Plato first attacked the Sophists for their inability to define and classify, rhetoricians have seen definition as a primary tool of effective speaking. In fact, Richard Weaver, representing the view of many modern scholars, has named definition as the most valuable of all lines of development.[1]

In this chapter we first look at the most common ways words are or can be defined. Then we look at preparation of a speech of definition.

---

[1] Richard Weaver, "Language is Sermonic," in *Contemporary Theories of Rhetoric: Selected Readings*, ed. Richard L. Johannesen (New York: Harper & Row, 1971), pp. 170–171.

HOW WORDS ARE DEFINED

We define words in many different ways. In this section we want to discuss some of the most common of those ways. The ultimate test of the effectiveness of a definition is whether the receiver or receivers can understand the meaning and can use the word appropriately.

Classification and Differentiation

When you define by *classification and differentiation,* you give the boundaries of a word and focus on the features that make the referent different from other members of that same class. For instance, a clarinet is a woodwind instrument. This statement defines *clarinet* by class. The definition is completed by saying it is a single-reed instrument consisting of a long tube made of wood, metal, or plastic that flares out at the end and contains both holes and keys for playing. Each of the additional details helps to define, stating aspects of the clarinet that differentiate it from some or all other woodwind instruments. Let us look at another example: A mansard is a roof (classification). The mansard has two slopes on each of the four sides—the lower slopes are steeper than the upper (descriptive and differentiating details).

Many dictionary definitions, especially definitions of nouns, are of the classification-differentiation variety. The success of the definition by classification is tested by the specificity of the differentiating details.

Synonym and Antonym

Synonyms are words that have the same or nearly the same meanings; *antonyms* are words that have opposite meanings. When you use synonym or antonym, you are defining by comparison or contrast. For instance, synonyms for *sure* are "certain," "confident," "positive." An antonym is "doubtful." Some synonyms for *prolix* are "long," "wordy," or "of tedious length." Antonyms are "short" and "concise." Synonyms and antonyms are often the shortest, quickest, and easiest ways to clarify the meaning of a new word. Thus we might define *to compute* as "to calculate"; *ebullient* as "bubbling" or "boiling"; *pacific* as "appeasing" or "conciliatory"; and *sagacious* as "keenly perceptive," "shrewd," or "wise." Of course, the use of synonym (and antonym) presupposes that the audience is familiar with the synonyms (and antonyms) selected.

Etymology and Historical Example

Etymology is the derivation of a particular word, or an account of its history. Depending on the word being defined, etymology may or may not be a fruitful method of definition. Since words change over time, origin may reveal very little about modern meaning. In many instances, however, the history of a word gives additional insight that will help the audience remember the meaning a little better.

Take the word *tantalize,* for instance. *Tantalize* means "to tease" (this is an example of definition by synonym). Does it mean exactly the same? If so, why use it? Definition by etymology or historical example may give a more complete meaning that will help a person remember the meaning and use it appropriately. In the case of the word *tantalize,* the following explanation adds considerable insight. Tantalus, the mythical king of Phrygia, was the son of Zeus. Tantalus committed the crime of revealing the secrets of the gods to mere mortals. For his punishment he was condemned to stand up to his chin in water that constantly receded as he stooped to drink and surrounded by branches of assorted fruit that eluded his grasp whenever he reached for them. Thus, for eternity Tantalus was *tantalized* by food and drink that were shown to him but were forever withheld.

In this and similar circumstances, etymology and historical example can give an excellent assist in the definition of a word. Like any illustration, anecdote, or story, etymology and historical example increase the vividness of the explanation.

Uses and Functions

A fourth way to define is to explain the use or the function of a particular object. Thus, when you say, "A plane is a hand-powered tool that is used to smooth the edges of boards," you are defining the tool by indicating its use. Since the use or function of an object may be more important than its classification, this is often an excellent method of definition. Thus, by saying that a harp is the metal hoop that supports a lampshade, that a quarrel is the diamond-shaped pane of glass that is used in lattice windows, and that a zarf is a holder for a handleless coffee cup, you are defining these most unusual words by use or function.

Examples and Comparisons

Regardless of the way you define, you are likely to have to supplement your definitions with examples and/or comparisons to make them truly understandable. This is especially true when you are defining abstract words. Consider the word *just* in the following sentence: "You are being just in your dealings with another when you deal honorably and fairly." Although you have defined by synonym, listeners are still likely to be unsure of the meaning.

If you add, "If Paul and Mary both do the same amount of work and we reward them by giving them an equal amount of money, our dealings will be just; if, on the other hand, we give Paul more money because he's a man our dealings will be unjust." In this case, you are clarifying the definition with both an example and a comparison.

For some words a single example and/or comparison will be enough. For other words or in communicating with certain audiences, you may need several examples and/or comparisons.

PREPARING A SPEECH OF DEFINITION In most of our communication, our definitions are, by necessity, short and to the point. Occasionally, however, for purposes of information or clarification we may feel a need to present an extended definition. The speech of definition provides excellent practice both for using one or more types of definition and for building a complete definition.

Topics The best topics for an extended definition are often general or abstract words, words that give you leeway in definition and allow for creative development. On your brainstorming lists look for words like the following:

Expressionism	Rhetoric	Logic
Existentialism	Epicurean	Acculturation
Status	Fossil	Extrasensory
Rolfing	Epistemology	perception
		Word processing

Organizing the Extended Definition Definition can be used in your speeches either as a form of support or as the framework for the speech itself. Since this chapter is concerned with an assignment of a speech of definition, we need to see how such a speech may be organized. One method is to organize the speech topically with coordinate headings, each of which stands as a part of the definition. The other method is to develop the speech topically with subordinate headings in which the first point defines the word in general and subsequent points define the word in specific.

COORDINATE DEVELOPMENT *Webster's Third New International Dictionary* defines *jazz* as "American music characterized by improvisation, syncopated rhythms, contrapuntal ensemble playing, and special melodic features peculiar to the individual interpretation of the player." Like most dictionary definitions, this one is of the classification-differentiation variety that requires an understanding of the various terms used within the definition. Before its meaning is clear, most people will have to look up "improvisation," "syncopation," "contrapuntal" (which refers to "counterpoint"), and "ensemble." Nevertheless, such a dictionary definition makes for a very good purpose sentence for a speech. By utilizing each aspect as a prospective topical development of the speech, a potentially sound organizational structure is provided with very little effort on your part. Assuming that you have the background to attest to the accuracy of the definition and to understand the various topics mentioned, your structural outline will look like this:

Specific Purpose: To explain the four major characteristics of jazz.

    I. Jazz is characterized by improvisation.
    II. Jazz is characterized by syncopated rhythms.
    III. Jazz is characterized by contrapuntal ensemble playing.
    IV. Jazz is characterized by special melodic features peculiar to the individual interpretation of the player.

With this method, then, the organization is suggested by the definition itself. The inventive process determines how you enlarge upon each aspect of the definition. Your selection and use of examples, illustrations, comparisons, personal experiences, and observations will give the speech original distinctive flavor. Furthermore, you will have the option of using other methods of definition to reinforce various parts of the speech.

You can achieve the same coordinate development by starting from a definition you have evolved for yourself. In this case, your purpose sentence is evolved from various existing definitions and from individual analysis of the subject. Suppose you wish to define or clarify the concept "a responsible citizen." A dictionary will indicate that *responsible* means "accountable" and *citizen* means a "legal inhabitant who enjoys certain freedoms and privileges." But this definition does not really tell what a "responsible citizen" is. As you think about citizenship in relation to responsibilities, you might begin to list such categories as social, civic, financial, and political. From this analysis, you could evolve the following subjective definition: "A responsible citizen is one who meets his or her social, civic, and financial obligations." Once you are satisfied with the soundness of your definition, you may proceed in much the same way as the person who has adopted a dictionary definition. Your organization, developed topically, will look like this:

Specific Purpose: To define "responsible citizen."

Thesis Statement: A responsible citizen is one who meets his or her social, civic, and financial obligations.

    I. A responsible citizen meets his or her social responsibilities.
   II. A responsible citizen meets his or her civic responsibilities.
  III. A responsible citizen meets his or her financial responsibilities.

This second method allows you to talk about concepts that have connotative or subjective meanings not usually found in dictionaries.

SUBORDINATE DEVELOPMENT   Sometimes you discover that the word you wish to define is most clearly defined through various examples and illustrations that *limit* the boundaries of the definition. Under these circumstances, rather than developing the speech topically, with each main point standing as a part of the definition, you may elect to develop the speech subordinately. In subordinate development, your first major point presents the total definition *in general.* Your remaining points present degrees, limits, or other specific aspects of the definition. For example, assume a speaker defines the word *norm.* The definition itself is rather simple—norms are rules that define accepted behavior in society. Much of the real understanding of the word, then, must come through examples that consider degrees of norms. The skeleton of an outline for such a speech would look like this:

Specific Purpose: To define the word *norm.*

Thesis Statement: A norm is a rule determining social behavior that grows from folkways or mores.

  I. Norms are rules that define what is required in certain situations in society.
 II. One degree of norms is illustrated by folkways.
III. Another degree of norms is illustrated by mores.

The strength of this kind of development is that in moving from general to specific, you give your audience a clear and vivid understanding of the word being defined.

In the following assignment you should not feel restricted to either of these procedures. Your goal is to give the clearest, most meaningful definition possible, using any method of definition suggested.

Assignment   *Prepare a two- to four-minute speech of definition. An outline is required. Select a word or concept that is not readily definable by most members of the class. Criteria for evaluation will include the clarity of the definition, organization of main points, and quality of the developmental material.*

Outline: Speech of Definition (2–4 minutes)

Specific Purpose: To define the Montessori method of education.

Introduction

  I. What kind of a school did you attend? Was it traditional? Or was it Montessori?
 II. In 1907 Maria Montessori opened her first school in the slums of Rome.
III. Today, the Montessori method is a system of teaching young children through individual guidance rather than through strict control.

Thesis Statement: The Montessori method is a hands-on approach to learning that gives children freedom of choice in a controlled environment where the child works at his or her own speed.

Body

I. Montessori is "hands-on."
   A. Children are encouraged to develop their senses by touching and experience.
   B. All experiences and exercises involve the student.
II. Montessori gives freedom of choice.
   A. The child is free to work on whatever he or she wishes.
   B. The child must work to complete the particular task.
III. Montessori creates a controlled environment.
   A. Beneath the colorful surface, everything is designed for a learning purpose.
   B. A Montessori class contains sets of prescribed objects.
IV. Montessori encourages the child to work at his or her own speed.
   A. The child is assigned a series of tasks to perform.
   B. The tasks are individualized.

Conclusion

I. The Montessori system teaches by giving freedom of action that helps the child develop through trial and error experiences: It is a hands-on system that gives freedom of choice in a controlled environment where the child develops at his or her own speed.
II. As Maria Montessori said, "Within the child lies the fate of the future."

Read the speech aloud. Then analyze it in terms of the clarity of the definition, the organization of the main points, and the quality of the development of each main point.[2] After you have read and analyzed the speech, turn to the analysis in the other column.

---

[2] Delivered in Speech class, University of Cincinnati. Printed by permission of Cookie McDonough.

Analysis	*Speech: The Montessori Method*
The opening does a good job of soliciting audience involvement.	Think back to your first years at school. Were you sitting at your desk longing to explore, only to have your teacher telling you what to do and when to do it? If so, you were a student of the traditional method of education. Tonight I'd like to talk with you about another method, the Montessori method.
The total introduction lays a nice groundwork for the definition.	
	It was developed back in 1907 by an educator named Maria Montessori, who began teaching school in the slums of Rome. I'd like to define for you tonight what the Montessori method is. Briefly, the Montessori method is a hands-on approach to learning, giving freedom of choice, in a controlled environment, which allows the child to develop at his or her own speed. Let's consider each of the four parts of this definition.
The definition of *Montessori* is clear and concise.	
Notice how the speech follows the coordinate plan explained on pp. 200–202.	The Montessori method is a hands-on approach. By "hands-on," I mean that children are encouraged to develop their senses through touching and experiencing. Children are encouraged to explore their school environment.
This first point develops the first concept in the definition. Each of the four concepts is clearly set forth as a main point.	
	Second, Montessori gives freedom of choice. The child learns by trial and error. Children are encouraged through individual guidance rather than through strict control.
This third main point is the best developed of the four. Good use of specifics to illustrate the "controlled environment."	Third, Montessori creates a controlled environment. It appears that the child is free to move about with no plan, but it is a very controlled environment. Everything there is for a special purpose. In the room you'll see colorful cubes and prisms, other geometric solids, alphabets, cards with numbers, sticks for counting, geography maps with nobs on places—in this case to develop prehensile grasp that enables the child to hold a pencil better and write better.
	Fourth, Montessori encourages the child to complete a task at his or her own speed. The teacher sets forth a series of tasks and the child can complete the tasks in any order he or she wishes, but the child has an allotted period of time, and must complete a task.
The summary puts emphasis back on the total definition.	In summary, then, the Montessori method is a hands-on approach, giving the child freedom of choice, in a controlled envi-

ronment, which allows the child to develop at his or her own speed. Many children have found that an exciting way to learn.

I would like to close with a quote by Maria Montessori. "Within the child lies the fate of the future."

Although the quotation does not further the definition per se, it does end the speech on a positive note—it emphasizes the importance of education. The speech is a good example of a classification method of extended definition.

Chapter 12 Expository Speeches: Using Resource Material

Throughout history people have had an insatiable need to know. Unanswered questions stimulate research; research yields facts; and facts, when properly ordered and developed, yield understanding. Oral communication of the understanding of these questions is often made through expository speeches.

Most expository speeches are referred to as reports or lectures. Whether you call your speech a report, a lecture, or an exposition, it should be a carefully prepared informative speech that depends on creative use of resource material for its effectiveness. The expository speech is differentiated from other speeches you have been giving by the kinds of material used. In some contexts, any explanation is considered expository; in this context, however, we are giving "expository" a very restrictive meaning—we are defining as expository a type of speech that depends on exploration of resource material for its substance. The narratives, processes, descriptions, and definitions you have given may have depended more on personal knowledge, experience, and observation than on research for speech development. Expository speaking, as we are defining it, places such emphasis on the understanding of an idea that outside source material is needed to give the speech depth.

We introduced sources of information in Chapter 3. In this chapter on expository speech preparation, we look at sample topics, library material, interviewing, and processing source material.

EXPOSITORY SPEECH TOPICS

Almost any topic on your brainstorming list can be worked into an expository speech. Still, some will be more likely candidates than others. The test is whether preparation for the speech requires extensive research. If the answer is yes, it is probably a good candidate for this assignment.

The following lists give examples of topics that are likely to qualify for the expository speech assignment. Perhaps some of the topics on these lists coincide with topics on your brainstorming list; perhaps one will remind you of a similar topic that you neglected to list; or perhaps the lists will only substantiate the point that many topics on your brainstorming list are indeed acceptable for an expository speech. The topics are listed under four broad categories to illustrate the variety of possibilities.

Political, Economic, and Social Issues

Methods of solving air pollution	Effects of marijuana
Modernization of police forces	Cable television
Progress on research on cancer	Women's rights
Alternate forms of school financing	Effects of TV on children
Urban renewal progress	Nuclear power

Historical Events and Forces

Pyramids	Oriental use of gunpowder
Circus Maximus	One-room schoolhouse
Roman roads	Pirates
Castles	Establishing trade routes
Chivalry	Napoleonic wars
Stonehenge	Witches

Theories, Principles, and Laws

Binomial theory	Magnetism
Archimedes' law	Condensation
Binary number system	Light refraction
Einstein's theory of relativity	X-rays
Harmonics	Multiplier effect

Critical Appraisals

Painting:	*Literature:*	*Music:*
Picasso	Poetry	Jazz
Van Gogh	Novels	New Wave

| Rembrandt | Short stories | Symphony |
| Rockwell | Science fiction | Concerto |

Speeches:	*Film:*
Inaugural addresses	Silent movies
Courtroom speaking	Foreign movies
Legislative speeches	

LIBRARY MATERIAL

In Chapter 3, we looked at the card catalog and *Readers' Guide to Periodical Literature* as two of the most popular sources for speech material; now we want to review these and look at other library sources that are basic to speech research and to discuss a strategy for using source material most advantageously.

Card Catalog

The card catalog indexes all your library's holdings by author, title, and subject. Your principal use of the card catalog will be to locate the best books on your topic.

Periodicals and Magazines

Periodicals are publications that appear at fixed periods: weekly, biweekly, monthly, quarterly, or yearly. The materials you get from weekly, biweekly, and monthly magazines are more current than those you will find in books. Of course, some magazines are more accurate, more complete, and more useful than others. Since you must know where and how to find articles before you can evaluate them, you should know and use three indexes: *Readers' Guide to Periodical Literature, Education Index,* and *Index to Behavioral Sciences and Humanities.*

Readers' Guide to Periodical Literature, the index of some 150 popular magazines and journals, is by far the most valuable source for topics of current interest. Nevertheless, you can probably make effective use of the other two important indexes to magazines and journals.

If your specific purpose is related directly or indirectly to the field of education, including such subject areas as school administration, adult education, film strips, intelligence, morale, tests and scales, Project Head Start, or ungraded schools, *Education Index,* a cumulative subject index to a selected list of some 150 educational periodicals, proceedings, and yearbooks, will lead you to the available sources.

In contrast to *Readers' Guide,* which will lead you to articles in popular journals, the *Index to Behavioral Sciences and Humanities,* a guide to some 150 periodicals, will lead you to articles in such scholarly journals as *American Journal of Sociology, Economist, Modern Language Quarterly,* and *Philosophical Review.*

Encyclopedias   Not only do encyclopedias give you an excellent overview of many subjects, but they also offer valuable bibliographies. Nevertheless, because the articles cannot possibly cover every topic completely, relatively few are very detailed. In addition, because of the time lag, an encyclopedia is seldom valuable for the changing facts and details needed for contemporary problems. Most libraries have a recent edition of *Encyclopaedia Britannica, Encyclopedia Americana,* or *World Book Encyclopedia.*

Biographical Sources   When you need biographical details, from thumbnail sketches to reasonably complete essays, you can turn to one of the many biographical sources available. In addition to full-length books and encyclopedia entries, you should explore such books as *Who's Who* and *Who's Who in America* (short sketches of British subjects and American citizens, respectively) or *Dictionary of National Biography* and *Dictionary of American Biography* (rather complete essays about prominent British subjects and American citizens, respectively).

Statistical Sources   When you need facts, details, or statistics about population, records, continents, heads of state, weather, or similar subjects, you should refer to one of the many single-volume sources that report such data. Three of the most noteworthy sources in this category are *World Almanac and Book of Facts* (1868 to date), *Statistical Abstract of the United States* (1878 to date), and *Statesman's Yearbook: Statistical and Historical Annual of the States of the World* (1867 to date).

Newspapers   Despite the relatively poor quality of reporting in many of our daily newspapers, newspaper articles should not be overlooked as sources of facts and interpretations of contemporary problems. Your library probably holds both an index of your nearest major daily and the *New York Times Index.*

Since the holdings of libraries vary so much, a detailed account of other bibliographies, indexes, and special resources is impractical.

Where to Go   If you knew you had to use library source material, where would you go first for information? Some people always try encyclopedias first—through their years of experience in schooling they have developed the belief that "you can find anything in an encyclopedia." Some people always start with the card catalog; some always start with *Readers' Guide.* The point of this section is to try to get you to think about your topic a little bit before you act. Where are you most likely to find the most and the best information on your topic? Consider the following questions before you set foot in the library:

1. Is the focus of the topic you are considering less than two years old? If so, use the magazine and newspaper indexes for articles. Since it usually takes one to three years for current topics to appear in books and encyclopedias, it may be a waste of time to search the card catalog or encyclopedias for information. *Occasionally* a book is rushed into print within six months of an event, but such speed is rare (and the worth of such a hastily prepared work is questionable).

2. If you decide on searching magazine or newspaper indexes, how should you proceed? Indexes are published yearly for years before the current edition and in monthly and quarterly supplements for the current year. In order to find appropriate articles about your topic, you need to determine when the events occurred or during what years the topic was actively discussed. For example, if you are preparing a speech on what it was like to be a television writer during the McCarthy era, it would be a waste of time to begin your research with indexes of the 1970s and work backward. Rather, you should begin your research in 1953, the height of the McCarthy era, and work forward and backward from there until the supply of articles dries up. If you are preparing a speech on the effects of the Arab oil embargo of the early 1970s, you would begin with 1973.

Moreover, you need to be creative in determining the headings you will research. Suppose you were researching the topic "minimum cash income." You may find little or nothing under that heading in either a periodical index or the card catalog. Within a few minutes of creative thinking, however, you should be able to come up with such additional headings as "economic assistance—domestic," "guaranteed income," "income," "negative income tax," "poverty," "war on poverty," "welfare," and other related headings.

3. **When is the card catalog the best place to start?** If you want a comprehensive analysis of a topic, books will provide your best material, and you should therefore begin with the card catalog. Although newer books are usually preferable to old ones, older books should not be ignored.

INTERVIEWING

Although written sources may provide most of the material for most of your speeches, you should not overlook the potential of the interview as a source for valuable material. Because good interviews do not "just happen," let us take a look at the principles that govern good interviewing for information. Interviewing involves selecting the best person to interview, determining a procedure, conducting the interview itself, and interpreting the results.

Selecting the Best Person

Somewhere on campus or in the larger community, there are persons who have expertise in the problem areas you want to research. Your first step should be to find out who they are so you can arrange to talk with them. Suppose you are interested in the selection and preparation of dormitory food. Whom should you interview? Perhaps one of the employees can tell you who is in charge of the dining hall. Perhaps you need to call a particular campus agency. After you have made a list of names, you would make an appointment with one or more persons on the list. Making an appointment is very important—you cannot just go walking into an office and expect the prospective interviewee to drop everything on the spur of the moment. You are not going to get much valuable information if the person is not willing to cooperate with you. To get an appointment you must know (1) why you need to interview this particular person and (2) what information you hope to get from the interview.

Before going in to conduct the interview, you should do some research on the person you will be interviewing. If you are going to interview the dietitian who makes out menus and orders the food, you should already know something about the job of dietitian and something about the problems involved in ordering and preparing institutional food. Not only will evidence of your preliminary research encourage the person to talk more openly with you (few people will either respect or talk in detail with a person who obviously knows nothing about the subject or the person), but also this familiarity with material will enable you to frame more penetrating questions. If for some reason you are unable to get any preliminary information, then at least approach the interviewee with a degree of enthusiasm and apparent interest in his or her job.

In addition, you should be forthright in your reasons for seeking the interview. If you are interviewing the person as part of a class project, if you are writing a newspaper article on campus food, or if you have some other reason, say so.

Determining a Procedure

Good interviewing results from careful planning. The plan includes an overall method and preparation of specific questions. Since questioning is the most important tool of a good interviewer, let us look at the kinds of questions you need to be prepared to ask. Questions may be phrased as open or closed, primary or secondary, leading or neutral.

OPEN AND CLOSED QUESTIONS   *Open questions* are broad-based; *closed questions* are those that can be answered with yes or no, or with only a few words. Open questions range from those with virtually no restrictions like "Will you tell me about cave exploring?" to those that give more specific direction like "Will you tell me about preparing yourself for the exploration of a new cave?" Why do interviewers use open questions? The open question encourages the responding person to talk, allowing the interviewer maximum opportunity to listen and to observe. Through the open question, the interviewer finds out about the interviewee's feelings, attitudes, values, and so forth in relation to the subject area. Open questions take more time, and the interviewer can lose direction if he or she is not careful.

Closed questions range from those requiring only yes and no answers ("Have you ever explored any caves that are uncharted?") to the short-answer variety ("How many caves have you explored this year?"; "What kinds of situations give a cave explorer the most problems?"). With the closed question the interviewer can control the interview; moreover, he or she can get large amounts of information in a short time. Still, the closed question seldom enables the interviewer to learn why a person gives a certain response; the closed question is also not likely to yield much voluntary information.

Which type of question is superior? The answer depends on what kinds of material you are seeking and how much time you have for the interview. An opinion poll interviewer who wants specific responses to specific questions will rely mostly or entirely on closed questions; a person who is primarily interested in the thoughts and feelings of another person might ask all open questions. In an information-getting interview for a speech, you will want enough closed questions to get the specifics you need and enough open questions to allow for the inclusion of anecdotes, illustrations, and personal views.

PRIMARY AND SECONDARY QUESTIONS *Primary questions* introduce topics, and *secondary questions* follow up on the answers to primary questions. Primary questions are determined beforehand; framing good secondary questions requires the interviewer to pay close attention to what is happening. Both primary and secondary questions may be phrased as open or as closed questions.

The major reason for secondary questions is to motivate the respondent to enlarge upon an answer that appears inadequate. Follow-ups are necessary because the respondent may be purposely trying to be evasive, incomplete, or vague, or because the interviewee may not really understand how much detail you are looking for.

As an interviewer, you must get used to asking certain kinds of questions under certain circumstances. If you want to encourage the respondent to continue, you should use such questions as "And then?", "Is there more?", and "What happened next?" If you want to probe more deeply into an area, you should use such follow-up questions as "What do you mean by 'frequently'?", "What were you thinking at the time?", or "Can you give me some examples?" If you want to plumb the feelings of the respondent, you might ask such secondary questions as "How did it feel to be stuck underground?", "Were you worried when you didn't find her?", or "Did you feel any resentment when you weren't selected?"

Your effectiveness with follow-up questions may well depend on your skill in asking them. Since probing questions can alienate the interviewee (especially when the questions are perceived as threatening), such in-depth probes work best after you have gained the confidence of the respondent and when the questions are asked within the atmosphere of a positive interpersonal climate.

NEUTRAL AND LEADING QUESTIONS *Neutral questions* are those in which the respondent is free to give an answer without direction; *leading questions* are those in which the interviewer suggests the answer that is expected or desired. A neutral question is "How do you like working on a team with a famous explorer?"; a leading question is "Being on a team with a famous explorer is intimidating, isn't it?" In the neutral question the respondent determines how to answer. In the leading question, the person feels some pressure to answer in a particular way.

Since leading questions are frequently used by persons who are intending to control the attitude or behavior of the respondent, the leading question is usually inappropriate for information-getting interviews.

Now let's consider the questions you should ask, and the order in which you should ask them.

In the opening stages of an interview you should start by thanking the person for taking time to talk with you. During the opening try to develop good rapport between you and your respondent. Start by asking questions that can be answered easily and that will show your respect for the person you are interviewing. For instance, in an interview with the head dietitian you might start with such questions as "How did you get interested in nutrition?" or "I imagine working out menus can be a very challenging job in these times of high food costs—is that so?" When the person nods or says yes, you can then ask for some of the biggest challenges he or she faces. The goal is to get the interviewee to feel at ease and to talk freely. Since the most important consideration of this initial stage is to create a positive communication climate, keep the questions easy to answer, nonthreatening, and encouraging.

The body of the interview includes the major questions you have prepared to ask. A good plan is to group questions so that the easy-to-answer questions come first and the hard-hitting questions that require careful thinking come later. For instance, the question "What do you do to try to resolve student complaints?" should be near the end of the interview. You may not ask all the questions you planned, but you don't want to end the interview until you have gotten all the important information you intended to get.

As you draw to the end of your planned questions, thank the

person for taking time to talk with you. If you are going to publish the substance of the interview, it is courtesy to offer to let the person see a draft of your reporting of the interview before it goes into print. If a person does wish to see what you are planning to write, get a draft to that person well before deadline to give the person opportunity to read it and to give you opportunity to deal with any suggestions. Although this practice is not followed by many interviewers, it helps to build and maintain your own credibility.

The following is an example of an interview question schedule. If you were planning to interview the dietitian, you might prepare the following question schedule:

•Background

What kinds of background and training do you need for the job?

How did you get interested in nutrition?

Have you worked as a dietitian for long?

Have you held any other food-related positions?

•Responsibilities

What are the responsibilities of your job besides meal planning?

How far in advance are meals planned?

What factors are taken into account when you are planning the meals for a given period?

Do you have a free hand or are constraints placed on you?

•Procedures

Is there any set ratio for the number of times you put a given item on the menu?

Do you take individual differences into account?

How do you determine whether or not you will give choices for the entree?

What do you do to try to answer student complaints?

Could a student get a comparable meal at a good cafeteria for the same money? Explain.

**Conducting the
Interview**

The best plan in the world will not result in a good interview unless you practice good interpersonal communication skills in conducting the interview. Let us focus on a few of the particularly important elements of good interviewing. Perhaps more than anything else, you should be courteous during the interview. Listen carefully—your job is not to debate or to give your opinion, but to get information from a person who has it. Whether you like the person or not and whether you agree with the person or not, you must respect his or her opinions—after all, you are the one who asked for the interview.

Put into practice your best receiver skills. If the person has given a rather long answer to a question, you should paraphrase what has been said to make sure your interpretation is correct. Also, keep the interview moving. You do not want to rush the person, but he or she is probably very busy with a full schedule of activities. It is usually a good idea to ask for a given amount of time when you first make the appointment. Sometimes the interviewee will want to extend the time. Ordinarily, however, when the time is up, you should call attention to that fact and be prepared to conclude.

Last, but certainly not least, you should be very much aware of the impression you make nonverbally. You should consider your clothes—you want to be dressed appropriately for the occasion. Since you are taking the person's time, you should show an interest in the person and in what he or she has to say. How you look and act may well determine whether or not the person will warm up to you and give you the kind of interview you want.

**Interpreting the
Results**

The interview serves no useful purpose until you do something with the material, but you should not do anything with it until you have reviewed it carefully. Especially if you took notes, it is important to write out complete answers carefully while information is still fresh in your mind. After you have processed the material from the interview, you may want to show the interviewee a copy of the data you are going to use. You do not want to be guilty of misquoting your source.

You may also find it necessary to check out the facts you have been given. If what the person has told you differs from material you have from other sources, you had better double-check its accuracy.

The most difficult part is interpreting and drawing inferences from the material. Facts by themselves are not nearly so important as the conclusions that may be drawn from the facts. Think through your analysis of the material carefully before you present the substance in a speech or for publication.

PROCESSING SOURCE MATERIAL

As you work with your materials in building your speech, you will have to test the quality of the material, determine how you will cite the source for information in the speech, and determine how you can use the material creatively.

Testing Material

The first test of the information gathered for a speech is to determine whether it is comprehensive. Your material meets the test of being comprehensive if it covers the areas that need to be covered in order to satisfy your purposes. Or, to put it another way, your material is comprehensive if you have researched the best available material on the subject. Although comprehensive research on any expository subject could take a team of researchers weeks or more, for a class assignment, the speech should be comprehensive "within reason," which might be defined as using at least four or more sources of information.

As you gather the sources, which will be included in your bibliography, you may find that you have discovered more material than you can possibly read completely. In order to locate and record the best material, you should develop a system of evaluation that will enable you to review the greatest amount of information in the shortest period of time. Most students find that with a little practice they can increase their efficiency by skip reading. If you are appraising a magazine article, spend a minute or two finding out what it covers. Does it really present information on the phase of the topic you are exploring? Does it contain any documented statistics, examples, or quotable opinions? Is the author qualified to draw meaningful conclusions? If you are appraising a book, read the table of contents carefully, look at the index, and skip-read pertinent chapters, asking the same questions you would for a magazine article. During the skip-reading period, you decide which sources should be read in full, which should be read in part, and which should be abandoned. Every minute spent in evaluation saves you from unlimited amounts of useless reading.

In addition to making your analysis comprehensive, a wide variety of sources are needed to ensure accuracy and objectivity. Because your goal is to find the facts regardless of what they may prove, you need to get material on all sides of the topic being explored. If your material reveals some contradictory aspects, your speech should reflect the nature of the conflict.

Any source that you read will be a representation of fact and opinion. A fact is anything that is verifiable; an opinion is an expressed view on any subject. That apples have seeds is a fact; that apples taste good is an opinion. Some opinions are related to, based upon, or extended from facts—some are not. Before you begin to develop, you need to test the accuracy of the "facts" you have discovered and the objectivity of opinions. Determining the accuracy of every item in a source can be a long and tedious and perhaps even an impossible job. In most cases accuracy can be reasonably assured if you check the fact against the original, or primary, source. If your source states that, according to the most recent Department of Labor statistics, unemployment went down 0.2 percent in December, you should look for those most recent Department of Labor statistics. If your history book footnotes the original source of an important quotation, you should go to that original source. Although checking sources in this way may seem to be unnecessary, you will be surprised at the number of errors that occur in using data from other sources.

If the original or primary source is not available, the best way of verifying a fact is to check it against the facts in a second source on the subject. Although two or more sources may on some occasion get their "facts" from the same faulty source, when two or more sources state the same fact or similar facts, the chances of verification are considerably better.

A second and equally important test is to determine the objectivity of an opinion. Facts by themselves are not nearly as important as the conclusions drawn from them. Since conclusions are more often than not opinions, they have to be weighed very carefully before they can be accepted. Researchers find that a good procedure is to study a variety of sources to see what they say about the same set of facts; then the researchers draw their own conclusions from the facts. Your conclusion may duplicate one source, or may be drawn from several sources, or occasionally may differ from the sources. Only after you have examined many sources are you in a position to make the kind of value judgment that a thinking speaker needs to make. In your research, you may be surprised how many times two sources will appear to contradict each other on the interpretation of a set of facts. Whether the issue is the cause of World War I, the effects of birth-control pills on women, or the importance of free trade to a nation's economic position, what the source says may depend on the biases of the author, the availability or selection of material, or the care taken in evaluation of material. As a result, expository speakers must be sure that they are not communicating a distorted, biased, or hastily stated opinion as fact.

Citing Source Material

A special problem of a research speech is how you can cite source material in your speech. In presenting any speech in which you are using ideas that are not your own personal knowledge, you should attempt to work the source of your material into the context of the speech. Such efforts to include sources not only will help the audience in their evaluation of the content but also will add to your credibility as a speaker. In a written report, ideas taken from other sources are designated by footnotes. In a speech, these notations must be included within the context of your statement of the material. In addition, since an expository speech is supposed to reflect a depth of research, citing the various sources of information will give concrete evidence of your research. Your citation need not be a complete representation of all the bibliographic information. In most instances, the following kinds of phrasing are appropriate:

> According to an article about Senator Glenn in last week's *Time* magazine . . .
>
> In the latest Harris poll cited in last week's issue of *Newsweek* . . .
>
> One conservative point of view was well summed up by William F. Buckley, Jr., in his book *God and Man at Yale.* In the opening chapter, Buckley wrote . . .
>
> But in order to get a complete picture we have to look at the statistics. According to the *Statistical Abstract,* the level of production for under-developed countries rose from . . .
>
> In a speech before the National Organization for Women given just last fall, Billie Jean King said . . .
>
> During an in-person interview last week, Raoul Gordon, a noted area cave explorer, said . . .

Although you do not want to clutter your speech with bibliographical citations, you do want to make sure that you have properly reflected the sources of your key information. If you practice these and similar short prefatory comments, you will find that they will soon come naturally.

Showing Creativity and Originality

If you have selected a worthwhile topic and have gathered sufficient reliable material, your speech should have the necessary depth. Because you are engaging your audience in a learning process, you also want to do what you can to make your ideas interesting. By thinking creatively you can add originality to your speeches. An original speech is new; it is not copied, imitated, or reproduced. To you, the lecturer, this means that your speech must be a product of, but entirely different from, the sources you used. You find material, you put it in a usable form, then you inject your insights and your personality into the speech.

Originality is a product of the creative process. Some people have the mistaken idea that creativity is a natural by-product of a special "creative individual." Actually, we all have the potential for thinking creatively—some of us just have not given ourselves a chance to try.

To be creative, you must give yourself enough time to allow the creative process to work. Creative thinking is roughly analogous to cooking. You just can't rush it. Have you ever tried to make a good spaghetti sauce? It takes hours and hours of simmering the tomatoes, herbs, and spices. A good cook knows that success with the best ingredients and the best recipes depends on allowing the proper length of time. So it is with speech making. Once you have prepared yourself fully (when you have completed your outline), you need two or three days for your mind to reflect on what you have gathered. Let us take the practice period as an example of the result of giving the creative process time to work. You may find that the morning after a few uninspiring practices you suddenly have two or three fresh ideas for lines of development. While you were sleeping, your mind was still going over the material. When you awoke, the product of unconscious or subconscious thought reached the level of consciousness. Had there been no intervening time between practice sessions and delivery, your mind would not have had the time to work through the material.

Time alone is not enough, however. You must be receptive to new ideas, and you must develop the capacity to evaluate comparable ideas. Too often we are content with the first thought that comes to mind. Suppose, for your speech on computers, you thought you would begin the speech with "Years ago even the simplest computer had to be housed in a large room; today you can hold a functioning computer in your hand. Let's examine some of the advances that have led to computer miniaturization." Now, there is probably nothing wrong with such an opening, but is it the best you can do? There is no way for you to know until you have tried other ways. Here is where you can usefully employ the brainstorming method for a goal other than selecting topics. Try to start your speech in two, three, or even five different ways. Although several attempts will be similar, the effort to try new ways will stretch your mind, and chances are good that one or two of the ways will be far superior and much more imaginative than any of the others.

Being receptive also means taking note of ideas that come to you regardless of the circumstances. Did you ever notice how ideas will come to you at strange times—perhaps while you are washing dishes, or shining your shoes, or watching a television program, or waiting for your date, or waiting for a stoplight to change? Also, have you noticed that often when you try to recall those ideas they have slipped away? Many speakers, writers, and composers carry a pencil and a piece of paper with them at all times, and when an idea comes, they take the time to write it down. They do not try to evaluate it; they only try to get the details on paper. Not all of these inspirations are the flashes of insight that are characteristic of creativity, of course, but some of them are. If you do not make note of yours, if you are not receptive to them, you will never know.

The greatest value of the creative process is to enable you to work out alternative methods of presenting factual material. In addition to methods already discussed, familiarity with possible lines of development will help guide your creative thinking. From a body of factual material, an infinite number of lines of development are possible. In any one speech, you may wish to follow one line of development or several, depending on the scope of the speech, the number of points you wish to make, and the time available to you. To illustrate the inventive process fully, let us suppose you are planning to give a speech on climate in the United States, and in your research you come across the data in Table 12.1.

We want to show the following: (1) Data, even one set, can suggest *several* lines of development on one topic—in this case climatic conditions—and (2) the same point can be made in different ways.

TABLE 12.1

City	Temperature Jan.		Year High	Low	Extremes		Precipitation July	Annual
	Max.	Min.	High	Low			July	Annual
Cincinnati	41	26	96	2	109	−17	3.3	39
Chicago	32	12	93	− 6	103	−39	3.4	33
Denver	42	15	100	− 5	105	−30	1.5	14
Los Angeles	65	47	88	39	110	28	T	14
Miami	76	58	96	44	100	28	6.8	59
Minneapolis	22	2	96	−21	108	−34	3.5	24
New Orleans	64	45	98	23	102	7	6.7	59
New York	40	17	97	11	106	−15	3.7.	42
Phoenix	64	35	114	27	118	16	T	7
Portland, Me.	32	12	93	− 6	103	−39	3.9	42
St. Louis	40	24	97	2	115	−23	3.3	35
San Francisco	55	42	86	33	106	20	T	18
Seattle	44	33	91	15	99	0	.6	38

1. Data can suggest several lines of argument. Before you read the following material, study Table 12.1. What conclusions can you draw from it? If you are thinking creatively, you can determine the following:

   a. Yearly high temperatures in American cities vary far less than yearly low temperatures.

   b. It hardly ever rains on the West Coast in the summer.

   c. In most of the major cities cited, July, a month thought to be hot and dry, produces more than the average $1/12$ of the precipitation you might expect.

Thus, this one table will produce at least three lines of development for a single speech on climate.

2. From the data presented, one point can be made in more than one way. Let's consider the statement "Yearly high temperatures in American cities vary far less than yearly low temperatures."

   a. Statistical development: Whereas, of the thirteen cities selected, ten of them (77%) had yearly highs between 90° and 100°, three cities (23%) had yearly lows above freezing; six of them (46%) had yearly lows between zero and 32°, and four of them (30%) had low temperatures below zero.

b. Comparative development: Cincinnati, Miami, Minneapolis, and New York, cities at different latitudes, all had yearly high temperatures of 96° or 97°; in contrast, the lowest temperature for Miami was 44°, and the lowest temperatures for Cincinnati, Minneapolis, and New York were 2°, −21°, and 11°, respectively.

c. Can you determine another way of making the same point?

PITFALLS OF DEVELOPMENT

The development of expository speeches can lead to two problems that should be considered and overcome if possible.

Jargon

When a speech is about a theory, principle, or law, there is a tendency to overuse or become dependent on scientific terminology, formulas, and jargon. This dependence is one reason why some engineers, mathematicians, economists, and behavioral scientists find it very difficult to talk with people outside their professions. Your problem, then, is to explain professional terminology in language that can be understood by lay persons. Popularizers such as Vance Packard, Margaret Mead, and Isaac Asimov have earned reputations for their ability to bridge the gap between the specialists and the common person. Good expository speakers must be such popularizers. They must understand the subject, and they must be able to discuss that understanding in an intelligible manner. Thus, a speaker discussing classical rhetoric would substitute synonyms for the terms *ethos, pathos,* and *logos;* the speaker explaining economics would find synonyms for *microeconomic and macroeconomic tendencies;* and the speaker discussing heart disease before an audience not made up of doctors would find synonyms for such terms as *myocardial infarction* and *myofibril contractile elements.*

Confusion of Theory and Fact

Whether your discussion is about history, economics, sociology, or any other subject, you must avoid misleading an audience by confusing theories with facts. People hypothesize about many things in this world. From these hypotheses they formulate theories. Be sure that you know whether the supporting material you offer is theory or fact. The formula πr^2 will give us the area of a circle, pure water boils at 212° Fahrenheit at sea level, and gravity can be measured. Relativity, evolution, and multiplier effects are theories that may or may not be valid. If you keep this differentiation in mind, you can avoid confusing yourself and your audience.

Assignment   *Prepare a four- to seven-minute expository speech. An outline and bibliography (at least four sources) are required. Criteria for evaluation will include how well you limit your topic, how substantial is your resource material, how well you have introduced bibliographical citations, and how creative and informative you have made the development. A question period of one to three minutes will follow (optional).*

Alternate Assignment   *Prepare a four- to seven-minute report using information gained through one or more interviews. Criteria for evaluation are the same as in the first assignment. Include a question schedule with your outline. Following are samples for both assignments.*

Outline: Expository Speech (4–7 minutes)

Specific Purpose: To discuss three common errors in the use of the English language.

Introduction

I. "Wishing to divest myself of all pomposity, I situate my presence before you in complete candor to speak in mellifluous tones, between you and I and, yes, even him whom is in that corner, in regards to a beguiling yet profound, substantive matter."

II. If you don't get the meaning, it's because of three common mistakes in English usage.

Thesis Statement: The three common mistakes of English usage are abuse of grammar, misuse of words, and circumlocution.

Body

I. Abuse of grammar is widespread.
   A. Commercials illustrate problems of English usage.
   B. Failure of students in English composition across the country points up the problem.
   C. Jean Stafford attributes much of the problem to television.

II. A more subtle problem is misuse of words.
   A. It's a sneaky malfunction because it sounds quite good.
      1. "Guestimate," "thrust," and "parameter" are widely used.
      2. "Viable" is the new superword of planning.
   B. Many of these uses are quite funny when analyzed.
      1. "In depth" is really meaningless.
      2. "I teach college" is all-encompassing.

III. Circumlocution, the art of using fifty words when ten would do, may be the most distressing problem.
   A. Edwin Newman asks where simple, direct speech has gone.
   B. Random samples of statements illustrate current abuse.
   C. The cap is former presidential press secretary Ronald Ziegler's meandering answer that means simply, "I need more time to think about it."

IV. Of course, the answer is not total purity.
   A. We need to have fun with language.
      1. Louis Armstrong's classic response to "What's jazz?"
      2. *Reader's Digest* column, "Toward More Picturesque Speech."
   B. Still, we must be conscious of problems that hinder communication.

Conclusion

 I. In most cases, abuse of grammar, misuse of words, and circumlocution hurt rather than facilitate communication.

II. To what extent and with what results seem to be the most important questions we can ask—"at this point in time," that is.

Bibliography

"Bonehead English." *Time,* 11 November 1974, p. 106.

Middleton, Thomas H. "Linguistic Inanities." *Saturday Review/World,* 13 July 1974, p. 56.

Newman, Edwin. *Strictly Speaking: Will America Be the Death of English?* Indianapolis: Bobbs-Merrill, 1974.

Stafford, Jean. "At This Point in Time, TV Is Murdering the English Language." *New York Times,* 15 September 1974, p. 23.

"Toward More Picturesque Speech." *Reader's Digest,* October 1974, p. 74.

Read the transcription of this speech at least once aloud.[1]
Examine the speech to see how well the topic has been limited,
how substantial is the research, how well bibliographical
citations have been introduced, and how creatively the
information has been presented.

Analysis

The speaker begins with a very clever opening sentence illustrating the problems she will discuss. The attention comes from the bewildering complexity and obscurity of the language. Incidentally, if you reread the sentence carefully you will see that it does tell you what she plans to do. At the end of the introduction the speaker states her goal quite smoothly.

She moves into her first point, abuse of grammar.

As the speech continues, we begin to see the strength of her development: clear, vivid examples.

Since such a point as abuse of grammar is difficult to illustrate with examples alone, the speaker makes good use of statistics to show the scope of the problem she is considering.

Notice the way the speaker cites her sources. Her references are short and unobtrusive, but they serve the purpose. They let us know the scope and depth of her research.

Speech: *Problems of Communication*

Wishing to divest myself of all pomposity, I situate my presence before you in complete candor to speak in mellifluous tones between you and I, and, yes, even him whom is in that corner, in regards to a beguiling yet profound substantive matter. Get the meaning? Well, neither do I. But as strange as it may sound to your ear, the sentence I just spoke may be more typical than we'd like to admit. It contained three common problems of everyday communication that some experts say are ruining the English language: abuse of grammar, misuse of words, and circumlocution.

Abuse of grammar is a criticism we've heard for years. And after all, we've come a long way since the controversy over "Winston tastes good, like a cigarette should." Now our commercials give us such sentences as "You get a lot of dirt with kids, you get a lot of clean with Tide."

Is the misuse of grammar really a problem? Well, a recent article in *Time* magazine stated, "Almost half the freshmen at the University of California at Berkeley failed the English composition test in the fall. Bonehead English was instituted to help them out." At the University of Houston, 60 percent of the current freshmen failed their first composition essay. At Harvard University, similar results are reported. Some people argue that schools have deemphasized grammar too much. Jean Stafford, a noted novelist, takes another view. In an article in the September 15, 1974, issue of the *New York Times* she pointed an accusing finger at television with the title, "At This Point in Time, TV Is Murdering the English Language." When asked during the recent Watergate hearings, "Who is 'We'?" a lawyer defendant replied, "We is us."

---

[1] Delivered in Speech class, University of Cincinnati. Printed by permission of Betty Zager.

The speaker moves smoothly into her second main point, misuse of words.
Another of the strengths of the speaker's lecture is her humor. Although her topic and her information are serious, the light touch adds to both interest and retention of her points. These two examples are excellent in making her points in a creative way.

Something more subtle than the outright abuse of grammar is the misuse of words. It's a rather sneaky malfunction because, when used expertly, the language sounds quite good. For instance, "Guestimate" now replaces an "educated guess." "Thrust" is a new "in" word, as in "What is the thrust of the situation?" "Parameter" is used to make you sound educated. The term was once confined to mathematics, but now it pops up everywhere. Rather than talking about the limits or boundaries, we have to know the "parameters of a problem." And the new superword of planning, "viable"—it has to be a viable alternative or a viable solution. Sometimes these misuses are pretty funny if we think about them. How about the common phrase, "This study will be conducted in depth"? Well, unless the researchers are conducting the experiments on the bottom of the ocean, the phrase is really very meaningless. Or think about the lovely lady on TV pushing headache tablets. She testifies, "I teach college"—with such an all-encompassing subject, no wonder she has a headache.

The third point, circumlocution, continues the topic order of the speech development.
In a speech that abounds with good examples, I consider the ones in this section the very best.
I believe the speaker is wise in making this the third point. Whereas abuse of grammar and misuse of words may still communicate, circumlocution short-circuits the communication process completely.

But perhaps the most distressing malfunction of language is circumlocution—the art of using fifty words when ten would do. Edwin Newman, NBC-TV correspondent, took pen in hand for the first time to write his book *Strictly Speaking: Will America Be the Death of English?*, which appeared on the market in 1974. Mr. Newman asked, "Where has simple direct speech gone?" I have jotted down a few examples for your review. If you listen closely to what people are saying, I'm sure you'll hear statements like these. Teachers are "busy constructing behavioral objectives that individualize instruction to the point where the learner's self-concept is enhanced." Business executives must "set up study groups to evaluate committees that have been created to delve into the cortex of complexities swirling in the power hierarchy in order to get at the parameters of the problem." Politicians are "concerned with the meaningful rethink of the issues, including specificity." Children when leaving the home nest "opt for life-styles or living situations allowing them the greatest feedback from their input in education, which in turn focuses the thrust of the future contributions to mankind." Mr. Newman's concern is that the stilted and pompous phrase, the slogan, and cliché are going to come to dominate the entire language. As a cap to this

This is an excellent example to use to conclude this point.

point, let's look at presidential press secretary Ron Ziegler's explanation when defending a request for a four-day extension on subpoenas for special files. He replied that James St. Clair, the president's attorney, "needed to evaluate to make a judgment in terms of a response.'' Why didn't Ziegler just say he needed more time to think about it?

This short point helps put the speaker's lecture in proper perspective—and it continues the humorous thread that runs throughout the speech.

Now, I'm not saying that these critics are calling for total purity in language. We have to be able to have some fun with language. For instance, no one should be concerned with Louis Armstrong's double negative in his answer to the question, ''What's jazz?'' Armstrong replied, ''If you got to ask what it is, you ain't never gonna know.'' Moreover, our language is enriched with many usages that stretch meanings to the breaking point. The *Reader's Digest* column ''Toward More Picturesque Speech'' has been collecting quaint usages for years. Who would question the value of the observation about the orchestra conductor ''who kept throwing tempo tantrums''?

These last sentences ably summarize the speaker's points. And, of course, this final sentence from the Watergate era is a kind of topper that ends the speech on a high note. The speaker uses excellent material, develops it creatively, and organizes it clearly. All in all this is an excellent expository speech on abuses of language.

Still, our language suffers abuses that we should be aware of and do our best to correct. In most cases, abuse of language, misuse of words, and circumlocution hurt rather than facilitate communication. To what extent and with what results would seem to be the most important question we can ask—''at this point in time,'' that is.

Outline   Interview speech (4—7 minutes)

Specific Purpose: To explain the danger of a ''backdraft.''

Introduction

I. On October 9, an explosion ripped through Simon Kenton High School killing sixteen-year-old Robert Williams; thirty minutes later, a second, stronger explosion injured thirty firefighters.

II. It is reasonable to assume that the first explosion was caused by a gas buildup due to an installation error by Union Light Heat and Power Company.

III. Fire officials thought the second explosion was the result of the firefighter's unseen enemy, the backdraft.

Thesis Statement: A backdraft is a cause of explosions at fires, it is a real and present danger to firefighters, and it is nearly impossible for the firefighters to protect themselves from it.

Body

I. A backdraft is an unseen cause of explosions at fires.
   A. According to Clarke's manual, a *backdraft* is a "fire phenomenon that involves the movement of air; it occurs when superheated gases suddenly receive an influx of fresh oxygen—the mixture causes an explosion."
   B. Lt. Hensley's elaboration of this definition further explains the nature of this phenomenon.
      1. Fire in a tightly sealed room exhausts the available oxygen.
      2. Without oxygen the fire continues to smolder.
      3. When oxygen is reintroduced as a nutriment, it creates instant ignition.

II. Backdrafts are a real and present danger that is heightened by our efforts to save energy and money.
   A. Their recent frequency gives an impression that backdrafts are a new phenomenon.
      1. They have always been known to firefighters.
      2. They are occurring with increased frequency.
   B. Our efforts to save energy and money are contributing to their frequency.
      1. Increased insulation of homes creates a tighter seal for rooms.
      2. Improved insulation materials provides greater opportunity for smoldering.
      3. Use of concrete blocks in inner walls lowers building costs, but increases drafts.

III. Firefighters can do very little to protect themselves from the dangers of backdrafts.
   A. Firefighters cannot cave in the roof to prevent a backdraft, because it would endanger the lives of those caught in the room.
   B. Firefighters cannot afford to ignore a search of a room just because it may be right for a backdraft.
   C. Firefighters' need for speed to fight fires and save lives of potential victims precludes their using measures that are effective in coping with backdrafts.

Conclusion

I. We can now understand the nature of and problem with backdrafts.

II. Yet threat of a backdraft is only one of the dangers a firefighter faces.

Read the following speech at least once aloud.[2] Examine the speech to see how well information gained from the interview is used to develop the speech. Although interview material can be used as one of many sources of information for a speech, in this particular assignment the goal is to feature the information gained from the interview.

Analysis

Excellent narrative opening to the speech. Initial audience attention is ensured. Notice the use of short sentences and specific, vivid images throughout the speech, but especially in the narration.

This orientation lays an excellent groundwork for the interview information.

This illustrates the use of definition in the context of the longer, expository speech.

Notice the way the speaker works in the information gathered from the interview.

Speech: Backdraft

At 11:45 A.M. Thursday, October 9, an explosion ripped through Simon Kenton High School. The explosion killed sixteen-year-old Robert Williams. Just thirty minutes later, a second much stronger explosion scattered firefighters like tenpins: it cracked walls; it blew windows out; it crumbled a set of concrete steps; it blew two metal doors from their hinges and hurled them more than 100 feet down a corridor impaling them on another set of doors; and it injured thirty firefighters.

The following day utility officials acknowledged that gas buildup from an installation error by Union Light Heat and Power contributed to the first explosion. Yet no cause was ever given for the second blast, the one of much greater intensity that injured thirty firefighters.

In an effort to determine what caused that second blast, I interviewed Lieutenant Ron Hensley of the Cincinnati Fire Department. Lieutenant Hensley indicated that fire officials thought the second blast was the result of a backdraft.

Just what is a backdraft, the unseen phenomenon that can result in such tremendous damage? Clarke's firefighting manual defines a backdraft as a fire phenomenon that occurs when superheated gases captured in an enclosed and unventilated space suddenly receive fresh oxygen and explode.

I asked Lieutenant Hensley to discuss that definition for me so that we could better understand the nature of a backdraft. He portrayed the process in the following way: A fire burning in a

---

[2] Presented by William G. Cherrington in Speech class, University of Cincinnati. Printed by permission.

tightly sealed room can literally burn up all the available oxygen. In the process of burning up this oxygen it superheats the remaining gases in the room. Even though there is no remaining oxygen present, material continues to smoulder very slowly. Then when oxygen is reintroduced into the room, be it by opening a door, or a window, there is an instantaneous explosion as this fresh oxygen mixes with the superheated gases and the smoldering embers.

Since none of the accounts that I read in any of the newspapers identified the cause as a backdraft, I asked Lieutenant Hensley if a backdraft was an unknown condition. He said it wasn't. He said that backdrafts have always been accepted as a real and present danger. It has been known as both a backdraft and a smoke explosion. But backdrafts are occurring with greater frequency. He indicated that the major reason for the greater frequency was our efforts at saving energy and money. As we become more concerned with energy conservation in our homes, in our attempts to keep out the cool air, we're better insulating our homes, creating a greater seal. This better seal produces better chances for a backdraft if a fire does occur. In addition to better insulation is the improvement of insulation materials. For example, a drop ceiling in a building has a sealing characteristic and a flame retarding characteristic that will permit a fire to burn above that ceiling area and burn up all the oxygen, but continue to smolder. The seal prohibits oxygen from feeding the fuel. Until a panel is removed you do not realize what's above that ceiling, but with removal of the panel comes the explosion. Cinder blocks or concrete block construction in commercial buildings decrease construction costs but also affect a greater seal, furthering the possibility of a backdraft occurring.

I asked the Lieutenant what firefighters could do to prevent being involved in such a situation. He said that the ways to avoid a backdraft were first to vent the room from overhead. If you cave in the roof of a room that has an abundance of these superheated gases, the heated gases will rise faster than the oxygen will come into the room (just as a hot air balloon will rise faster than oxygen), decreasing the possibility of an explosion. A firefighter can also determine whether a room is right for a backdraft by touching the doors to see if they're hot. Even though these methods can help to protect the firefighter, his job prohibits his making good use of them. The firefighter's primary objective, along with put-

Throughout the speech, the speaker continues the dramatic development of ideas.

Although main points are not made 1, 2, 3, they are clearly revealed through the use of good transitions.

The speech continues to deliver solid information.

The use of example helps clarify a point.

The third point, like the second, is revealed through a good transition statement.

Throughout the speaker incorporates information gained from his interview quite well.

ting out the fire, is to ensure that no one is trapped in a burning building. If he cannot see into the room because it is smoke-filled, he can't cave the roof in on potential victims. To touch the door and find it is hot does not tell whether there's a potential backdraft or whether there is a fire in the room.

I think now we can understand what a backdraft is, what causes it, and the danger it represents to firefighters. We can also, I think, understand why the profession of firefighter runs second only to underground miner as most dangerous profession.

Good indirect summary. It does not restate the information, but it does remind the audience of the main points. Final sentence gives the speech that "final touch" that leaves the speech on a high note.

Suggested Readings: Part Three

The following books are recommended as additional reading for the informative speaking unit.

Braun, J. Jay and Darwyn E. Linder, *Psychology Today*. 4th ed. New York: Random House, 1979. See especially Chapter 4 Learning and Chapter 5 Memory. Nearly any recent introduction to psychology textbook will have information related to how people learn.

Downs, Cal W., G. Paul Smeyak, and Ernest Martin. *Professional Interviewing*. New York: Harper & Row, 1980 (paperback). Some excellent advice for planning the interview. Also considers the interview as a research tool.

Good, Thomas L. and Jere E. Brophy. *Educational Psychology*. 2d ed. New York: Holt, Rinehart and Winston, 1980 (paperback). See especially the four chapters in Part 2 Learning.

Guth, Hans P. *Words and Ideas*. 4th ed. Belmont, Calif.: Wadsworth, 1975. Although this is a book on writing, chapters on observation, personal experience, definition, tone and style, and the research report present material that can be adapted to the study of informative speaking.

Petrie, Charles. "Informative Speaking: A Summary and Bibliography of Related Research." *Speech Monographs* 30 (June 1963), 79–91. This nearly 20 year old summary is still a useful source.

Stewart, Charles J. and William B. Cash. *Interviewing: Principles and Practices*. Dubuque, Iowa: Wm. C. Brown, 1978 (paperback). Another excellent book on interviewing.

PART FOUR

PERSUASIVE SPEAKING

Perhaps some of your most important speeches will be those given to persuade. Your study of persuasion presupposes an understanding of fundamentals and informative principles. After the presentation of principles of persuasion, the unit considers the skills of reasoning, motivating, and refuting.

"STOP KILLING THE SEALS!"

"logic plus emotion makes the argument"

"I feel that the slaughter of birds and animals for their furs and feathers in order to satisfy some fashion notion should be totally banned."

Chapter 13 Principles of Persuasive Speaking

Have you ever had a fantasy involving your persuasive powers? You imagine that as a result of a stirring speech given by you war is averted, poverty abolished, or you get a date with that person you have had an eye on for six weeks. Although everything works superbly in our fantasies, our real-life attempts at changing attitudes or modifying behavior are not always so successful. Let us face it: speaking persuasively is perhaps the most demanding of speech challenges. Moreover, there is no formula for success—no set of rules to guarantee effectiveness. In the centuries during which people have been studying the process, however, they have learned to identify many of the variables of persuasion.

In this opening chapter of the persuasive-speaking unit, I want to suggest the modifications and extensions of informative speech preparation that must be made to increase your chances of persuading. Then, in the following three chapters the skills of reasoning, motivating, and refuting will be discussed in detail and speech assignments giving you an opportunity to put those skills into practice will be introduced. For now, we want to deal with the elusive answer to that question: What makes a speech persuasive? A speech is more likely to be persuasive (1) if the specific purpose does not call for too large a change in belief or does not call for action that is contradictory or inconsistent with audience attitude; (2) if the speech uses materials that are logical, emotional, credible, and ethical; (3) if the speech is organized to adapt to audience attitudes; and (4) if the speech is delivered with conviction.

DETERMINING YOUR PURPOSE   Although persuasion may occur unintentionally (merely saying "The team's having a great year, isn't it?" may "persuade" another person to go to a game), persuasive speaking is basically an intentional activity. The successful persuader does not leave the effect of the message to the interpretation of the receiver. The persuasive speaker starts his or her planning with a clearly stated specific purpose firmly in mind.

The persuasive purpose statement, often called a *proposition*, indicates specifically what you want your audience to do or to believe. Ordinarily, the proposition will be phrased in one of three ways; it will be phrased: to *reinforce a belief* held by an audience, to *change a belief* held by an audience, or to *move the audience to act*. Speeches to reinforce a belief (often called *inspirational speeches*) are usually based on the universally held beliefs and values of society. They are likely to grow from the broad-based themes of patriotism, moral-ethical guidelines, and so forth. Thus, "America is the land of opportunity" and "We have the freedom of worship" are examples of such propositions. In both instances, the speaker will try to strengthen a prevailing attitude.

Speeches to change or alter a belief are usually those for which a speaker stands a chance of establishing a logical position in favor of the belief or attitude. The change of belief may provide a springboard for action, but the focus of the speech is on intellectual agreement. "Capital punishment should be reinstated" and "The Ohio State Lottery should be abolished" indicate the purpose of changing the beliefs of the audience. Even though some classmates will favor the propositions before the speech is given, each calls for a change from current policy. Speeches of this kind are often referred to as *speeches to convince*.

Speeches to get action are motivational. The audience may or may not already believe in the logic of the proposition. But the speaker wants more than intellectual agreement—he or she wants us to act. "Buy Easter Seals" and "Eat at the Manor Restaurant" are both propositions of action.

This discussion has already used several words that are basic to an understanding of persuasion. Although you probably know these words and use them frequently, so that we all understand the same meaning, let us examine the definition and application of the words *attitude, belief, value, opinion,* and *behavior*.

Every textbook on persuasion discusses the importance of understanding the meaning of *attitude* and the importance of identifying audience attitude toward a topic. An *attitude* is a predisposition for or against people, places, or things—it is a tendency or an inclination to feel or to believe a certain way. If, for example, I asked you, "What's your attitude toward physical fitness?" you might say, "I think it's important." Attitudes have three essential characteristics: *direction* (from favorable to unfavorable), *intensity* (from strong to weak), and *saliency* (from very important to not-so-important). Your statement of attitude about physical fitness is favorable; it may be a very strongly held attitude or it may be subject to change, and the whole subject might be a minor issue to you even though you used the word *important*.

A *belief* is an acceptance of truth based upon evidence, opinion, and experience. Beliefs are outgrowths of attitudes. Although we use the word *belief* rather loosely, we are likely to *believe* that something is true if someone can prove it to our satisfaction. On the subject of physical fitness, I might believe that keeping in good physical condition increases a person's chances of avoiding heart disease. My belief may be based on statistics and examples that I read in a recent magazine. How are beliefs an outgrowth of attitudes? If I hold a favorable attitude toward physical fitness in general, it will be easier for me to hold a belief that being in good physical condition does in fact lower the likelihood of heart disease.

A *value* is a cluster of attitudes or beliefs. This cluster serves as a guideline for measuring the worth of various aspects of our lives. In practice, we hold economic, aesthetic, social, political, and religious values. Thus a person's attitudes and beliefs about physical fitness may lead to *or* grow from a set of aesthetic or social values. A person who believes in physical fitness may come to value a trim, solid, healthy body; *or* valuing a trim, solid, healthy body may lead to favorable attitudes and beliefs about physical fitness.

An *opinion* is a verbal expression of an attitude, belief, or value. Earlier I used a hypothetical situation in which I asked your attitude about physical fitness. The reply "I think it's important" is an opinion reflecting a favorable attitude.

A *behavior* is an action related to or resulting from a belief, attitude, or value (or some combination of the three). As a result of attitudes, beliefs, and values, the person who believes in the value of physical fitness "works out" at least three times a week in order to stay in good physical condition.

Let us quickly summarize the relationship among these terms: A person has a favorable *attitude* toward physical fitness. Given supporting evidence, the person is willing then to *believe* that good physical condition lowers the likelihood of heart disease. Both the *attitude* and the *belief* fit well into the person's aesthetic and social *values* concerning the human body. In conversation, the person will give the *opinion* that good physical conditioning is in fact important. As a result of these *attitudes* and *beliefs*, the person works out at least three times a week and eats sensibly in order to maintain physical fitness.

The goals of persuasive speeches are usually to change beliefs and bring to action. To be successful, you must take into account the attitudes and values of members of your audience as revealed in their opinions and behaviors. Attitudes can be changed and behavior can be modified, but to expect 180-degree shifts in attitude or behavior as a result of a single speech is unrealistic and probably fruitless. William Brigance, one of the great speech teachers of this century, used to speak of "planting the seeds of persuasion." If we present a modest proposal seeking a slight change in attitude, we may be able to get an audience to think about what we are saying. Then later when the idea begins to grow, we can ask for greater change. For instance, if your audience believes that taxes are too high, you are unlikely to make them believe that they are not. However, you may be able to influence them to see that taxes are not really as high as they originally thought or not as high as other goods and services. Or you may be able to persuade them to support a program that involves even slightly higher taxes.

The more distant your goal is from the focus of audience belief, the more time it will take you to achieve that goal. Major attitude change is more likely to be achieved over a period of time than in a one-shot effort. One author encourages "seeing persuasion as a campaign—a structured sequence of efforts to achieve adoption, continuance, deterrence, or discontinuance."[1] Attitude change is most effective over a long-range, carefully considered program in which each part in the campaign is instrumental in bringing about later effects. Still, much of your speaking allows for only one

---

[1] Wallace Fotheringham, *Perspectives on Persuasion* (Boston: Allyn and Bacon, 1966), p. 34.

effort—and you want to make the most of it. So, we have to look for principles to guide us when we have just one opportunity.

There are two important guidelines for phrasing the specific purpose for a speech of persuasion. A speech is more likely to be persuasive (1) if it does not call for too large a change in belief or (2) if it does not call for action that is contradictory to or inconsistent with prevailing audience attitude.

We consider strategies for coping with audience attitudes and needs in Chapter 15, which deals with motivation. Now let us turn our attention to using the materials of persuasion.

USING MATERIALS OF PERSUASION

The materials of persuasion are the same as those you have used in your informative speeches: the examples, illustrations, statistics, quotations—the facts and the opinions—that you get from surveying your own personal experience, observing, interviewing, and reading. The difference between the materials in informative and in persuasive speeches lies in their use. Whereas in the informative speech the materials are used to explain, clarify, and promote understanding, in the persuasive speech the materials are used to prove and to motivate, to change beliefs, and to bring others to action. These goals are accomplished through materials that provide logical proof, that arouse the emotions, that are perceived as being delivered by a credible source, and that are used ethically. Let us consider each of these in turn.

Logical Proof

We human beings differ from other mammals in that we have powers of reasoning. We take pride in considering ours as a "rational" species. As individual persons, we seldom do anything without some sort of reason. Sometimes these reasons are not clearly articulated—or even realized. Sometimes the reasons we give for our behavior are neither the real ones nor very good ones. Sometimes the reasons we give come after the fact rather than before (this tendency has led some to say that human beings are *rationalizing* creatures). Whether the reasons are good or bad or whether they come before or after the fact, we human beings are not likely to believe or to act unless we have some reason to do so. In your persuasive speeches, then, it is vitally important that you provide reasons. Reasons are statements that give the answer to the question *Why?* For instance, today I am thinking about buying a video tape recorder. Why? Because I could tape public speeches that are televised; because I could record shows that I want to see, but would miss otherwise; because I could be more selective in my television viewing; because stores are having year-end sales and I can get a good price; and because I am in a mood to buy something. These statements I offer in support of buying a video tape recorder are reasons.

Think over one of your actions during the past couple of days. You probably can identify a reason or a set of reasons that impelled you to take that action *or* to explain later why you did it. Did you watch a little television last night? Why? Because you needed a little relaxation? Because the program you watched is almost always good? Because a friend wanted to watch? Because you were bored and had nothing else to do? Each of these is a reason.

If you want to influence other people's beliefs or actions, you must present those people with reasons to modify their beliefs or actions. You must determine a number of possible reasons and choose the ones that seem to you best for persuasion.

How do you compile a list of reasons? Sometimes the reasons will become apparent if you just think about the issue. What are some reasons for buying a video recorder? Let us summarize the ones mentioned earlier:

1. I could tape public speeches that are televised.
2. I could record shows that I would miss otherwise.
3. I could be more selective in my television viewing.
4. I can get a good price now.
5. I am in the mood to buy something.

For most topics you must do more than just think about the issue. Although creative thinking will supply some reasons, others will be suggested by observing, interviewing, and reading. If you wished to give a speech in support of the proposition that the United States should overhaul the welfare system, you might, through thinking and research, arrive at the following list of possible reasons:

1. The welfare system costs too much.
2. The welfare system is inequitable.
3. The welfare system does not help those who need help most.
4. The welfare system has been grossly abused.

5. The welfare system does not encourage people to seek work.

6. The welfare system does not provide means for people to better their lot.

In a speech you cannot use (nor would you want to use) all the reasons you can think of. Remember that any speech should have only two to five main points—for this persuasive speech you want to build upon two to five reasons. This leads to the question: How do you decide which reasons to use? The reasons you decide to use must meet the following three criteria:

1. **The reason must really give support to the proposition.** Sometimes statements look like reasons, but really are not. The statement "I'm in the mood to buy something" is not a good reason in support of buying a video tape recorder.

2. **The reason must itself be supportable.** Some reasons sound very good; but, if they are not supportable, they will not work in the speech. For instance, the reason "The present system has been grossly abused" is a good reason in support of a proposition calling for "overhauling the welfare system." However, if you cannot find, in your reading, material that really indicates *substantial* abuse of the system, then you would not want to use that reason. If you argue that "we should go to The Sternwheeler for dinner," offering as a reason that "the prices are reasonable," you should find material indicating that, in fact, the prices are reasonable. If, however, you discover that most comparable restaurants in the same area as The Sternwheeler offer many of the same dishes at *lower* prices, then you should either drop the reason that "the prices are reasonable" or change the wording of that reason to something like "the slightly higher prices are justified."

You cannot be sure that a reason is supportable until you have done some research. If you think you have a good reason, you may have to work very hard to find the support you need. Nevertheless, if a reason is not itself supportable, you should drop it from consideration.

3. **The reason must be one that will have impact on the intended audience.** Let us say that in support of the statement "We should eat at The Sternwheeler," you consider the reason "The seafood is excellent" and are able to support that reason fully. Nevertheless, "The seafood is excellent" would be a poor reason to use in the

speech if you were aware that most of the people in the audience *did not like seafood!*

A reason will have impact on an audience if it is a reason that the audience is likely to accept. Sometimes you cannot be sure about a reason; but most of the time you can anticipate probable impact by thinking about the nature of your audience. In Chapter 3 we spoke about the importance of good audience analysis—nowhere is that analysis more important than in the selection of the reasons for your speech of persuasion. Go back to the material on pages 45–46 in that chapter. On the basis of your audience analysis, make the final decision as to which reasons you will use in the speech. We analyze reasoning in more depth in Chapter 14.

Emotional Appeals   As we think back over causes for our actions we may hear ourselves saying that something impelled us to act. It is as if something inside of us took control of us and directed our actions. That something is often our emotional response to various stimuli. What is an emotion? *Webster's* says it is a "strong feeling" or a "psychological excitement." We recognize the presence of such emotions as love, sadness, happiness, joy, anxiety, anger, fear, hate, pity, and guilt. We hear ourselves and others say, "I'm feeling anxious about the test," "I feel anger toward him for slighting me," "I feel sad that he's no longer able to work." Many of these emotions we feel are triggered by physical happenings: a dog jumps from behind a tree and frightens us, a friend falls and sprains his ankle and we feel sad, that person puts his or her arm around us and we feel joy. However, emotions are also triggered by words. A person says, "You idiot, what did you do a dumb thing like that for?" and we feel angry. A person says, "I'd love to go with you," and we feel happiness. A friend says, "Go ahead with the gang—I'll be all right alone," and we feel guilty. We are interested in the conscious effort of a speaker to phrase ideas in a way that appeals to the emotions of the audience.

Various researchers[2] have attempted to determine the effect of emotional appeals in persuasive communication. So far, the results of such research have been inconclusive and at times contradic-

---

[2] See Ronald L. Applbaum and Karl W. Anatol, *Strategies for Persuasive Communication* (Columbus, Ohio: Charles E. Merrill, 1974), pp. 102–103, for a summary of conflicting research studies.

tory. The effectiveness of emotional appeals seems to depend a great deal on other related factors, such as mood of the audience, attitude of the audience, and construction of the appeals. My experience has been that the ethical value of emotional appeal is as a supplement to logical proof. Good speech development then is logical-emotional development. I like to look at logic and emotion as inseparable elements within an argument. Thus, we should not look for some additional material that will arouse fear or pity or joy or anger or guilt or love—we should look for a good, logical, supportable argument that will, *if properly phrased,* arouse fear or pity or joy or anger or guilt or love.

Suppose you are to give a speech calling for more humane treatment of the elderly in our society. In the speech, you want to make the point that older people often feel alienated from the society that they worked so many years to support and develop. In so doing, you can present facts and figures to show how many older citizens are not employed, how many are relegated to "old people's homes," how many skills and talents are lost by present procedures. These are all good points. If, in addition, you can cause your listeners to *feel* guilty, to *feel* responsible for treatment of the elderly, and to *feel* sad about that treatment, you can add effective dimension to the material. The role of emotional appeal in a speech is to compel members of the audience to *feel* as well as to *think* about what is being said. This is done by making statements in language that stimulates emotional reactions.

This procedure does not call for you to use emotional appeals the way you use statistics or examples. To think "I'll put in one angry statement here" will not work. Emotional appeal grows out of an emotional climate. You are the catalyst to developing that climate. The best use of emotional appeals comes out of your sincere feelings about the topic. If you can really imagine the elderly suffering from lack of food, money, or shelter; if you can visualize their pleading eyes and constant sad looks; if you can picture living in a world where bare existence is all you dare hope for each day, perhaps you can find the words to describe that feeling to your audience. If you can, you can bring out that feeling in the audience.

Now, emotional appeals can go too far. If we as listeners are too aware of obvious or clumsy attempts to appeal to our emotions, we may put up our defenses so strongly that the appeals have no effect; sometimes, in fact, we may even react in a way that is the opposite of what was intended. A poor try at making us sad may make us laugh.

In Chapter 5, we discussed the means of making language clear, appropriate, and vivid. These language skills are the basis of emotional appeal. You must select the right words, you must speak vividly, and you must involve the audience directly to bring the emotional reactions you seek. In developing a speech with emotional appeal, then, try the following procedure:

1. **Get in touch with your own feelings about the topic.** When you think of the increased bite that taxes take from your pay, or the increase in the number of rapes in the cities, or the success of certain social action programs, do you feel anger? joy? sadness? guilt? pleasure? remorse?

2. **Picture what you see when you are thinking about the topic.** When you think about Barney's restaurant, do you picture a cozy atmosphere? a juicy steak? a dent in your pocketbook? Or when you think about inflation, can you picture the pain of decreased expectations? putting off new purchases? struggling to make ends meet?

3. **Practice describing your feelings and your mental pictures so the audience can get the same feeling or picture.** Your first attempts may be clumsy. However, as you work with your descriptions, you will find yourself speaking more and more vividly. For instance, how would you describe your feelings about what inflation does to your pocketbook?

In your speech, you are likely to find that, in addition to supplementing the logical development of the speech, emotional appeals tend to serve you best in the introduction and the conclusion of the speech. Let us give an example of emotional appeal in each of these situations.

1. **Emotional appeal to supplement logical statements.** Consider each of the following statements:

> Television commercials portray women primarily as housewives whose major thoughts are restricted to the comparative cleanliness of their wash and their floors.

> And tell me, what is a woman as seen through the eyes of a television commercial? Primarily a housewife—a housewife with two deep all-consuming prayers: "Oh, that my clothes will come out white!" and "Oh, that my floors will be spotless!"

Notice that each of the statements makes the same point. Each could then be developed with the same examples, illustrations, or quotations. The difference is that in the second case the phrasing is designed to have an emotional impact.

2.   Emotional appeal in speech introductions and conclusions. Recently a young woman in class began her speech as follows:[3]

> Let's pretend for a moment. Suppose that on the upper righthand corner of your desk there is a button. You have the power, by pushing that button, to quickly and painlessly end the life of one you love: your brother, or sister, or father. This loved one has terminal cancer and will be confined to a hospital for his remaining days. Would you push the button now? His condition worsens. He is in constant pain and he is hooked up to a life-support machine. He first requests, but as the pain increases he pleads for you to help. Now would you push that button? Each day you watch him deteriorate until he reaches a point where he cannot talk, he cannot see, he cannot hear—he is only alive by that machine. Now would you push that button?

After giving reasons for changings our laws on euthanasia, she ended her speech as follows:

> I ask again, how long could you take walking into that hospital room and looking at your brother or father in a coma, knowing he would rather be allowed to die a natural death than to be kept alive in such a degrading manner? I've crossed that doorstep—I've gone into that hospital room, and let me tell you, it's hell. I think it's time we reconsider our laws concerning euthanasia. Don't you?

Regardless of your beliefs about the subject of euthanasia I think you will have to agree with me that you would be inclined to feel the sadness.

A speech that has emotional wallop is going to motivate the audience.

Credibility of Source   Consider the following situation. A group is at an impasse. Several members favor the motion before the group and several are opposed. So far, Jack Edwards has said nothing. In the midst of the heated debate, the chair looks at Edwards and says, "Jack, we haven't heard from you yet—what do you think?" Jack rises, looks

---

[3] Speech on euthanasia delivered in Persuasive Speaking, University of Cincinnati. Portions reprinted by permission of Betsy R. Burke.

slowly from person to person, and says, "I'm convinced we should go ahead." As if by magic, a solidarity can be sensed in the group. The chair says, "Are we ready to vote? All those in favor say aye"; and the group votes its unanimous support.

What happened? Before Edwards's statement, the group was stalemated in heated debate. Jack Edwards presented no information, offered no reasons, made no emotional pleas—he did nothing but state his support for the motion. Then why did the group vote as they did? The group considered Edwards as an opinion leader, a person of high status—in short, they saw him as a credible source whose words were worth heeding.

I think that this is not a far-fetched example. It may be more dramatic than most instances of its kind, but in every group, however large or small, there are some members whose opinions carry far more weight than those of others. When we identify such a person (or persons), we are inclined to let our behaviors be directed (or at least influenced) by opinions expressed by that person. I have given money to a particular charity because my best friend asked me to; I have voted for a particular plan because a person I trusted favored it; I did what certain of my professors asked, without question, because I respected their competence to suggest what was best for me—and I imagine that you have behaved similarly.

The Greeks had a word for this concept—they called it *ethos.* Whether we call it ethos, image, charismatic effect, or the word I prefer—credibility—the effect is the same: Almost all studies confirm that speaker credibility has a major effect on audience belief and attitude.[4]

Why are people willing to take the word of someone else on various issues? Since it is impossible for us to know all there is to know about everything (and even if it were *possible,* few of us would be willing to spend the time and effort), we seek shortcuts in our decision making—we rely on the judgment of others. Our thinking often goes something like this: Why take the time to learn about the new highway when someone we trust tells us it is in our best interest? Why take the time to try every restaurant in town when someone we rely on tells us that Barney's is the best? Why

---

[4] Kenneth E. Andersen and Theodore Clevenger, Jr., "A Summary of Experimental Research in Ethos," *Speech Monographs* 30 (1963), 59–78.

take time to study the candidates when our best friend tells us to vote for Smith for council representative? Each of us places trust in certain people in order to take shortcuts in our decision making.

How do we determine on whom we will rely? Is it blind faith? No, the presence (or our *perception* of the presence) of certain qualities will make the possessor a *high credibility* source. Although aspects of credibility differ somewhat in every analysis of that quality, most analyses include competence, intention, character, and personality.

Competence is a quality that commands our respect. Your admiration of your favorite professor may be based on his or her competence. Although all professors are supposed to know what they are talking about, some are better able to project this quality in their speaking. What they say "makes sense" in comparison to all we have read or heard; likewise, we believe people are competent when they can give factual support for their statements. In a school setting competence may also be perceived by the belief that a person knows far more than he or she is telling us now. For instance, when a student interrupts with a question, the competent professor has no difficulty in discussing the particular point in more detail—perhaps by giving another example, or by telling a story, or by referring the student to additional reading on the subject. Perhaps most of all, our judgment of competence is based on a past record. If we discover that what a person has told us in the past is true, we will tend to believe what the person tells us now.

A second important aspect of credibility is *intention*. People's intentions or motives are particularly important in determining whether another person will like them, trust them, have respect for them, or believe them. For instance, you know that clothing salespersons are trying to sell you the garments they help you try on, so when they say to you, "This is perfect for you," you may well question their intentions. On the other hand, if a bystander looks over at you and exclaims, "Wow, you really look good in that!" you are likely to accept the statement at face value because the bystander has no reason to say anything—the person's intentions are likely to be good. The more positively you view the intentions of the person, the more credible his or her words will seem to you. A past record of consideration for others builds confidence in a speaker; a past record of selfishness makes us question the speaker's motives.

A third important aspect of credibility is *character*. Character is sometimes defined as what a person is made of. We believe in people who have a past record of honesty, industry, and trustworthiness. Notice, however, that now we are not asking whether our professor knows the subject matter; instead, we are judging the professor as a person. Would he or she give good advice on a personal problem? Prepare an exam that is a good test of our knowledge? Grade us on what we do and not on extraneous factors? Judging another's character comes down to our basic respect for the individual.

The fourth important aspect of credibility is *personality* (called *dynamism* by some). Sometimes we have a strong "gut reaction" about a person based solely on a first impression. Some people strike us as being friendly, warm, nice to be around. Some would argue that personality or likeability is the most important of all aspects of credibility. Whether we are talking about public speakers or people we meet at a party, we make a judgment about whether we like them. If we do, we are more likely to buy their ideas or products. If we do not, we are likely to shun them.

Credibility is not something that you can gain overnight or turn off or on at your whim. Nevertheless, you can avoid damaging your credibility and perhaps even strengthen it somewhat during a speech or series of speeches. You will probably see the cumulative effect of credibility during this term. As your class proceeds from speech to speech, some members will grow in stature in your mind and others will diminish. Being ready to speak on time, approaching the assignment with a positive attitude, showing complete preparation for each speech, giving thoughtful evaluation of others' speeches, and demonstrating sound thinking—all of these contribute to classroom credibility. Some people earn the right to speak and to be heard. Having once earned that right, they command the confidence of their listeners. Others never earn the right, and nothing they do will have a very real, lasting effect on their audience. Think about how you are representing yourself to your audience. What kind of a person are you projecting to the class? Credibility is an important means of persuasion.

Although credibility takes time to build, there are some things you can do during your speech. Personality and character are projections of what you are, but competence and intention can be demonstrated by what you say. How do you illustrate your competence and your intention? You should try to establish your credentials during the speech. A few sentences of explanation of your point of view, your concern, or your understanding may make a big difference. For instance, if you were speaking on prison reform, you might say, "I read articles about conditions in prisons, but before I came before you with any suggestions, I wanted to see for myself, so I spent two days observing at. . . ." Assuming you had visited the prison, this short statement would help to increase your credibility with the audience. Or to show the amount of work you have done you might say, "I had intended to read a few articles to prepare for this speech, but once I began, I became fascinated with the subject. I hope word doesn't get around to my other teachers, but quite frankly this past week I've put everything else aside to try to find the most accurate information I could." Or a speaker might show fairness by saying "It would be easy for me to say we could get by without new taxes—such a move might get me elected, but I just don't see any way out of new taxes."

The key to the effectiveness of these and similar statements is the honesty of your representation. Whereas an arrogant, know-it-all approach will often backfire, a short, honest statement of qualifications, experience, or ability may build your speaker credibility.

Ethics in Persuasion   In the short run, success may be achieved by any means, but persuasion is more likely to have a lasting effect if it is ethical. In the final analysis, we must ask whether our efforts are within the limits of the ethical standards set by society. Often when we believe strongly in the righteousness of our cause, we are faced with the temptation of bowing to the belief that the end justifies the means—or to put it into blunt English, that we can do *anything* to achieve our goals. As we observe the world around us, we are all well aware of the many people who have ridden roughshod over the moral or ethical principles operating within the society. Yet, just when we appear to be ready to give up on humanity, something happens that proves that a society does set and observe ethical limits.

Ethics are the standards of moral conduct that determine our behavior. Ethics include both how we ourselves act and how we expect others to act. Whether or how we punish those who fail to meet our standards says a great deal about the importance we ascribe to our ethics. Although ethical codes are personal, society has a code of ethics that operates on at least the verbal level within that society. In Chapter 1, we outlined the major ethical responsibilities of the speaker. In this section we want to look at specific behaviors that affect your persuasive speaking.

What is your code of ethics? The following five points reflect the standards of hundreds of students that I have encountered in my classes during the past few years. I believe that these five make an excellent starting point in helping you determine your standards. These are not rules someone made up. They are statements of attitudes held by large numbers of individuals within our society.

1. **Lying is unethical.** Of all the attitudes about ethics, this is the one most universally held. When people *know* they are being lied to, they usually reject the ideas of the speaker; if they find out later, they often look for ways to punish the speaker who lied to them.

2. **Name calling is unethical.** Again, there seems to be an almost universal agreement on this attitude. Even though many people name-call in their interpersonal communication, they say they regard the practice by public speakers as unethical.

3. **Grossly exaggerating or distorting facts is unethical.** Although some people seem willing to accept "a little exaggeration" as human nature, when the exaggeration is defined as "gross" or "distortion," most people regard it as lying. Because the line between "some" exaggeration and "gross" exaggeration or "distortion" is often so difficult to distinguish, many people see *any* exaggeration as unethical.

4. **Damning people or ideas without divulging the source of the damning material is unethical.** Where ideas originate is often as important as the ideas themselves. And although a statement may be true regardless of whether a source is given, people want more than the speaker's word when a statement is damning. If you are going to discuss the wrongdoing of a person or the stupidity of an idea by relying on the words or ideas of others, you must be prepared to share the sources of those words or ideas.

5. **Suppression of key information is unethical.** If you have material to support your views, you should present it; if you have a motive that affects your view, you should divulge it. An audience has a right to this information—its members have the right to make a choice, but they must have the information in order to exercise that right.

Remember, these are but starting points in your consideration of ethical standards. Effective speaking should be ethical speaking.

ORGANIZING TO ADAPT TO YOUR AUDIENCE

Although the nature of your material and your own inclination may affect your organization, the most important consideration is expected audience reaction. Let us first look at means of classifying audience reaction and then at various organizational patterns.

Classifying Audience Reaction

Earlier in this chapter we defined attitude in terms of direction, strength, and saliency (importance). Since much of your success depends on the kind of audience you face for the particular speech, you must find out whether the members favor your proposition, to what degree they favor it, and how important their attitude is to them. Audience attitude may be distributed along a continuum from hostile to highly in favor (see Figure 13-1). Even though any given audience may have one or a few members at nearly every point of the distribution, audience attitude will tend to cluster at a particular point on the continuum.

Except for polling the audience, there is no way of being sure about your assessment. However, by examining the data in the way described in Chapter 3, you will be able to make reasonably accurate estimates. For instance, skilled workers are likely to look at minimum wage proposals differently from business executives; men will look at women's rights proposals differently from women; Protestants are likely to look at property tax levy for schools differently from Catholics. The more data you have about your audience and the more experience you have in analyzing audiences, the better are your chances of judging their attitudes relatively accurately. By and large, a very precise differentiation of opinion is not necessary.

Through a sample of attitude, an insight into audience behavior, or a good guess, you can place your audience in one of the

FIGURE 13-1

| Hostile | Opposed | Mildly Opposed | Neutral, No Opinion, Uninformed | Mildly in Favor | In Favor | Highly in Favor |

following classifications: *no opinion*—either no information or no interest; *in favor*—already holding a particular belief; *opposed*—holding an opposite point of view. These classifications may overlap. Since you will, however, have neither the time nor the opportunity to present a line of development that will adapt to all possible attitudes within the audience, you should assess the prevailing attitude and knowledge and work from there.

NO OPINION   With some topics, your audience will have no opinion. Often this lack of opinion results from a lack of knowledge on the subject. Suppose you wanted to persuade the class "that elementary schools should explore the feasibility of ungraded primary schools." Unless your class is composed of prospective elementary teachers, only a few will know what an ungraded primary school is. Even those who know the term may not have enough knowledge to formulate an opinion. In this instance, yours will be a problem of instruction before you can hope to create a favorable attitude. Since they lack preconceived biases, you can usually approach uninformed listeners directly. If you can show enough advantages to meet their requirements, you have a good chance of persuading them. Despite this advantage, you may have the burden of trying to explain, which must precede argumentation. If you have only five minutes to speak and it takes that long to explain the program, you will have a very difficult time creating any attitudes.

A lack of audience opinion may also result from apathy. When apathy is the problem but knowledge does exist, you can spend your entire time in motivation. Although an apathetic audience is difficult to motivate, you will have nearly the entire speech time to create interest and commitment. An apathetic audience presents a challenge and an opportunity for the persuasive speaker.

IN FAVOR   In your analysis, you may find that the audience is already favorably disposed toward the proposition. Although this sounds like an ideal situation, it carries with it many hazards. When an audience is already in favor, they are seldom interested in a rehash of familiar material and reasons. Because of an ill-considered approach, a favorable audience can become hostile or apathetic to you as a speaker—a result as undesirable as negative commitment. If your campus is typical, a common complaint is the lack of on-campus parking. The subject matter of a speech in favor of increased parking space would, therefore, already be accepted. In situations of this kind, the best line of argument is to develop a specific course of action satisfying the felt need. A speech on the need for an underground garage or a high-rise parking garage on a present site or a new system of determining priority would build on the existing audience attitude. The presentation of a well-thought-out specific solution increases the potential for action. In summary, when you believe your listeners are on your side, do not just echo their beliefs. Try to crystallize their attitudes, recommit them to their direction of thought, and bring the group to some meaningful action that will help solve or alleviate the problem.

OPPOSED   With many of the kinds of propositions that call for a change in existing attitudes and procedures, your audience attitude may range from slightly negative to thoroughly hostile. Such a range of negative attitudes requires a slightly different handling. For instance, with the proposition "The United States is spending too much for space exploration," most people have an opinion. Since this is a debatable proposition, about half the audience will probably be at least slightly negative. The other half may be slightly favorable to strongly favorable. Usually, the best way to proceed is with the generalization that your listeners can be persuaded to your point of view if you can give good reasons and if you can motivate them. A straightforward, logically sound speech may convince those who are only slightly negative and will not alienate those who already agree with you.

However, suppose the topic were "The federal government should guarantee a minimum annual income to all its citizens." With this proposition, there is an excellent chance that most of the audience will be negative to hostile. Hostile audiences can seldom be persuaded with one speech. In fact, a hostile audience may well turn itself off when it hears the topic. To get this kind of an audience even to listen requires a great deal of motivation. If you have done a good job, you will be able to plant the seeds of persuasion. Next week, next month, or even next year, one or more members of that audience might well come to your way of thinking—but do not expect too much to happen during the speech.

Methods of Organization   The goal of a good persuasive speech organization is to organize the materials in such a way that they maximize the probability of success with the particular audience. As we consider various possible organizations, we will consider the audience attitude for which the organization seems most appropriate.

STATEMENT-OF-REASONS METHOD We first outlined the statement-of-reasons method on page 69 when we were talking about standard patterns of organization. In summary, the statement-of-reasons method is a topic order in which each main point is a statement of a reason that justifies the proposition. When you believe your audience has no opinion on the subject, is apathetic, or perhaps is only mildly in favor or mildly opposed, the straightforward topical statement of reasons may be your best organization. (To illustrate the similarities and differences in organization, the same subject, supporting the part of the population living in poverty, will be used in examples to show the various methods of organization.)

Specific Purpose: To convince the audience that a minimum annual cash income should be guaranteed to families living below the poverty income level.

    I. A minimum cash income would guarantee every family a living income.

    II. A minimum cash income would be the same regardless of where the person lived.

    III. A minimum cash income would be easy to administer.

COMPARATIVE-ADVANTAGES METHOD As you look at your list of reasons, you may see that the best reasons can be phrased as advantages over the procedure that is now in practice or the procedure most people consider. This being so, the best organization may be a statement of reasons in comparative-advantage form. What is the present system for dealing with the segment of Americans living below the poverty level? We have a welfare system. Your reasons may show that a guaranteed minimum cash income would be better than the welfare system. If so, you might want to organize your speech as follows:

Specific Purpose: To convince the audience that a minimum annual cash income should be guaranteed to families living below the poverty income level.

I. A minimum cash income is more equitable than the welfare system.

II. A minimum cash income is less likely to be abused than the welfare system.

III. A minimum cash income will cost less money than the welfare system.

The comparative-advantages method is also a good organization when the audience agrees with you that something needs to be done—the issue is how to do it. For instance, we all take some of our clothes to a dry cleaner—either a regular or a do-it-yourself establishment. If you were trying to get us to take our clothes to Ace Dry Cleaners, you would perhaps try to show how it is better. Your speech might develop the following two advantages:

I. Ace always does the little bit extra for no additional charge.

II. Ace gives students a 10 percent discount.

The comparative-advantages method works well when there is agreement that something needs to be done or when the audience is neutral, apathetic, or only slightly for or against the proposition.

THE PROBLEM-SOLUTION METHOD We outlined the problem-solution method on page 70 when we were talking about standard patterns of organization. The problem-solution method is always organized to show (1) that there is a problem that requires a change in attitude or action, (2) that the proposal you have to offer will solve the problem, and (3) that your proposal is the best solution to the problem. Let us see how the problem-solution method works on the specific purpose we are considering:

Specific Purpose: To convince the audience that a minimum annual cash income should be guaranteed to families living below the poverty income level.

I. Nearly 20 percent of the people in the United States are living on incomes below the poverty level of $6,000.

II. A guaranteed cash income would eliminate the problem of poverty with these people.

III. A guaranteed cash income is a much better solution than the present welfare system.

Each of the main points could of course be developed with additional subpoints in the speech outline.

A problem-solution method is especially good when you believe you are dealing with a rational audience that is not hostile to your proposition. The neutral, apathetic, or only slightly pro or con audience is also likely to hear you out.

CRITERIA-SATISFACTION METHOD   In some situations, particularly with hostile audiences, you may find it to your advantage to establish audience agreement—a yes-response—before you attempt to present the proposition and reasons. Although reasons are still the basis for the persuasion, the preliminary statement of criteria is essential to the method.

Specific Purpose: To convince the audience that a minimum annual cash income should be guaranteed to families living below the poverty income level.

I. We all want a system of dealing with the nation's poor that we can support.
   A. We want a system that is equitable.
   B. We want a system that is truly helpful.
   C. We want a system that is subject to the least amount of abuse.
II. A minimum annual cash income is a system we can all support.
   A. A minimum annual cash income is equitable.
   B. A minimum annual cash income is helpful.
   C. A minimum annual cash income is difficult to abuse.

THE NEGATIVE METHOD   The other method that is particularly effective for hostile audiences is the negative method. In this, you show that something must be done but that the alternative suggestions just will not work. Of course, this method will work only when the audience must select one of the alternatives.

To persuade a hostile audience to support a minimum cash income, you might develop your speech as follows:

Specific Purpose: To convince the audience that a minimum annual cash income should be guaranteed to families living below the poverty income level.

I. The present system of state welfare is not really solving the problems of the poor.
II. An overhauled system of state welfare still would not work to solve the problems of the poor.
III. A negative income tax system would not work to solve all the problems of the poor.
IV. A minimum annual cash income, the only other reasonable choice, would solve the problems of the poor.

The negative method works best when you have excellent material to show that the other reasonable choices cannot or will not work. A topic that seems particularly suited to this method is one like the following:

Specific Purpose: To convince the audience that taxes must be increased to provide the state with needed services.

I. Saving money by reducing services will not help us.
II. The federal government will not help us.
III. The state government will not help us.
IV. All we have left is to raise taxes.

PROJECTING CONVICTION

Effective delivery for persuasion is no different from effective speaking for any speech. Still, because delivery is so important it is worth a moment to focus on one key aspect of delivery that is especially relevant to persuasion: The effective persuader shows conviction about the subject. With some people, conviction is shown through considerable animation. With others, it is shown through a quiet intensity. However it is shown, though, it must be perceived by the audience. If the audience does not perceive some visual or auditory sign of conviction, what you say is likely to be suspect. If you really do have a strong conviction about the subject, there is a good chance that your voice and your bodily action will reflect it.

At the beginning of this chapter we said that no formula for success could be given. However, we have discussed certain principles that can serve as guidelines for your procedure. Let us summarize these basic principles in terms of steps of preparation:

1.   Determine a specific statement of the belief or action you seek.

2.   Gather the materials you will use ethically to develop your credibility, prove your points, and arouse the emotions of your audience.

3.   Organize your speech following some pattern that adapts to the prevailing audience attitude.

4.   Deliver your speech with conviction.

The assignment that follows is appropriate for several situations: (1) as an assignment for a persuasive speech when time permits only a single persuasive speech assignment for the term; (2) as a diagnostic persuasive speech assignment that precedes one or more of the skills assignments that follow; or (3) as a final assignment for the persuasive speech unit to be given after students have practiced with one or more of the following chapter assignments.

Assignment   *Prepare a four- to seven-minute persuasive speech. An outline is required. Criteria for evaluation will include appropriateness of proposition to this audience's needs, interests, or attitudes; quality of information provided to explain the proposal, to demonstrate speaker credibility, to prove soundness of argument, and to motivate; clarity and appropriateness of organization; and convincing delivery.*

Outline: Persuasive Speech (4–7 minutes)

Specific Purpose: To persuade the audience of their need to be aware of the symptoms of Reye's Syndrome.

Introduction

I. On Tuesday evening in February 1979, seven-year-old Carrie Anne felt feverish.
    A. As time went on, her condition worsened.
    B. Dissatisfied with the prescribed treatment, her mother called Children's Hospital.

  II. What followed was a living nightmare.
     A. Within thirty-five minutes of her arrival at Children's, Carrie had a spinal, a liver biopsy, X rays, multiple blood tests, and an IV.
     B. The doctors diagnosed her as having Reye's Syndrome.
       1. Many recover—some with permanent brain or liver damage.
       2. Forty percent die!
 III. Carrie is my daughter—she recovered.
 IV. But such is not the case with most Reye's patients.

Thesis Statement: You must be aware of the symptoms of Reye's Syndrome because you cannot count on a correct diagnosis from a regular doctor and because medication for the illness being treated masks the potential real problem.

Body
  I. You cannot always count on your child's doctor to make a correct diagnosis.
     A. In Carrie's case the doctor believed she had chicken pox—he had seen it hundreds of times.
       1. Carrie's mother wanted another opinion.
       2. We were lucky she did.
     B. According to the Center for Disease Control, Reye's is frequently misdiagnosed.
       1. It acts like many other diseases.
       2. It is most often mistaken for chicken pox encephalitis, post influenza encephalitis, hepatitis, and drug reaction.
     C. It is estimated that for every reported case there are two or three unreported because of misdiagnosis.
     D. It is impossible to estimate the total number of cases and deaths because of the similarity of symptoms with other diseases.
  II. Medication that is taken for the assumed disease masks the potential real disease.
     A. When accurate diagnosis is made, it is often too late.
     B. Death can occur in just three days.

Conclusion
  I. Be aware of the symptoms.
  II. My daughter is alive today because of her mother's suspicion.

III. Two weeks after Carrie's dismissal her five-year-old brother was admitted.
   A. This time we were aware—we rushed him to the hospital immediately.
   B. Had we waited we might not have been as lucky the second time.

Read the following speech aloud.[5] Then, analyze it on the basis of reasoning and evidence, motivation, and speaker credibility. After you have read and analyzed the speech refer to the analysis in the other column.

Analysis

This narrative opening both gains attention and leads into the nature of the problem being considered.

Notice how the drama is built through specifics, vivid language, and suspense.

Speech: Reye's Syndrome

On a Tuesday evening in February 1979, seven-year-old Carrie Anne felt feverish. Her mother put her to bed that night and when she awoke Wednesday morning with chicken pox, her parents thought, "Just another childhood disease—nothing to be alarmed about. It will run its course." Thursday and Friday Carrie played at home with her brother Albert. Saturday afternoon she began to vomit. Her mother called the doctor. He said, "It's nothing to worry about." Carrie vomited through the night. Sunday morning when she awoke, she was near dehydration; her lips were cracked and bleeding; she was listless; she was combative. Her mother called the doctor again. He said, "It's chicken pox in the stomach lining; I'll send her out some medication to stop the vomiting." But her mother was not satisfied with that answer. She wanted another opinion. She called Children's Hospital and described the symptoms. They said it may be Reye's Syndrome, "Bring her to the hospital immediately." What followed was a living nightmare. A team of doctors awaited Carrie at the hospital. Within thirty-five minutes of her arrival they had done a spinal tap; they had done a liver biopsy; they had done multiple blood tests; they had X-rayed her; they had started an IV; and they had admitted her to the intensive care unit. The doctors approached her parents and said, "Your daughter has Reye's Syndrome. We do not know its cause—we do not know its cure. She has a 30 percent chance of nearly complete recovery; a 30 percent chance

---

[5] Delivered in Speech class, University of Cincinnati. Printed by permission of William G. Cherrington.

of permanent brain or liver damage; and a 40 percent chance of dying. Luckily, you got her in quickly—but we'll know nothing for forty-eight hours."

Carrie is my daughter. She lived. She had minimal memory loss—the only side effect. Today, Carrie studies hard; she brings home good grades. We were lucky. But such is not the case with many Reye's patients. Don't hope for luck. We don't know the cause or cure, but we know that if the child is brought in for treatment quickly enough, doctors have a chance to save the child. But, you must be aware—you must know the symptoms. Why? for many reasons.

First, because you cannot count on your pediatrician to diagnose Reye's Syndrome. They just are not familiar enough with it. Doctors treat thousands of children each year, but they may never see a case of Reye's Syndrome. In Carrie's case the doctor believed that she had chicken pox in the stomach. Luckily her mother felt something else was wrong. She wanted a second opinion.

According to the Ohio Department of Health Center for Disease Control, Reye's Syndrome is often misdiagnosed. It's diagnosed as chicken pox encephalitis, post influenza encephalitis, hepatitis, and drug reaction. For every reported case of Reye's Syndrome there are likely to be two or three unreported cases. Dr. John Parton, Head of the Reye's research at Childrens' Hospital told me it was impossible to estimate the actual number of Reye's Syndrome cases or resulting deaths because of the frequent misdiagnosis.

Yet there is another reason why you must be aware of the symptoms. Speed of diagnosis is essential. Reye's Syndrome usually follows a viral infection. We as parents may feel that even though our child may appear to be worsening, since the child is on medication, the disease, whatever it is, will run its course. As a result, precious time is lost. According to the National Reye's Syndrome

---

This startling revelation had tremendous impact on the audience.

Nothing is more powerful than personal involvement. But it does not take near tragedy to make material worth sharing. If you have firsthand information, don't be reluctant to share it. It is not likely to be as dramatic as the information in this speech, but use of personal information will make you more "human" and will add to overall effectiveness.

Although the personal-experience approach continues throughout the speech, there is plenty of factual information presented.

This speech is an excellent example of how speaker credibility can affect an audience. The audience was held spellbound throughout as a result of a strong feeling of empathy with the speaker—but equally important, the experience added to the audience's sense of speaker competence, which further added to credibility.

Speech blends logical information, emotional appeal, and credibility quite well.

Foundation, in a nine-year study there's no child that has reached what they call stage five of the disease that has lived. The disease progresses rapidly—these final stages come within a matter of days.

We must be aware of the symptoms: persistent or recurrent vomiting, listlessness, personality change, disorientation or confusion, delirium and/or convulsions.

This is a picture of my daughter. We are lucky. She is alive today because her mother suspected something was wrong. She never suspected Reye's, but we still got her to the hospital in time.

Just two weeks after Carrie's dismissal from the hospital, her five-year-old brother was admitted—also with Reye's Syndrome. This time we were aware of the symptoms. At first sign we got him to the hospital, and he too recovered. When Al was admitted to the hospital his motor senses were impaired; he could not walk. Today, I manage his knothole team just to watch him run.

In total this is a powerful persuasive speech. Perhaps too powerful, for it may give the impression that good persuasion can come only from such dramatic circumstances. If that is your perception, I ask you to reread the speech to be more aware of the speaker's use of the dramatic material. I have heard many speeches that grew from dramatic circumstances that were dull and unimpressive speeches. In this case, the speaker maximizes the power of the material to give very good reason for being alert to the possibility of Reye's Syndrome. A really persuasive speech is a combination of good material and careful development.

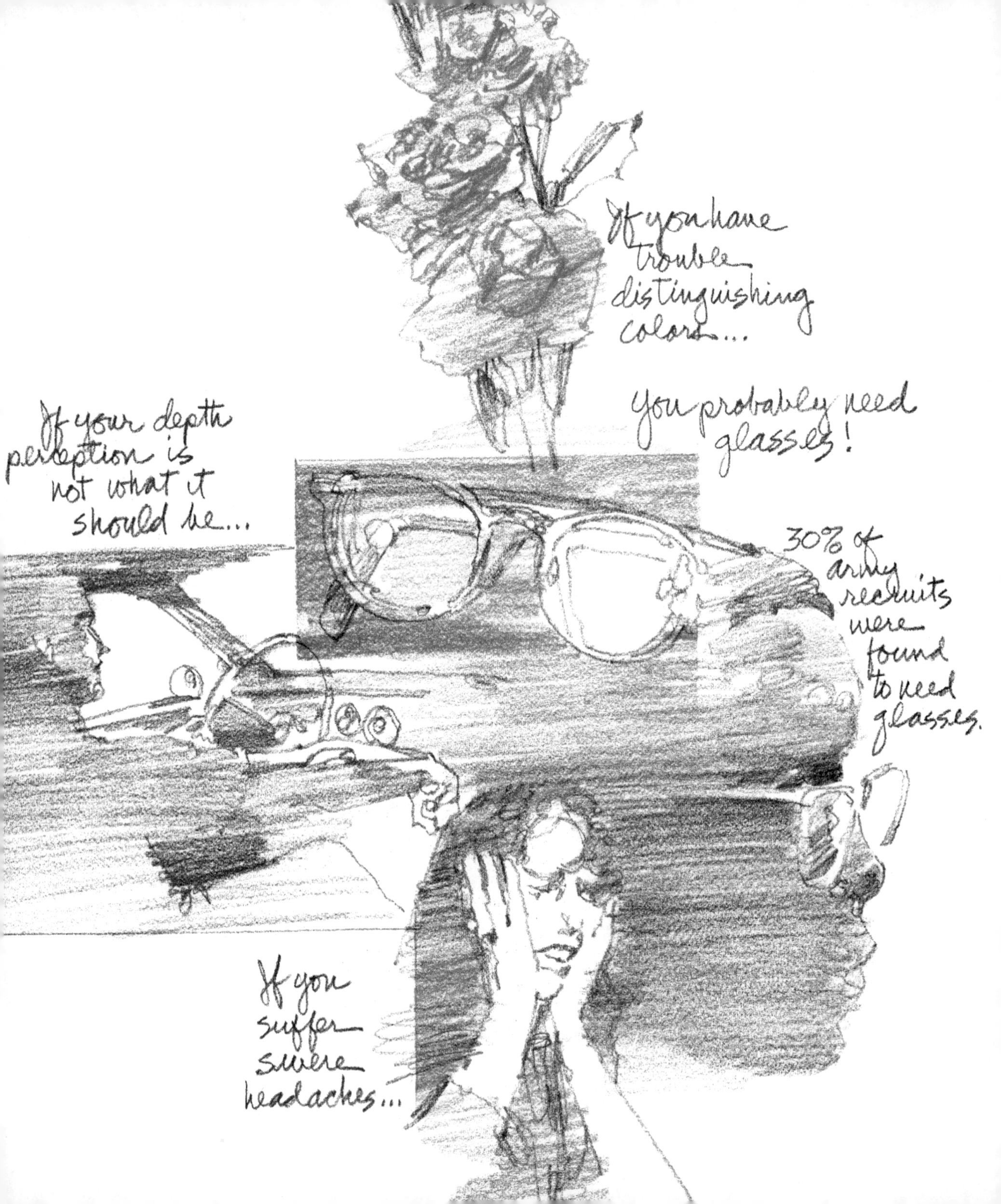

If you have trouble distinguishing colors...
You probably need glasses!
If your depth perception is not what it should be...
30% of army recruits were found to need glasses.
If you suffer severe headaches...

Chapter 14 Reasoning with Audiences: Speeches of Conviction

When Lyndon Johnson was president, he often began his discussions with colleagues by saying, "Let's reason together." In a public speaking context "reasoning" with an audience means presenting arguments and evidence in support of your proposition. The goal of your reasoning? To achieve conviction—to get your audience to believe that what you say is true on the basis of the power of the argument.

In this chapter we define reasoning, look at the means of analyzing reasoning, examine the formation and testing of typical speech arguments, and then, for practical application of the principles, we discuss a speech-of-conviction assignment that requires presentation of sound arguments.

REASONING DEFINED

Reasoning is the process of drawing inferences from facts *or* proving propositions with arguments and facts. We draw inferences to help determine our attitudes and behaviors; we form arguments to convince others of the soundness of those attitudes and behaviors. Let us consider this relationship between drawing inferences and forming arguments.

Suppose that as you drive to school you become aware that the car is "missing" at slow speeds and stalling at lights. You think to yourself that gas mileage has been below normal lately, and the car has not seemed nearly as peppy as it should. As you think about these things, you *reason* to draw some conclusion from the information you have available. You say to yourself, "I think the car needs a tune-up." From these facts and opinions, you become convinced that the car needs a tune-up.

Further, suppose that to get the money for a tune-up you have to convince your wife, husband, father, mother, or whoever is in charge of the purse strings that the car does in fact need a tune-up. Now you use the product of your reasoning to form the arguments you will use to convince that other person. You state your proposition as "The car needs a tune-up." Your arguments are the reasons and evidence you use in support of that proposition. Specifically, you argue: that (1) the car is "missing" at slow speeds; (2) it is stalling at lights; (3) it is getting lower mileage than usual; and (4) it is not nearly as peppy as usual. With each of the reasons you present, you supply appropriate facts and figures in support.

ANALYZING REASONING
Whether you draw inferences from facts or whether you form arguments with facts in support, you need a method of examining the reasoning process. The method we suggest is to break the reasoning process down into its three essentials—data, conclusion, and warrant—and lay the three essentials out on paper. Although in our discussion we present a rather traditional analysis of the types of reasoning, we show the nature of the process using the diagrammatic method developed by Stephen Toulmin.[1]

Data are the evidence, assumptions, or assertions that provide the basis for a conclusion. In the car example, the data are: "missing at slow speeds," "stalling at lights," "lower gas mileage than usual," and "lack of pep." The *conclusion* is the product of the reasoning, the inference drawn, or the inference to be proved. In our example, the conclusion is "the car needs a tune-up." The *warrant* is a statement denoting the substantive relationship between data and conclusion. It is the verbal statement of the reasoning. Now, you will need to think carefully about the warrant, because it is the key that shows how the conclusion follows from the data that have been presented. The warrant is usually implied rather than stated, but before we can test the soundness of the reasoning, the warrant must actually be stated. If you find that you cannot word a sentence that shows how the conclusion follows from the data, the reasoning may well be fallacious. How can the

---

[1] This analysis is based on the ideas set forth by Stephen Toulmin, *The Uses of Argument* (Cambridge, England: Cambridge University Press, 1958).

warrant be stated for the car example? One way would be to say that "missing at slow speeds, stalling at lights, lower gas mileage than usual, and lack of pep are all signs of a need of a tune-up."

To examine reasoning critically it is valuable to set the entire example down on paper so that you can look at each part carefully. Using (D) for data, stated or observed; (C) for conclusion; (W) for warrant; and an arrow to show the direction of the reasoning, our example could be set down on paper as follows:

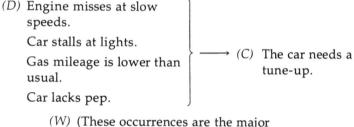

(D) Engine misses at slow
    speeds.

    Car stalls at lights.

    Gas mileage is lower than
    usual.

    Car lacks pep.

        ⟶ *(C)* The car needs a
                tune-up.

    (W) (These occurrences are the major
       signs of a need for a tune-up.)

The warrant is written in parentheses because it is implied rather than actually stated. The warrant, then, indicates how you arrived at the conclusion from the data supplied.

So far you have seen how you can lay out a unit of reasoning. Now you need to see how you can test the essentials in order to judge the validity of the reasoning.

The tests you apply to reasoning are twofold. First you test the data. For a logical conclusion to follow, the data must be sufficient in quantity and quality. If either no data or insufficient data are presented, you must supply more; if the data are inaccurate, biased, or from a questionable source, the conclusion will be suspect. If you are satisfied that "engine misses," "car stalls," "low gas mileage," and "lack of pep" are accurate, you can examine the logic of the warrant. The warrant is tested by casting it as a yes-or-no question: "Is it true that engine missing, stalling at lights, low gas mileage, and lack of pep are the major indications for a tune-up?" If the answer is yes, the reasoning is sound; if the answer is no, the reasoning process is fallacious.

Analyzing reasoning schematically in the data-conclusion-warrant framework does not ensure the infallibility of the logic. However, if you take the time to write the process out in this manner and ask whether the warrant is supported by research, the chances of discovering illogical reasoning are increased considerably.

FORMS OF ARGUMENT

Although a number of different kinds of warrants can be phrased, most of the arguments you will use in your speeches can be placed under six headings. Five of the headings may be classified as inductive; the other is deductive. Inductive reasoning forms have in common a conclusion based on "pattern or resemblance."[2] We determine what was true in the past, and then we predict that something similar will be true in the present or future. The conclusions of inductive arguments are tested on the basis of probability. That is, we predict that the conclusion will be true most of the time. The higher the probability (the closer to 100 percent), the better the argument. Deductive patterns, on the other hand, move from premises to conclusions. If the premises are true, then the conclusion is not just probable as in inductive argument, but *certain*. Since most of our everyday reasoning is inductive we look first at generalization, analogy, causation, sign, and definition; then we look at deduction.

Generalization

In reasoning by *generalization* we say that what is true in some instances is true in all instances (or at least enough instances to validate the generalization). One or more minor exceptions to the generalization do not necessarily invalidate it. If, however, exceptions prove to be more than rare or isolated instances, the validity of the generalization is open to serious question. The following illustrates an argument by generalization about athletic programs in Ohio:

Athletic programs in Ohio universities are losing propositions.

 I. Miami U. lost substantial amounts of money in its athletic program.

 II. Ohio U. lost substantial amounts of money in its athletic program.

---

[2] Howard Kahane, *Logic and Contemporary Rhetoric*, 3d ed. (Belmont, Calif.: Wadsworth, 1980), p. 10.

III. Cincinnati U. lost substantial amounts of money in its athletic program.

Now let us lay the generalization argument out diagrammatically to test the reasoning:

(D) Miami U. lost substantial amounts of money in its athletic program.

Ohio U. lost substantial amounts of money in its athletic program.

Cincinnati U. lost substantial amounts of money in its athletic program.

→ *(C)* Athletic programs in Ohio universities are losing propositions.

(W) (What is true in representative universities in the state will be true in all universities.)

A generalization warrant (the verbal statement of the reasoning process) may be tested by asking these questions:

Are enough instances cited? Are Miami, Ohio, and Cincinnati enough universities? Since instances cited should represent most to all possible, enough must be cited to satisfy the listeners that the instances are not isolated or hand picked.

Are the instances typical? Are the three Ohio universities typical of all universities in Ohio? "Typical" means that the instances cited must be similar to or representative of most or all within the category. If instances are not typical, they do not support the generalization.

Are negative instances accounted for? Are there athletic programs in Ohio that did *not* lose money? Although negative instances by themselves may not invalidate a generalization, if negative instances are numerous and typical, no valid generalization can be drawn from those cited.

Analogy   *Analogy* is a special kind of generalization. In reasoning by analogy, we are attempting to show that similar circumstances produce similar conclusions. A warrant in the form of an analogy would be stated, "What is true or will work in one set of circumstances will be true or will work in another comparable set of circumstances."

The following illustrates an argument by analogy about off-track betting.

Ohio should adopt off-track betting.

I. Ohio is similar to New York in many key respects.

II. New York is making money from off-track betting.

Now let us lay the analogy argument out diagrammatically to test the reasoning:

(D) Ohio is similar to New York
in many respects.   → (C) Ohio should adopt
New York is making money   off-track betting.
from off-track betting.

(W) (Since off-track betting is working
well in New York and since New
York and Ohio are similar in many
respects, off-track betting will work
in Ohio.)

An analogy warrant (the verbal statement of the reasoning process) may be tested by asking these questions:

Are the subjects being compared really similar in all important ways? Are New York and Ohio similar in form of government? capability of handling betting? attitudes of residents? If subjects do not have significant similarities, then they are not really comparable.

Are any of the ways that the subjects are dissimilar important to the outcome? Is Ohio's dissimilarity in size a factor? Is the dissimilarity in concentrations of population a factor? If dissimilarities exist that outweigh the subjects' similarities, then conclusions drawn from the comparisons are not necessarily valid.

Causation   *Causation* is a form of reasoning that validates a conclusion on the basis of a special connection between the data and the conclusion. In causation, we assume that one or more circumstances listed always (or at least usually) produce a predictable effect or set of effects. The following illustrates a causation argument you might make about a fellow student.

Paula will pass the course.

   I. Paula is intelligent.

   II. Paula has studied hard.

   III. Paula has a good attitude.

Now let us lay the causation argument out diagrammatically to test the reasoning.

(D) Paula is intelligent.

     Paula has studied hard.   →   (C) Paula will pass the course.

     Paula has a good attitude.

        (W) (Intelligence, study, and good attitude are causes of or result in passing grades.)

A causation warrant (the verbal statement of the reasoning process) may be tested by asking these questions:

Are the data alone important enough to bring about the particular conclusion? Are intelligence, study, and attitude by themselves important enough to result in passing a course? If the data are truly important, it means that if we eliminate the data, we would eliminate the effect. If the effect can occur without the data, then we can question the causal relationship.

Do some other data that accompany the data cited really cause the effect? Are there some other factors (like luck, whim of a professor, attendance) that are more important in determining whether a student passes? If accompanying data appear equally or more important in bringing about the effect, then we can question the causal relationship between cited data and conclusion.

Is the relationship between cause and effect consistent? Do intelligence, study, and attitude always (or usually) yield passing grades? If there are times when the effect has not followed the cause, then we can question whether a causal relationship really exists.

Sign   *Sign* is a form of reasoning that validates a conclusion on the basis of a connection between symptoms and the conclusion. When the presence of certain events, characteristics, or situations always or usually accompanies other unobserved events, characteristics, or situations, we say that the observed events are a *sign*. Signs are often confused with causes, but signs are indicators, not causes. A fever is a sign of sickness. It occurs when a person is sick, but it does not cause the sickness.

You may have used a sign argument in a situation like the following:

The recession is over.

I. New car sales are skyrocketing.

II. Housing starts are up.

Now let us lay the sign argument out diagrammatically to test the reasoning:

(D) New car sales are skyrocketing.   } → *(C)* The recession is over.

Housing starts are up.

   (W) (Dramatic increases in car sales and
housing starts are signs of a healthy
economy.)

A sign warrant (the verbal statement of the reasoning) may be tested by these questions:

Do the data cited always or usually indicate the conclusion drawn? Do skyrocketing car sales and increases in housing starts always (or usually) indicate a healthy economy? If the data can occur independently of the conclusion, then they are not necessarily indicators.

Are sufficient signs present? Are skyrocketing new-car sales and increases in housing starts enough to indicate a healthy economy? Events or situations are often indicated by several signs. If enough of them are not present, then the conclusion may not follow.

Are contradictory signs in evidence? Is unemployment up? If signs that usually indicate different conclusions are present, then the stated conclusion may not be valid.

Definition   The preceding four are usually considered the major forms of reasoning. We will, however, often observe the use of reasoning from definition, a minor form of reasoning. A *definition* is a verbal classification that follows the application of specific criteria for that classification. A definition warrant is usually stated, "When a situation has all the characteristics that are usually associated with a term, then we can use that term to describe the product of those characteristics."

The following illustrates an argument by definition about a leader.

> Bill is an excellent leader.
> I. He takes charge.
> II. He uses good judgment.
> III. His goals are in the best interest of the group.

Now let us lay the definition argument out diagrammatically to test the reasoning:

(D) He takes charge.

He uses good judgment.

His goals are in the best interest of the group.

$\rightarrow$ *(C)* Bill is an excellent leader.

> *(W)* (Taking charge, showing good judgment, and considering the best interests of the group are the characteristics most often associated with excellent leadership.)

A definition warrant (the verbal statement of the reasoning process) may be tested by asking these questions:

> Are the characteristics mentioned the most important ones in determining the definition? Are taking charge, good judgment, and sensitivity to group goals the most important criteria of excellent leadership? If the data presented are not usually considered criteria for the classification, then the definition does not follow.

> Is an important aspect of the definition omitted in the statement of the definition? Do we need to consider Bill's influence or power? His desire to lead? If items that are ordinarily a part of the definition are missing, then the conclusion does not necessarily follow from the criteria listed.

Are those criteria best labeled by some other term? Are taking charge and judgment better labeled by "autocrat" rather than "leader"? If another label fits the criteria better, then the conclusion is not valid.

Deduction   As we have mentioned, a *deduction* is a form of reasoning that is used in moving from statements that are true to a related statement that must be true. A deductive warrant may be stated, "If two related premises are true, then a conclusion based on those two premises must be true."

The following is an argument based on deduction:

Jones passed the state bar exam.

  I. Lawyers must pass the state bar exam to practice in that state.

  II. Jones is practicing in that state.

Now let us lay the deductive argument out diagrammatically to test the reasoning:

(D) Lawyers must pass the state bar exam to practice law in that state.

Jones is practicing law in that state.

$\longrightarrow$ *(C)* Jones passed the state bar exam.

    (W) (If it is true that lawyers must pass the bar to practice and that Jones is practicing, then it is certain that Jones passed the bar.)

A deduction warrant (the verbal statement of the reasoning process) may be tested by asking these questions:

Are the premises true? If it is not true that lawyers must pass the bar to practice or if Jones is in fact not practicing in that state, then the conclusion would not be true. A sound conclusion cannot be drawn from untrue premises.

Is the conclusion based on the premises? Does the conclusion concern itself with Jones? With practicing law? With passing the bar?

As you study your resources you try to draw conclusions from the data. Then, when it comes time to prepare the speech, you use the product of your reasoning to form arguments. Now we consider the process of preparing a speech in which the emphasis is on reasoning with the audience.

PREPARING A SPEECH OF CONVICTION

You can put what you have learned about reasoning into practice by preparing and presenting a speech of conviction. A *speech of conviction,* or a *speech of reasons* as it is sometimes called, is an attempt to develop a proposition with clear reasons and sound support for the reasons. Your goal in accomplishing this assignment is to gain conviction by presenting sound arguments.

This assignment is not without real-life application. When you consider your persuasive strategy, you may decide that as a result of the audience position on a proposition or as a result of the nature of the audience itself, presenting the merits of the proposition is your best procedure. Under these circumstances the speech-of-conviction model will be the one you will follow. This does not mean your speech will be devoid of motivation or that you as a speaker can ignore the value of your credibility. It does mean that the final evaluation of your effort will be on the soundness of your case.

Determining the Specific Purpose

The specific purpose of a speech of conviction is usually a proposition phrased to change a belief held by an audience—for example, "All states should adopt a no-fault automobile insurance program" or "Jones is the best man for president." In both cases, the assumption is that the propositions are in opposition to the attitude or belief of the audience to which the speeches will be given.

Determining the Main Points

In order to determine what should be the main points of a speech of conviction, you go through the reasoning process discussed earlier in the chapter. As a result of examining data, you draw conclusions. You then put the product of your thinking in argument form. Sometimes the sources you read suggest your arguments for you by presenting clearly stated reasons in support of the proposition. How can you recognize reasons? You look for statements that answer *why* a proposition is justified. These statements are reasons. If you were doing research on the subjects of product safety, the most valuable player in the NBA, and guaranteed incomes, you might well find the sources suggesting the following reasons:

Proposition: You should read labels on products carefully before you use them. (Why?)

I. Taking time to read labels saves time in the long run.

II. Taking time to read labels may save money.

III. Taking time to read labels prevents errors.

Proposition: Julius Erving is the best player in the National Basketball Association. (Why?)

I. He is one of the leading scorers in the league.

II. He is an outstanding playmaker.

III. He is an excellent rebounder.

Proposition: The federal government should guarantee a minimum annual cash income to all its citizens. (Why?)

I. A minimum cash income would eliminate the present poverty conditions that breed social unrest.

II. A minimum cash income would eliminate the need for overlapping state and federal welfare agencies.

III. A minimum cash income would go directly to the people in need.

If the reasons given to justify the proposition are sound, then the attempted persuasion is logical; if the reasons satisfy the audience, then the reasons are persuasive. Thus, in developing a speech of conviction, you have two goals in mind: (1) to select reasons that prove the proposition and (2) to limit the speech to the reasons that are likely to be most persuasive—the reasons that are likely to have the greatest impact on your audience.

After you have a list of five or more reasons, you can select the best ones on the basis of which are most adaptable to your audience. You may discard some reasons on your list because you do not have and cannot get material. From those that are left, you can determine which will probably have the greatest effect on your specific audience. For most speeches, you need at least two and probably not more than four of the best, most applicable reasons.

However, your job is not finished with the discovery and selection of reasons. They in turn must be supported with further data—with evidence.

Basically, all supporting material may be reduced to two kinds of statements: *fact* and *opinion*. For instance, in one of our examples, we stated that Julius Erving is the best player in the National Basketball Association because he is one of the leading scorers in the league. If this statement were supported by quotations from other players, sports journalists, and fans, the support would be opinion. On the other hand, if we checked the records and found him second in scoring this year, first last year, and third the year before, our support would be fact.

The best support for any reason is fact. Facts are statements that are verifiable. That metal is heavier than air, that World War II ended in 1945, and that marijuana is a mild hallucinatory drug are all facts. If you say, "It's warm outside; it's 60°," and if the thermometer registers 60°, then your support is factual.

Although factual support is the best, there are times when facts are not available or are inconclusive. In these situations, you will have to support your conclusions with opinion. The quality of opinion depends on whether the source is expert or inexpert. If your gasoline attendant says it is likely that there is life on other planets, the opinion is not expert—the attendant's expertise lies in other areas. If, on the other hand, an esteemed space biologist says there is a likelihood of life on other planets, the opinion is expert. Both statements are only opinions, not facts, but some opinions are more authoritative than others. Opinions are also more trustworthy when they are accompanied by factual data. If it is an automotive engineer's opinion that a low-cost electric car is feasible, the opinion is valuable, since automotive engineering is his or her area of expertise. If the engineer also explains the advances in technology that are leading to a low-cost battery of medium size that can run for more than 200 hours without being recharged, the opinion is worth even more.

TESTING THE LOGIC OF YOUR DEVELOPMENT

Since the speech of conviction is an exercise in logical development, you must assure yourself that the speech development is sound. First you make sure your speech representation meets the tests of the speech outline; then you subject the outline and its parts to a data-conclusion-warrant analysis.

Testing the Logic of Structure

The logic of structure of a speech is tested by use of the speech outline. If the outline meets the key tests discussed on pages 85–88, you know the proposition is clear, the main points are support for the proposition, and that data are present. In slightly abbreviated form, an outline on the subject of direct election of the president might look like this:

Proposition: To prove that the United States should determine the president by direct election.

Introduction

I. In 1968, we barely avoided the electoral catastrophe of selecting the president in the House of Representatives.
II. The time to reform the electoral system is now.
III. Direct election of the president offers the best alternative to the electoral college.

Body

I. Direct election of the president is fair.
   A. It follows the one-person, one-vote policy laid down by the Supreme Court.
   B. It allows every vote to count equally, regardless of where it is cast.
   C. It eliminates the possibility of the election of a candidate who receives a lesser number of popular votes.
II. Direct election of the president is certain.
   A. The identity of the new president would be public knowledge once the votes were counted.
   B. The election of the president would not be subject to political maneuvers.
III. Direct election of the president is a popular plan.
   A. A recent Gallup Poll showed that the majority of people favor direct election.
   B. Many political leaders have voiced their approval of this plan.

Conclusion

I. The time to anticipate possible catastrophe is now.
II. Support direct election of the president.

This outline meets the key tests. It illustrates sound idea relationships, but it does not describe the reasoning process or test the logic. These goals are accomplished by subjecting the outline to a data-conclusion-warrant analysis.

Testing the Logic of Argument

In subjecting the outline to a data-conclusion-warrant analysis, the first step is to examine the logic of the entire speech. In schematic form, the speech in its entirety looks like this:

(D) Direct election is fair.

Direct election is certain.

Direct election is popular.

→

(C) The United States should determine the president by direct election.

(W) (Fairness, certainty, and popularity are the three major criteria for determining how a president should be elected.)

To test this warrant, you ask, "Is it true that fairness, certainty, and popularity are the criteria for selecting a method of election?" If experience, observation, and source material indicate that these three are of fundamental importance, the speech is logical. If, on the other hand, source material indicates that some other criterion is more important, or that two or three others are of equal importance, then the warrant does not meet the test of logic, and the argument should be reconsidered.

Assuming that this warrant does meet the test of logic, you can be assured that the overall structure of the speech is logical. But what of the individual units that make up the speech? Each of the three items of data listed in the schematic is itself the conclusion of an argument that must be tested. Let's make a schematic examination of the first of those statements, "Direct election is fair":

(D) Direct election follows the one-person, one-vote policy.

Direct election allows every vote to count equally.

Direct election eliminates the possibility of the election of a candidate who receives a lesser number of popular votes.

→ (C) Direct election is fair.

(W) (Fairness of election procedure
requires that all votes must count
equally and that the majority rules.)

First, you should test the data. Since you are working with an abbreviated outline (probably only half as detailed as an outline you would be working with), for purposes of this analysis, assume the data are representative and accurate. Next, you will test the warrant by asking, "Is it true that election-method fairness requires that all votes must count equally and that majority rules?" If you find from experience, observation, and source material that election-system fairness does require these, then the argument is logical. However, if election fairness is determined by criteria apart from those included as data, the warrant is faulty and the argument needs to be revised.

Assignment   *Prepare a three- to six-minute speech of conviction. An outline is required. Criteria for evaluation will include the clarity of the proposition, the clarity and quality of the reasons, the quality of the data used to support the reasons, and the logic of the units of argument presented.*

Outline: Speech of Conviction (3–6 minutes)

Proposition (*Specific Purpose*):   To prove that the administering of Scholastic Aptitude Tests to high school seniors should be abolished.

Introduction

 I. Every year 1½ million high school students across the country take the Scholastic Aptitude Test (SAT).
 II. An aptitude test is an intelligence test that measures the results of general and incidental learning experiences and is used as a frame of reference for the future.

Thesis Statement: The administering of the Scholastic Aptitude Tests to high school seniors should be abolished because these tests are an unreliable measure of intelligence or aptitude and because the tests are unfair and biased.

Body

I. The SATs should be abolished because they are an unreliable measure of aptitude.
    A. The Federal Trade Commission has proved that test scores are inaccurate due to inconsistent results.
    B. The Educational Testing Service admits that results are not reliable.
    C. On the local level, a high school counselor verifies that SATs' results do not provide solid information.

II. The SATs should be abolished because they are unfair and biased.
    A. First, SATs are economically unfair.
        1. The more money a student's parents earn, the better will be his or her scores on SAT tests.
        2. Students with more money can afford to boost their scores.
            a. They can afford tutoring for tests.
            b. They can afford to take the tests several times until they improve their score.
    B. Second, SATs are culturally biased.
        1. Tests are geared to students of one environment.
            a. Students from the "wrong" schools can't do well.
            b. A lack of English mastery is devastating to scores.
        2. Culture-free tests are not a solution.
            a. None has been developed.
            b. Attempts cannot be properly tested.

Conclusion

I. In summary, SATs are unreliable for measuring intelligence or aptitude and they are both economically unfair and culturally biased.

II. Because of these two reasons, administration of these tests to high school seniors should be abolished.

Bibliography

"Coaching Daze." *Time,* June 11, 1979, p. 57.

Selegman, D. "Rich Are Different." *Fortune,* May 5, 1980, p. 84.

Shah, D. K. "SAT Cramming: Does it Work?" *Newsweek,* June 11, 1979, p. 113.

As you analyze this speech of conviction, judge whether each of the reasons is clearly stated in the speech and whether the developmental material supports the reasons clearly, completely, and interestingly.[3] After you have made your own analysis, study the analysis given here.

Analysis

Since a speech of conviction is usually a straightforward presentation of reasons, the opening needs to get attention quickly.

This is a good clear statement of speaker position. A speech of conviction usually takes a direct approach.

Speaker clearly identifies the first reason.

This section represents a good compilation of key evidence. Still, sources need to be documented more specifically. See pp. 222–223 for directions on citing sources.

If an agency that would be expected to give information on the other side gives information that proves your point, you should make sure you use it. It stands as strong support.

Use of restatement adds emphasis to the point.

Speech: SATs

Every year 1½ million high school students across the United States take the Scholastic Aptitude Test. Why? To help determine whether they are capable of handling college material; to help determine what college, if any, they should attend; and finally to help determine what program they should pursue.

The SAT is an intelligence test which is supposed to measure the results of general and incidental learning. I believe administration of these SATs to high school seniors should be abolished for two reasons: (1) the test results themselves are an unreliable measure of intelligence or aptitude and (2) because the tests are biased.

My first reason for abolishing the SATs is because the scores are unreliable for measuring intelligence or aptitude. Higher education places great stock in the results of these tests. But in the last couple of years, evidence that questions the reliability of these tests has begun to mount. A study by the Federal Trade Commission proved that the scores are inaccurate due to inconsistencies of the results. The study says, "Special coaching can improve SAT scores by an average of 25 points out of 800, and such a difference is large enough to matter to the college admissions office." Educational Testing Service, which is the service that administers the tests even admits the unreliability. Due to luck and other external forces such as tutoring, an individual's score can vary from one occasion to another on the same test from plus or minus 30 to 35 points. That's up to a 70 point difference! In reaction to the new coaching industry that has sprung up in the past decade to tutor students to take the SAT test, the FTC reports that if a ten-week

---

[3] Presented in Speech class, University of Cincinnati. Printed by permission of Jennifer Payne.

coaching course can systematically improve a student's scores on a test, the test's validity as a measure of aptitude becomes totally dubious. I spoke with Mr. Gordon, who is a high school guidance counselor at Hughes High School in Cincinnati, and I asked him his professional opinion about SAT tests and he said, quote, "Aptitude testing is not strong enough—it does not judge intelligence or provide enough consistent or accurate results to give students substantial information about what they are suited for."

Good transition to second main point.

So far, I've told you that I think SATs for high school seniors should be abolished because the scores are an unreliable measure of intelligence or aptitude.

Speaker clearly states the second main point.

Another reason in support of my proposition is that SATs are biased. First, the SATs are economically biased. According to Ralph Nader, who did a study on the Educational Testing Service, higher income students do better than lower income students on SATs. Let me quote from his report. He says, "Every time you move from one income group to the next highest, the mean SAT on verbal and mathematical scores increases." There are basically two reasons why the test is economically unfair. First of all, according to Mr. Gordon, white suburban communities teach the student a curriculum that gears them toward taking the test— plus, these schools also have a 98 percent attendance rate to work with. Secondly, students who have money can afford to take and retake the tests (which cost approximately $10 each time) as many times as they wish in order to get the score they want.

Good support, but again, I'd like to see more specific documentation.

Another clear transition—this time to the second subpoint under the main reason.

Not only are the SATs to be abolished because they are economically unfair, but second, it is also proven that they are culturally biased. Remember, an aptitude test is an intelligence test which measures the results of general and incidental learning through the individual's total life experience; the goal of these tests is to predict what can be learned in the future. According to Berkely Rice, who did an investigation and reported it in *Psychology Today* magazine, generations of Black, Chicano, and other minority students have been measured by intelligence tests that assume that everyone grows up in the same white culture; therefore, English can be a barrier to some students if they have not grown up in communities like those being assumed. Berkely further states that any written test in English discriminates against those for whom English is a second language. Now, in order to alleviate this problem, experts have tried to produce an aculture-free test

This support all comes from one source. This section of the speech would be strengthened with the use of material from other sources as well.

that would not discriminate. But they have not been successful in creating one. And even the ones that they have tried to create have proved to be unverifiable.

The speech ends with a good, clear summary. Speech offers two clearly stated reasons. The two reasons strike at major criteria for determining the value of any test. The support offered is good. This stands as a solid speech of conviction.

In conclusion, I believe that the administration of the SATs to high school students should be abolished because, as shown by the Federal Trade Commission and admitted by the Educational Testing Service, the test results are not reliable in indicating a student's aptitude and, furthermore, as shown by the FTC, the tests are both economically and culturally biased.

And keep your favorite uncle happy.
More inside room and more available accessories
Save some hard-earned money.
Better made
"Why to buy an American front-wheel drive compact."

Chapter 15 Motivating Audiences: Speeches to Actuate

Reasoning provides a solid logical base for your persuasion and a sound rationale for change of audience attitude. But what if sound reasoning is not enough to bring action? What can you do to complement or supplement reasoning? What can you do when your listeners recognize the relative merits of your proposition—but they are not acting? The catalyst for firing the imagination, causing commitment, and bringing to action is the psychological aspect of persuasion called *motivation*.

In this chapter we consider three psychological approaches that will help you determine your overall strategy; then we consider language patterns that can be used to help you carry out your overall strategy; and finally we consider a specific speech assignment, the speech to actuate, to help you put what you have learned into practice.

STRATEGIES
Through the years many individuals have set forth rhetorical and psychological theories of persuasion. To help you formulate an overall strategy for motivation, we examine here the basic theory and material in support of three such strategies. These are, of course, not the only ones available—nor are they necessarily the only ones that will work.

What is likely to bring an audience to action? We can summarize the strategies involved as follows:

1. People are more likely to act when they see the suggested proposition as presenting a favorable cost-reward ratio.

2. People are more likely to act when the suggested proposition creates dissonance.

3. People are more likely to act when the proposition satisfies a strong unmet need.

Now let us examine the theories behind these statements.

Cost-Reward John Thibaut and Harold Kelley explain social interactions in terms of rewards received and costs incurred by each member of an interaction.[1] Rewards are the benefits received from a behavior. Rewards can be economic gain, good feelings, prestige, or any other positive outcome. Costs are units of expenditure. They can be perceived in terms of time, energy, money, or any negative outcomes of an interaction.

According to Thibaut and Kelley, each of us seeks situations in which our behaviors will yield us rewards in excess of the costs; or, conversely, each of us will continue our present behaviors unless we can be shown that either lower costs or higher rewards will come from changing those behaviors. Let us consider an example. Suppose you are asked to give money to a charity. The money you are asked to give is a negative outcome; however, giving money may be rewarding in that you can feel civic-minded, responsible, or helpful. Will you then give to the charity? The answer may depend on whether the potential for rewarding feelings outweighs the potential for negative feelings caused by the absence of the money given. For some, the rewards of good feelings are worth only small amounts of money—for others the rewards of good feelings may be worth considerably more.

Strategies growing from this theory are easy for most people to understand because the theory is so easily supported by our own "commonsense" observations. What makes this theory work for you is your ability to understand the cost-reward ratios in relation to the particular topic operating within your particular audience. Suppose that you are in fact trying to motivate the audience to give money to a particular charity. Assuming that this audience has nothing against this particular charity, and assuming they agree that giving to this charity has merit, how do you proceed? You

---

[1] J. W. Thibaut and H. H. Kelley, *The Social Psychology of Groups* (New York: Wiley, 1959).

could ask each person to give ten cents. Since the cost is very low, you are unlikely to meet much resistance and you will probably get a high percentage of donations; but you will not be making much money for that charity. What if you decide to ask for a donation of $10 from each person! Since $10 is likely to represent a lot of money to members of a college audience, they must be shown that $10 really is not that much money (a difficult point to make for any audience) or they must be shown that the reward for giving $10 is worth that $10 investment. For most of your audience, a portrayal of a momentary good feeling will not be enough. You will have to demonstrate some very tangible rewards.

In general, then, the higher the cost to the individual, the greater the reward must be. Thus, the higher the perceived cost, the harder you will have to work to achieve your goal. In summary,

1. People look at calls for action on the basis of a cost-reward ratio.

2. You must show that the time, energy, or money investment is minimal.
or

3. You must show that the benefits in good feelings, prestige, economic gain, fulfillment of emotional needs, or other possible rewards is high.

In your speech then, you are looking at ways to minimize cost and maximize gain. The speech at the end of this chapter is an excellent example of this strategy in action.

Cognitive Dissonance   A second theory on which persuasive strategies may be developed is the theory of cognitive dissonance. *Cognitive dissonance* is an inconsistency that occurs between two or more cognitive elements. A *cognition* is a thought or a knowledge about some situation, person, or behavior. For example, if you had worked hard to save $35 for a gift for your friend, the amount you had saved to spend on that gift would be one cognitive element. If you proceed to spend $75 for the gift, the amount you have actually spent would be a second cognitive element. The inconsistency between money available and money spent would create a discomfort. This discomfort is what Leon Festinger, the originator of this theory, calls cognitive dissonance.[2] Notice that, as he sees the situation, this discomfort or dissonance can occur only after you have done something.

Festinger holds that whenever you get yourself in one of these states of discomfort (and some of us may find ourselves in this state quite often), you have a great desire to *reduce the discomfort*. The greater the degree of discomfort experienced, the greater the desire to reduce it.

What determines the degree of discomfort? According to Festinger the amount of dissonance you are likely to feel depends on at least two factors. The first is the number of elements in each cognition. You are likely to experience less dissonance if there are only two conflicting cognitions than if there are several. For instance, high pay for a job combined with low prestige for that job may create cognitive dissonance. The degree will be relatively low because only two cognitions are in competition. On the other hand, if higher pay and a better location are in competition with low prestige, little chance for advancement, and less desirable duties, the degree of dissonance will be considerably greater.

The second factor determining the degree of discomfort is the importance of the entire issue. For instance, less dissonance is usually experienced after making a decision to buy a certain pair of shoes than after making a decision to buy a new car.

When a person experiences dissonance, what can be done to relieve it? Festinger suggests four methods of reducing or relieving dissonance: (1) A person may change his or her attitude toward the decision. If you bought your friend a present that cost more than you had planned to pay, you can reduce the dissonance by telling yourself that your friend is really worth every penny you spent. (2) A person can change his or her behavior. If you smoke excessively and the smoking is hurting your relationship with your friend, you can stop smoking. (3) A person can change the environment in which the dissonance occurs. If you are an actor of only average ability, but wish to have major parts in plays, you can go to a smaller school where it is more likely that you can get better parts. (4) A person may add new cognitive elements. If you have paid too much for your friend's gift, you might tell

---

[2] Leon Festinger, *A Theory of Cognitive Dissonance* (Evanstown, Ill.: Row, Peterson, 1957).

yourself that you can cut expenses by avoiding evening snacks for a month.

Now that you can see what cognitive dissonance is, you may be asking what it has to do with developing a persuasive strategy. As a speaker, you have it within your power to create dissonance in the mind of each person in the audience. Once the audience becomes aware of dissonance, you can show them ways to relieve it.

Consider a situation in which you as a speaker wish to motivate the audience to stop buying cigarettes and liquor from people who obtain their merchandise from out of state. People may buy these products because they are cheaper; people may know that the reason they are cheaper is because the taxes for those products are lower in the other state—and these savings are being passed along to them. How can you create dissonance in the minds of these people? You may develop a line of argument linking trafficking in out-of-state cigarettes and liquor with organized crime. Most people believe that supporting organized crime is wrong. If you can show that what looks like small savings to them mounts up to really big business for the "smugglers," you may well create dissonance between the cognition of saving money and the cognition of supporting organized crime. Although the members of the audience may choose to repress a perception of the information you cite, or bury that dissonance, or devalue the issue (three common ways of rationalizing), if you can make the point strongly enough, at least some members of the audience may feel compelled to do something to relieve that dissonance by not buying the products under the circumstances described. We can summarize as follows:

1. People will look for ways to relieve dissonance when confronted with conflicting cognitions.

2. You can create dissonance through presentation of conflicting cognitions.

3. The proposition of your speech can be perceived as a way of relieving the dissonance you have created.

Basic Needs A third theory on which persuasive strategies may be developed is based on Abraham Maslow's theory of the hierarchy of needs. Persuasion is more likely to occur when the proposition meets a specific need of members of the audience. If people have a need for food, they are more likely to be receptive to a message about where to eat, where to shop, or what to buy than if they do not have that need. Thus, if you are able to identify audience needs, you have a good start for planning your persuasive strategy.

Abraham Maslow[3] classifies basic human needs in five categories:

1. Physiological needs
2. Safety needs
3. Belongingness and love needs
4. Esteem needs
5. Self-actualization needs

Notice that Maslow places these needs in a hierarchy: One set of needs must be met or satisfied before the next set of needs emerge. Our physiological needs for food, drink, temperature are the most basic; they must be satisfied before the body is able to consider any of its other needs. The next level consists of safety needs—security, simple self-preservation, and the like; they emerge after basic physiological needs have been met, and they hold a paramount place until they, too, have been met. The third level includes our belongingness or love needs; these involve the groups that we identify with—our friends, our loved ones, our family. In a world of increasing mobility and the breakdown of the traditional family, however, it's becoming more and more difficult for individuals to satisfy this need. Nonetheless, once our belongingness needs are met, our esteem needs predominate; these involve our quest for material goods, recognition, and power or influence. The final level is called, by Maslow, the self-actualizing need; this involves developing one's self to meet its potential. When all other needs are met, this need is the one that drives people to their creative heights, that urges them to do "what they need to do."

What is the value of this analysis to you as a speaker? First, it provides a framework for and suggests the kinds of needs you may appeal to in your speeches. Second, it allows you to understand why a line of development will work on one audience and fall flat

---

[3] Abraham H. Maslow, *Motivation and Personality* (New York: Harper & Row, 1954), pp. 80–92.

with another. For instance, if our audience has great physiological needs—if they are hungry—an appeal to the satisfaction of good workmanship, no matter how well done, is unlikely to impress them. Third, and perhaps most crucial, when our proposition is going to come in conflict with an operating need, we will have to be prepared with a strong alternative in the same category or in a higher-level category. For instance, if our proposition is going to cost money—if it is going to take money in the form of taxes—we will have to show how the proposal satisfies some other comparable need.

Let us try to make this discussion even more specific by looking at some of the traditional motives for action. The few we will discuss are not meant to be exhaustive—they are meant to be suggestive of the kind of analysis you should be doing. You have a proposition; you have determined reasons for its acceptance. Now try to relate those reasons to basic needs and discover where you may be getting into difficulty by coming into conflict with other motives or other needs.

WEALTH   Wealth, the acquisition of money and material goods, is a motive that grows out of an esteem need. People are concerned about making money, saving it, losing it, or finding it. People who do not have money may be motivated by a plan that will help them gain money, save money, or do more with what they have. People who already have money may be motivated by a plan that will enable them to enlarge it or to use it in a way that will indicate their wealth. For example, those who have little money can perhaps be motivated to buy a Toyota or a Chevette primarily because they are economical; on the other hand, those who have a great deal of money can perhaps be motivated to buy a Rolls-Royce or a Cadillac because they are prestigious. Does your proposition affect wealth or material goods in any way? If it does in a positive way, you may want to stress it. If your plan calls for giving up money, you will need to be prepared to cope with an audience's natural desire to resist giving it up—you will have to involve another motive from the same category (esteem) or from a higher category to override the loss of any money the audience will have to give up.

POWER   For many people, personal worth depends on their power over their own destiny, the exercising of power over others, and the recognition and prestige that comes from such recognition or power. Recognition, power, and prestige are all related to people's identity, to their need for esteem. If people control things, if they are well known, these feelings of control and recognition will raise their self-esteem and make them feel important. Consider whether your speech allows the person, group, or community to exercise power; if it does, it may offer a strong motivation. On the other hand, if your speech proposition takes away power from part or all of your listeners, you will need to provide strong compensation to be able to motivate them.

CONFORMITY   Conformity is a major source of motivation for nearly everyone. It grows out of people's need for belongingness. People often respond in a given way because a friend, a neighbor, an acquaintance, or a person in the same age bracket has so responded. Although some will be more likely to do something if they can be the first one to do it or if it makes them appear distinctive, most people feel more secure, more comfortable when they are members of a group. The old saying that there is strength in numbers certainly applies. If you can show that many favor your plan, that people in similar circumstances have responded favorably, that argument may well provide motivation.

PLEASURE   When you give people a choice of actions, they will pick the one that gives them the greatest pleasure, enjoyment, or happiness. On at least one level, pleasure is a self-actualizing need—more often it is an esteem need. Pleasure sometimes results from doing things you are good at. If you are able to shoot a basketball through the basket a higher percentage of times than most others, you probably enjoy the experience. At other times, pleasure is a result of accomplishing something that is difficult. Getting an A in a class you regard as difficult may give you more pleasure than getting an A in a class that you regard as easy— challenges often give people pleasure. Just as you respond to things that are pleasurable, so will your classmates respond favorably when they see that your proposition will give them pleasure. If your speech relates to something that is novel, promises excitement, is fun to do, or offers a challenge, you can probably motivate your audience.

As we have already said, these are only a few of the possible motives for action. Freedom, recognition, security, workmanship, sex, responsibility, justice, and many other motives operate within each of us. We can and should have an understanding of such motives and some idea of which of these are likely to be most easily aroused in our audience on the specific proposition. Then we need to determine the hierarchy of the motives operating to make sure that the audience will be free to be receptive to the need we appeal to.

However, knowing which motives are in operation and appealing to them are two different things. To maximize our effectiveness we need to understand how to trigger these motives.

What happens when your proposition does not meet a specific audience need? Either you can change the wording of your proposition so that it is in tune with audience needs, or you can work to create or uncover an audience need that this proposition will meet. For instance, if you are giving a speech intended to motivate the audience to go to dinner at Le Parisian (a very expensive restaurant), your proposition may be meeting a need to eat out occasionally but it is in opposition to most people's need to eat at reasonable prices. So for this speech to work for you, you will either have to change the proposition to recommend a more modest restaurant (The River Captain's, for instance) or you must arouse some needs that would be met by going to Le Parisian.

In planning strategy in terms of basic needs, consider the following:

1. What needs are in operation within this audience at this time?

2. If the proposition meets those needs, stress how.

3. If the proposition does not meet those needs, either change the proposition or work to activate unexpressed and perhaps unrealized needs.

LANGUAGE STRATEGIES

In addition to the potential for developing motivational strategies, you must also consider language strategies that can add to the motivational effect of your message. Three such language strategies are yes-response, common ground, and suggestion. Please be aware that these language strategies are two-edged swords. When used ethically, they can work on your behalf—but unethical use will work against you even if you appear to achieve short-term gains. Learn to use these language strategies ethically and learn to recognize their unethical use by others.

Yes-Response   A favorable climate for persuasion is built upon audience agreement. Psychologists have found that when listeners get in the habit of saying yes, they are likely to continue saying yes. If you can phrase questions that establish areas of agreement early in your speech, the audience will be more likely to listen to you and perhaps to agree with you later. In contrast, if you create areas of disagreement earlier, you may not be able to get agreement later. For instance, an insurance salesperson might phrase the following questions: "You want your family to be able to meet their needs, don't you? You want to be able to provide for them under all circumstances, don't you? You want your family to have the basic needs, don't you? Then of course you want to have an insurance program that meets all these criteria, don't you?" With this set of yes-responses, potential clients are led to a yes-response they might not have made earlier; that is, they may well say yes to the suggestion that they buy an insurance policy.

The criteria-satisfaction organization we considered in Chapter 13 illustrates a yes-response organization. Thus, in a speech trying to get the audience to support a bill providing more funds for hiring more police you might follow this pattern:

> You want a safe community? (Yes)
>
> You want your sons and daughters to be able to walk the streets at night? (Yes)
>
> You want to be able to leave your house without the constant fear of loss from burglary? (Yes)
>
> Then you want a police force that can help make these a reality. (Yes!)

Common Ground   Common ground relates to credibility and commonality of experience. Why is it that a good friend can tease us about a mistake we make, but a stranger or an enemy cannot? Why are we leery of "outsiders" trying to solve "our" problems? Because we respect, believe in, and trust those with *common experience.* When we meet someone from home when we are out of state or out of the country, why do we treat him or her like a long-lost friend, when perhaps back at home we hardly ever see each other? Because under a certain special set of circumstances (strangers in a strange land), we share a common experience; when those special circumstances no longer exist (when we are back home), that bond is no longer a strong common experience.

When you can show your audience that you have common experiences, you can build an affinity between you and your audience that lays a groundwork for bridging differences of opinion. Let us see how two different speakers build and use common ground.

This speaker, in her commencement address to the women of Hartford College, attempted to build common ground early in her speech this way:

> I do commend you for what you have accomplished thus far. Working with you during the past year, I identified with many of you and recalled my own struggles, lacking financial and emotional support, to get a college education. I learned in my time, as you have learned in your day, that the president of Hartford College had her own affirmative action program for women long before it was fashionable. I am only one of many products of that program.
>
> I know what some of you have sacrificed for your achievement.[4]

Notice that the emphasis is on common experience. What is the implication of her words? If we have had the same experiences, then we can talk together as equals.

Vernon Jordan, a black, uses common ground to make an appeal to his audience of Jews. Throughout his speech he shows what blacks and Jews have in common. Then he says:

> Because I feel at home with you, because I am among friends, I wish to speak with the bluntness of a true friend; with the honesty that must characterize relations between friends who respect each other and who have each other's interests at heart. To the degree that tensions or misunderstandings exist between Jews and blacks today, some of the responsibility must be laid upon the indifference to issues touching the very core of black interests on the part of some Jews.[5]

In effect, Jordan is criticizing some members of his audience—he could not have made his criticism and been heard without first building the common ground. Did the Jews in the audience accept the criticism as coming from a friend? No doubt much better than if he had made the criticism without building common ground.

Suggestion   Suggestion involves planting an idea in the mind of the listener without development. It is an idea stated in such a way that its acceptance is sought without analysis or consideration.

---

[4] Mary Lou Thibeault, "The Hazards of Equality," *Vital Speeches,* July 15, 1974, p. 588.

[5] Vernon E. Jordan, Jr., "The Black and Jewish Communities," *Vital Speeches,* August 1, 1974, p. 630.

Suggestion may be direct, as in bumper stickers that say SEE MAMMOTH CAVE or VOTE FOR SMEDLEY. Suggestion may also be indirect. The speaker who says, "Let's see, we could act now—a stitch in time often saves nine" has found an indirect way of saying, "If I were you I'd act now before the problem gets any worse, causing us to take even more drastic action later." Suggestion may be positive ("Play soccer") or negative ("Don't walk on the grass"). Positive suggestion is usually more effective. Negative suggestion often leads to the very behavior it decries. Who can avoid putting a finger on the wall when the sign says DO NOT TOUCH—WET PAINT? Suggestion may be in the form of counter-suggestion. *Countersuggestion* is a manipulative form that can and often does backfire. You use countersuggestion when you want to go swimming, and you say to a bullheaded friend, "Let's go fishing"—and he replies, as you hoped, with "Naw, let's go swimming." Of course, if he said yes to fishing, your counter-suggestion would have backfired.

One writer, Robert Oliver, says that suggestion works best when "(1) the audience is inclined to be favorable to the proposition; (2) the audience is in a generally agreeable state; and (3) the audience is polarized to such a degree that judgment is inhibited."[6]

As an example of a program of suggestion, see what the following speaker says about his hotel's efforts to boost sales of dessert in the restaurants. His point is that the waiter can try for other goodies, but no matter what, he can sell strawberries:

> "So sell 'em strawberries!" we said. "But sell 'em." And then we wheeled out our answer to gasoline shortages, the dessert cart. We widened the aisles between the tables and had the waiters wheel the cart up to each and every table at dessert time. Not daunted by the diet protestations of the customer, the waiter then went into raptures about the bowl of fresh strawberries. There was even a bowl of whipped cream for the slightly wicked. By the time our waiters finish extolling the virtues of our fresh strawberries flown in that morning from California, or wherever he thinks strawberries come from, you not only had an abdominal orgasm, but one out of two of you order them.[7]

---

[6] Robert T. Oliver, *The Psychology of Persuasive Speech* (New York: David McKay, 1957), pp. 151–152.

[7] James Lavenson, "Think Strawberries," *Vital Speeches*, March 15, 1974, p. 348.

As an ethical speaker, however, you will find your use of suggestion limited. One prevalent use of suggestion in speech making is the use of directive. Such expressions as "I think we will all agree," "As we all know," and "Now we come to a most important consideration" are forms of suggestion that will help you direct audience thinking. Another use of suggestion is to associate the name of a prominent individual to add prestige to a proposal. Of course, ethical use of this method is limited to individuals who have given their backing to that particular proposal. In contrast to saying that a proposal is favored by notable people, you can say that Senator X, who received an award for his work on air pollution control, favors the proposal to curb air pollution. This kind of use helps the audience make the association between the proposal and responsible public officials. A third way to use suggestion is to phrase ideas in specific, vivid language. Audiences are drawn to favor proposals that are phrased in memorable language. In 1946 Winston Churchill, regarded by many as the most effective speaker of the twentieth century, introduced the term *Iron Curtain* in a speech at Fulton, Missouri. This term suggested an attitude about Russian ideology that has permeated Western thinking for more than thirty years. Because the subtle, less obvious statement of an idea may be more easily accepted by an audience, suggestion is an aid to persuasive speaking.

PREPARING A SPEECH TO ACTUATE

Practice with motivation may be best accomplished with a speech-of-actuation—a speech calling for the speaker to bring the audience to action—assignment.

Preparing a speech to actuate requires that you think creatively about your overall plan and about the specific means you can use to implement the plan. This preparation will involve (1) wording the proposition (specific purpose) in a way that gives you the best opportunity to achieve success, (2) analyzing your audience's attitude toward the subject matter to determine where you will have common ground and where you will have to work to meet objections to the action you call for, (3) writing an outline that is organized to take into account what you have learned from your audience analysis, (4) developing vividness of language that will motivate, (5) placing special emphasis on introduction and conclusion, and (6) practicing the delivery.

The following is an example of the way you might approach

such planning. Although it considers only one topic, the method will be the same for any topic you select.

For the past decade, foreign imports have placed increased pressure on our economy. Our choosing to buy foreign-made products over American-made has contributed to recessions and high levels of unemployment. Suppose you were determined to persuade your audience to buy American-made products.

What would be an effective phrasing for your proposition? If you are content with phrasing the proposition "To persuade the class to buy American-made products," you are confronted with the reality that even if the audience agreed in principle, the action called for is so sweeping that it might hurt the chances of your achieving action. So, you might ask yourself, what is a key to our economy? Where is foreign buying hurting the most? The answer, of course, is the auto industry. As a result of these questions, you might better select the phrasing, "To persuade the class to buy a small, front-wheel drive American car." This wording has a chance of succeeding.

What will be your audience's reaction toward such a proposition? Instead of trying to get one overall view, it is usually better to look at several aspects of the topic to determine intensity, importance, and direction of audience attitude. For instance, in this case you might be wise to raise at least four questions that will reveal where there may be common ground and where there is likely to be the greatest amount of objection. These relevant questions, and their answers, are as follows: (1) Is the audience likely to have a favorable attitude toward buying American in general? Yes—few people are opposed to American-made products in general. (2) Is the audience likely to favor purchase of a small, front-wheel drive car? Yes. This is one of the reasons for wording the proposition in this way. During the past decade Americans have been buying more and more smaller and front-wheel drive cars. (3) Is the audience likely to have a favorable attitude toward American-made front-wheel drive small cars? Yes, but only in the abstract. That a wider selection of small, front-wheel drive cars is available is applauded, but sales have not been as good as expected. (4) What is keeping people from purchasing the small, front-wheel drive American car? At least three factors seem to be involved: gas mileage, quality of workmanship, and habitual buying practices. Let us consider each of these negative reactions in order to determine a strategy for dealing with them.

"The American made car doesn't get comparable gas mileage." This has been true—but the difference is narrowing. If the motive of the American buyer is to save energy, even a few miles per gallon difference can make a difference; but if the motive is saving money, a good point can be made in favor of the American car. Since American cars begin with a lower base price, the small amount of gasoline saved with the highest mileage foreign cars will not offset the original price difference.

"The American small car is not quality made." Again, this appears to have been very true in the past. But evidence is accumulating that American small car workmanship is improving, resulting in a car with a record comparable to the imports on such important indexes as frequency of repair and buyer satisfaction.

"Americans are out of the habit of looking for the small, front-wheel drive American-made car." This seems to be especially true, and is probably the area you will have to work on the hardest. Yet, if you are able to show a competitive product, you should be able to meet this problem.

Such an analysis shows you where to put the major emphasis in development and shows you how you can manage the major objections.

Let us look at a tentative (and shortened) outline that you can construct that takes this analysis into consideration.

Proposition (Specific Purpose): To persuade the class to buy a small, front-wheel drive American car.

Introduction

 I. In these times of expensive energy and high taxes, each of us is looking for ways to save money.

 II. Our indignation with American auto companies that have been trying to sell us shoddy merchandise has virtually forced many of us to turn to foreign cars.

 III. At the same time, we realize our entire nation is facing perilous economic disorders that are at least partly brought about by our purchase of imports.

 IV. What can we do to meet our own needs to save money and energy and still help the nation with its economic problems?

Thesis Statement: Buy small, front-wheel drive cars because American manufacturers are now providing high mileage, small, front-wheel drive cars and because at last the quality is going back into the American new car product.

Body

I. At last, American car manufacturers are producing a product that is truly competitive.
   A. The small, front-wheel drive American car gets comparable mileage to foreign small cars.
   B. The small, front-wheel drive American car is often *safer* to drive.
   C. The small, front-wheel drive American car carries the kind of extras we want and need.
   D. Even in those instances where mpg is not as good, the American car is much less expensive.

II. Most of all, manufacturers are putting quality back into the American car.
   A. Frequency of repair records are much better.
   B. Workmanship is much improved.
   C. Buyer satisfaction is much higher.

Conclusion

I. It would be foolish to shout "buy American" solely to support poorly made, noncompetitive products.

II. But at last, in the small, front-wheel drive car, America is back on target.

III. When you start looking for that new car, go to the American manufactured car first—I think you'll buy one!

Notice how the organization speaks to your audience analysis. You start by developing some common ground. You try to establish that Americans will buy American if the product is competitive. Then, you show that the product is competitive.

While you are constructing your outline, you can also be deciding on the specific means of motivation you can use. The driving force of such a speech will be the points selected and the wording. In various places in this text we have spoken of vividness, description, narration, common ground, yes-response, and suggestion—any or all of these can be considered for development of this speech.

If you look again at the outline, you will see that the wording was selected because it is motivational as well as logical. Since the introduction and conclusion of this kind of speech are so important, look especially at how those were outlined. In this speech you want to develop patriotism, but you also want to stress the needs of saving money and having a product a person can be proud of.

Let us summarize the special steps you will want to take as you prepare this speech:

1. Word the specific purpose in a way that gives you the best opportunity to achieve success.

2. Analyze your audience's attitude toward the subject matter to determine where you will have common ground and where you will have to work to meet objections to the action you call for.

3. Write an outline that is organized to take into account what you have learned from your audience analysis.

4. Develop vividness of language that will motivate.

5. Place special emphasis on the introduction and conclusion. You cannot persuade an audience that is not listening; likewise, you must leave your audience excited about the action you call for.

6. Practice the delivery of the speech until it adds to the force of motivation you are trying to develop.

Assignment   *Prepare a four- to seven-minute persuasive speech on a topic designed to bring your audience to action. An outline is required. In addition to clarity of purpose and soundness of rationale, criteria for evaluation will include your credibility on the topic, your ability to satisfy audience needs, and your ability to phrase your ideas in a way that will motivate.*

Outline: Speech to Actuate (4–7 minutes)

Proposition (Specific Purpose): To persuade listeners to donate their eyes to an eye bank.

Introduction

   I. Close your eyes and imagine living in a world of darkness.

  II. Millions live in this world.

Thesis Statement: People should donate their eyes to an eye bank because corneas are necessary for sight, because corneas can be transplanted, and because donors know that through a donation a part of them lives on and they can be as useful to humanity in death as in life.

Body

   I. The windows through which we see the world are the corneas.

     A. They are tough, dime-sized, transparent tissues.

     B. Normally they are clear.

     C. When they are distorted, they blot out the light.

  II. Those with injured corneas have the hope of normal sight through a cornea transplant.

     A. The operation works miracles, but it cannot work without donors.

     B. If eyes are transplanted within seventy-two hours after death of the donor, the operation can be 100 percent successful.

     C. The operation has turned tragedy into joy.

 III. There are many reasons for donating.

     A. The donor knows a part of him goes on living.

     B. The donor knows he can be as useful to humanity in death as in life.

 IV. I hope you will consider becoming a donor.

     A. Leaving your desire in your will is not enough—the operation must come within seventy-two hours of death.

     B. Get forms and details from a Cincinnati eye bank.

     C. Then, when you die, someone who needs the chance can see.

Conclusion

   I. Close your eyes again—now open them.

  II. Won't you give someone else the chance to open theirs?

Read this speech at least once aloud and analyze the use of motivation.[8] *What motives is the speaker appealing to? What are her methods of heightening motivation? After you have analyzed the speech, read the analysis given here.*

Speech: Open Your Eyes

Analysis

Much of the strength of this speech is a result of the speaker's ability to involve members of the audience personally and get them to feel what she is saying. This opening is a striking example of audience involvement. She does not just tell the audience what it would be like—she has them experience the feeling. The speaker very successfully lays the emotional groundwork for total audience reception of her words.

Would all of you close your eyes for just a minute. Close them very tightly so that all the light is blocked out. Imagine what it would be like to always live in a world of total darkness such as you are experiencing right now, though only for a moment. Never to see the flaming colors of the sunset, or the crisp green of the world after the rain—never to see the faces of those you love. Now open your eyes, look all around you, look at all of the things that you couldn't have seen if you couldn't have opened your eyes.

Here the speaker begins the body of her speech by telling us about the role of the cornea. Notice throughout the speech the excellent word choice, such as "The bright world we awake to each morning is brought to us by. . . ."
Here again she does not just tell us what it is like but asks us to imagine for ourselves what it would be like if. The "rain-slashed window pane" is an especially vivid image.

The bright world we awake to each morning is brought to us through two dime-sized pieces of tough, transparent, semielastic tissue; these are the corneas, and it is their function to allow light to enter the lens and the retina. Normally, they are so clear that we don't even know they are there; however, when they are scratched or scarred either by accident or by disease, they tend to blur or blot out the light. Imagine peering through a rain-slashed window pane or trying to see while swimming under water. This is the way the victims of corneal damage often describe their vision.

The speaker continues in a very informative way. After asserting that corneal transplants work, she focuses on the two key points that she wants the audience to work with—the operation works, but it must be

"To see the world through another man's eyes." These words are Shakespeare's, yet today it can literally be true. Thanks to the research by medical workers throughout the world, the operation known as a corneal transplant or a corneal graft has become a reality, giving thousands of people the opportunity to see. No other generation has held such a profound legacy in its possession. Yet,

---

[8] Speech given in Speech class, University of Cincinnati. Printed by permission of Kathleen Sheldon.

done within seventy-two hours. Notice that there is still no apparent direct persuasion. Her method is one of making information available in a way that will lead the audience itself to thinking about what effects the information might have on them personally.

In this segment of the speech, she launches into emotional high gear. Still, her approach remains somewhat indirect. Although we stress the importance of directness in language in this speech, the use of "no one" repeatedly throughout the examples is done by design. Although a more direct method might be effective, in this case the indirectness works quite well. The real effectiveness of the section is a result of the parallel structure and repetition of key phrases: "no one who has seen . . . human tragedy . . . great joy . . . can doubt the need or the urgency." As this portion of the speech was delivered, the listeners were deeply touched by both the examples themselves and their own thoughts about the examples. Also note how the examples themselves are ordered. The first two represent a personal effect; the final one a universal effect.

At this point in the speech the audience should be sympathetic with the problem and encouraged by the hope of corneal transplants. Now the speaker must deal with the listener's reactions of "That may be a good idea for someone else, but why me?" It

the universal ignorance of this subject of cornea donation is appalling. The operation itself is really quite simple; it involves the corneas of the donor being transplanted into the eyes of a recipient. And if this operation takes place within seventy-two hours after the death of the donor, it can be 100 percent effective.

No one who has seen the human tragedy caused solely by corneal disease can doubt the need or the urgency. Take the case of a young woman living in New Jersey who lost her sight to corneal disease. She gave birth to a baby and two years ago, thanks to a corneal transplant, she saw her three-year-old baby girl for the first time. And no one who had seen this woman's human tragedy caused solely by corneal disease nor her great joy at the restoration of her sight can doubt the need or the urgency. Or take the case of the five-year-old boy in California who was playing by a bonfire when a bottle in the fire exploded, flinging bits of glass, which lacerated his corneas. His damaged corneas were replaced with healthy ones in an emergency operation, and no one who had seen this little boy's human tragedy caused solely by corneal laceration nor the great joy to his young life of receiving his sight back again can doubt the need or the urgency. Or take the case of Dr. Beldon H. Scribbner of the University of Washington School of Medicine. Dr. Scribbner's eyesight was damaged by a corneal disease that twisted the normally sphere-shaped corneas into cones. A corneal transplant gave Dr. Scribbner a twenty-twenty corrective vision and allowed him to continue work on his invention—the artificial kidney machine. And no one who has seen this man's human tragedy caused solely by corneal disease, nor the great joy brought not only to Dr. Scribbner but to the thousands of people his machine has helped save, can doubt the need or the urgency.

There are many philosophies behind such a gift. One of them was summed up by a minister and his wife who lost their daughter in infancy. They said, "We feel that a part of her goes on living." Or take the case of the young woman who was dying of cancer. She donated her eyes and did so with this explanation: "I want to be useful; being useful brings purpose and meaning into my life." Surely if being useful is important there are few better is in this section that she offers reasons for our acting. If the speech has a weakness, it may be here. I'd like to have heard a little further development of the reasons or perhaps the statement of an additional reason.

Here she brings the audience from ''Good idea—I'll do something someday'' to ''I'd better act now.''

She reminds them of the critical time period. And tells them how they can proceed to make the donation. In this section it might be worth a sentence to stress that the donation costs nothing but a little time.

Here the speaker brings the audience full circle. Although she could have used different images, the repetition of those that began the speech takes the emphasis off the images themselves and places it in what the audience can do about those who are in these circumstances.

The last line of the speech is simple, but in the context of the entire speech it is direct and quite moving. This is a superior example of a speech to actuate.

ways than to donate your eyes to someone who lives after you. But no matter which philosophy you do adopt, I hope each of you will consider donating your eyes to another who will live after you and who otherwise would have to survive in the abyss of darkness. It will do you no good to leave your eyes in your regular will if you have one; for as I mentioned earlier, there is a seventy-two-hour critical period. If you wish to donate your eyes, I would suggest you contact Cincinnati Eye Bank for Sight Restoration at 861–3716. They will send you the appropriate donor forms to fill out, which should be witnessed by two of your closest friends or by your next of kin so that they will know your wishes. Then, when you die and no longer have need for your sight someone who desperately wants the chance to see will be able to.

Will all of you close your eyes again for just a moment? Close them very tightly, so that all the light is blocked out. And once more imagine what it would be like to live always in a world of total darkness such as you are experiencing right now, never seeing the flaming colors of a sunset, or the crisp green of the world after a rain—never seeing the faces of those you love. Now open your eyes . . . Won't you give someone else the chance to open theirs?

Ad Hominem

Questionable Cause

Hasty Generalizations

Misleading Statistics

Chapter 16 Counterattack: Speeches of Refutation

For every assignment suggested in this book so far, you have been concerned with preparing a speech, delivering it to the audience, and then retiring to your seat to listen to either another speech or an evaluation of your speech. Although your professor may provide question or discussion periods for some speeches, he or she probably has not asked you to defend or attack any position taken. A useful assignment in a persuasive speaking unit is one that provides an opportunity for students to confront ideas directly, a speech of refutation. In order to make the best use of your potential in social, legislative, vocational, and other decision-making bodies, you must develop some confidence in your abilities to reply.

Specifically, refutation means disproving, denying, or invalidating an idea that was presented. A speech-of-refutation assignment gives you an experience with confrontation without all the trappings of formal debate. In this chapter we focus on what can be refuted and on how refutation is prepared and presented. Then we consider three assignments that allow for differing amounts of direct refutation, and present a debate illustrating the use of refutation.

WHAT CAN BE REFUTED: FALLACIES

Refutation involves attacking your opponent's arguments. What is it that serves as the basis for these attacks? In one word: *weaknesses*. Basically you are looking for weaknesses in data, both quantity and quality, and weaknesses in reasoning. More often than not these weaknesses occur in the form of fallacies. Although books written on the subject of fallacies usually investigate ten to twenty or more possibilities, in this section I wish to focus on five common fallacies that you are likely to find in your opponents' speeches.

Hasty Generalization

A *hasty generalization* is a fallacy that is based on quantity of data. As you review argument from generalization covered in Chapter 14, you will recall that to meet the tests of logic, generalization must be based on both a sufficient number of instances and a representative sample of instances. Thus, before a person can generalize that teenagers are in favor of decriminalizing marijuana, that person will have to examine a cross-section of teenage opinion that includes both enough teenagers and teenagers from a variety of backgrounds. As we listen to arguments presented in real-life situations, however, we are likely to find generalizations asserted that are based on only one example or at most a few examples. In support of the argument that teenagers are in favor of marijuana, a person might cite the opinions of two teenagers who live next door. Such a generalization would be based on a "cross-section" that is neither large enough nor representative enough. In a speech, the argument may sound more impressive than it is—especially if the person can dramatize the one example.

If your opponent asserts with no substantiation—no data—you have the opportunity to refute his or her argument on that basis alone. There is no way an assertion can stand as proof if it is not supported.

Likewise, you can refute an argument if you think that the data presented were insufficient. For instance, if a person says, "Food prices are terrible, the price of a dozen eggs has gone up ten cents in the last week," you could question whether the price of eggs is indicative of other products. Perhaps last week eggs were on sale at ten cents below normal price. Perhaps other food products have actually gone down in price. A single item of data is seldom enough to support a major conclusion.

Attacking quantity of data is the easiest form of refutation. Although students who understand argumentative speaking should not make the mistakes of asserting or using too few data, you may still find an opportunity to refute a speech on that basis.

Appeals to Authority

Appeal to authority is a fallacy based on quality of data. When a speaker supports an argument with the testimony of an authority, you can refute it as being fallacious if the use of the testimony fails to meet either of the following tests: (1) Is the source really an authority on the issue being discussed? and (2) Is the content of the testimonial out of line with other expert opinion?

Let us consider the first criterion: Is the source really an authority on the issue being discussed? Advertisers are well aware that because of adulation of athletes, movie stars, and television performers, the public is willing to transfer the entertainer's credibility to areas in which there is no logical reason for accepting that credibility. So, because Robert Young praises Sanka coffee and Laura Baugh, the golfer, praises Ultra Bright, people are led to buy those products. Robert Young's expertise in acting and Laura Baugh's in golfing do not qualify them to make authoritative statements about coffee or toothpaste.

Of course, the fallacy of authority in these two examples is easy to spot. At other times this fallacy is not so easy to pinpoint. Economists, politicians, and scientists often sound off about subjects outside their areas of expertise; sometimes neither they nor we realize how unqualified they are to speak on such subjects. A scientist's statement is good evidence only in the area of science in which he or she is an expert. Thus, a geneticist's views on the subject of the world food supply may or may not be fallacious, depending on the point he or she is trying to make.

The second test question is "Is the content of the testimonial out of line with other expert opinion?" Even when an authority states an opinion relevant to an area in which he or she is an authority, citing that opinion may be fallacious if the opinion is one that is not supported by a majority of other authorities in that field. If a space biologist contends that there must be life like our own on other planets, his or her opinion is no more logical proof than any other opinion; it is not even an authoritative opinion if a majority of other equally qualified space biologists believe otherwise. If you look long enough you can always find someone who has said something in support of even the most foolish statements. Try to avoid the mistake of accepting any statement as valid support for an argument just because some alleged authority is cited as the source of the statement.

Appeals Based on Statistics

Fallacies in use of statistics may be based on quantity of data, quality of data, or reasoning from data. The potential fallacies from statistics are so numerous that there is no way I can do total justice to the subject in this short analysis. To be safe, you should look at any statistical proof as potentially fallacious. The old saying, "Figures don't lie, but liars figure," is so applicable to the general use of statistics that I for one have become very cynical and am suspicious of any argument that is made solely on the basis of statistics. Now, I am not saying that every use of statistics is a conscious effort to trick the listener. Often statistics that are used honestly and with the best of motives are still fallacious. I believe this is true mostly because clear, logical use of statistics is difficult.

Statistics are nothing more than large numbers of instances. Yet, statistics seem to have bewitching force—most of us seem conditioned to believe that instances cast in statistical form carry a real weight of authority. As you examine your opponent's arguments look for at least the following uses:

1. Statistics that are impossible to verify. If you are like me, you have read countless startling statements such as "Fifteen million mosquitoes are hatched each day in the Canadian province of Ontario" or "One out of every 17 women in ancient Greece had six fingers." Now, don't go around quoting these—I made them up; but they are no more unlikely than many other examples I have seen. The fact is we have no way of verifying such statistics. How does anyone count the number of mosquitoes hatched? How can we test whether anyone counted the fingers on women of ancient Greece? Statistics of this kind are startling and make for interesting conversation, but as support for arguments they are fallacious.

2. Statistics used alone. Statistics by themselves do not really mean much. "Last season the Cincinnati Reds drew about 2.7 million fans to their seventy home games." Although at face value this sounds like (and it is) a lot of people, it does not tell much about the club's attendance. Is this figure good or bad? Was attendance up or down? Often, statistics are not meaningful until they are compared with other data.

3. Statistics used with unknown comparative bases. Comparisons between and among statistics do not mean much if the comparative base is not given. Consider the following statement: "While the Zolon growth rate was dawdling along at some 3 percent last year, Allon was growing at a healthy 8 percent." Now this statement implies that Allon is doing much better than Zolon; however, if Zolon's base was larger, its 3 percent increase could be much better than Allon's 8 percent. We cannot know unless we understand the entire economic base.

Ad Hominem
Argument

An *ad hominem argument* can reveal a fallacy based on quality of data. Literally, *ad hominem* means "to the man." The fallacy occurs when an attack is made on the person making an argument rather than on the argument itself. For instance if Bill Bradley, the highly intelligent and very articulate former New York Knicks basketball player, presented the argument that athletics are important to the development of a total person, the reply "Great, all we need is some jock justifying his own existence" would be an example of ad hominem argument.

When a personal attack is made, you will find more often than not that it is used as a smokescreen to cover up for a lack of good reasons and evidence—ad hominem, name calling, is then used to try to encourage the audience to ignore the lack of evidence. Make no mistake, ridicule, name calling, and other personal attacks are at times highly effective—but they are almost always fallacious.

Questionable Cause

Questionable cause involves fallacy based on weakness of reasoning. It seems to be human nature that we seek causes for events we experience or learn about. If we are having a drought, we want to know what caused it; if the school is in financial trouble, we want to seek the cause; if the crime rate has gone up during the year, we want to find out the cause. In our haste to discover causes for behavior, we sometimes identify something that happened or existed before the event or at the time of the event, and label that something as the cause of the event. This tendency leads to the fallacy of questionable cause.

Think of the people who blame loss of money, sickness, and problems at work on black cats that ran in front of them or mirrors they broke or ladders they walked under. You recognize these as superstitions. Nevertheless, they are excellent examples of attributing cause to unrelated events.

Superstitions are not the only examples of questionable cause. Consider a situation that occurs yearly on many college campuses. One year a coach's team has a winning year and the coach is lauded for his or her expertise. The next year the team does poorly and the coach is *fired*. Has the coach's skill deteriorated that much in one year? It is quite unlikely. But it's much easier to point the finger at the coach as the cause of the team's failure than it is to admit that the entire team or the program itself is inferior. The fact is that examples of this kind of argument abound.

How do you cope with the fallacy of questionable cause? You

should keep in mind that an event is seldom a result of a single cause. Attribution of an event to one cause is almost always fallacious. When you find a speaker attempting this form of argument, you should refute it on the basis of weakness in reasoning.

HOW TO REFUTE

Refutation, like all other aspects of speech making, can and should be handled systematically. A speech of refutation begins with anticipation of what the opponent will say. If you research your opponent's side of the proposition as carefully as you research your own, you will seldom be surprised by his or her arguments. The second step of refutation is to take careful notes on your opponent's speech. The key words, phrases, and ideas should be recorded accurately and as nearly as possible in the actual words used. You do not want to run the risk of being accused of distorting what your opponent really said. Divide your note paper in half vertically and outline your opponent's speech in the one column. Use the other column to note your line of refutation on each of the particular points.

At this stage you will have anticipated your opponent's preparation and you will have a reasonably accurate account of all your opponent said. Now, how are you going to reply? You will present refutation based on the quantity of the data, the quality of the data, and the reasoning from the data. Although you do not have as long to consider exactly what you are going to say, your refutation must be organized nearly as well as your planned informative and persuasive speaking assignments. If you will think of refutation in terms of units of argument, each of which is organized by following four definite steps, you will learn to prepare and to present refutation effectively:

1. State the argument you are going to refute clearly and concisely. (Or as the advocate replying to refutation, state the argument you are going to rebuild.)

2. State what you will prove; you must tell your listeners how you plan to proceed so that they will be able to follow your thinking.

3. Present the proof completely with documentation.

4. Draw a conclusion; do not rely on the audience to draw the proper conclusion for you. Never go on to another argument before you have drawn your conclusion.

In order to illustrate the process of refutation, let us examine both a small portion of a typical note sheet and a short unit of refutation directed to that one particular argument. Notice that in the notes the proposition is written out in full, the main point is written out as a complete sentence, and subpoints include enough to reflect the content. In the "Comment" column, the speaker sketches his or her thoughts related to each point made.

Comments	*Outline of One Argument*
(Thoughts recorded by the opponent while listening to advocate's speech)	*Proposition (Specific Purpose):* To prove that students should purchase insurance while they are young.
True, but are these necessarily beneficial?	I. Buying insurance while you are young provides a systematic, compulsory savings.
True, but what if you miss a payment?	A. Each due period you get a notice—Banks, etc., don't provide service.
True, but what if you need money? You can borrow, but you have to pay interest on your own money! Cash settlement results in loss of money benefits.	B. Once money is invested it is saved—there's no put and take with insurance.

In the following abbreviated statement, notice how the four steps of refutation (stating the argument, stating what you will prove, presenting proof, and drawing a conclusion) are incorporated. For purposes of analysis, each of the four steps is enumerated.

> [1] The speaker has said that buying insurance provides a systematic, compulsory savings. [2] Her assumption is that "systematic, compulsory savings" is a *benefit* of buying insurance while you are young. But I believe that just the opposite is true—I believe that there are at least two serious disadvantages resulting from this. [3] First, the system is so compulsory that if you miss a payment you stand to lose your entire savings and all benefits. Most insurance contracts include a clause giving you a thirty-day grace period, after which the policy is canceled . . . [evidence]. Second, if you need money desperately, you have to take a loan on your policy. The end result of such a loan is that you have to pay interest in order to borrow your own money . . . [evidence]. [4] From this analysis, I think you can see that the "systematic, compulsory saving" is more a disadvantage than an advantage for young people who are trying to save money.

Assignment A   *Working with a classmate, select a debatable proposition and clear the wording with your professor. Phrase the proposition so that the first speaker is in favor of the proposal. Speaker A presents a four- to six-minute speech of conviction in support of the proposition. Speaker B presents a four- to six-minute speech of conviction in refutation of the proposal.*

Assignment B   *Working with a classmate, select a debatable proposition and clear the wording with your professor. Phrase the proposition so that the first speaker is in favor of the proposal. Speaker A presents a two- to four-minute speech of conviction in support of the proposal. Speaker B presents a two- to four-minute speech of conviction in refutation of the proposal. Each speaker then gets two minutes to question the opponent, after which each speaker gets two minutes to summarize his or her case.*

Assignment C   *Working with a classmate, select a debatable proposition and clear the wording with your professor. Phrase the proposition so that the first speaker is in favor of the proposal. Speaker A presents a four-minute speech in support of the proposal; Speaker B presents a five-minute speech in refutation; Speaker A presents a two-minute speech of summary-refutation.*

Criteria for evaluation will include soundness of argument and skill in refutation.

SPEECHES   The following two speeches are presented to illustrate the debate format. The first speech is a speech of conviction with two reasons in support of the proposition. The second is a speech of refutation.[1]

Instead of analyzing this first speech on the basis of its effectiveness as a speech, analyze it as if you were to give the speech of refutation. That is, consider its strengths and weaknesses, but do so in a context of how you would develop your refutation. After you have determined a strategy for refuting the speech, read the analysis.

---

[1] These two speeches are based on a debate between Sheila Kohler and Martha Feinberg presented at the University of Cincinnati, and are printed with their permission.

| *Analysis* | *Speech of Conviction: Use of Lie Detector Tests* |

Analysis

The negative speaker should outline as clearly as possible the key affirmative points.

Special care should be taken to write affirmative reasons accurately.

Accuracy of tests is very important. Is there confirmation for this estimate? If so, accept it and/or work around it. If not, correct it.

Decision on how to deal with ''misleading'' will depend on development.

These two examples are very emotional and may be persuasive. But, (1) only two examples have been given. Nothing has been presented to show that the examples are representative. (2) The examples do not necessarily indicate a problem with the mechanics of testing.

Assuming that testers are relatively incompetent, how

Speech of Conviction: Use of Lie Detector Tests

Lie detector or polygraph tests used either to screen job applicants or to uncover thefts by employees have become a big business. Hundreds of thousands are given each year, and the number is steadily rising. What I propose to you today is that employers should be prohibited from administering lie detector tests to their employees either as a condition of employment or as a condition of maintaining the job. I support this proposition for two reasons. First, despite technological improvement in equipment, the accuracy of results is open to question; and second, even if the tests are accurate, use of lie detector tests is an invasion of privacy.

First, let's consider the accuracy. Lie detector tests just have not proved to be very accurate. According to Senator Birch Bayh, tests are only about 70 percent accurate. And equally important, even the results of this 70 percent can be misleading. Let's look at two examples of the kinds of harm that come from these misleading results.

One case involves a young girl named Linda Boycose. She was at the time of the incident a bookkeeper for Kresge's. One day she reported a dollar and fifty cents missing from the previous day's receipts. A few weeks later the store's security man gave her a lie detector test. He first used the equipment with all its intimidating wiring and then he used persuasion to get information. He accused her of deceiving him and actually stealing the money. After this test, Boycose was so upset she quit her job—she then spent the next two years indulging in valium at an almost suicidal level. Last year a Detroit jury found Boycose's story so convincing that they ordered the Department Store chain to award her $100,000. Now, almost six years later, she is still afraid to handle the bookkeeping at the doctor's office she manages.

The next example is of a supermarket clerk in Los Angeles. She was fired after an emotional response to the question, "Have you ever given discount groceries to your mother?" It was later discovered that her mother had been dead for five years, thus showing that her response was clearly an emotional one.

Much of the inaccuracy of the tests has to do with the examiner's competence. Jerry Wall, a Los Angeles tester, said that out of

does this information affect
negative case? Can this be
either admitted or ignored? If
not, how can it be refuted?

Reemphasis of importance of
level of accuracy.

Can instances of abuse be
admitted without concluding
that tests should be abolished?
How?

This material demonstrates a
threat of government
intervention. But has
government intervened? Has
government determined what
constitutes "invasion of
privacy"?

Strong emotional appeal in this
summary. How can effect of
this be countered?

three thousand estimated U.S. examiners, only fifty are competent. Some polygraph operators tell an interviewee that he or she has lied at one point even if the person has not, just to see how the person will handle the stress. This strategy can destroy a person's poise, leading to inaccuracies. With these examples of stress situations and inefficient examiners, the facts point to the inaccuracy of polygraph test results.

My second reason for abolishing the use of these tests is that they are an invasion of privacy. Examiners can and do ask job applicants about such things as sexual habits and how often they change their underwear. The supposed purpose of lie detector tests is to determine whether an employee is stealing. These irrelevant questions are an invasion of privacy, and not a way to indicate whether someone is breaking the law.

Excesses are such that the federal government has been conducting hearings on misuse. Congress is considering ways to curtail their use.

That they are an invasion of privacy seems to be admitted by the companies that use them. Employers are afraid to reveal too much information from tests because they have a fear of being sued. Because of an examiner's prying questions on an employee's background, and because government has shown such a concern about the continued use of polygraphs, we can conclude that they are an invasion of privacy.

In conclusion, let me ask you how, as an employee, you would feel taking such a test. You'd probably feel nervous and reluctant to take the test. Couldn't you see yourself stating something that would be misconstrued, not because of the truth, but because of your nervousness? Also, how would you feel about having to answer very personal and intimate questions about yourself in order to get a job.

Because lie detector tests are inaccurate and an invasion of privacy, I believe their use should be prohibited.

In this speech, we would expect the speaker to say something about the two reasons that were presented in the first speech. In your analysis, look to see how the groundwork for refutation is laid; then look for the use of the four step method of refutation.

Analysis

Good opening. Speaker has clearly stated her position.

Speaker has clearly laid the groundwork for her negative position. This material establishes a need for some measures to be taken against theft. It shows that tests are not being used without good reason.

This represents further clarification of what affirmative has done and what negative proposes to do. It helps to place affirmative attack in proper perspective.

Good direct attack on level of accuracy. Notice she states opponent's point, states her position on the point, and then presents the evidence. She needs a concluding statement to tie the unit of refutation together.
But why are Kelley's figures better than Bayh's? She needs to show us.

Good job of debating the conclusion to be drawn from the example. Still, I would like to have heard her make a closer examination of the examples themselves.

That businesses use the tests does not prove that businesses are convinced they are

Speech of Refutation: *Use of Lie Detector Tests*

My opponent has stated that the use of lie detector tests by employers should be abolished. I strongly disagree; I believe employers have to use these tests.

Before examining the two reasons she presented, I'd like to take a look at why more than 20 percent of the nation's largest businesses feel a need to use these tests and why the number is growing each year. Employers use lie detector tests to help curb employee theft. According to the National Retail Merchants Association, employees steal as much as $40 billion of goods each year. Moreover, the figure increases markedly each year. The average merchant doesn't recognize that he loses more to employees than to outsiders. Fifty to seventy percent of theft losses go to employees, not to shoplifters. This use of lie detector tests is a necessity to curb this internal theft.

Now, I do not believe that my opponent ever tried to show that there is not a problem that lie detector testing solves; nor did she try to show that lie detector testing doesn't help to deter internal theft. Notice that the two reasons she presented are both about abuses. Let's take a closer look at those two reasons.

First, my opponent said that the accuracy of results is open to question; in contrast, I would argue that these tests are remarkably accurate. She mentioned that Senator Bayh reported a 70 percent level of accuracy. Yet the literature on these tests as reported by Ty Kelley, Vice President of Government Affairs of the National Association of Chain Drug Stores argues that the level is around 90 percent, not 70 percent.

She went on to give two examples of people who were intimidated and/or became emotional and upset when subjected to the test. And on this basis she calls for them to be abolished. I would agree that some people do become emotional, but this is hardly reason for stopping their use. Unless she can show a real problem among many people taking the test I think we'll have to go along with the need for the tests.

If these tests are so inaccurate, why are one-fifth of the nation's largest companies using them. According to an article in *Business Week*, "Business Buys the Lie Detector," more and more businesses each year see a necessity for using the tests because they deter crime. These tests are now being used by nearly every type of accurate. Need more factual data here.

company—banks, businesses, drug stores, as well as retail department stores.

Her second reason for why the tests should be abolished is that they are an invasion of privacy. I believe, with Mr. Kelley, whom I quoted earlier, that there must be some sort of balance maintained between an individual's right to privacy and an employer's right to protect his property. In Illinois, for instance, a state judge ruled that examiners could ask prying questions—there has yet to be any official ruling that the use is "an invasion of privacy."

This is a further attempt to put affirmative argument into proper perspective. Judge's ruling gives strong support to her position.

Good line of argument. Any attempt at refuting alleged abuses would be damaging to negative position.

Here speaker does a nice job of bringing emphasis back to the need for the tests.

My opponent used the example of asking questions about sexual habits and change of underwear. In that regard, I agree with her. I think that a person is probably pretty sick who is asking these kinds of questions—and I think these abuses should be checked. But asking questions to screen out thieves, junkies, liars, alcoholics, and psychotics is necessary. For instance, an Atlanta Nursing Home uses polygraph tests to screen out potentially sadistic and disturbed nurses and orderlies. Is this an invasion of privacy? I don't think so.

Good summary.

This is a good speech of refutation. It illustrates the importance of showing the negative position before launching into refutation; it illustrates good form for refutation; and it provides several approaches to refutation.

It is obvious to me that some type of lie detector test is needed. Too much theft has gone on and something must be done to curtail this. I say that lie detector tests are the answer. First, they are accurate. Companies have been using them for a long time, and more and more companies are starting to use them. And second, it is only an invasion of privacy when the wrong types of questions are asked. I agree that these abuses should be curbed, but not by doing away with the tests. Employers cannot do away with these tests and control theft; the benefits far outweigh the risks.

Suggested Readings: Part Four

Brembeck, Winston L., and William S. Howell. *Persuasion: A Means of Social Influence,* 2d ed. Englewood Cliffs, N.J.: Prentice-Hall, 1976. This is a new edition of one of the oldest and most widely used contemporary books on persuasion.

Huff, Darrell, and Irving Geis. *How to Lie with Statistics.* New York: W. W. Norton, 1954. This older book is still an excellent source—not for showing you how to use statistics, but for showing you what to look for in their use.

Kahane, Howard. *Logic and Contemporary Rhetoric,* 3d ed. Belmont, Calif.: Wadsworth, 1980 (paperback). This excellent source gives you some outstanding pointers on the use and development of logical argument and a considerable emphasis on identifying and eliminating the fallacies of reasoning.

Kiesler, Charles A., Barry E. Collins, and Norman Miller. *Attitude Change.* New York: Wiley, 1969. A comprehensive analysis of theories of attitude change pointing out strengths, weaknesses, similarities, and differences.

Larson, Charles U. *Persuasion: Reception and Responsibility,* 2d ed. Belmont, Calif.: Wadsworth, 1979. A solid textbook that places more emphasis on the receiver of the persuasive message rather than on the persuader.

Packard, Vance O. *The Hidden Persuaders.* New York: Pocket Books, 1975 (paperback). This popular book, first published in the 1950s, still makes for excellent reading about the problems and excesses of persuasion.

PART FIVE

ADAPTING TO OTHER OCCASIONS AND FORMATS

The speaker will, at times, have to apply his or her skills to group contexts and ceremonial occasions, sometimes using different delivery modes. The material in this unit provides the speaker with the means to meet the challenge of these different goals.

Questions of fact

Questions of value

Questions of policy

CHAIRPERSON

Chapter 17 Speaking in Problem-Solving Groups

The characteristic American response to problem solving is "Let's form a committee." Despite the many jokes about committees and the often justified impatience with them, the committee system and the group discussion it encourages can and should be an effective way of dealing with common problems. For our purposes, *discussion* is defined as a systematic form of speech in which two or more persons meet face to face and interact orally to arrive at a common goal. The goal may be to gain understanding of a topic, it may be for the entertainment of the participants, and in some situations it may be for therapeutic purposes, but in this chapter we focus on problem-solving discussion. By *problem-solving discussion* we mean one in which the group meets to accomplish a particular task (for example, recommend whether the group should donate to Easter Seals and if so, how much) or to arrive at a solution to a common problem (for example, consider what the group can do to enlarge its membership). In addition to competence in the use of fundamental speech principles, effective problem-solving discussion requires knowledge of the forms of discussion, an understanding of the problem-solving method, and guidelines for leadership and participation in problem-solving discussion.

THE FORMS OF DISCUSSION

Practically speaking, group discussions are either public or private. Since these two basic forms influence goals and procedures, let us examine each to show their characteristics and some of their advantages and disadvantages.

Public Discussion   In a public discussion, the group is discussing for the information or enjoyment of a listening audience, as much as they are for the satisfaction of the participating members. As such, public discussions have much in common with traditional public speaking. Two common forms of public discussion are the symposium and the panel.

SYMPOSIUM   A symposium is a discussion in which a limited number of participants (usually three to five) present to an audience individual speeches of approximately the same length dealing with the same subject. After the planned speeches, the participants in the symposium may discuss their reactions with each other or respond to questions from the listening audience. Although the symposium is a common form of public discussion, participation in one can be a dull and frustrating experience. Despite the potential for interaction, a symposium is usually characterized by long, sometimes unrelated individual speeches. Moreover, the part designated for questions is often shortened or deleted because "our time is about up." Discussion implies interaction—a symposium often omits this vital aspect. If the participants make their prepared speeches short enough so that at least half of the available time can be spent on real interaction, a symposium can be interesting and stimulating. In terms of meeting the goals of discussion, a good symposium is much more difficult to present than it appears; however, as a public speaking assignment, the symposium may be very beneficial. Rather than solving a problem, a symposium is more effective in shedding light on or explaining various aspects of a problem.

PANEL DISCUSSION   A panel discussion is one in which the participants, usually from four to eight, discuss a topic spontaneously, under the direction of a leader and following a planned agenda. After the formal discussion, the audience is often encouraged to question the participants. So the discussion can be seen and heard by the audience, the group is seated in a semicircle, with the person chairing it in the middle, to get a good view of the audience and the panelists. Since the discussion is for an audience, the panelists are obliged to make good use of traditional public speaking skills. Because a panel discussion encourages spontaneity and interaction, it can be very stimulating for both a listening audience and the participants themselves. The panel works as a form of problem-solving discussion.

Private Discussion

Although your classroom assignment may be in the form of a panel, the majority of discussions that you participate in will be private. Private discussions are ones in which the participants meet to solve a problem or exchange ideas on a particular topic without the presence of an onlooking or participating audience. Committees convened for the purpose of formulating a recommendation to be submitted to the larger legislative body, to another committee, or to various individuals or agencies authorized to consider such recommendations engage in private discussion. Likewise, individuals who meet informally for the purpose of sharing ideas on topics of mutual interest engage in private discussion. Private discussions are most productive when they are conducted in an atmosphere where all members of the group have equal prominence. The best seating arrangement is a full circle, so that each person can see and talk with everyone else. Sometimes, as a stimulant for study groups, a "resource" person sits in with the group to suggest ideas and to add needed information. Because of the proximity of the participants in private discussion, the group need not be as concerned with all the traditional public speaking skills. Furthermore, since no audience is present, the group can adjust its time to meet the needs of the topic. If the question cannot be resolved in one sitting, the group can meet later.

PREPARATION FOR PROBLEM-SOLVING DISCUSSION

For either public or private discussion, preparation is likely to follow a problem-solving method: phrasing the problem, analyzing the problem, suggesting solutions, and selecting the best solution. This method serves not only as a guideline to preparation but also as a basic outline for the discussion itself.

Phrasing the Problem

Although problems for discussion may be drawn from any subject area, they should be (1) of interest to the group, (2) controversial, (3) capable of being discussed within the time available, and (4) written in question form. Participants' interest is a primary test of a topic for all forms of speech making, including group discussion. Discussion, however, also requires that the topic, the problem, should be controversial. If all discussants have approximately the same point of view or if the subject matter leaves little room for interpretation, there is really very little need for discussion. "How to make a book" may be a satisfactory topic for an informative speech; for a discussion, however, the problem would generate very little collective reaction. On the other hand, the problem "Should *Catcher in the Rye* be included on the required reading list for tenth grade English?" would leave room for various viewpoints. Even if a problem is interesting and controversial, it should not be considered for discussion unless it can be discussed within the time available. In an informal social discussion, there is value in coping with a problem regardless of whether consensus can be reached. For most group discussions, however, the resolution of the problem is the reason for meeting, and until or unless a satisfactory conclusion is reached, the discussion is for nought. If the problem is so broad that discussion can only begin to scratch the surface, then a more limited aspect should be considered.

Finally, a discussion problem should be stated in question form. Questions elicit response. Since the goal of discussion is to stimulate group thinking, the problem itself and all of the subheadings are phrased as questions. In phrasing the question, make sure it considers only one subject, that it is impartial, and that the words used can be defined objectively. "Should the United States cut back the foreign aid program and welfare?" considers two different questions; "Should the United States recognize those wretched Palestinians?" would be neither impartial nor definable.

As you consider various phrasings, you will discover that changes in wording affect the kind of response you are seeking. In order to test whether your wording correlates with your intentions, you should understand the implications of questions of fact, questions of value, and question of policy.

QUESTIONS OF FACT   These determine what *is*. Implied in such a question is the possibility of determining the facts by way of direct observed, spoken, or recorded evidence. For instance, "How much rain fell today?" is a question of fact because rain can be measured and recorded. "Is Smith guilty of robbing the warehouse?" is also a question of fact. Smith either committed the crime or he did not.

QUESTIONS OF VALUE   These consider relative goodness and badness. They are characterized by the inclusion of some evaluative word such as *good, cool, reliable, effective, worthy.* The purpose of the question of value is to compare a subject with one or more members of the same class. "What was the best movie last year?" is a question of value. Although we can set up criteria for "best" and measure our choice against those criteria, there is no way of verifying our findings. The answer is still a matter of judgment, not a matter of fact. "Is socialism superior to capitalism?" "Is a small-college education better than a large-college education?" are both questions of value.

QUESTIONS OF POLICY These questions judge whether a future action should be taken. The question is phrased to arrive at a solution or to test a tentative solution to a problem or a felt need. "What should we do to lower the crime rate?" seeks a solution that would best solve the problem of the increase in crime. "Should the university give equal amounts of money to men's and to women's athletics?" provides a tentative solution to the problem of how we can achieve equity in financial support of athletics. The inclusion of the word *should* in all questions of policy makes them the easiest to recognize and the easiest to phrase of all discussion questions.

The applicability of the next three points, analyzing the problem, suggesting possible solutions, and selecting the best solution, vary depending on the kind of question being discussed.

Analyzing the Problem Once the group is in agreement about exactly what the problem is, it should move on to the next step, analyzing the problem. Analysis means determining the nature of the problem: its size, its causes, the forces that create or sustain it, the criteria for evaluating solutions. Sometimes analysis takes only a few minutes; at other times it may take longer. Both in preparation and in the discussion itself, analysis is the stage of problem solving that is most easily sloughed off. It is the natural tendency of the researcher or the group to want to move directly to possible solutions. For instance, if your problem is to determine what should be done to solve the campus parking problem, you may be inclined to start by listing possible solutions immediately. Because this procedure sounds as if it is the logical beginning, the tendency is then to pursue these prematurely offered solutions. However, a solution or a plan can work only *if* it solves the problem at hand. Before you can shape a plan you must decide what obstacles the plan must meet, what symptoms the plan must eliminate, and with what other criteria the plan must deal. Before you even begin to suggest a solution, you should check to make sure that the following questions about the problem have been answered:

I. What is the nature of the problem?
  A. What are its size and scope? (What can we identify that shows that something is wrong or needs to be changed?)
  B. What are its causes? (What forces created it, sustain it, or otherwise keep it from being solved?)
II. What criteria should be used to test the solutions? Specifically, what checklist must the solution meet to best solve this problem? Must the plan eliminate the symptoms, be implemented within present resources, and so on?

Suggesting Possible Solutions

For most problems, there are many possible solutions. If, however, you are considering a problem that needs only a single yes or no solution, your procedure may be altered. Should support for women's sports be increased? This question has only two possible answers. Still, you may need to suggest other solutions for comparison.

How do you come up with solutions? One way is to use brainstorming, stating ideas at random until you have compiled a long list. In a good ten- to fifteen-minute brainstorming session you may think of ten to twenty solutions by yourself. Depending on the nature of the topic a group may come up with 100 possibilities. Of course, some solutions will come through your reading, your interviews with authorities, or from your observation.

Determining the Best Solution

In your preparation you probably will not want to spend much time trying to figure out the best solution, for the best solution should emerge through the group discussion itself. During actual discussion, if the group has analyzed the problem carefully and has suggested enough solutions, then the final step involves only matching each solution against the criteria. For instance, if you have determined that hiring more patrols, putting in closed-circuit television, and locking outside doors after 9:00 P.M. are three possible solutions to the problem of reducing crime on campus, then you begin to measure each against the criteria. The one meeting the most criteria or that meets several criteria most effectively is then selected.

Now let us put these all together with a sample (and somewhat abbreviated) outline that will help the individual get his or her own thoughts together and help the group proceed logically. The group is being convened to discuss "meeting the needs of the commuter."

1. State the problem—suggested wordings:

    What should be done to improve the commuter's campus life?

    What should be done to increase or enlarge commuter opportunities on campus?

    What should be done to better integrate the commuter into the social, political, and extracurricular aspects of student life on campus?

2. Analyze the problem of integrating commuters.

    I. What are size and scope of the problem?
        A. How many commuters are there?
        B. What is the ratio between students living on or close by campus and commuters?
        C. How do commuters spend their campus time?
            1. Are commuters involved in social organizations? How many? What ratio?
            2. Are commuters involved in political organizations? How many? What ratio?
            3. Are commuters involved in extracurricular organizations? How many? What ratio?

    II. What are the causes of the problem?
        A. Do commuters want to be involved?
        B. Do on-campus students discriminate against commuters?
        C. Does the commuters' work life or home life inhibit them?
        D. Is commuting time or method a problem?
        E. Are meeting times for groups discriminatory against the commuter?

    III. What criteria should be used to test solutions?
        A. Will commuters favor the solution?
        B. Will it cope with discrimination (if discrimination exists)?
        C. Will it interfere with commuter needs (work, travel, and the like)?
        D. Will it fit into commuters' time schedules?

3. State possible solutions.

   (The list can be begun at this point—other possible solutions will be revealed later.)

   A commuter information center?

   Commuter representation on Social Board? University Student Union Board?

   Others to be added as they come to mind.

4. Determine the best solution.
   (To be completed during discussion.)

LEADERSHIP IN PROBLEM-SOLVING DISCUSSION

A problem-solving discussion will not work well without effective leadership. Ordinarily we think of an appointed or elected individual acting as leader and all others in the group acting as contributors of content. Although that is the way it is often done, it does not have to be that way. A group can be so organized that everyone shares the burden of leadership. Thus, a group can have leadership whether or not it has a designated leader. In order to decide whether your group should vest leadership responsibilities in one person or not, you must understand the advantages and disadvantages of each kind of situation.

When someone is appointed or elected leader, the group looks to him or her for leadership. If the individual is a good leader, the group will benefit. Each participant can concentrate on considering the issues being raised, confident that the leader will guide the group justly. Disadvantages are related to inadequacy of the leader: When that person is unsure, the group may ramble about aimlessly; when the leader dominates, participants do not feel free to contribute spontaneously and the discussion follows a path predetermined by the leader; when the leader is unskilled, the group can become frustrated and short-tempered. Good leadership is a necessity. When the appointed leader cannot provide it, the group suffers.

When the group is leaderless, everyone has the right and the obligation to show leadership. Ordinarily, leadership will emerge from one, two, or perhaps three members of the group. Since no one has been given the mantle of leadership, everyone is on equal footing, and the discussion can be more spontaneous. Disadvantages are seen in a group where no one assumes leadership or where a few compete for leadership. In such situations, the discussion becomes "leadershipless." Depending on the qualities of the participants, a leaderless discussion can arrive at truly group decisions or it can be a rambling, meaningless collage of fact and opinion. If you have only one round of discussion, I suggest beginning with the method the group will have most confidence in.

Regardless of whether a leader is appointed or whether several members of the group share leadership, certain leadership responsibilities must be met. In this next section, let us assume that you have or wish to assume the responsibilities of leadership.

Establish a Climate   Your first job is to set up a comfortable physical setting that will encourage interaction. The leader is in charge of such physical matters as heat, light, and seating. Make sure the room is at a good comfortable temperature. Make sure that there is enough lighting, and most important, make sure the seating arrangements are conducive to spirited interaction.

Too often, seating is too formal or too informal for the best discussion. By too formal, I mean board-of-directors style. Imagine the long polished oak table with the chairperson at the head, principal lieutenants at right and left, and the rest of the people down the line. Since seating may be an indication of status, how the seating is arranged can facilitate or kill real interaction. In the board-of-directors style, a boss-and-subordinates pattern emerges. People are less likely to speak until they are asked to do so. Moreover, no one has a really good view of all the people present. However, an excessively informal seating may also inhibit interaction—especially if people sit together in small groups or behind one another.

The ideal is the circle. Here, everyone can see everyone else. At least physically, everyone has equal status. If the meeting place does not have a round table, you may be better off with either no table at all or a setting of tables that make a square at which the members can come close to the circle arrangement.

Plan the Agenda   A second leader responsibility is to plan the agenda. You may do this alone or in consultation with the group. When possible, the agenda should be in the hands of the group several days before the discussion. How much preparation any individual member makes depends on many factors, but unless the group has an agenda beforehand, members will not have an opportunity for careful preparation. Too often, when no agenda is planned, the group discussion is a haphazard affair, often frustrating and usually unsatisfying.

What goes into the agenda? Usually a sketch of some of the things that need to be accomplished. In a problem-solving discussion, the agenda should include a suggested procedure for handling the problem. In essence it is an outline form of the steps of problem solving discussed earlier in this chapter. If you are leading a discussion on what should be done to better integrate the campus commuter into the social, political, and extracurricular aspects of student life, the following would be a satisfactory agenda:

I. What is the size and scope of the commuter problem?

II. What are the causes for commuters' not being involved in social, political, and extracurricular activities?

III. What criteria should be used to test possible solutions to the problem?

IV. What are some of the possible solutions to the problem?

V. What one solution or combination of solutions will work best to solve the problem?

Direct the Flow of Discussion   The leader is responsible for directing the flow of discussion. It is in this area that leadership skill is most tested. Let us examine carefully several of the most important elements of this responsibility.

DISCUSSANTS SHOULD HAVE EQUAL OPPORTUNITY TO SPEAK   Conclusions are valid only when they represent the thinking of the entire group. Yet, in discussions some people are more likely or more willing to express themselves than others. For instance, if a typical eight-person discussion group is left to its own devices, two or three may tend to speak as much as the other five or six together; furthermore, one or two members may contribute little if anything. At the beginning of a discussion, at least, you must operate under the assumption that every member of the group has something to contribute. To ensure opportunity for equal participation, those who tend to dominate must be held somewhat in check, and those who are content to observe must be brought into the discussion more.

Accomplishing this ideal balance is a real test of leadership. If an ordinarily reluctant talker is embarrassed by another member of the group, he or she may become even more reluctant to participate. Likewise, if a talkative yet valuable member of the group is constantly restrained, he or she may become less valuable.

Let us first consider the handling of the shy or reluctant speaker. Often, apparently reluctant speakers want to talk but cannot get the floor. As leader you may solve this problem by clearing the road for that speaker. For instance, Mary may give visual and verbal clues of her desire to speak; she may come up on the edge of her seat, she may look as if she wants to talk, or she may even start to say something. Because the reluctant speaker in this posture may often relinquish the opportunity if another more aggressive person competes to be heard, you can help considerably with a comment such as "Just a second, Jim, I think Mary has something she wants to say here." Of course, the moment that Mary is sitting back in her chair with a somewhat vacant look is not the time for such a statement. A second method of drawing out the reluctant speaker is to phrase a question that is sure to elicit some answer and then perhaps some discussion. The most appropriate kind of question is one requiring an opinion rather than a fact. For instance, "Mary, what do you think of the validity of this approach to combatting crime?" is much better than "Mary, do you have anything to say here?" Not only is it specific, but it also requires more than a yes or no answer. Furthermore, such an opinion question will not embarrass Mary if she has no factual material to contribute. Tactful handling of the shy or reluctant speaker can pay big dividends. You may get some information that could not have been brought out in any other way; moreover, when Mary contributes a few times, it builds up her confidence, which in turn makes it easier for her to respond later when she has more to say. Of course, there are times when one or more members do not have anything worth saying, because they are just not prepared. Under such circumstances it is best for you to leave them alone.

As a leader you must also use tact with the overzealous speaker. Remember that Jim, the talkative person, may be talkative because he has done his homework—he may have more information than any other member of the group. If you turn him off, the group may suffer immensely. After he has finished talking, try statements such as: "Jim, that's a very valuable bit of material; let's see whether we can get some reactions from the other members of the group on this issue." Notice that a statement of this kind does not stop him; it suggests that he should hold off for a while. A difficult kind of participant to deal with is the one who must be heard regardless of whether he has anything to say or not. If subtle reminders are ineffective with this individual, you may have to say, "Jim, I know you want to talk, but you're just not giving anyone else a chance. Would you wait until we've heard everyone else on this point?" Of course, the person who may be the most difficult to control is the leader. Leaders often engage in little dialogues with each member of the group. They sometimes exercise so much control that participants believe they can talk only in response to the leader.

There are three common patterns of group discussion (see Figure 17-1, in which the lines represent the flow of discussion among the eight participants). Discussion A represents a leader-dominated group. The lack of interaction often leads to a rigid, formal, and usually poor discussion. Discussion B represents a more spontaneous group. Since three people dominate and a few are not heard, however, conclusions will not represent group thinking. Discussion C represents something closer to the ideal pattern. It illustrates a great deal of spontaneity, a total group representation, and theoretically at least, the greatest possibility for reliable conclusions.

KEEP THE DISCUSSION ON THE TOPIC   Not only must the leader see to it that the key ideas are discussed, but also he or she needs to get maximum value out of each point that is made. The skill that best helps here is appropriate questioning.

Although the members of any group bring a variety of skills, information, and degrees of motivation to the group, they do not always operate at peak efficiency without help from the leader.

FIGURE 17-1   Patterns of Group Discussion

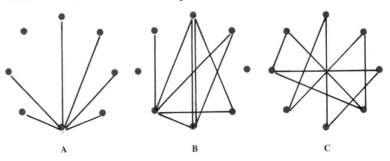

A   B   C

Perhaps one of the most effective tools of effective leadership is the ability to question appropriately. This skill involves knowing when to ask questions and knowing what kinds of questions to ask.

By and large, the leader should refrain from questions that can be answered yes or no. To ask a group member whether he or she is satisfied with a point that was just made will not lead very far, for after the yes or no answer you must ask another question to draw the person out or you must change the subject. The two most effective types of questions are those that call for supporting information and those that are completely open-ended, giving the member complete freedom of response. For instance, rather than asking John whether he has had any professors who were particularly good lecturers, you could say, "John, what are some of the characteristics that made your favorite lecturers particularly effective?" or, "John, from your experience in listening to speakers, what would you select as most important elements of speaker effectiveness?"

When to ask questions is particularly important. Although we could list fifteen to twenty circumstances, let us focus on four purposes of questioning:

1. **To focus the discussion:** Individual statements usually have a point; the statements themselves relate to a larger point being made; and the general discussion relates to an issue or to an agenda item. You can use questions to determine a speaker's point or to determine the relationship of the point to the issue or agenda item; for instance: "Are you saying that the instances of marijuana leading to hard-drug use don't indicate a direct causal relationship?" Or, to what has just been said: "How does that information relate to the point that Mary just made?" Or, to ask about an issue or an agenda item: "In what way does this information relate to whether or not marijuana is a problem?"

2. **To probe for information:** Many statements need to be developed, supported, or in some way dealt with. Yet, members of a group often apparently ignore or accept a point without probing it. When the point seems important, the leader should do something with it. For instance, on a question of source, you can say: "Where did you get that information, Sonia?" Or, to develop a point: "That seems pretty important—what do we have that corroborates the point?" Or, to test the strength of a point: "Does that statement

represent the thinking of the group?" Or, to generate discussion: "That point sounds rather controversial—why should we accept the point as stated?"

3.   To initiate discussion: During a discussion, there are times when lines of development are apparently ignored, when the group seems ready to agree before sufficient testing has taken place. At these times, it is up to the leader to suggest a starting point for further discussion; for instance: "OK, we seem to have a pretty good grasp of the nature of the problem, but we haven't looked at any causes yet. What are some of the causes?"

4.   To deal with interpersonal problems that develop: Sometimes the leader can help a member ventilate very personal feelings; for instance: "Ted, I've heard you make some strong statements on this point. Would you care to share them with us?" At times, a group may attack a person instead of the information that is being presented. Here you can say: "I know Marie presented the point, but let's look at the merits of the information presented. Do we have any information that goes counter to this point?"

Questions by themselves are not going to make a discussion. In fact, some questions can hurt the discussion that is taking place. The effective leader uses questions sparingly but decisively.

SUMMARIZE FREQUENTLY   Often a group talks for a considerable period, then takes a vote on how they feel about the subject. A good problem-solving discussion group should move in an orderly manner toward intermediate conclusions represented by summary statements seeking group consensus. For instance, on the question "What should be done to lower the crime rate on campus?" the group would have to reach consensus on each of the following questions:

> What is the problem?
>
> What are the symptoms of the problem? (Draw intermediate conclusion; ask whether group agrees.)
>
> What are the causes? (Draw intermediate conclusion on each cause separately or after all causes have been considered; ask whether group agrees.)
>
> What criteria should be used to test the solution?
>
> What is one criterion? (Draw conclusions about each criterion.)
>
> What are some of the possible solutions? (Determine whether all possible solutions have been brought up.)

What is the best solution?

How does each of the solutions meet the criteria? (Discuss each and draw conclusions about each; ask whether group agrees.)

Which solution best meets the criteria? (The conclusion to this final question concludes the discussion; ask whether all agree.)

During the discussion the group might draw six, eight, ten, or even fifteen conclusions before it is able to arrive at the answer to the topic question. The point is that the group should not arrive at the final conclusion until each of the subordinate questions is answered to the satisfaction of the entire group.

It is up to the leader to point up these conclusions by summarizing what has been said and seeking consensus on a conclusion. Everyone in the group should realize when the group has really arrived at some decision. If left to its own devices, a group will discuss a point for a while, then move on to another before a conclusion is drawn. The leader must sense when enough has been said to reach a consensus. Then he or she must phrase the conclusion, subject it to testing, and move on to another area. You should become familiar with phrases that can be used during the discussion:

"I think most of us are stating the same points. Are we really in agreement that . . ." (State the conclusion.)

"We've been discussing this for a while and I think I sense an agreement. Let me state it, and then we'll see whether it does summarize group feeling." (State the conclusion.)

"Now we're getting on to another area. Let's make sure that we are really agreed on the point we've just finished." (State the conclusion.)

"Are we ready to summarize our feelings on this point?" (State the conclusion.)

MAINTAIN NECESSARY CONTROL   A leader must maintain control of the discussion. Remember, absence of leadership leads to chaos. Group members need to feel that someone is in charge. If the group has a set of formal rules, be sure the rules are followed (at times rule bending is necessary, but breaking all the rules does not help the group). As leader, remember that some members will be playing negative roles in the discussion; do not let them spoil the outcome. You are in charge. You are responsible. You have authority. You need to exercise it on occasion for the benefit of the group. If John is about to talk for the fortieth time, it is up to you to harness him. If Jack and Mary are constantly sparring with each other, it is up to you to harmonize their differences. If something internal or external threatens the work of the group, it is up to you to deal with it. Also, when the group has solved its problem, end the discussion smoothly. Some discussion groups meet by time instead of by problem. Just because you are scheduled to discuss for an hour does not mean that you cannot stop in forty-five minutes if you have the job done.

RESPONSIBILITIES OF DISCUSSANTS

Even the most successful leader will fail if the members of the discussion group do not fulfill their responsibilities. Good discussion is characterized by members accomplishing various task and maintenance roles and avoiding various negative roles.

Discussants Should Fill Positive Roles

Everyone in the group has a responsibility to fill certain roles within the group. A role is a kind of behavior that you determine for yourself or that is determined for you by the expectations of the group. Sometimes a person plays only one role throughout the duration of the discussion. At other times a person may play several roles simultaneously or alternately, and, of course, more than one person can play a given role in a discussion. In a successful group discussion all the positive roles are usually played sometime during the discussion; an unsuccessful discussion group may be one in which no one plays the positive roles or one in which negative role playing predominates. Let us examine the most common and most essential positive roles.

Group roles consist of both task and maintenance functions. The *task function* involves doing the job in the best manner; the *maintenance function* involves how the group handles the way they talk about their task, the nature of the interaction, and dealing with the feelings of the group. In a successful group discussion, both functions are usually satisfied. Thus, when we analyze a discussion, we look first to see how and whether they solved the problem; second, we look to see how well the group worked together, and whether members liked, respected, and understood other members of the group.

TASK ROLES In most groups there are at least four major task roles that can be identified.

1.   The information or opinion giver provides content for the discussion. Actual information provides about 50 percent of what is done in a group. Without information and well-considered opinions, the group will not have the material from which to draw its decisions. Probably everyone in the group plays this role during the discussion. Nevertheless, there are usually one or more persons who have really done their homework. Either as a result of past experience with this or a related problem, long conversations with people who have worked with similar problems, or a great deal of study, these persons are relied upon or called upon to provide the facts. In some groups, a designated resource person or consultant is called in solely to fulfill the information-giving role. In most groups, one or more persons take it upon themselves to be especially well prepared.

Playing the information-giving role well requires solid preparation. The more material you have sampled, the better knowledge you will have of the subject, and the more valuable your contributions will be. As a guideline to quantity of resource material, you should have access to considerably more than you could get into the discussion. It is not uncommon for discussants to be familiar with eight or ten sources. Since, of course, you cannot predict all of the ideas that will be covered in the discussion or when you will be speaking, you cannot prepare your actual contributions ahead of time. Nevertheless, you should be familiar enough with the material that you can find any item you need when you need it. Usually, you will bring your sources with you to the discussion. If you are disallowed the use of the actual sources by your professor, then make notecards containing all the material you are likely to need for the discussion.

Not only should you have sound information, but you should also be prepared to draw conclusions from information that has been presented. Discussants must pool information to provide a basis for conclusions about the topic question. Students sometimes blame the sterility of their discussion on the need to present information responsibly. Yet sterility is a result of poor discussants, not the format. You can still offer opinions, but unlike social sessions in which opinions substitute for data, in discussion, your opinions are based on the previously tested materials.

Perhaps most important, the discussant must be as objective as possible with the presentation of material. Let us focus on two recommendations for ensuring objectivity of approach. First, report data, don't associate yourself with it. If you reported that crime has risen 33 percent in the past five years, don't feel that because you presented the data that you must defend it. An excellent way of presenting data with a degree of disassociation is illustrated by the following: "According to *U.S. News & World Report,* crime has risen 33 percent in the past five years. That seems like a startling statistic. I wonder whether anyone else found either any substantiating or any contradictory data?" Presenting data in this way tells the group that you want discussion of the data and that, whether it is substantiated or disproven, you have no personal relationship with it. Contrast that disassociative approach with the following statement: "I think crime is going up at a fantastic rate. Why, I found that crime has gone up 33 percent in the past five years, and we just can't put up with that kind of thing." This speaker is taking a position with the data. Since anyone who questions the data or the conclusions is going to have to contend with the speaker, there's a good chance that the discussion that follows will not be the most objective.

A second recommendation for ensuring objectivity is to solicit all viewpoints on every major issue. Suppose you were discussing the question "Should financial support of women's sports be increased?" Suppose that after extensive reading you believed that it should. If in the discussion you spoke only to support your position and you took issue with every bit of contrary material, you would not be responding objectively. Although there is nothing wrong with formulating tentative opinions based on your research, in the discussion you should present material objectively whether it supports or opposes your tentative claims. If the group draws a conclusion that corresponds to your tentative conclusion, fine. At least all views have had the opportunity to be presented. If the group draws the opposite conclusion, you are not put in a defensive position. By being objective, you may find that during the discussion your views will change many times. Remember, if the best answer to the topic question could be found without discussion, the discussion would not be necessary.

The information giver identifies himself by such statements as: "Well, when Jones Corporation considered this problem, they found. . . ." Or, "That's a good point you made—just the other day I ran across these figures that substantiate your point." Or, "According to Professor Smith, it doesn't necessarily work that way. He says. . . ."

2.   The information seeker, the opposite of the information giver, is a role played by the member of the group who sees that at a given point the group needs data in order to function. Again, in most groups more than one person takes this role during the discussion; yet, one or more are often especially perceptive in seeing where more information is needed.

The role of information seeker may be accomplished by raising questions about and probing into the contributions of others. Your obligation does not end with the reading of items of information into the record. Once an item of data has been submitted, it is the obligation of the membership to determine whether the item is accurate, typical, consistent, and otherwise valid. Suppose that in a discussion on reducing crime, a person mentioned that, according to *U.S. News & World Report*, crime had risen 33 percent in the past five years; the group should not leave this statement until they have explored it fully. What was the specific source of the data? On what were the data based? What years are being referred to? Is this consistent with other material? Is any countermaterial available? Now, the purpose of these questions is not to debate the data, but to test them. If these data are partly true, questionable, or relevant only to certain kinds of crime, a different conclusion or set of conclusions would be appropriate.

The information seeker may be identified by such questions as: "What did we say the base numbers were?" Or, "Have we decided how many people this really affects?" Or, "Well, what functions does this person serve?" or, "Have we got anything to give us some background on this subject?"

3.   The expediter is the individual who perceives when the group is going astray. Whether the group is meeting once or is an ongoing group, almost invariably some remarks will tend to sidetrack the group from the central point or issue in front of them. Sometimes apparent digressions are necessary to get background, to enlarge the scope, or even to give a person an opportunity to get something off his or her chest. Often in a group these momentary digressions lead to tangents that take the group far afield from their assignment. Because tangents are sometimes more fun than the task itself, a tangent often is not realized for what it is and the group discusses it as if it were important to the group decision. Expediters are the people who help the group stick to its agenda; they help the group stay with the problem at hand. When the group has strayed, they help lead it back to the mainstream. This role is revealed by such statements as: "Say, I'm enjoying this, but I can't quite see what it has to do with whether permissiveness is really a cause." Or, "Let's see, aren't we still trying to find out whether these are the only criteria that we should be considering?" Or, "I've got the feeling that this is important to the point we're on now, but I can't quite get hold of the relationship—am I off base?" Or, "Say, time is getting away from us and we've only considered two possible solutions. Aren't there some more?"

4.   The analyzer is the person who is the master of technique. He or she knows the problem-solving method inside out. The analyzer knows when the group has skipped a point, has passed over a point too lightly, or has not taken a look at matters they need to. More than just *expediting,* the analyzer helps the group penetrate to the core of the problem they are working on. In addition, the analyzer examines the reasoning of various participants. The tests he or she applies may be seen by looking at the explanation of common forms of reasoning discussed on pages 274–281. The analyzer may be recognized from such statements as: "Tom, you're generalizing from only one instance. Can you give us some others?" Or, "Wait a minute, after symptoms, we have to take a look at causes." Or, "I think we're passing over Jones too lightly. There are still criteria we haven't used to measure him by."

MAINTENANCE ROLES   In most discussion groups at least three major maintenance roles facilitate good working relationships.

1.   The active listener feeds back specific reactions to group members. People participating in groups are likely to feel better about their participation when their thoughts and feelings are recognized. In any group we expect that nearly everyone will exhibit active listening traits at some time, but people tend to get so wrapped up in their own ideas that they may neglect to reward the positive comments that are made. The true active listener responds verbally, or at least nonverbally, whenever a good point is made.

The active listener is recognized through such nonverbal cues as a smile, a nod, or a vigorous head shake. Verbally he or she is recognized by such statements as "Good point, Mel," "I really like that idea, Susan," "It's obvious you've really done your homework, Peg," and "That's one of the best ideas we've had today, Al."

2.   The harmonizer brings the group together. It is a rare group that can expect to accomplish its task without some minor if not major conflicts. Even when people get along well they are likely to get angry over some inconsequential points in heated discussion. Most groups experience some classic interpersonal conflicts caused by different personality types. The harmonizer is responsible for reducing and reconciling misunderstanding, disagreements, and conflicts. He or she is good at pouring oil on troubled waters, encourages objectivity, and is especially good as a mediator for hostile, aggressively competing sides. A group cannot avoid some conflict, but if there is no one present to harmonize, participation can become an uncomfortable experience. The harmonizer may be recognized by such statements as: "Bill, I don't think you're giving Mary a chance to make her point." Or, "Tom, Jack, hold it a second. I know you're on opposite sides of this, but let's see where you might have some agreement." Or, "Lynne, I get the feeling that something Todd said really bugged you, is that right?" Or, "Hold it, everybody, we're really coming up with some good stuff; let's not lose our momentum by getting into a name-calling thing."

3.   **The gatekeeper is the person who helps to keep communication channels open.** If a group has seven people in it, the assumption is that all seven have something to contribute. However, if all are to feel comfortable in contributing, those who tend to dominate need to be held in check and those who tend to be reticent need to be encouraged. The gatekeeper is the one who sees that Jane is on the edge of her chair, ready to talk, but just cannot seem to get in, or that Don is rambling a bit and needs to be directed, or that Tom's need to talk so frequently is making Cesar withdraw from the conversation, or that Betty has just lost the thread of discussion. As we said earlier, a characteristic of good group work is interaction. The gatekeeper assumes the responsibility for facilitating interaction. The gatekeeper may be recognized by such statements as: "Joan, I see you've got something to say here. . . ." Or, "You've made a really good point, Todd; I wonder whether we could get some reaction on it. . . ." Or, "Bill and Marge, it sounds like you're getting into a dialogue here; let's see what other ideas we have."

Discussants Should Avoid Negative Roles	The following are the four most common negative roles that group discussants should try to avoid.

1.   **The aggressor is the person who works for his or her own status by criticizing almost everything or blaming others when things get rough.** His main purpose seems to be to deflate the ego

or status of others. One way of dealing with the aggressor is to confront him. Ask him whether he is aware of what he is doing and of the effect it is having on the group.

2.   The joker's behavior is characterized by clowning, mimicking, or generally disrupting by making a joke of everything. This person, too, is usually trying to call attention to himself. He must be the center of attention. A little bit of a joker goes a long way. The group needs to get the joker to consider the problem seriously, or he will constantly be an irritant to other members. One way to proceed is to encourage him when tensions need to be released but to ignore him when there is serious work to be done.

3.   The withdrawer refuses to be a part of the group. She is a mental dropout. Sometimes she is withdrawing from something that was said; sometimes she is just showing her indifference. Try to draw her out with questions. Find out what she is especially good at and rely on her when her skill is required. Sometimes complimenting her will bring her out.

4.   The monopolizer needs to talk all the time. Usually he is trying to impress the group that he is well read, knowledgeable, and of value to the group. He should, of course, be encouraged when his comments are helpful. However, when he is talking too much or when his comments are not helpful, the leader needs to interrupt him or draw others into the discussion.

Group Assignment   *Participants select a question of fact, value, or policy for a 20- to 40-minute discussion. Determine method of leadership, and establish an agenda. Criteria for evaluation of the discussion will include quality of participation, quality of leadership, and ability to arrive at group decisions.*

Chapter 18 Adapting to Special Occasions

Most of your speaking time in and out of class will be spent exchanging information or persuading. At times, however, you may be called upon to speak under more ceremonial circumstances.

Although no speech can be given by formula, these occasions require at least the knowledge of some conventions expected by many audiences. Of course, speakers should always use their own imagination in developing their thesis; they should never adhere slavishly to those conventions. Still, one should know the conventions before trying to deviate from them.

This chapter gives the basics for accomplishing five common types of special speeches: introductions, presentations, acceptances, welcomings, and tributes. In addition, the chapter considers alternate forms of delivery for these and other speeches.

INTRODUCTIONS

The occasion calls for a short but important speech.

Purpose

The purpose of the introduction is to pave the way for the main speaker. If you make the introduction in such a way that the audience is psychologically ready to listen to the speech, then you have accomplished your purpose.

Procedure

An audience wants to know who the speaker is, what he or she is going to talk about, and why they should listen. Sometime before the speech you will want to consult with the speaker to ask what he or she would like to have told. Usually, you want the necessary biographical information; this includes who the speaker is and why he or she is qualified to talk on the subject. The better known the person is, the less you need to say. For instance, the introduction of the President is simply, "Ladies and gentlemen, the President of the United States." Ordinarily, you will want enough information to allow you to talk for at least two or three minutes. Only on rare occasions should a speech of introduction last more than three minutes. The audience assembled to hear the speaker, not the introducer. During the first sentence or two, then, you should establish the nature of the occasion. In the body of the speech you should establish the speaker's credibility. In the conclusion you should usually include the name of the speaker and the title of the talk.

Considerations   There are some special considerations concerning the speech of introduction. First, do not overpraise the speaker. If expectations are too high, the speaker will never be able to live up to them. Overzealous introducers may be inclined to say: "This woman is undoubtedly one of the greatest speakers around today. You can look forward to one of the greatest speeches you have ever heard. See whether you don't agree with me." This appears to be paying a compliment, but it is doing the speaker a disservice by emphasizing comparison rather than speech content. A second caution is to be familiar with what you have to say. Audiences question sincerity when an introducer has to read the praise. You may have been present when an introducer said, "And now it is my great pleasure to present that noted authority . . . ," and then had to look down at notes to recall the speaker's name. Third, get your facts straight. The speaker should not have to spend time correcting your mistakes.

Assignment   *Prepare a two- to three-minute speech of introduction. Criteria for evaluation will include creativity in establishing speaker credibility and in presenting the name of the speaker and the title of the speech.*

PRESENTATIONS   Next to introductions, presentations are the kind of ceremonial speech you are most likely to give.

Purpose   The purpose of a speech of presentation is to present an award, prize, or gift to someone. In most cases, the speech of presentation is a reasonably short, formal recognition of some accomplishment.

Procedure   Your speech usually has two goals: (1) to discuss the nature of the award, including history, donor, and conditions under which it is made; and (2) to discuss the accomplishments of the recipient. If a competition was held, you should describe what the person did in the competition. Under other circumstances, you should discuss how the person has met the criteria for the award.

Obviously, you must learn all you can about the award and about the conditions under which such awards are made. The award may be a certificate, plaque, or trophy. The contest may have a long history and tradition that must be mentioned. Since the audience wants to know what the recipient has done, you should know the criteria that were met. For a competition, you should know the number of contestants and the way the contest was judged. If the person earned the award through years of achievement, you should know the particulars of that achievement.

Ordinarily, the speech is organized to show what the award is for, to give the criteria for winning, and to state how the person met the criteria. If the announcement of the name of the recipient is meant to be a surprise, all that is said should build up to the climax, the naming of the winner.

Considerations   For the speech of presentation there are only two special considerations: (1) Be careful of overpraise during the speech; do not explain everything in such superlatives that the presentation lacks sincerity. (2) In handing the award to the recipient, hold the award in your left hand and present it to the left hand of the recipient; shake the right hand in congratulations. If you practice, you will find that you can present the award and shake the person's hand smoothly and avoid those embarrassing moments when the recipient does not know quite what he or she is supposed to do.

Assignment   *Prepare a three- to five-minute speech of presentation. Criteria for evaluation will include showing what the award is for, criteria for winning, and how the person met the criteria.*

ACCEPTANCES   When an award is presented, it must be accepted. This speech is a response to speeches of presentation.

Purpose   The purpose of the speech of acceptance is to give brief thanks for receiving the award.

Procedure   The speech usually has two parts: (1) a brief thanks to the group, agency, or people responsible for giving the award; (2) if the recipient was aided by others, he or she gives thanks to those who share in the honor.

Considerations   Unless the acceptance is the lead-in to a major address, the acceptance should be brief. (A politician accepting a gift from the Chamber of Commerce may launch into a speech on government, but the audience will probably be expecting it.) As the Academy Awards program so graphically illustrates, however, when people are honored, the tendency is to give overly long and occasionally inappropriate speeches. The audience expects you to show your gratitude to the presenter of the award; they are not expecting a major address.

Assignment   *This assignment may well go together with the speech of presentation assignment. Prepare a one- to two-minute speech of acceptance in response to another speaker's speech of presentation. Criteria for evaluation will be how imaginatively you can respond in a brief speech.*

WELCOMINGS   Another common ceremonial speech is the welcoming.

Purpose   A speech of welcome expresses your pleasure in greeting a person or organization. In a way, the speech is a double speech of introduction: you introduce the newcomer to the audience, and you introduce the audience to the newcomer.

Procedure   You must be familiar both with the person or organization you are welcoming and with the situation you are welcoming them to. It is surprising how little many members of organizations and communities really know about their community. Although you may not have the knowledge on the tip of your tongue, it is inexcusable not to find the material you need to give an appropriate speech. Likewise, you want accurate information about the person or organization you are welcoming. The speech should be brief, but you need accurate and complete information to draw from.

After expressing pleasure in welcoming the person or organization, tell a little about your guests and give them the information about the place or organization to which they are being welcomed. Usually the conclusion is a brief statement of your hope that the person or organization has a pleasant and profitable visit.

Considerations   Again, the special caution is to make sure the speech is brief and honest. Welcoming guests does not require you to gush about them or their accomplishments. The speech of welcome should be an informative speech of praise.

Assignment   *Prepare a short speech welcoming a person to the community, organization, or institution. Criteria for evaluation will include how well you explain the nature of the institution and how well you introduce the person being welcomed.*

TRIBUTES   The final ceremonial speech we will consider is the tribute.

Purpose   The purpose of a speech of tribute is to praise someone's accomplishments. The occasion may be a birthday, the taking of office, retirement, or death. A formal speech of tribute given in memory of a deceased person is called a *eulogy.*

Procedure   The key to an effective tribute is sincerity. Although you want the praise to be apparent, you do not want to overdo it.

You must know the biographical information on your subject in depth. Since audiences are primarily interested in new information and specifics that characterize your assertions, you must have a mastery of much detail. You should focus on the person's laudable characteristics and accomplishments. It is especially important to note, if true, that the person had to overcome some special hardship or meet some particularly trying condition. All in all, you must be prepared to make a sound positive appraisal.

One way of organizing a speech of tribute is to focus on the subject's accomplishments. How detailed you make the speech depends on whether the person is well known or not. If the person is well known, you will be more general in your analysis. If the person is little known, you will have to provide more details so the audience can see the reasons for the praise. For prominent individuals, you will be able to show their influence on history.

Considerations   Remember, however, that no one is perfect. Although you need not stress a person's less glowing characteristics or failures, some allusion to this kind of information may make the positive features even more meaningful. Probably the most important guide is for you to keep your objectivity. Overpraise is far worse than understatement. Try to give the subject his or her due, honestly and sincerely.

Assignment   *Prepare a four- to six-minute speech of tribute to a person living or dead. Criteria for evaluation will include how well you develop the person's laudable characteristics and accomplishments.*

TWO ALTERNATE FORMS OF DELIVERY   Throughout this course we have been stressing the value of extemporaneous speaking, a form of speaking that depends on careful preparation but that leaves the actual wording until time of delivery. Still, there are times when you must speak without preparation or times when the way you phrase your ideas is as important or perhaps more important than the message itself. To help with these two kinds of situations, let us look at impromptu speeches and speeches from manuscripts.

Impromptu Speeches   By far most "speeches" you give are impromptu. When you answer a question posed by a professor in class, when you rise to speak on a motion made at a club meeting, when you talk about the events of your vacation at a party, you are giving an impromptu speech. Just because a speech is impromptu (given on the spur of the moment) does not mean that it need not be prepared. However, the preparation time is reduced to a matter of seconds or at most a matter of a few minutes.

If all the time we spent on speech preparation, information exchange, and persuasion is going to prove worthwhile, we must be able to carry over some of what we learned into these impromptu settings. Even in a few seconds you can give your thoughts structure. First, determine specifically the point you want to make. Although your specific purpose is not going to be as well thought out as for a fully prepared speech, it can at least give you necessary direction. If time permits, you can determine the one, two, or three points you will make to develop that purpose. If you have additional time you can search your mind for examples, illustrations, or stories that will help illustrate or prove your point. Usually, you must accomplish this third aspect while you are speaking. If at all possible, try to think of a way to start that will get a little attention. Just as extemporaneous speaking improves with practice, so does impromptu speaking. The following assignment can help you test your preparation and delivery facility even when preparation time is minimal.

Assignment   *Present a two- to three-minute impromptu speech.*
Topics: The best topics for impromptu speeches are those that each of you in class will be able to discuss without going beyond your own knowledge and experience. For topics, your instructor will have twenty to twenty-five 3-by-5-inch cards with words and phrases such as "Violence on television," "Feminism," "Does the end justify the means?" "Sex in the movies," "The 'in' fashions," and so forth.

Procedure: To begin the round, one student draws three of the cards, selects one for his or her topic, and begins preparation. The first person in the round has three minutes to prepare. The second person in the round draws three cards just before the first person begins talking. The second person, and each subsequent speaker, has the same length of time to prepare as the previous speaker, and does so while the previous speaker is talking.

Speeches from Manuscripts   During this course, you have learned the value of speaking extemporaneously. Occasionally, however, you may want to make sure that the wording of your speech is just right. Remember that what you gain in style may be lost in lack of spontaneity or in lack of specific audience adaptation if you do not prepare the manuscript carefully.

The final draft of your manuscript should be extremely well worded. You will want to show all that you have learned about making ideas clear, vivid, emphatic, and appropriate. In your preparation, you should proceed as if you were giving an extemporaneous speech. Then record what you would ordinarily consider your final speech practice. Type up the manuscript from your recorded practice, and then work on polishing the language. This procedure will ensure that you work from an oral style rather than from a written essay style.

After the manuscript is fully prepared, you should practice using it effectively. You should be sufficiently familiar with the material that you do not have to focus your full attention on the manuscript as you read. I suggest going over the manuscript at least three times in these final stages of practice. You will discover that even when you are reading you can have some eye contact with your audience. By watching audience reaction, you will know when and if to deviate from the manuscript.

So that the manuscript will be of maximum value to you I offer the following tips for preparing the manuscript:

1.   The manuscript should be typed, preferably on a typewriter that is pica sized or larger. Some radio, television, or student newspaper rooms are equipped with typewriters that have extra large type. You may be able to gain access to such a machine. Whatever size type you use, however, it is wise to double- or even triple-space the manuscript.

2.   For words that you have difficulty pronouncing you should use phonetic spelling, accent marks, or diacritical marks to help you in your pronunciation.

3.   Make markings that will help you determine pauses, places of special emphasis, or where to slow down or speed up. Also, make sure that the last sentence on each page is completed on that page; you want no unintended pauses.

4.   Number pages boldly so that pages are kept in their proper order. You may also find it valuable to bend the corner of each page slightly to help you turn the pages easily.

5.   Make sure to double-check that there will in fact be a lectern or speaker's stand upon which the manuscript can be placed.

Assignment   *Prepare a four- to six-minute manuscript speech (your professor will indicate the kind of speech by purpose or occasion). Criteria for evaluation will include clarity, vividness, emphasis, and appropriateness of language, as well as the quality of delivery.*

Chapter 19 Speeches for Evaluation

Throughout this textbook we have been considering the issue of speech criticism. In Chapter 2, "Listening to Speeches," we outlined an overall approach to speech criticism that could be applied to any speech; throughout the remainder of the book we presented critiques of student speeches and called for you to compare them with your own analyses. It seems fitting in this final chapter that we return to the subject of speech criticism, giving you one final chance to exercise the critical judgments that you have been developing as you have been improving your own speech preparation and presentation.

The following three speeches illustrate how three contemporary speakers met the challenge of effective speaking. I think you will find two potential benefits from your analyses of these speeches: (1) All four speeches speak to some aspect of communication. Therefore, to some extent they lend credence to the guidelines discussed throughout this text; they also supplement some of the ideas that were alluded to but not necessarily explored. (2) The three speeches were presented by people from different walks of life. This fact seems to further substantiate the point that speech making is important in a variety of contexts. Through the spoken word these people had an opportunity to exert influence on their audiences. I have selected these speeches because I believe they exhibit many of the principles we have discussed. None of the speeches is perfect—no speech ever is. What I look for you to do is seek out both the strengths and the weaknesses. In addition to supplying background for the speech, two of the speakers have offered information about their speech preparation and presentation, and have suggested "pointers" they believe a speech student should consider. I have included some of this pertinent data in the preface to each speech.

Analyze each of the speeches using the questions asked on pages 29–30.

NO ARTS, NO LETTERS— NO SOCIETY[1]

A speech by Harvey C. Jacobs, Editor, The Indianapolis News, delivered at Indiana-Purdue University, Indianapolis, Indiana, April 17, 1980.

This is a hard-hitting speech on the importance of written communication skills. Consider the speech on the basis of how effective Jacobs is at making his point. Notice the touches of humor throughout. How do they affect his message?

Mr. Jacobs reported that he carried a manuscript to the stand, but varied from it considerably as he spoke. He offers these comments: "Everything I write uses my college English teacher's formula: A thesis—what is my central thought? What do I want to prove? Then, I immerse myself in the facts I've accumulated (clips, files—masses I've accumulated—I read and clip), then I try to lift out three or four main points for the speech (or article) outline. The final research has to do with finding statistics, anecdotes, whatever to support the main points and the thesis. Facts and anecdotes make a speech 'listenable.'"

1   It is flattering to me, a newspaper man, to be invited to talk about the arts and letters, and especially under the sponsorship of a group dedicated to excellence. Newspapers are not generally held in high esteem today. Norman Mailer wrote some time ago that half the stories in the newspaper are 50 percent incorrect. The rest are 75 percent incorrect. "If a person is not talented enough to be a novelist," he said, "not smart enough to be a lawyer and his hands are too shaky to perform operations, he becomes a journalist."

---

[1] Reprinted from *Vital Speeches,* July 1, 1980, pp. 562–565. By permission.

2   Therefore, I am honored to be asked to share some thoughts about a few problems journalists have in common with the academic community. Our respective futures depend upon a sizable number of Americans being able to communicate—to be able to read and write and, above all, to think and form conclusions based upon reason and knowledge. I feel sure you share my pessimism—that all is not well in this process of gathering facts and drawing logical conclusions. Many of you may be victims of such failures. Others are engaged in rectifying these failures, but all of us are in the boat together—sinking into the sloppy swamps of neglect and carelessness in language and communication.

3   I was invited, I understand, partly because of something I wrote in *The News* about the lost art of letter-writing. From time to time I view with alarm the tilt toward poor scholarship, fuzzy language and tongue-tied students. I happen to be a letter writer; I like to receive good letters, and I also know how out of step I am: hardly anyone writes letters any more. Why write, even my own children say, when it's so easy to make a telephone call?

4   Writing letters, we are told by the anti-letter crowd, is a bother and also costs too much money. In some offices letters may cost up to $12 to $15 each—dictation, transcribing, typing, mailing. But the real reason more letters aren't written is that most Americans do not know how to write a letter. Since I have been editor of *The News* I have learned the most effective way to deal with irate callers. After the caller has spewed invective for a minute or two I say: "That's well said. Now put those thoughts in a letter and we'll be glad to publish it."

5   The silence is deafening. "Put it in a letter? Oh, no, I couldn't do that. I don't write very well. When I sit down to write, my brain goes into cerebral arrest"—or words to that effect.

6   In the letter-less society of the future how shall we acquire insights into our heroes? The hands of all biographers would be tied without letters. The best in literature, the best in biography, the best in creative and candid comments have been preserved in letters. Imagine, for example, the void left if a letterless society had existed in Bible times. Paul said in his letter to the Galatians: "Ye see how large a letter I have written unto you with mine own hand." No ghost writers, no telegrams, no telephone calls, no keying into a computerized data bank—just a plain letter in which a man's heart is laid bare.

7   Mostly because Americans cannot express their noblest and tenderest thoughts in a letter, a gigantic greeting card industry has come to dominate the most intimate channels of communication. This industry thrives on a laziness that would have shattered our forefathers. The attitude toward the art of letter writing is well summarized by one card which, on the cover, says: "I should write," and inside it exclaims: "But you'd probably write back!" Such a communication puts an end to all exchange of opinions and sentiment and reduces what could be a pleasurable experience to a salable absurdity.

8   Why is the letter such a neglected form of communication? English classes once elevated the letter to distinctive forms and required students to compose all of them. Perhaps a few teachers still do, but students report that not many dwell long on the letter. Perhaps they don't because of their own ineptitude.

9   I received a lengthy letter from a veteran Indianapolis high school teacher with 13 misspelled words in it. Bear with me while I run a few of them by: VIGEROUS, YOUND, FRAM, IRRATATING, IMPLACATIONS, CAREFULL, SENCE, CAUGHING, BREATH(E), AUDIANCE and DISPITE. A letter from another teacher began: "I was shigrinned to learn . . ." and so on for a page or two.

10   It's fashionable to blame Johnny because he can't read or write, but I suspect he does about as well as his father or mother—or perhaps even as well as his teachers. Trying to place the blame for our communications problems brings back a little rhyming explanation:

The college professor says:
Such rawness in a pupil is a shame;
High school preparation is to blame.
The high school teacher says:
Good heavens, what crudity—the boy's a fool!
The fault of course is the grammar school.
The grade teacher cries:
From such stupidity may I be spared;
They send them to me so unprepared.
The kindergarten teacher says:
Such lack of training did I never see;
What kind of woman must the mother be?
But the mother laments:
Poor helpless child—he is not to blame;
His father's folks are just the same.

11 The head of a language arts department told me that she can sense when a child begins "to tune me out when I talk about reading and writing." Reading and writing are twins, you know, but too many parents and teachers do not know this. Or they just don't really care. So, the home is at fault in the beginning. At home the child has probably never seen his or her parents sitting down and quietly reading a book or a magazine or a newspaper. This does not mean that the parents are dumb or uncultured or not interested in current affairs. It may merely mean that it is not at all essential that they read anything. They get their news, such as it is, from the television or the radio. The limits of their reading, of following any kind of words on a printed page, may be the perusal of their junk mail.

12 It is, then, a simple transition from a family that doesn't write letters or write anything else beyond a grocery list, to one that doesn't read much beyond the salutation of a letter selling mail order insurance. If this is a thumbnail portrait of the average TV family—parents and school age children—what are the implications for society as a whole? Who are the models for the typical American family?

13 Well, one model would be that lovable kid on television who talks about loving the pudding because "it ain't got no lumps." The advertising agency that created the words of the commercial and recruited the innocent lad to mouth them should be blacklisted and charged with contributing to the language delinquency of a minor. The company that approved the agency's so-called creative efforts and authorized the distribution of the commercial should be subjected to a national boycott and charged publicly with contributing to the decline of good grammar.

14 No one seems to care about the boy's giving respectability to "ain't" and elevating a double negative as a model for 220 million Americans. Television newscasters, caught without a script, say "between you and I" or "neither candidate have commented . . ." or "some Iranian students are laying in the streets." If we tell our children not to say "ain't," for example, they come back at us with, "Larry Bird says 'ain't' and 'have went'—and he's a millionaire." Tick off the top TV and motion picture heroes. Mork and Mindy, the Fonz, Laverne and Shirley, Archie Bunker—all of them glorify rotten English. It is easy to understand the frustration of the few parents and teachers who despair over the models their children are emulating. It's a feeling of utter helplessness, akin to holding back an avalanche with a spoon.

15   The avalanche spills over into colleges and universities. A former newspaper man now in his first year of college journalism teaching recently told me that he was puzzled by many of his students who are well-informed, have good basic abilities to reason, are charming and personable—but can't recognize or write a complete English sentence. They write mostly fragments.

16   Many students—and a few teachers—defend this kind of writing as colorful and creative. Some communication faddists may call it "subculture dialect," typified, I suppose, by the California cult-language reproduced in the 1976 bestseller, *The Serial,* and currently in the movie of the same name. Cyra McFadden, the author of *Serial,* recently told about incidents in her teaching experience at San Francisco State. Once when she had assigned the reading of a Ray Bradbury short story a student responded: "I picked up his vibes. Just couldn't get behind him." When she threatened to flunk another student for not completing an assignment, he said, "I'm not into value judgments, so don't lay your power trips on me."

17   This is Marin County English, satirized in *The Serial.* Asked to comment on it, Edwin Newman, the national defender of grammar and good writing, called it "hooey," and continued: "What worries me isn't so much the effect of Marin County English on the language but its larger effect upon society. A society must be affected if a number of its members spend their time talking drivel."

18   Let's repeat that sentence, for it leads to a consideration of the next step in our discussion—the broader impact upon society of a culture that shows little respect for standards of communication. "A society," says Ed Newman, "must be affected if a number of its members spend their time talking drivel."

19   Talking drivel—it's on the tube, on the radio, in some magazines and newspapers, in the classroom, on the courts and fields of athletic contests and in casual conversation. The national state of the art of communication is somewhere between "you know, you know, you know" and "expletive deleted." "You know" and profanity have become substitutes for the exact word to express the exact meaning.

20   There is a college professor teaching at Glassboro (N.J.) State College who believes that split infinitives are the first step toward

moral decay. His name is Richard Mitchell, and he publishes a monthly newsletter called "The Underground Grammarian." He attacks the misuse of English wherever he finds it, mostly in publications and memoranda issued by the academic community. Because of the deplorable state of the art of clear communication, and especially in professional journals, he is kept busy with satire and ridicule in his little circle of alarmists. But there are much wider implications, he thinks, and I agree. Students who ignore the mastery of skills in language will ignore mastery in other things. They tend to become shoddy workers in whatever field they enter, because they have slid past the guideposts without direction. Prof. Mitchell believes that if English had been taught well and learned in the schools, the accident at Three Mile Island could have been prevented. An in-bred in-attention to detail found its inevitable climax at Three Mile Island and will be repeated again and again, he thinks. He says careless, non-reading, non-comprehending college graduates—and high school graduates, too—take jobs with power companies, chemical manufacturers, railroads, and in a hundred other similar settings where instructions are complex and where attention to detail and to standards are absolutely essential.

21   Thomas Sticht, of the National Institute of Education, tells us that, contrary to widespread belief, the effect of modern technology is not to reduce but to increase an individual's need for literacy. In 1939, he noted, the Navy's first weapons system came with a total of 500 pages of documentation; the last one came with 300,000 pages. For those facing the computerized world, it should be noted that the principal function of computers is to put writing in front of people—usually in a coded form that, in effect, requires knowledge of not one but two languages. Walter Davis, director of education for the AFL-CIO, estimates that very soon anyone who doesn't have at least a 12th grade reading, writing and calculating level "will be absolutely lost."

22   Well, how are we doing in meeting these demands of the future? Here are some answers. A high school graduate on Long Island sued the local school system because he couldn't read above third grade level. A testing group showed a group of 17-year-olds a replica of a traffic ticket and more than half could not ascertain the last day on which the fine could be paid. The Navy reported that $250,000 damage was done to a diesel engine because a sailor working on it could not read the maintenance manual.

23   Yes, these are extreme cases, and I have not mentioned the millions of success stories. But looking at the mass record is almost as disturbing. In a study underwritten by The New York Times Foundation, educators tested a group of college freshmen at the University of Minnesota by giving them a reading exam used in testing students in 1928. The 1978 students made decidedly poorer grades than their counterparts in 1928. The test asked students to select synonyms for words like *surplus, affirm, eternal, restrain* and *silhouette*. It also asked them to choose correct interpretations of reading matter and, in a race against the clock, to delete redundant and unrelated phrases in paragraphs. In every aspect the 1928 students were better. Even the best of the 1978 class were less literate than the best in 1928 and there were many fewer superior scores in the 1978 generation. This particular test merely corroborates scores of other tests given in many different settings.

24   Turning from the communications skills, how do the teenagers measure up in political literacy? According to the Gallup Youth Survey, only 6 of 10 can identify the Vice President of the United States. Only 11 percent of the nation's young people can name the chief justice of the Supreme Court. Only half of them know whether people who cannot read or write may vote in national elections, and only 23 percent know the length of a U.S. senator's term.

25   There are chilling inferences to be drawn from such statistics, although I am well aware of the danger of basing judgments on polls. But one inference relates to the competence of the electorate to participate fully and intelligently in the political process. This republic was founded on the principle of an informed citizenry being essential to intelligent voting. Postal rates, tax rates, and a long list of built-in incentives were established with the view that both public education and self-education were essential elements of self-government. It is a sad piece of irony if, possessing all the tools of modern communication arts, we should fail at self-government because we have not been taught to use these tools.

26   Moving to another inference, let us think briefly about the American educational retreat into provincialism and isolation in a time when the global village shrinks with every passing day. If sloppy education is at least partially responsible for what might have been a holocaust at Three Mile Island, is it reaching too far to infer that this nation's incredible bungling in Iran was related to our de-emphasis of foreign language and foreign culture? I have

read that only two of the scores of Americans employed at the embassy in Iran could speak the language. There may have been others who knew a little bit, but the point is that a failure to understand the language and the culture of Iran provides part of the background for our present dilemma. A failure of cultural perception has contributed to our failures in many overseas areas, including Vietnam.

27   The U.S. is not alone among the nations that neglect to study the languages and cultures of other nations, but we are among the most negligent. The 35 nations that signed the Helsinki accord on East-West cooperation in 1975 agreed "to encourage the study of foreign language and civilization as an important means of expanding communication among peoples." But we have not done well in our follow through.

28   Only 15 percent of all the high school students in the land study a foreign language. The figure was 24 percent in 1965. Only one public high school of 20 offers French, Russian or German beyond the second year. Only 8 percent of all American colleges and universities now require a foreign language for graduation. The figure was 34 percent in 1966. The federal government cannot recruit enough language-trained personnel for its overseas and domestic staffs; it now spends $100 million a year to train them. When I visited Japan a few years ago it was difficult to find any upperclass Japanese salesmen who could not speak some English. There are 10,000 Japanese salesmen in the U.S. who speak English, but there are only 900 American business representatives in Japan who can speak Japanese.

29   Setting aside the cultural growth achieved in the study of foreign languages, the practical demands of burgeoning international business should be reason enough for the restoration of foreign languages to the curriculum.

30   One more international comment about a culture which may be sliding off the peak it once held. Allow me to turn to former ambassador George F. Kennan to put the capstone on this segment. "Show me," said Kennan, "an America which has successfully coped with the problems of crime, drugs, deteriorating educational standards, urban decay, pornography and decadence of one sort or another—show me an America that has pulled itself together and is what it ought to be, then I will tell you how we are going to defend ourselves from the Russians. But as things

are, I can see very little merit in organizing to defend ourselves to defend from the Russians the porno shops in central Washington." Then George Kennan placed parentheses after his indictment of his homeland. "Please understand," he continued, "that, for the purposes of argument, I am given to overstating a case."

31   Perhaps I, too, have overstated the negative case against the communication and language arts. Perhaps it is going too far to contend that because we have neglected the disciplines of such lowly topics as grammar and spelling that we are also endangering the national interest both at home and abroad. But I see a connection. I sense a dulling of the tools of expression. I sense a loss of confidence in language that translates to a loss of confidence in literature. I see students escaping the discipline of writing and re-writing and thereby escaping the discipline of thinking. I see students settling for the easy word and the loose sentence, and I am reminded of Mark Twain's saying that the difference between the right word and almost-right word is the difference between lightning and a lightning bug. I see only a few teachers who can impart the love of language and clear expression. When students encounter a teacher who loves the language, they are more likely to learn to appropriate its riches for themselves.

32   There is magic in good literature—a magic, I suspect, uncultivated by greater proportions of the American populace than ever before in our history. Who has the time to sit quietly for the single purpose of reading a book? Reading in America has become a challenge to physical as well as mental discipline. There are few places in the typical modern house for reading or for solitary reflection. Furniture is arranged to face the tube or around the stereo speakers.

33   But a family does not have to be rich to have a library. Almost anyone can afford paperback books. Being informed or being *transformed* by a good book is not proscribed by a lack of wealth; it is purely a matter of choice. The literature dropouts, both in and out of schools, turn off literature because they say it does not provide a convincing answer to their consuming question: What's in it for me?

34   Answers to that question abound, but they are difficult to translate into Marin County English. Literature can help us to converse with better minds than our own, can help us to lay hold upon

better ideas than we now possess. It stretches our imagination, plumbs our depths, hits us with sledge hammers, teaches us to roll with the punches and gives us something beyond today's headlines. Literature—good literature—can give this anti-hero age heroes to emulate, a pattern for stability. It is the best antidote against alienation. Literature, art and communication can help us avoid mental bankruptcy.

35   *Mental bankruptcy.* These two words summarize the threat I have been talking about and what all of us should be concerned about. My feeling, I'm sad to say, is that we may be teetering on the brink of mental bankruptcy. We can avoid it, I'm certain, if some students and educators enlist, as you have, in the cause of excellence. Your commitment is our one best hope.

STANDARD ENGLISH[3]
A speech by Benjamin H. Alexander, President, Chicago State University, delivered to the Fellows, American Council on Education, South Bend, Indiana, September 23, 1979.

This is a strong argument in support of the teaching of standard English to all students. How well does Alexander make and develop his points?

Mr. Alexander reported that he delivered his speech from notes. About his methods he wrote: "I started giving speeches just after graduation from college to important church, civic and civil rights groups. I knew that poor speakers were not invited back, so I strove to be a good and interesting speaker.

"Prior to any significant speaking engagement, I write the speech, read it aloud, and change it repeatedly until the speech satisfies me. It is then edited for grammatical errors, interest, coherence etc., and typed in final form.

"Key topic sentences are written on 3" by 5" index cards. The speech is not read, but given from these note cards after rehearsing it about six times prior to delivery."

1   Thank you for that kind introduction. And you beautiful people in the audience—keep up the applause; I like it. Americans have a peculiar habit: they applaud a speaker before he has uttered a

---

[3] Reprinted from *Vital Speeches*, May 1, 1980, pp. 437–440. By permission.

single word. I hope you will applaud just as loudly when I have finished this address.

2   I understand that the theme of this conference is "College Access for the Non-traditional Student: A Glimpse of Tomorrow." Well, let me say immediately that the process of education, whether traditional or non-traditional, is not my concern here. What is important to me is that the goal of education—traditional or non-traditional—be *excellence*. No student who strives to succeed in today's competitive world, who wants a *share* of tomorrow, and not just a glimpse, can be satisfied with anything but academic excellence. And as educators we must insist on that excellence.

3   The achievement of academic excellence is not possible without first mastering Standard English, and that is *my* theme this afternoon.

4   In one basic phase of that academic excellence, I am a traditionalist. I refuse to recognize that the achievement of excellence is possible without mastery of Standard English. I will not accept the legitimacy of Black English or any other kind of non-standard English—no matter what many of my colleagues may say.

5   As you heard from the speaker who introduced me, I was born in the South, in Roberta, Georgia. My roots go back to plantation days, and an important part of my growing up was the training my parents gave me to make me overcome the plantation mentality they could still see in the South.

6   In the plantation days, blacks were expected to think of themselves as inferior. They were expected to believe that their role in life was established when they were born. Whites *and* blacks took it for granted that the standards and values of the slave society were inferior. Blacks in those days were supposed to know their place and to act accordingly.

7   My parents did not believe in this plantation mentality and encouraged me and my brothers and sisters to become educated and find our place in society. As a result of my parents' encouragement, I did earn an education and gradually have risen and have been accepted in society. Personally, I have had little occasion to feel that society has treated me in any way which has reflected the plantation mentality about which my parents were so concerned.

8   However, my parents' words came back to me when I read of the recent ruling by U.S. District Judge Charles W. Joiner in Ann Arbor, Michigan. His ruling, which calls for implicit recognition of Black English, is nothing more than blatant plantation mentality. I cannot support it.

9   This ruling is criminal, a travesty of justice, because it implies that blacks are still on the plantation—despite the passage of over 100 years—that blacks are basically inferior and must be treated differently. If such a ruling stands and its acceptance becomes widespread, the poor of Ann Arbor and elsewhere are certain to become the next "boat people" drifting from port to port, accepted nowhere. If people cannot communicate in Standard English and have not developed their talents and skills—then who wants them?

10 When the German, Russian, Polish, Greek, Italian immigrants and even African slaves came to America, unable to speak the language, there was no recognition given their non-standard broken English. The immigrants and slaves were compelled to learn Standard English and without specially trained teachers, despite the fact that each day those immigrants returned from work to homes where only non-standard English was spoken. That is why I consider it a cheap insult to see educational standards lowered in Ann Arbor schools—solely for black students. How can we justify recognition of their non-standard broken English and then ask teachers to learn it? Was it necessary for teachers of the immigrants to be given formal training in Polish English, German English, Italian English or any *non-standard English?*

11 The answer, of course, is no! Then, why train teachers in non-Standard English when the English applies to blacks.

12 Many blacks in America deeply resent the fact that the non-Standard English that is spoken by the students in Ann Arbor, Michigan, is called Black English. These blacks feel the term is racist, since the non-Standard English spoken by the white immigrants, earlier, was not called White English.

13 Moreover, they are aware, particularly the educated blacks, that whenever society wants to take a perfectly good word or noun and make it negative, it too often only has to add the word black as an adjective. For example, the good word mail plus black becomes blackmail, list becomes blacklist, hand becomes black

hand, flag becomes black flag, art becomes black art, market becomes black market, and, of course, English becomes Black English.

14   The above is one of the main reasons so many blacks prefer the name Afro-American over black, particularly the young college black.

15   This summer *The Chronicle of Higher Education* carried the results of a national study on foreign languages which reported that 10 percent of all Americans grew up in homes where either a language other than English was used predominantly or where a second language was spoken as much as was English. As far as I could determine from the report, none of that 10 percent consisted of those who spoke the so-called Black English. Ironically, the source of this study was the University of Michigan in *Ann Arbor*.

16   On the one hand, one institution in Ann Arbor has determined that 10 percent of the populace apparently has grown up and has been educated without their teachers being required to adjust to the languages spoken in their homes. At the same time, another institution in Ann Arbor—the judicial system—has determined that Black English should be made legitimate to the extent that teachers of black children need take special training to communicate with them.

17   I sense that some of you out there are getting uncomfortable. Aren't some of you saying—how can an educated, seemingly successful black like myself be so lacking in compassion? Well, I don't believe that the judge's ruling in Ann Arbor is based on compassion for those children at all. I see it as paternalism, unintentioned perhaps, but still just a modern version of the paternalism which my ancestors experienced on the plantation.

18   I do believe in compassion, but not misguided compassion. I saw the results of such compassion at my own institution, Chicago State University. For several years before I became president, CSU had a policy, developed out of compassion for the difficulties the inner city CSU students—mostly black—were having in adjusting to college studies. This policy called for an R (Repeat) grade rather than an F or even a D grade. At CSU a student couldn't fail. Did this policy help these inner city students adjust to college? Not at all, human nature being what it is. Instead there were hundreds of students who were doing little more than just "hanging around," gathering R grades on their transcripts.

19   The faculty wisely voted to reinstate the normal grading system, drop the R grade, and insist upon a passing grade point average. During the next year it became necessary to expel several hundred students and place well over one thousand students—more than a quarter of the undergraduate student body—on academic probation with the admonition "shape up or ship out."

20   On the surface, this position may have seemed cruel, but let me tell you from experience, false compassion is criminal; it only serves to doom the poor to the junk heap of failure. To our great pleasure the student body was very supportive of this new demand for academic excellence; students wanted to be proud of a degree from CSU. Fortunately, most of those on probation rose to the new standards, and a surprising number of those expelled followed our recommendation to go to a community college and get good grades, and many of them did come back to CSU.

21   Did this insistence on academic excellence chase students away? No, today CSU has the highest enrollment in its history, and our students are competing with the best in the nation—and winning. For example, one of our business students recently tallied the highest written score in the nation on the "GMAT," the General Management Entrance Examination, and he also earned the third highest law school admissions test score in the country. Please know that students from Harvard, Yale, Princeton, etc., also took these two written tests.

22   We produced another student who graduated number one in his class at John Marshall Law School. And this fall fourteen of our graduates will enter medical and dental school programs, another first for CSU students. Most of these were black students from Chicago's inner city who thrived on the demand for academic excellence.

23   You may say that my remarks are based only on my experience in *higher* education—that the public schools are different. I may not have worked in the public schools, but I was a member of the Board of Education in Washington, D.C. I know that the public school children of Washington and their parents, almost all of whom are black, would have been highly indignant if our school board had insisted that the teachers in Washington treat the speech of the poor as a foreign language which must be studied.

24   Given the proper incentive and inspiration, those black Washington, D.C. youngsters did not need the crutch of compassion for

their English because they were taught Standard English—and many excelled.

25   And Chicago inner city children are no different, according to research by Dr. Earl Ogletree of Chicago State University and Marie Chambers of the Chicago public schools, which appeared in the April 1978 *Phi Delta Kappan.* This article reported on responses from inner city students on conduct in the classroom. I would like to take just a moment to read some of the results of that survey, particularly those responses connected with freedom of speech in the classroom.

26   A question: "Should students have the freedom of speech in the classroom, i.e., should they be able to talk when they wish?" 59 percent said No.

27   "Should students be allowed to use abusive language in the classroom?" 74 percent of these inner city students said No.

28   "Should students have the right to argue with their teachers?" 81 percent said No.

29   Finally—and I think pertinent to today's subject: "Should students be allowed to use informal slang (street language) in the classroom?" 71 percent of these inner city students said No.

30   That street language is probably what some are calling Black English. These students seemed to realize that there is a way they may talk on the street and even at home, but they also apparently know that in the classroom Standard English is required.

31   Dr. Lloyd Leverton, a Chicago Board of Education psychologist, seems to concur. On the subject of Black English, he has commented that children learn to dress one way for home and in a more formal way for school, and they learn they can run around at home but not in school. Similarly, he said, "They can learn there is one way of talking at home and another—Standard English—in school."

32   I don't want you to think that I am misinterpreting the Ann Arbor ruling, as it appears that a number of those commenting on it have done. I realize that the ruling is not calling for the *teaching* of Black English in the schools. Rather it calls for the recognition of Black English as a formal dialect with roots and grammatical rules and requires the faculty to be trained to teach so-called Black English students. I understand the program which has

evolved from that ruling is costing the Ann Arbor schools $42,000. That, to my way of thinking, is a nonsensical waste of money, a waste which clearly tells these children: You are so different that our teachers must take special courses in order to deal with you in the classroom. Isn't this just another way of confirming their inferiority or relating dumb to slum.

33 This isn't my idea of compassion in the classroom, a compassion which singles out certain students *based on their race* as being inferior. Each child in a classroom *is* different, and a good elementary school teacher must recognize those differences. But black children do not all differ in the same way, whether on the basis of their dialect or whatever. Such a racist generalization prompts me to think that the judge in Ann Arbor may one day order the music teachers to put all the black children in the *rhythm* band. (On that subject, my wife would say that any one who thinks all blacks have rhythm should dance with me just once.)

34 Based on that same misguided compassion, some so-called experts claim that correcting a black child's speech in the classroom will upset him about his parents and home life. I believe that a black child who speaks non-Standard English is already very aware of it. While I do not condone the amount of time that children, and particularly disadvantaged children, spend in front of the television, those children from the time they are one and two have been exposed to hours and hours each week of relatively Standard English spoken by both white, black and brown performers. Those children need not have a teacher tell them that they don't speak Standard English.

All children should be taught Standard English from the moment they enter the classroom, and the numbers who cannot speak Standard English in this country are legion. However, the race of the children is not the cause of their deficiency. The cause is their socio-economic status; they are poor and come from environments discouraging education. In total numbers there are no doubt more whites, than blacks and browns, who cannot speak

35 Standard English because in number there are *more poor whites* than there are poor blacks and browns. Should we set up special programs which recognize all the various white dialects? Must we teach the teachers all the various white dialects? If there had been white and Latino children in the Ann Arbor housing project, would the teachers have to be trained in their dialects also?

36   Attorney Gabe Kaimowitz, who brought the Ann Arbor case to court, is quoted as saying: "There was either something wrong with these kids, or with the school system. We proved it was the school system." As we educators sit idly by, Mr. Kaimowitz and the courts resolved this simplistic proposition with a simplistic solution—as always, blame the school system.

37   Blame the school system, but not the economic, social and political system of this country which provides so little encouragement and inspiration to the poor and disadvantaged—be they black, brown or white. And if we educators continue to be passive, the lawyers and judges will continue to decide what is best for education. They will continue to look for ways by which it appears that equal educational opportunity is being given to the poor. But in fact, by lowering standards for poor children and easing their ways through our schools, judges are merely condoning the old concept of social promotion.

38   If we educators do not protest this Ann Arbor ruling, we are encouraging the next lawyer to sue to suspend college requirements, to lower standards because college lectures are unintelligible to those who speak Black English. (And why not those also who speak Polish English, Italian English, Vietnamese English?)

39   Success in this competitive marketplace is hard work—everyone who has succeeded knows that. So I urge you as educators to use your status to uplift the poor. Men and women of scholarship must lead the way—not judges and lawyers. People who believe in themselves ask only for equal breaks—not more breaks. Thirty years ago educators were asking that the doors to an education be opened equally for all; we supposedly have that now. Recognition of Black English will give us closed doors again. With this ruling, this judge is saying he doubts the ability of the poor blacks, because if the poor blacks really need recognition of their Black English, they are hopelessly inferior. They will also need doctored math, doctored reading, doctored history, doctored science—and finally meaningless doctored diplomas and even doctored college degrees.

40   I use this occasion as a forum to present my views because you are in the forefront of non-traditional education. It is important that you as believers in non-traditional education speak out when the non-traditional approach to education is being bastardized. The non-traditional student, as well as the traditional student,

cannot succeed unless he has been trained from the beginning in Standard English. Standard English—not Black English or Brown English or White English—is the only foundation for effective reading, speaking, writing and learning.

41 As an educator and a black man who as a child was very poor himself, I plan to speak out on every occasion against this blatant plantation mentality. The poor blacks of this nation are not inferior; they do not need the crutch of Black English. Most of them are able and willing to meet standards. They don't want to turn back the calendar to plantation days.

42 I urge you to join me in battling this paternalism in education. Join with me in saying—Standard English—the hell with anything else! As educators, we must set as our objectives the raising of standards, not their lowering. In my view, to do otherwise is to admit that we are not educators—we are *hustlers.*

Thank you.

THINK STRAWBERRIES[4]

This final speech by James Lavenson, President of the Plaza Hotel, was delivered before the American Medical Association on February 7, 1974.

I have included this speech in three editions of **Challenge of Effective Speaking.** *As you read the speech I believe you will agree with me that it is a truly excellent informative speech—one of the best you will find. Notice how Lavenson blends humor, excellent specific instances, informal language, and clear, vivid language to form an extremely interesting and very informative speech about the hotel business.*

1 I came from the balcony of the hotel business. For ten years as a corporate director of Sonesta Hotels with no line responsibility, I had my office in a little building next door to The Plaza. I went to the hotel every day for lunch and often stayed overnight. I was a professional guest. You know nobody knows more about how to run a hotel than a guest. Last year, I suddenly fell out of the corporate balcony and had to put my efforts in the restaurants where

---

[4] Reprinted from *Vital Speeches,* March 15, 1974, pp. 346–348. By permission.

my mouth had been, and in the rooms and night club and theater into which I'd been putting my two cents.

2   In my ten years of kibitzing, all I had really learned about the hotel business was how to use a guest room toilet without removing the strip of paper that's printed "Sanitized for Your Protection." When the hotel staff found out I'd spent my life as a salesman and that I'd never been a hotelier, never been to Cornell Hotel School, and that I wasn't even the son of a waiter, they were in a state of shock. And Paul Sonnabend, President of Sonesta, didn't help their apprehension much when he introduced me to my executive staff with the following kind words: "The Plaza has been losing money the last several years and we've had the best management in the business. Now we're going to try the worst."

3   Frankly, I think the hotel business has been one of the most backward in the world. There's been very little change in the attitude of room clerks in the 2,000 years since Joseph arrived in Bethlehem and was told they'd lost his reservation. Why is it that a sales clerk at Woolworth asks your wife, who points to the pantyhose if she wants three or six pairs—and your wife is all by herself—but the maître d' asks you and your wife, the only human beings within a mile of the restaurant, "How many are you?"

4   Hotel salesmanship is retailing at its worst. But at the risk of inflicting cardiac arrest on our guests at The Plaza when they first hear shocking expressions like "Good Morning" and "Please" and "Thank you for coming," we started a year ago to see if it was possible to make the 1,400 employees of The Plaza into genuine hosts and hostesses. Or should I say "salesmen?"

5   A tape recorder attached to my phone proved how far we had to go. "What's the difference between your $85 suite and your $125 suite?" I'd ask our reservationist, disguising my voice over the phone. You guessed it: "$40!"

6   "What's going on in the Persian Room tonight?" I asked the Bell Captain. "Some singer" was his answer. "Man or woman?" I persisted. "I'm not sure" he said, which made me wonder if I'd even be safe going there.

7   Why is it, I wondered, that the staff of a hotel doesn't act like a family playing hosts to guests whom they've invited to their house? It didn't take too long after becoming a member of the family myself, to understand one of the basic problems. Our

1,400 family members didn't even know each other! With that large a staff, working over eighteen floors, six restaurants, a night club, a theater, and three levels of subbasement, including a kitchen, a carpentry shop, plumbing and electrical shops, a full commercial laundry—how would they ever know who was working there, and who was a guest or just a purveyor passing through? Even the old-timers who might recognize a face after a couple of years would have no idea of the name connected to it. It struck me that if our own people couldn't call each other by name, smile at each other's familiar face, say good morning *to each other,* how could they be expected to say amazing things like "Good Morning, Mr. Jones" to a guest? A year ago The Plaza name tag was born. The delivery took place on my lapel. And it's now been on 1,400 lapels for over a year. Everyone, from dishwashers to the General Manager, wears his name where every other employee, and of course every guest, can see it. Believe it or not, our people say hello to each other—by name—when they pass in the halls and the offices. At first our regular guests thought The Plaza was entertaining some gigantic convention, but now even the old-time Plaza regulars are able to call our bellmen and maids by name. We've begun to build an atmosphere of welcome with the most precious commodity in the world—our names. *And* our guests' names.

8   A number of years ago, I heard Dr. Ernest Dichter, head of the Institute of Motivational Research, talk about restaurant service. He had reached a classic conclusion; when people come to a fine restaurant, they are hungrier for *recognition* than they are for food. It's true. If the maître d' says "We have your table ready, Mr. Lavenson," then as far as I'm concerned the chef can burn the steak and I'll still be happy.

9   When someone calls you by name and you don't know his, a strange feeling of discomfort comes over you. When he does it twice you *have* to find out *his* name. This we see happening with our Plaza name tags. When a guest calls a waiter by name, the waiter wants to call the guest by name. It will drive him nuts if he doesn't know. He'll ask the maître d', and if he doesn't know he'll ask the bellman, who will ask the front desk . . . calling the guests by name has a big payoff. It's called a *tip.*

10   At first there was resistance to name tags—mostly from the old-time, formally trained European hoteliers. I secretly suspect they liked being incognito when faced with a guest complaint. We

only had one staff member who said he'd resign before having his dignity destroyed with a name tag. For sixteen years he'd worn a rosebud in his lapel and that, he said, was his trademark and everyone knew him by it. His resignation was accepted along with that of the rosebud. Frankly, there are moments when I regret the whole idea myself. When I get on a Plaza elevator and all the passengers see my name tag, they know I work there. Suddenly, I'm the official elevator pilot, the host. I can't hide, so I smile at everybody, say "good morning" to perfect strangers I'd ordinarily ignore. The ones that don't go into shock, smile back. Actually, they seem to mind less the fact that a trip on a Plaza elevator, built in 1907, is the equivalent of commuting to Manhattan from Greenwich.

11   There are 600 Spanish-speaking employees at The Plaza. They speak Spanish. They don't read English. The employee house magazine was in English. So was the employee bulletin board. So were the signs over the urinals in the locker rooms that suggest cigarette butts don't flush too well. It was a clue as to why some of management's messages weren't getting through. The employee house magazine is now printed one side in English, the other in Spanish. The bulletin board and other staff instructions are in two languages. We have free classes in both languages for departmental supervisors. It's been helping.

12   With 1,400 people all labeled and smiling we were about ready last June to make salesmen out of them. There was just one more obstacle to overcome before we started suggesting they "ask for the order." They had no idea what the product was they would be selling. Not only didn't they know who was playing in the Persian Room, they didn't know we had movies—full-length feature films without commercials—on the closed-circuit TV in the bedrooms. As a matter of fact, most of them didn't know what a guest room looked like, unless they happened to be a maid or a bellman.

13   The reason the reservationists thought $40 was the difference between two suites was because they'd never been in one, much less actually slept there. To say our would-be salesmen lacked product knowledge would be as much an understatement as the line credited to President Nixon if he had been the Captain of the Titanic. My son told me that if Nixon had been Captain of the Titanic, he probably would have announced to the passengers

there was no cause for alarm—they were just stopping to pick up ice.

14   Today, if you ask a Plaza bellman who's playing in the Persian Room he'll tell you Ednita Nazzaro. He'll tell you because he's seen her. In the contract of every Persian Room performer, there's now a clause requiring him to first perform for our employees in the cafeteria before he opens in the Persian Room. Our employees see the star first, before the guests.

15   And if you ask a room clerk or a telephone operator what's on the TV movies, they'll tell you because they've seen it—on the TV sets running the movies continuously in the employees' cafeteria.

16   Believe me, if you are having your lunch in our cafeteria and watch "Female Response" or "Swedish Fly Girls" on the TV set, you won't forget the film. You might, however, suspect the chef has put Spanish fly in your spaghetti.

17   Our new room clerks now have a week of orientation. It includes spending a night in the hotel and a tour of our 1,000 guest rooms. They can look out the windows and see the $40 difference in suites, since a view of the Park doesn't even closely resemble the back of the Avon building.

18   As I mentioned, about six months ago, we decided it was time to take a hard look at our sales effort. I couldn't find it. The Plaza had three men with the title "salesman"—and they were good men. But they were really sales-*service* people who took the orders for functions or groups who came through the doors and sought us out. Nobody, but nobody, ever left the palace, crossed the moat at Fifth Avenue, and went looking for business. We had no one knocking on doors, no one asking for the order. The Plaza was so dignified it seemed demeaning to admit we needed business. If you didn't ask us we wouldn't ask you. So there! Our three sales-service people were terrific once you voluntarily stepped inside our arena. You had to ring our doorbell. We weren't ringing yours or anyone else's.

19   This condition wasn't unique to our official Sales Department. It seemed to be a philosophy shared by our entire staff—potentially larger sales staff of waiters, room clerks, bellmen, cashiers, and doormen. If you wanted a second drink in the Oak Bar, you got it by tripping the waiter. You asked for it. If you wanted a room you were quoted the minimum rate. If you wanted something

better or larger, you had to ask for it. If you wanted to stay at the hotel an extra night, you had to ask. You were never invited. Sometimes I think there's a secret pact among hotelmen. It's a secret oath you take when you graduate from hotel school. It goes like this: "I promise I will never ask for the order."

20   When you're faced with as old and ingrained a tradition as that, halfway countermeasures don't work. We started a program with all our guest contact people using a new secret oath: "Everybody sells!" And we meant everybody—maids, cashiers, waiters, bellmen—the works. We talked to the maids about suggesting room service, to the doormen about mentioning dinner in our restaurants, to cashiers about suggesting return reservations to departing guests. And we talked to waiters about strawberries.

21   A waiter at The Plaza makes anywhere from $10,000 to $20,000 a year. The difference between those two figures is, of course, tips. When I was in the advertising agency business, I thought I was fast at computing 15 percent. I'm a moron compared to a waiter. Our suggestions for selling strawberries fell on responsive ears when we described a part of the Everybody Sells program for our Oyster Bar restaurant. We figured, with just the same number of customers in the Oyster Bar, that if the waiters would ask every customer if he'd like a second drink, wine, or beer with the meal, and then dessert—given only one out of four takers we'd increase our sales volume by $364,000 a year. The waiters were way ahead of the lecture—they'd already figured out that was another $50,000 in tips! And since there are ten waiters in the Oyster Bar, even I could figure out it meant five grand more per man in tips. It was at that point I had my toughest decision to make since I've been in this job. I had to choose between staying on as President or becoming an Oyster Bar waiter.

22   But, while the waiters appreciated this automatic raise in theory, they were quick to call out the traditional negatives. "Nobody eats dessert anymore. Everyone's on a diet. If we served our chocolate cheesecake to everybody in the restaurant, half of them would be dead in a week."

23   "So sell 'em strawberries!" we said. "But sell 'em." And then we wheeled out our answer to gasoline shortages, the dessert cart. We widened the aisles between the tables and had the waiters wheel the cart up to each and every table at dessert time. Not daunted

by the diet protestations of the customer, the waiter then went into raptures about the bowl of fresh strawberries. There was even a bowl of whipped cream for the slightly wicked. By the time our waiters finish extolling the virtues of our fresh strawberries flown in that morning from California, or wherever he thinks strawberries come from, you not only have had an abdominal orgasm but one out of two of you order them. In the last six months we show our waiters every week what's happening to strawberry sales. This month they have doubled again. So have second martinis. And believe me, when you get a customer for a second martini you've got a sitting duck for strawberries—with whipped cream. Our waiters are asking for the order.

24 "Think Strawberries" is The Plaza's new secret weapon. Our reservationists now think strawberries and suggest you'll like a suite overlooking Central Park rather than a twin-bedded room. Our bellmen are thinking strawberries. Each bellman has his own reservation cards, with his name printed as the return addressee, and he asks if you'd like him to make your return reservation as he's checking you out and into your taxi. Our Room Service order takers are thinking strawberries. They suggest the closed-circuit movie on TV ($3.00 will appear on your bill) as long as you're going to eat in your room. Our telephone operators are even thinking strawberries. They suggest a morning Flying Tray breakfast when you ask for a wake-up call. You just want a light breakfast, no ham and eggs? How about some strawberries?

25 We figure we've added about three hundred salesmen to the three sales-service team we had before. But most important, of course, is that we've added five pure sales people to our Sales Department. Four of them are out on the street calling—mostly cold—on the prospects to whom they're ready to sell anything from a cocktail in the Oak Bar to a Corporate Directors meeting to a Bar Mitzvah. The chewing gum people sell new customers by sampling on street corners. The Plaza has chewing gum licked a mile. Our sales people on the street have one simple objective: get the prospect into the hotel to sample the product. With the Plaza as our product, it isn't too difficult. And once you taste The Plaza, frankly, you're hooked.

26 In analyzing our business at the hotel we found, much to my surprise, that functions—parties, weddings, charity balls, and the like—are just about three times more profitable than all our six restaurants put together. And functions are twice as profitable as

selling all 1000 of our rooms. Before we had this analysis, we were spending all our advertising money on restaurants, our nightclub, and our guest rooms. This year we're spending 80 percent of our advertising money to get function business—weddings instead of honeymoons, banquets instead of meals, annual corporate meetings instead of a clandestine romantic rendezvous for two. We've added a fulltime Bridal Consultant who can talk wedding language to nervous brides and talk turkey to their mothers. Retailers like Saks and Bonwit's and Bergdorf's have had bridal consultants for years. Hotels have Banquet Managers. Banquet Managers sell wedding dinners. Bridal Consultants sell strawberries—everything from the bridal shower, the pictures, the ceremony, the reception, the wedding night, to the honeymoon, to the first anniversary.

27   When you fight a habit as long standing as the hotel inside salesman, you don't just wave a wand and say "Presto: now we have four outside salesmen." We want our new salespeople to know how serious we are about going out after business. We started an Executive Sales Call program as part of our "Everybody Sells" philosophy. About forty of our top and middle-management executives, ones who traditionally don't ever see a prospect, are assigned days on which they make outside calls with our regular salesmen. People like our Personnel Director, our Executive Housekeeper, our Purchasing Director, and our General Manager are on the street every day making calls. Our prospects seem to like it. Our salesmen love it. And our nonsales "salesmen" are getting an education about what's going on in the real world—the one outside the hotel.

28   As a matter of fact, that's why I'm here today. I made a sales call myself with one of our salespeople. We called on your program chairman and tried to sell him strawberries. He promised that if I showed you a strawberry he'd book your next luncheon at The Plaza. I'm looking forward to waiting on you myself. Thank you very much.

Suggested Readings: Part Five

Brilhart, John K. *Effective Group Discussion.* 3d ed. Dubuque, Iowa: Wm. C. Brown, 1978.

Campbell, Karlyn Kohrs. *The Rhetorical Act.* Belmont, Calif.: Wadsworth, 1982. Analyzes the speaker's obstacles and strategies in detail and provides tools for developing critical-analytical skills.

Johnson, David W., and Frank P. Johnson. *Joining Together.* Englewood Cliffs, N.J.: Prentice-Hall, 1975 (paperback). This book contains many exercises and games to illustrate the points it makes.

King, Robert G. *Forms of Public Address.* New York: Bobbs-Merrill, 1969 (paperback). This short paperback is quite inexpensive. See particularly pp. 58–113.

Rogge, Edward, and James C. Ching. *Advanced Public Speaking.* New York: Holt, Rinehart and Winston, 1966. This comprehensive book on public speaking formats has a good section on speeches for special occasions.

Shaw, Marvin E. *Group Dynamics: The Psychology of Small Group Behavior,* 3d ed. New York: McGraw-Hill, 1981. A superior source.

Verderber, Rudolph F. *Working Together: An Introduction to Group Decision Making.* Belmont, Calif.: Wadsworth, 1982.

INDEX